The Christian Therapist's Notebook

Homework, Handouts, and Activities for Use in Christian Counseling

HAWORTH Practical Practice in Mental Health
Lorna L. Hecker, PhD
Senior Editor

101 Interventions in Family Therapy edited by Thorana S. Nelson and Terry S. Trepper

101 More Interventions in Family Therapy edited by Thorana S. Nelson and Terry S. Trepper

The Practical Practice of Marriage and Family Therapy: Things My Training Supervisor Never Told Me by Mark Odell and Charles E. Campbell

The Therapist's Notebook for Families: Solution-Oriented Exercises for Working with Parents, Children, and Adolescents by Bob Bertolino and Gary Schultheis

Collaborative Practice in Psychology and Therapy edited by David A. Paré and Glenn Larner

The Therapist's Notebook for Children and Adolescents: Homework, Handouts, and Activities for Use in Psychotherapy edited by Catherine Ford Sori and Lorna L. Hecker

The Therapist's Notebook for Lesbian, Gay, and Bisexual Clients: Homework, Handouts, and Activities for Use in Psychotherapy by Joy S. Whitman and Cynthia J. Boyd

A Guide to Self-Help Workbooks for Mental Health Clinicians and Researchers by Luciano L'Abate

Workbooks in Prevention, Psychotherapy, and Rehabilitation: A Resource for Clinicians and Researchers edited by Luciano L'Abate

The Psychotherapist as Parent Coordinator in High-Conflict Divorce: Strategies and Techniques by Susan M. Boyan and Ann Marie Termini

The Couple and Family Therapist's Notebook: Homework, Handouts, and Activities for Use in Marital and Family Therapy by Katherine A. Milewski Hertlein, Dawn Viers, and Associates

The Therapist's Notebook for Integrating Spirituality in Counseling: Homework, Handouts, and Activities for Use in Psychotherapy edited by Karen B. Helmeke and Catherine Ford Sori

The Therapist's Notebook for Integrating Spirituality in Counseling II: More Homework, Handouts, and Activities for Use in Psychotherapy edited by Karen B. Helmeke and Catherine Ford Sori

Interactive Art Therapy: "No Talent Required" Projects by Linda L. Simmons

Therapy's Best: Practical Advice and Gems of Wisdom from Twenty Accomplished Counselors and Therapists by Howard Rosenthal

The Christian Therapist's Notebook: Homework, Handouts, and Activities for Use in Christian Counseling by Philip J. Henry, Lori Marie Figueroa, and David R. Miller

The Group Therapist's Notebook: Homework, Handouts, and Activities for Use in Psychotherapy edited by Dawn Viers

Introduction to Complementary and Alternative Therapies edited by Anne L. Strozier and Joyce Carpenter

The Christian Therapist's Notebook
Homework, Handouts, and Activities for Use in Christian Counseling

Philip J. Henry, PhD
Lori Marie Figueroa, MS
David R. Miller, PhD
and Associates

The Haworth Press
New York • London • Oxford

For more information on this book or to order, visit
http://www.haworthpress.com/store/product.asp?sku=5334

or call 1-800-HAWORTH (800-429-6784) in the United States and Canada
or (607) 722-5857 outside the United States and Canada

or contact orders@HaworthPress.com

PUBLISHER'S NOTE
The development, preparation, and publication of this work has been undertaken with great care. However, the Publisher, employees, editors, and agents of The Haworth Press are not responsible for any errors contained herein or for consequences that may ensue from use of materials or information contained in this work. The Haworth Press is committed to the dissemination of ideas and information according to the highest standards of intellectual freedom and the free exchange of ideas. Statements made and opinions expressed in this publication do not necessarily reflect the views of the Publisher, Directors, management, or staff of The Haworth Press, Inc., or an endorsement by them.

Cover design by Kerry E. Mack.

Library of Congress Cataloging-in-Publication Data

Henry, Philip J.
The Christian therapist's notebook : homework, handouts, and activities for use in Christian counseling / Philip J. Henry, Lori Marie Figueroa, David R. Miller.
p. cm.
ISBN: 978-0-7890-2594-4 (soft : alk. paper)
1. Pastoral counseling—Handbooks, manuals, etc. I. Figueroa, Lori Marie. II. Miller, David R., 1941- III. Title.

BV4012.2.H427 2007
253.5'2-dc22

2006033839

CONTENTS

ABOUT THE AUTHORS

Philip J. Henry, PhD, is the director of the Graduate Counseling Psychology Program and associate professor of psychology in the School of Education & Behavioral Studies at Palm Beach Atlantic University, West Palm Beach, Florida. He has taught in psychology and counseling programs at several schools, including Temple University, Chestnut Hill College, and Eastern College, where he also served as the coordinator of the graduate program in school counseling. His experience includes counseling, research, training, and supervision of counselors and family therapy at Philadelphia Child Guidance Center. In addition, he is a licensed psychologist who has been in private practice for eight years with Diane Langberg and Associates, focusing on the treatment of addictions, school related problems, marriage and family counseling, and issues relating to physical and sexual abuse.

Lori Marie Figueroa, MS, is a teacher at Trinity Christian Academy and an adjunct professor at Palm Beach Atlantic University in West Palm Beach, Florida. She is pursuing her Doctorate at Regent University.

David R. Miller, PhD, is a professor of psychology in the Catherine T. MacArthur School of Continuing Education at Palm Beach Atlantic University, West Palm Beach, Florida. He is a Licensed Professional Counselor in Virginia and a Licensed Mental Health Therapist in Florida. He is certified as a school guidance counselor in Florida as well as nationally certified by the National Board for Certified Counselors. His books include *Parent Power, Single Moms, Single Dads, Help! I'm Not a Perfect Parent, A Parent's Guide to Adolescence, Tough Kids, Breaking Free,* and *Counseling Families After Divorce.* He has also authored numerous articles for both secular refereed journals and Christian magazines. He has conducted Christian counseling training in Ukraine and held parenting and family workshops in South America as well as holding parenting seminars and workshops in scores of churches across America. He has also served as Deacon and Head Usher at his two most recent churches and has provided free counseling services through those churches.

The Christian Therapist's Notebook

doi:10.1300/5334_a

NOTES FOR PROFESSIONAL LIBRARIANS AND LIBRARY USERS

This is an original book title published by The Haworth Press, Inc. Unless otherwise noted in specific chapters with attribution, materials in this book have not been previously published elsewhere in any format or language.

CONSERVATION AND PRESERVATION NOTES

All books published by The Haworth Press, Inc., and its imprints are printed on certified pH neutral, acid-free book grade paper. This paper meets the minimum requirements of American National Standard for Information Sciences-Permanence of Paper for Printed Material, ANSI Z39.48-1984.

DIGITAL OBJECT IDENTIFIER (DOI) LINKING

The Haworth Press is participating in reference linking for elements of our original books. (For more information on reference linking initiatives, please consult the CrossRef Web site at www.crossref.org.) When citing an element of this book such as a chapter, include the element's Digital Object Identifier (DOI) as the last item of the reference. A Digital Object Identifier is a persistent, authoritative, and unique identifier that a publisher assigns to each element of a book. Because of its persistence, DOIs will enable The Haworth Press and other publishers to link to the element referenced, and the link will not break over time. This will be a great resource in scholarly research.

Contributors

Judith T. Casey, EdD, is an assistant professor of psychology in the School of Education and Behavioral Studies at Palm Beach Atlantic University, West Palm Beach, Florida. She holds Florida State certification in the areas of School Guidance Counseling Pre-K–12, Early Childhood, Elementary, and English for Speakers of Other Languages. She has been in the combined fields of counseling and education since 1969. Prior to her work at Palm Beach Atlantic University, she worked as a guidance counselor and educator with the Palm Beach County School District for fifteen years. She has held numerous positions of leadership in both school and church settings. She has served as a Citizen Ambassador to Spain for a joint U.S./Spain Educational Conference. She and her husband currently facilitate *Home Builders Series* classes for Palm Beach Gardens Christ Fellowship Institute.

Gene A. Sale, EdD, is an associate professor of psychology in the School of Education and Behavioral Studies at Palm Beach Atlantic University, West Palm Beach, Florida. He has worked in various Christian counseling settings in the Washington, DC, area as a Licensed Professional Counselor and National Certified Counselor for over fifteen years. He was the founder of a counseling center in Washington, DC, and later became the director of counseling at Youth for Tomorrow, a residential boys' home in Manassas, Virginia. He served as a Congressional Fellow in the U.S. House of Representatives with the Select Committee on Children, Youth and Families, and later as a professional staff member of that committee, investigating the impact of federal policy on children, youth, and families. He currently serves as the president of the South Florida Association of Christian Counselors.

Ronald L. Sumner, MA, MFA, is an associate professor of digital arts and multimedia in the School of Music and Fine Arts at Palm Beach Atlantic University, West Palm Beach, Florida. He has worked as a freelance illustrator in children's literature and graphic art for twenty years and as a freelance scenic artist, painting sets and backdrops for theatre, television, and movies, for over fifteen years.

Emery D. Twoey, EdD, is a professor of education in the School of Education and Behavioral Studies at Palm Beach Atlantic University, West Palm Beach, Florida. His specialization is in Adolescent Psychology, Special Education, and Teacher Training in Middle School. He writes and speaks on areas concerning family relationships, adolescent development, counseling, special-needs children, and teaching social and academic skills while counseling families with adolescents. He speaks through a variety of venues, such as churches, district associations, schools and colleges, and regional and national conventions. His writing includes his book *ProTeen: A Positive Approach to Understanding Adolescents,* and articles in professional journals and magazines. He is the Director of Crossroads Counseling Ministry in Jupiter Farms, Florida.

Steven T. Zombory, PhD, is an assistant professor of psychology in the School of Education and Behavioral Studies at Palm Beach Atlantic University, West Palm Beach, Florida.

The Christian Therapist's Notebook

doi:10.1300/5334_b

Acknowledgments

I will be forever grateful to God for using me as His pencil to positively impact His children, both big and small.

I dedicate this book to Andrés, my son, who gave me kisses while I typed my chapters; to the two daughters, Janelle and Alina, whom I inherited from God the day I married my husband; to my husband, Angel "June," for his encouragement; to Tara, for her joyful help with the glossary; to Daniella Suarez, for her assistance with the resources for adolescents and adults; to Keren Roessner, for her excitement and help with the children's resources; to my mom, for her help editing resources; to my dad, for his everlasting faith; to Palm Beach Atlantic University, for the inspiration to integrate faith; to Lorna Hecker, for the opportunity to be a part of her series; to the pastors who will use this book as a reference with their congregation; to new counselors in the field who are seeking innovative ways to work with their clients; to interns in graduate counseling programs throughout the United States; to my classmates at Palm Beach Atlantic University; and, last but not least, to Philip Henry, for being a great mentor and source of inspiration.

Lori Figueroa, MS

First, I would like to recognize my family for their support and patience. To Paul, Jessica, and my wife, Celia, a big, big "thank you." Celia, you are, and will always be, the love of my life. To my colleagues at Palm Beach Atlantic University: Gene Sale, Judi Casey, Julie Harren, Eric Jones, Don McCulloch, Angie McDonald, and Billy Lewter, thanks for creating an atmosphere where true integration and love can take place.

Special thanks to Henry Virkler, for his advice and wisdom throughout the years; and to Joe Kloba, for his leadership and vision, and for reviewing the initial manuscript and offering suggestions; and to Ron Sumner, who is a master artist. Thanks also to Krystal Larkin, Tara Sununu, and all of the students in internship classes. To Lori Figueroa, thanks for your perseverance and faith; it has and will be rewarded. To Cathi Stegall, who hit it out of the park in the final innings to bring the manuscript home—thanks. To Jim Palmer, thank you for the vision to recognize the value of this project. To Lorna Hecker, thanks so much for working hard to make this book better; your wise advice and guidance have been an invaluable asset along the way.

Finally, I would like to thank God for dropping this idea on my desk and insisting that I persevere. I cannot be grateful enough for the many gifts I have been given.

Philip J. Henry, PhD

doi:10.1300/5334_c

Thanks are due to my wife, Linda, and our three children, Laurie, Douglas, and Jennifer, for allowing me to learn the lessons of Christian living with and through them. Thanks are also due to the many people who have trusted me as their counselor and, through sharing, have allowed me to learn from their experiences in life. Most of all, thanks be to God, who loves me and provides opportunities to help more than I could ask or think.

David R. Miller, PhD

Introduction

Why *The Christian Therapist's Notebook*? Because, despite the plethora of theological, theoretical, and philosophical books about Christian counseling that are available, few help answer the question, "What do I do with the client in the therapeutic session?"

Beginning counselors are inundated with theory and related training. They are taught everything from counseling theories, diagnosis, and human development to ethics, all of which are good. But, above all, new counselors desire to know what to do when the doors to their offices close.

Beginning Christian counselors have an added burden: they feel the additional weight and God-given responsibility of being representatives of God's truth. Often, the techniques they have been taught to use in session lack strong biblical roots or relevant real-world connections. In either case, knowing what to do in the session is often a struggle.

However, the struggle of knowing what to do in a session is not just an issue for the neophyte or Christian counselor. After being trained at universities and seminaries, and after being involved in providing counseling and ministry for over twenty years as a minister, and then as a counselor and psychologist, I began to see the main difficulty for me as not theological, theoretical, or philosophical; rather, it involved finding fresh and innovative ways to connect my clients and their worlds with the truth of God. I often found myself using the same interventions over and over. I also struggled to find interventions that touched the main issue of clients' lives and then aided them in understanding how their issues and their world could be seen anew in a more godly light.

What do we do with clients in our sessions? This book was written to help answer that question.

Christian Counseling

Everyone is concerned about success, and Christian counselors are no exception. The exercises in this book can be helpful toward that end, but it must be understood that success has many definitions, and that the exercises, while they may aid, will not be the crucial mover or the curative factor in treatment.

This book posits that success is promised, though, on the basis of three sure foundations: the truth of scripture, the centrality of Christ, and the guidance of the Holy Spirit. We believe that, to the extent that counselors will build on the truths presented here, success will follow.

The Truth of Scripture

> All scripture is God breathed [inspired] by God and is useful for teaching, rebuking, correcting, and training in righteousness, so that the men [and women] of God may be thoroughly equipped for every good work. (2 Timothy 3:16 NIV)

The Christian Therapist's Notebook

doi:10.1300/5334_01

All counseling must be consistent with the inspired word of God, in both precept and practice, and informed by it, for even the most complex or perplexing case. Scripture is the ruler by which all things are measured, the light by which even dark things are exposed, and the objective truth that does not change in an unreliable world. As a result, scripture and scriptural principles should inform and direct each step of the counseling process. Good clinical practice should and will never go against what the word of God teaches. The exercises presented in this book should be used with this in mind.

Finally, there are huge benefits to memorizing, meditating on, considering, and hiding God's word in our hearts. This benefit is not only for the client, but also for us, as counselors. As God promised Joshua, "Do not let this Book of the Law depart from your mouth, meditate on it day and night, so that you may be careful to do everything written in it. Then you will be prosperous and successful" (Joshua 1:8 NIV).

The Centrality of Christ

> Remember there is one foundation, the one already laid, Jesus Christ. (1 Corinthians 3:11 MSG)

At the center of any good session, any positive intervention, or any positive change is a person. The second step in the Twelve-Step Program of Alcoholics Anonymous (AA) has it right: "We came to believe that a power greater than ourselves could restore us to sanity." While some techniques may arrest psychopathology for awhile or trade one illness for another, there is ultimately no answer to the human dilemma, other than Jesus Christ.

Having said this, one must not only preach Jesus; one must be like Jesus. We must meet people where they are, have love and passion to care for them, be creative in our presentation of gospel truth, and have great patience for God to work in their lives, realizing that "it is God who works in you to will and to act according to his good purpose" (Philippians 2:13 NIV). This book is to aid those who do the work of God. We have the wonderful opportunity to be, as Paul writes, "co-laborers with God" (1 Corinthians 3:9 KJV).

The Guidance of the Holy Spirit

> But when He, the Spirit of truth comes, He will guide you into all truth. (John 16:13 NIV)

In therapy, the counselor can sometimes become as confused as the client. Like those children in the C. S. Lewis book *The Silver Chair,* we become confused, enchanted, and forget who we are, where we are going, and what our task should be. It is at these times that Christ has promised to provide a helper who will guide us into all truth.

This is not a minor point. The flow, the energy, the empowering to do the work of counseling is simply not within us. Technique, theory, and a host of other specific factors make up only a small percentage of the variants in successful therapy outcomes. Nonspecific factors, such as the therapist-client relationship, the communication of empathy, the instillation of hope and a host of other intangibles, make up the greatest portion of these outcomes. It is in these unknowns that God can guide us. It is our desire that the reader ask the Holy Spirit to lead her or him, not only to choose the best exercise, but also to understand its use.

As Isaiah writes, "Whether you turn to the right or the left, your ears will hear a voice behind you, saying, 'This is the way walk in it'" (Isaiah 32:3 NIV).

The Purpose of This Book

The purpose of this book is to provide Christian therapists with a resource that bridges the gap between the real world of the client and the truth of God. It seeks to be passionately Christian while remaining clinically professional.

To that end, the book offers scripturally sound exercises, handouts, and homework that aim to be professionally sound and principled. While no particular secular perspective has been integrated with the scriptural principles, there is some obvious influence of cognitive therapy, behavioral therapy, family and systems therapy, reality therapy, solution-focused therapy, and other more traditional therapies.

In therapy, as in life, the delivery of truth often has much to do with its effectiveness. Through the exercises and handouts, counselors can guide clients to consider their pasts, their thoughts, and their actions, and then to ponder how the truth of God is relevant to their situations and can provide the answers to their individual needs.

The Format of This Book

The exercises, handouts, and homework that make up this book are divided into three sections: the first is for use with individuals; the second for couples and families; and the third for children and adolescents.

Section I focuses on the Christian counselor working with individuals. Some exercises direct the clients to reexamine the past, others are present directed, and still others consider the future as a means to provide insight. Each exercise has a particular focus that is based on a key scripture and a key scriptural principle aimed toward growing repentance or birthing a new way of thinking and doing. In all cases, the word and truth of God and the Lordship of Christ are preeminent.

Section II provides interventions to aid in therapy with families and couples. Often, the most challenging therapy a counselor will face is with couples. Scripture clearly delineates the importance of this *one-flesh* relationship and uses it as a physical example of our ultimate relationship with Christ. In our world today, the greatest witness of the power of God in the life of any two believers may be their love relationship. The exercises here focus, not just on building communication skills, but on developing the spiritual life of the couple to support them in weathering the storms that all too frequently beset a marriage.

Working with families is similarly challenging and increasingly needed. The Bible has much to say about the importance of families and of the shaping of individuals from family interactions. The family is arguably one of the places where God's redemptive grace is most visible. Forgiveness, mercy, patience, and courage all are mandates for families to be successful. Exercises in this section seek to help families identify strengths while modifying dysfunctional patterns of interaction that have a negative effect on both the individual members and the family as a whole.

Section III provides interventions geared toward children and adolescents. Since much of a child's world is nonverbal, the chosen interventions involve broader, more creative communication styles. Exercises were carefully developed with the child's intellectual, emotional, and social development in mind. Adolescence is a developmental period where change is the norm. Because resistance is so common, exercises focus on minimizing the resistance or using it to explore its root and intention.

Who Should Read and Use This Book?

It is our hope that this book will serve as a helping hand to many different professionals, such as the following:

- Practicing therapists who are looking for creative homework activities for their clients
- Professors who would like to provide students with examples of different ways to approach counseling
- Christian counselors who want one book in which they can find the resources and daily forms they need
- Interns who are seeking hands-on examples to present to and use with clients
- Pastors who serve in a dual capacity as they counsel their congregations

How to Use the Exercises in This Book

Scripture has much to say about the place of wisdom; in fact, a whole book of the Bible (Proverbs) is devoted to developing wisdom in every aspect of our lives. It is our belief that this book is a tool that can be used effectively only with God's help and wisdom.

Several types of wisdom are necessary to conduct therapy:

- Wisdom in discerning the attitude of the heart
- Wisdom in recognizing responsibility
- Wisdom in recognizing key issues
- Wisdom in recognizing your own issues
- Wisdom in timing
- Wisdom in the relationship

Wisdom in Discerning the Attitude of the Heart

Jesus helps us to understand that clients will respond in unique ways to truth or, more specifically, to the spiritual truth hopefully revealed in the exercises in this book. The possible responses of clients may be grouped in categories that indicate the clients' hearts and openness to the presentation of positive spiritual change.

> What do you make of this? A farmer planted seed. As he scattered, some fell on the road, and the birds ate it. Some fell in the gravel; it sprouted quickly, but it didn't put down roots, so when the sun came up it withered just as quickly. Some fell in the weeds; as it came up, it was strangled by the weeds. Some fell on good earth, and produced a harvest beyond his wildest dreams. (Matthew 13:3-8 MSG)
>
> Jesus identifies four types of responses: road-hard, gravel-rootless, weed-choked, and listening-fruitful responses. Jesus explained the story later to his disciples:
>
> When anyone hears the good news of the kingdom and doesn't take it in, it just remains on the surface, so the Evil One comes along and plucks it right out of that person's heart. This is the seed that the farmer scattered on the road.
>
> The seed cast in the gravel—this is the person who hears the word and instantly responds with enthusiasm. But there is no soil of character, so when the emotion wears off and some difficulty arrives, there is nothing to show for it.
>
> The seed cast in the weeds is the person who hears the kingdom news, but weeds of worry and illusions about getting more and wanting everything under the sun strangle what was heard, and nothing comes of it.

> The seed cast on good earth is the person who hears and takes in the news, and then produces a harvest beyond his wildest dreams. (Matthew 13:19-23 MSG)

Road-hard. Those who are road-hard lack the ability to take in the truth, like a path that has been walked on over and over again until it becomes like rock. The truth, when planted, sits on the hard surface, until it is carried away by the evil one.

At times therapy can be like hosing down a duck. At the end of the session, a lot of water has been sprayed, but the duck is still dry. Denial is a primitive response; nonetheless, it is quite powerful. If there is no felt need to change, then change will not come.

Gravel-rootless. Some hear the truth and find faith quickly growing in them. Unfortunately, their belief is short-lived. Their hearts are shallow and so when the heat of life comes, they lack the roots to be consistent. In the end, their lives become dry and lifeless.

A half-hearted client can be especially disheartening because, in the early sessions, there is commitment and change. The future looks good and both the therapist and client are hopeful. However, as time goes on, the client may not be willing to dig down to do the hard work of therapy or to deal with the hard core issues of the heart. Without continued commitment on the part of the client, relapse is likely and the client will not be able to meet her or his goals.

Weed-choked. Some people also hear the truth and find faith quickly growing inside. Soon, however, the cares and concerns of their lives take over and they lose heart. Eventually, the change that had begun is gradually diminished until they return to the state in which they began.

This client is overwhelmed by his or her life and often in constant crisis. She or he has never learned to do things differently, responding impulsively to the immediate problem and lacking direction and focus. Eventually, this client may drop out of counseling because of more pressing problems.

Listening-fruitful. This response is organic; the good seed finds good soil. When this happens, the response is natural and steady. Consistent growth results in the soil being productive and producing a bountiful harvest.

This client may have some denial and begin slowly. The client may at times be unfocused, but she or he stays with it. The truth in the client's heart begins to change him or her. The client begins to grow and in the end bears little resemblance to the person who started. Fruitfulness is seen in the client's life and spirit, and in the lives of those with whom the client comes in contact.

Some overall observations:

1. The seed can be good but the response not so good.
2. The soil reveals the temporary situations of the heart. While the heart is like soil, it is not soil. God has a way of changing people through situations, pain, kindness, love, and patience.
3. The sower's/farmer's responsibility is to plant the seed. Jesus was the perfect sower/farmer. This parable of Jesus provides insight and proper perspective for the therapist sower/farmer. If we expect the same response from each client, we might question our sowing method or the seed. Similarly, if we see only a one-in-four response when we expect better, we may lose heart in sowing.
4. On some occasions it is better not to give more truth. Often spiritual truth, especially scripture, overwhelms the client and he or she may need time or space to digest or reject it. Scripture is described as a mirror. Those who do not like what they see in the mirror may be motivated to change, or they may stop looking in the mirror. Jesus was clear that we are not to cast our "pearls" before those who refuse to receive them (see Matthew 7:6).

Wisdom in Recognizing Responsibility

Therapists also need the wisdom to recognize who is responsible for what. An example:

> There was a woman who had gained fame due to her wisdom. One day a man who also considered himself wise came to visit this woman. The goal of the visit was to trick the woman and to show that she was not as wise as others had thought. The man brought with him a small bird in his hand. After greeting the woman with great flair, the man asked the woman to tell him and the others who were watching if the bird in his hand was alive or dead. He planned that if she said that the bird was dead, he would open his hand and let the bird go free. If, however, she said that the bird was alive, he would squeeze his hand, crush the bird and reveal it to be dead. To his dismay, the wise woman thwarted his plan. She calmly looked into his eyes and quietly replied, "It is as you wish it to be."

Scripture clearly teaches that individuals are responsible for choices in their own lives. Caring Christians sometimes have problems with boundaries. The Christian counselor must therefore constantly keep in mind that it is the client's responsibility to choose the way that he or she will go.

Wisdom in Identifying Key Issues

The wisdom to identify the client's key issues is necessary for effective therapy. An example:

> A man who worked on sophisticated machines was called in one day to fix a huge, complicated, and ridiculously expensive machine that had stopped running. After spending several hours looking at the machine, he took out a hammer and tapped on a certain part. To everyone's amazement, the machine immediately began to run and continued to run well.
>
> There was great rejoicing until the man submitted the bill for his work. The amount of the bill was one thousand dollars, which at that time was an unbelievable amount. The irate owner did not refuse outright to pay for the bill; he was happy that the machine was running well. However, he protested that he should not have to pay the exorbitant rate when the man had only "tapped." He asked the man for an itemized bill of the work. The invoice he received stated:

Tapping	$1.00
Knowing where to tap	$999.00

Therapy resembles this illustration in many ways. It is often difficult to identify the key issues that will make the "machine" work again. Experience and wisdom are needed because human beings are much more complicated than machines. In addition, client uniqueness compounds the challenge of therapy.

Wisdom in Recognizing Our Own Issues

We are able to see the faults of others quite clearly, or so we think. Wisdom, however, is the ability to recognize our own limitations and issues, and the humility to act in accordance with that truth. Jesus said that, before we take the speck out of someone's eye, we should take the plank out of our own (see Matthew 7:3).

Counselors grow up in a variety of families with, undoubtedly, had their own sets of problems. This is the result of a fallen world. Christian therapists must recognize that we all have issues deep down in our roots. In fact, the book of I John warns us that if we say that we have no sin, no shortcomings, no transgressions, no areas of weakness, then we are just liars. We must start with the truth that everyone has had some type of trauma or trials. Like Superman with his weakness to kryptonite, we all have feet of clay. Even though we grow up strong and heal, these issues nonetheless tend to reemerge.

Jesus warns us that before we begin working on the faults we so clearly see in others, we should start with the things that block our own vision. Interestingly, the speck and the log are both made of the same material: we may have the tendency to see mistakes and faults in others' lives that we have not yet dealt with ourselves.

Wisdom, like a compass, can set our direction because it demands and presumes honesty. The therapist's honesty must be developed. Then, during the journey of therapy, appropriate client honesty can be developed, both internally and externally. As we set the compass of wisdom, success will follow.

Wisdom in Timing

Another type of wisdom that the effective therapist must possess is wisdom in timing. "Timing is everything," or so they say. The truth is that, no matter what the process and regardless of the goal, timing is important. In counseling, timing plays a key role. It determines which therapeutic interventions or techniques will be effective toward progress. It is often not a question of which technique to use, but rather whether it is the right time to utilize it.

As a supervisor and counselor trainer, I have observed three common mistakes that new counselors make in regard to timing. Indeed, even experienced counselors can make these blunders, if we are not careful. The following discussion considers these mistakes and then examines two overall guidelines for the appropriate timing of therapeutic techniques.

The first mistake is haste created by being overzealous or overconfident. Proverbs 19:2 (NIV) instructs us, "It is not good to have zeal without knowledge nor to be hasty and miss the way." Training as a therapist involves paying close attention to some information and disregarding other details. In some counselor-training programs, students are taught to pursue emotion like a jaguar heading for the jugular vein. I have seen professors almost salivate because a student had a client in tears. Other programs ignore emotions, preferring to decipher the schemata of cognitions or judiciously hunt the "sinful patterns" of the client. Like computers crunching data, we often forget to stop to listen.

The commercial tag line "Can you hear me now?" is humorous to many cellular phone service customers who can relate to the annoyance of dropped calls and miscommunication. Such interruptions in service are not humorous in the context of therapy, however. As therapists, we cannot afford to make our clients wonder whether we can hear them, if we are to be effective. We must listen. This requires a special focus on the client.

> Sitting behind a one-way mirror with colleagues, watching a therapist during a family therapy session, I became involved in the discussion of the case. I was sure that I knew, not only the family's pattern of interaction, but also the best course of treatment to follow. When asked, however, my wise supervisor said, "We don't know yet." At his urging, we waited, watched, and listened longer and then we began to understand. I learned an important lesson that day about timing. Had we jumped in to address the issues that the client first began to talk about, we would have missed the natural unfolding of the deeper issues that emerged as the client was encouraged to talk and explore her thoughts and feelings.

This mistake can and does happen with more experienced counselors as well.
Overconfidence has the same result.

> Recently, I was working with a client who was addicted to a prescription medication. Despite having taught many graduate classes on substance abuse, lectured on substance abuse for churches and other organizations, and counseled hundreds of addicted clients, I needed to learn from this client about *her* addiction. After about four sessions, during which I taught her about substance abuse recovery and relapse prevention, I finally *shut up* and *listened.*
>
> What I heard was the story of a woman who had beaten an addiction to prescription drugs, staying clean for seven years. Now, however, she was faced with a mentally handicapped son who was struggling at school and failing. I listened as she told how she sat for hours with him, trying to help him with homework, only to have him begin banging his head on the kitchen table in frustration. Finally, I began to understand.

A second mistake is to fail to consider seriously the developmental nature of therapy. It is a process with a beginning, a middle, and an end. Each of these seasons has a distinct quality, a lesson I learned well during my internship at a state mental hospital.

> Although I had worked as a therapist for some time, I had never worked with the severely mentally ill. The ward to which I had been assigned was a research unit, composed of treatment-resistant patients. Early in my internship, I was walking around the grounds of the hospital, introducing myself to patients. When I walked up to one young man and introduced myself, he answered, "Hello. Glad to meet you. I'm Satan." Well, not quite knowing what to do or say, I said, "Glad to meet you, Satan," shook his hand, and turned away, thinking "Oh, my, my." In about three minutes, he walked back up to me, took my hand and said, "My name isn't really Satan; my name is Bob." It was obvious from that interaction that Satan, or Bob, had gotten quite a rise from the others with his "demonic" introduction. However, to respond to Satan was to miss Bob. The initial cry or scream of pain may not tell us what is really going on.

Based on my research, I believe that sessions with clients follow a pattern in regard to time, beginning with a significant focus on the therapist-client relationship in the first session. Other issues of a less defensive and more personal nature unfold over time. If we rush in with a verse, lecture, or a quick fix without understanding the core issue, we may miss the person. By doing this, we become useless to the client because we simply repeat the same relational interactions as everyone else in the client's life. The timing of therapy gives us a clue to the meaning of the interactions. Timing helps us initiate something new.

My second experience with the timing of therapy occurred with a group of women from the same research unit at the state hospital.

> I met on a weekly basis with about eight to twelve women for one year. Initially, this was extremely slow going. At first they would not talk or recognize me at all. Then I would get only a nod. Finally, they began to talk. I learned about the craziness, mistrust, and internal torture that they had been hiding. I learned that their journey with me was so slow because they had been hurt by so many already, and because they knew that I was there for only a year.
>
> As we moved from the initial stage of therapy to the middle stage, each woman moved at her own pace. The entire women's group was on its own time schedule, and, as the leader, I had to wait for them. Here was the "meat" of therapy, the "teachable moment," time to be with them, to work on and in their relationships. At this point, it became important to sense the flow of therapy. We moved from issues of inclusion, to issues of trust, vulnerability, and control. Eventually, in time, the women's personalities, like turtles' heads, came slowly peeping out of their shells. Gradually they began to develop trust and became more open.

As time in therapy progresses, and hopefully before termination, we begin to deal with issues of affection and how that fits within the confines of counseling. We may express care before this time, but signs of affection seem disingenuous, at best, and manipulative, at worst, if expressed too soon. The women of the group at the mental hospital were accustomed to being devalued, manipulated, and used. How could I be real and helpful? It is here where caring can be confused. These women were desperate to be loved, and relationally dependent, yet also fiercely independent. How could I offer love, while maintaining boundaries and respecting the inequality of relationships inherent in therapy? Only through consistency, respect, and caring, founded on trustworthiness, could these questions be answered during this time period.

The final stage of therapy, termination, leads us back to the reason for coming to therapy, and to the conclusion of inclusion, the finale—disengagement. Here we provide honesty concerning what has been accomplished and a blessing for future endeavors. For this group of women, this meant some final notes and shared hugs, a party, and good-bye.

An understanding of the seasons of therapy helps us know when to do what. Techniques and interventions, as with other tools, are chosen by the task we want them to perform. The tasks are dictated in part by where we are at in that moment in the therapeutic relationship.

A third mistake that we all make is that we simply are not patient. Healing takes time. I remember my early counseling sessions, when I was buoyed up by courses focusing on brief therapy, problem-solving therapy, and training in quick structural family interventions, and intoxicatingly high on my readings of the one-session cures of Milton Erickson. I was brought to my senses, as if with the proverbial bucket of ice water in the face, when I was confronted with a survivor of sexual abuse.

> She was a person who did not want to cooperate. Let me be specific. She did want to cooperate, deeply, truly, and sincerely, but I could not help her progress any faster. She was tired—sick and tired of therapy, as well as the variety of counselors, techniques, and interventions. She wanted me to help her be done with counseling and move on with her life. I wanted to help her be done, but we were not done after the first, second, third, fourth, or fifth session, nor after many more sessions that followed. Sometimes there was progress, and then regression. Sometimes I could not help at all. I merely had to sit there and listen. My powerful, sure-fire, one-shot, one-size-fits-all methods were brushed aside like flies. When I did feel I was being helpful, it was slow, tedious, painstaking work. I wondered at times if we were getting anywhere. Healing did come, by God's grace, but it took its own sweet time.

Growth and healing do take time. Despite managed care and insurance protocols, the gestation of a human being takes nine months. Broken bones do not mend faster just because the insurance has run out. Great harm can be done by trying to push physical healing before its time. The same is true for emotional healing. In recovery, those who are pushed too fast can easily become overwhelmed and relapse. With post-traumatic stress disorder (PTSD), for example, poor timing may trigger flashbacks or encourage self-destructive or even psychotic-like behavior. "Better a patient man . . . than one who takes a city" (Proverbs 16:32 NIV).

There is another part of patience that is not about endurance but wisdom. A chess game cannot be won on every move. In fact, the best players sacrifice power for position or a lesser piece for a better piece later. An angry adolescent who distrusts adults, the shame-filled woman who has had an abortion, the sexually addicted church leader are all afraid. They can become grandmasters at distancing others and at hiding. Proverbs 20:5 (NIV) says that "the purposes of a man's heart are deep waters, but a man of understanding draws them out." We are reminded that it is a patient woman or man who "has great understanding" (Proverbs 14:29 NIV).

If there is "a time for everything . . . under heaven" (Ecclesiastes 3:1 NIV), how then do we know when to act and when not to act? How can we act wisely? Two things are helpful in guiding the overall decision-making process in counseling. The first is the timing of the client's life:

Where is the client developmentally?
Where is he or she in regard to, say, Erickson's stages?
What is the task that life is asking from the client at this time?
Where is the client in his or her marriage or singleness?
Where is the client in recovery?
Where is the client in terms of career path or spiritual life?
How has time weathered the client—aged to perfection like a fine wine, faded like comfortable jeans, or worn out like an old blanket?

The timing and flow of clients' lives gives us insight into how their world appears to them. It shows the context that influences them and the appropriate intervention to be used with them.

The second guideline is God's timing. This begins with the realization that you are entering a work in progress. You are not the first to work in this field. God has been there continually working, and so have others. Paul tells us, "I planted the seed, Apollos watered it, but God made it grow" (1Corinthians 3:6 NIV). As therapists, we need to develop a sense of what God is doing in our clients' lives. Is he refining, pulling up weeds, drawing them closer to Him, letting them reap what they have sown? What is God up to in their lives? How can you verbalize this and participate with it?

Sometimes understanding and supportive words can hinder God's work. Jesus' reply to Peter, "Get behind me, Satan" (Matthew 16:23 NIV) when Peter encouraged him to avoid suffering, certainly indicates that we can miss the intent of God in a big way. Not sensing God's direction always leads to disaster. Sometimes repentance is needed or a warning needs to be sounded, even though no one will hear. Sometimes clients, like us, must wait on God's timing. Whatever the need, God's timing is a must. The difference between obedience and disobedience is often timing.

> Recently, I worked with a client who had lost over 100 pounds in a year and was recovering from compulsive binging (quite a feat for her and a tribute to God's work in her life). With her newfound body and self, she faced a new challenge; she now had a relationship with a man for whom she deeply cared. After a while, it became clear that she could not maintain both her abstinence in regard to binging and the relationship. Although I had guessed that this was the case early on, she wanted to try to keep them both. I encouraged her to try, but it was not yet time. After a while, she came to the conclusion that God had better timing in mind for her. She believed that recovery was a priority. With that, she decided to break off the relationship for the time being. My response toward accountability and her commitment became a sacred trust. Like Abraham, she had put what she loved on the altar. She knew that in time God had a better plan. For her, obedience was a question of timing. My support of this timing was necessary in helping her expectantly wait on God's plans for her life.

As a final note, during the time that I was writing this chapter, I went with my family to a fast-food restaurant. While waiting in line, I heard the woman behind us curse and belittle her son of twelve or thirteen for several minutes. Now all of us have heard a parent yell at a child in a store, mall, or restaurant, but this was one of the most demeaning lectures that I have ever heard. In any case, I turned to ask the woman to please stop. She informed me that it was her child and she could do what she wanted. Nonetheless, she stopped. I guess there is a time to speak and a time to be silent.

God has appointed a time for everything under heaven. May our counseling and lives conform to His time and may we help others to make the most of their time.

Wisdom in the Relationship

A final component of wisdom necessary for effective therapy is wisdom in the therapeutic relationship. In the gospel of John, we find records of the only extended dialogues between Jesus and another person found in scripture, therapeutic sessions, if you will. Jesus' first "session" is with Nicodemus, a member of the Jewish ruling council (see John 3). Then, in chapter 4, John records Jesus' interaction with a woman whose only distinguishing feature is that she was from Samaria. These are two of the most unique, amazing "sessions" found in scripture. They give us a sense of what it was like to sit in a room and be with Jesus. Together they reveal the wonder of His healing work as a counselor and His wisdom as the "Master Therapist."

As one who has practiced the art of therapy and now teaches the craft, I am drawn to these accounts on many levels. The first point that draws my attention is the issue of power, status, and culture. I have seen literally hundreds of people in therapy, from millionaires, corporate leaders, scientists, and powerful politicians, to street people, indigents, and prisoners in a state mental hospital, and quite a few individuals in between. I know from experience that status, power, and cultural issues run deep in the course of therapy and in the context of life. In many ways, status and power can both impede and promote change. Who you are as a person and therapist is revealed as you encounter life and other people. Jesus' interactions with Nicodemus and the Samaritan woman are a wonder with regard to issues of power.

Jesus is met by Nicodemus, a member of the Sanhedrin, a powerful spiritual and political leader of the Nation of Israel. He is a bright man, a scholar. He is politically astute. He knows when to visit a controversial figure—at night. He is someone who knows how to find and use the right words; he is a politician's politician. Listen to him as he liltingly begins, "Rabbi, we know you are a teacher who has come from God. For no one could perform the miraculous signs you are doing if God were not with him" (John 3:2 NIV).

After this powerful, scholarly politician opens with such a glowing appraisal, a proper response might be this, "Well, thank you very much, Dr. Nicodemus. I have heard of your work on the Sanhedrin. I have read and admired your writings, and have watched your political exploits, and it is so very nice to finally meet you."

Instead, Jesus gives this response: "I tell you the truth, no one can see the kingdom of God unless he is born again" (John 3:3 NIV). This response is direct, challenging, and provoking. Jesus not so covertly says to Nicodemus:

> With all your wisdom and knowledge, with all of the chapters of the Bible you have memorized, with all your wealth, power, and understanding, you cannot even begin to see God's kingdom, unless you start all over again. You have been completely wrong! The things you have counted on to get you points spiritually mean nothing. You have missed the target. You must start again from ground zero!

Contrast this to Jesus' interaction with the Samaritan woman at the well. She, unlike Nicodemus, had almost no status. She was a woman in a culture where men, daily, publicly thanked God that they were not women. She was a Samaritan, part of a hated minority. In addition, she was divorced at a time when being divorced was worse than wearing a scarlet letter. The choices of vocation for divorced women in that time were often slavery or prostitution, not high-status, high-paying jobs. She is not what we might consider a "religious woman." Most likely, she visited the well at the sixth hour (about noon) to avoid meeting others in the town. They would often go for water in the morning and evening because it was too hot to go at noon. She was an outcast, an untouchable.

Contrary to his opening with Nicodemus, Jesus begins the conversation with the woman from Samaria by taking the initiative because she could not. He does this by asking a question: "Will you give me a drink?" he asks, calling on the one thing that she could perhaps morally and ethically provide him. The effect and genius of this short question is immense.

First, it is a subtle and indirect way to connect and build a relationship. Unlike his direct confrontation of Nicodemus, rather than lower the woman's status, he raises it. I often tell my students that it is possible to bridge gaps associated with status, gender, race, and culture. However, it is like going to bat with two strikes already against you. You must swing at the next pitch and hit it. Jesus connects solidly across gender and race. Jesus indicates that he is ready to enter her world on her level: "I will dialogue with you." "You and I are not so different that we cannot communicate." "I don't care about the man-made rules. I care about you." These are the underlying messages Jesus communicated when he broke the rules of religious heritage, culture, social etiquette, and public decorum to talk with this woman. He raised her up and gave her dignity.

Second, Jesus' question humanizes her. She is not the naughty little girl or the seductive woman at the well in Jesus' eyes, but a person who has something to offer. She has value to be known as a person. We find out later that she knows how to be seductive with men. Jesus lets her know there will be no games from the start.

Third, his question throws her off base. As with Nicodemus, the opening is unexpected. Its uniqueness allows or forces the person into a unique response. Often, we fall into the trap of repeating techniques that do not work. We lecture the alcoholic; we shy away from telling the truth to the powerful. We so easily fall into the uncreative mediocrity that comes from complacency and fear.

Jesus is the great connector. Rather than avoiding status, power, and issues of gender and culture, he transcends them. He does this, not by ignoring differences, but by using himself as a tool to forge a relationship that goes beyond the expected. He does this not to be different, but because he seeks to be faithful to the standard the Father has set. What we learn from the Master Therapist is that we are to use our own status and power wisely, understanding the position of the person seeking help.

Jesus knew who he was first of all. We must know who we are. He did not bow to Nicodemus's flattery or position, nor did he fall to the seduction of the Samaritan woman. Knowing them, he built a relationship and challenged them toward truth. Jesus also never forgot what he was to be about. "My food," he says, "is to do the will of him who sent me and to finish his work" (John 4:34 NIV). The Master Therapist showed us that even brief encounters can open the door to life-changing communication.

The second issue that draws my attention as a therapist is Jesus' handling of resistance. Resistance, at its simplest level, is the act of being uncooperative. In therapy, this uncooperativeness is revealed through denial or when a person becomes argumentative. Freud and others after him have seen working with defenses and the countering of resistance as the heart of therapy. Jesus, in these two accounts, uses the individual's resistance to guide the person to truth. After Jesus' declaration that he needs to be "born again," Nicodemus pleaded ignorance. "How can a man be born when he is old? Surely he cannot enter a second time into his mother's womb to be born!" (John 3:9 NIV). Now, I believe Nicodemus knew very well that Jesus was not talking about a physical birth. However, sticking with Jesus' analogy, he resists the idea by stating the impossible. In other words, "How can all that I have done be wrong? I can't start over." He is effectively saying, "I am a dog too old to learn a new trick." Later, as if repeating a mantra, he lamely says, "How can this be?" He is dumbstruck. It is not that he does not understand, but rather that he understands all too well. He is unable to fathom it. It is new wine in old wineskins.

Jesus clarifies with an illustration: "Flesh gives birth to flesh, but the Spirit gives birth to spirit" (John 3:6 NIV). Jesus often uses analogies to remove resistance. He is patient. However, following the second objection, Jesus takes Nicodemus to task. "You are Israel's teacher and do you not understand these things?" (John 3:10 NIV). Here he says, "You should be getting this." Like a teacher chiding a bright student for lessons that should have been mastered, Jesus' words offer both an exhortation and a condemnation. They recognize Nicodemus's status and ability but also demand, however, that he be much more honest and humble.

I remember earlier in my life playing chess with a friend's father who was a chess master. He was always ahead of me; while I was thinking of the current move, he was thinking at least five or six moves beyond the present. He was always teaching me to think beyond what I currently understood. Like a great chess master, Jesus is far ahead of Nicodemus, and yet he challenges and attempts to educate him. He tries to get him to open up, to understand, and to be not so rigidly resistant.

The Samaritan woman, while low in status, is no slouch when it comes to resistance. In fact, in some ways, she puts up a better fight than Nicodemus. Some of the most simple resistance strategies can be the most difficult to breach. Addictions and personality disorders are two examples of simple, effective defense strategies.

After Jesus asks for water, the Samaritan woman reminds him of the obvious: "You are a Jew and I am a Samaritan woman" (John 4:9 NIV). You can almost hear in her sarcasm the hatred toward those who have put her down for her race: "Oh, you are talking to me? Should I jump for joy? What is it that you really want from me? Normally we don't talk, you know."

Often anger and hurt are behind the best schemes of resistance. Layer upon layer of hurt and anger can provide a tough shell. Some people, like tanks, run over all those who dare cross their paths. Yet, this resistance is itself a kind of a trap. Like the crazed tank driver who welds the hatch of the tank closed, such people become sealed in by their hurt and anger, becoming prisoners to both emotions. This held true for the Samaritan woman.

Interestingly, rather than react, Jesus begins to speak to her graciously about who he was and about "living water": "If you knew the gift of God and who it is that asks you for a drink, you would have asked him and he would have given you living water" (John 4:10 NIV). Rather than speak to the tank, he speaks to the person trapped inside. "Yes, I am someone," he says, "someone with something you need. I am here not to hurt you nor take from you like other men have, but to refresh you beyond the water of this well."

The woman counters this appeal by suggesting that the well is deep, that he has nothing with which to draw water out (you are not able to help me), and by the way, "Are you greater than our father Jacob, who gave us the well and drank from it himself, as did also his sons and his flocks and herds?" (John 4:12 NIV). Jesus claims that he is greater: "whoever drinks the water I give him will never thirst. Indeed, that water I give him will become in him a spring of water welling up to eternal life" (John 4:14 NIV). Even Jacob could not make this claim.

As therapy often goes, what once has been continues. Life tends to repeat itself, and so it does with this woman. She is stuck, and so she responds in the only way she can. The woman resists again. She counters artfully by making fun or mocking Jesus. She asks for this living water so that she will not get thirsty again. Jesus, knowing and probing the heart of the matter, asks her to call her husband and return to him. Here it gets edgy. Like a child being prodded by a physician's examining fingers, she feels the probing of deeply guarded emotional wounds, and the woman pulls back, instinctively replying: "I have no husband" (John 4:17 NIV).

Jesus, with great compassion and firmness, replies, "You are right when you say you have no husband. [Thank you for your honesty, but you are not telling the whole truth.] The fact is, you have had five husbands, and the man you have now is not your husband" (John 4:17b-18 NIV). You can almost see her eyes pop out on this one, yet she regains her composure, for she has been trained in all circumstances to resist. Keeping people away, keeping the lid of the tank closed, is the only way to remain safe and secure in her misery.

So, again, she creatively resists. In a sense, she desperately tries to pick a fight with Jesus and push him away. It is possible that she has avoided many unpleasant situations in the past by distracting men with a discussion aimed to camouflage her hurt, while avoiding disagreements. The most unpleasant thing for her right then, of course, is to let someone get close or to talk about her failed marriages.

What she chooses to do is to bring up the oldest dispute between the Jew and the Samaritan. She asks Jesus whether he thinks worship should be done in Samaria or in Jerusalem. Today, this would be like asking a Jew if he or she should worship in the Holy Land or in Mecca. She hopes that in bringing the subject up, Jesus will be angered, or at least will stop focusing on her. Instead, he responds that there is a deeper truth than location. The place to worship, Jesus says, is in the town of "spirit and truth" (John 4:24 NIV). There is something more important than me fighting with you. The underlying message is, "Relax. I want you to understand there is a way of connecting with God that has nothing to do with doing things right. You still have a chance."

Jesus' goal of confronting resistance in Nicodemus and the Samaritan woman is not to bend their wills or to break them, but to lead them toward repentance. Repentance conjures up ideas of groveling and weeping. In fact, it means something much more simple and powerful. In the original Greek, the word repentance, or *metanoia,* comes from the words *meta,* meaning "change," and *noia,* meaning "mind." The goal of the Master Therapist is to free the client from an unproductive position, to move through resistance to a deeper relationship that leads to repentance (a changed mind), resulting in faith.

The final key element that I am drawn to as a therapist is the honest compassion of Jesus. It opens the door to a deep revelation of him and of others. This begins with empathy, one of the first skills we try to teach new counselors. It is a learned skill. For some, it is a difficult skill to learn, especially if a person has never been the recipient of empathy.

With Nicodemus, Jesus is direct from the start, yet compassionate. There is a wonderful sense of caring and teaching, with no faultfinding. James reminds us, "If any of you lacks wisdom, he should ask God, who gives generously to all without finding fault" (James 1:5 NIV). Jesus does this. Nicodemus says that he does not understand. Jesus gives the illustration of Moses in the wilderness, holding up the snake for physical salvation, pointing to spiritual salvation. Jesus is open and asks Nicodemus to come along for the ride. Finally, he gives the clearest picture of himself, his mission, and the plan of salvation. "For God so loved the world that He gave His one and only Son, that whoever believes in him shall not perish but have eternal life" (John 3:16 NIV).

Jesus, unlike Freud, is willing to reveal and give of himself. He gives and asks for much. His compassionate honesty calls both Nicodemus and the Samaritan woman to go far beyond their comfort levels. He does this as an act of grace. With the woman, he simply admits, "I who speak to you am he" (John 4:26 NIV). Jesus' simple act of "speaking the truth in love" (Ephesians 4:15 NIV) reveals his revelation compassion.

As we know, much of what we communicate to others is nonverbal (facial expression, body language, eye movement) or non-content-related cues (verbal tone, pitch, speed, and timing). As a result, clients usually can sense the extent of caring. They know whether we are being honest with them and can be trusted with their deepest feelings.

Although these are brief encounters, Jesus, from beginning to end, shows an honest compassion that draws the individual out. His timing of compassionate truth and his revelations about them is remarkable. It begins in his addressing of power and status issues, flows through the wrestling with resistance, and ends with an honest, compassionate presentation of the truth.

When the truth does arrive, it does so in such a clear nonthreatening manner that Nicodemus and the Samaritan woman accept it, not because of miracles or wonders, but because of who Jesus was with them. As those who seek to help others, we must possess a willingness to be both compassionate and honest in a way that reveals who we are, while also encouraging others to delve deeper within themselves.

The result of any brief therapy is always left in God's hands. What can we say concerning the outcomes of these two one-session therapies? The woman, we can see, had an immediate change. She moved from a resistant individual to a person compelled to invite others to come and meet Jesus (see John 4:29). Nicodemus is counted among the believers who later recover the body of Christ.

The brief therapy of Jesus, the Master Therapist, reveals God's therapeutic work in our lives. It moves us to a deeper relationship through repentance. Let us learn from Jesus and follow His example as we face the needy men and women of our world. He can give us the complete wisdom we need to help our clients.

THE MASTER THERAPIST

As Christian counselors, times seem unclear
Encouraging clients, diffusing fear

We learn the theories, they help in a way
but true insight comes to us only after we pray

We remove bandages as people heal
we explore the cause, we help them feel

From mild depression to severe abuse
to angry couples who need to call a truce

Words are not always needed, as we listen with care
treating everyone equal as they sit in the chair

The Bible has an answer to every sin and issue
wiping tears from the hurting with the softest tissue

This book is only the beginning, only a lamp in the mist
for true revelation comes from the Master Therapist

Lori Marie Figueroa (2004)

SECTION I: HOMEWORK, HANDOUTS, AND ACTIVITIES FOR INDIVIDUALS

– 1 –

A New Creation

Philip J. Henry

Guiding Scripture

If anyone is in Christ, they are a new creation.

2 Corinthians 5:17 (NIV)

Type of Contribution: Exercise, Handouts

Objective

Although the Bible contains wonderful promises for the Christian, sadly, many are not experiencing the abundant life Jesus promised to give to those who believe. The objective of this exercise is to help the client realize who he or she is in Christ, to learn all that is available to him or her as a Christian and to facilitate his or her beginning to live in that faith.

Rationale for Use

The "A New Creation" exercise uses a "Christogram" to personalize the biblical promises and truths of the spiritual transformation. The result is becoming the new creation that is in Christ. A Christogram is a pattern of verses containing promises for the Christian about the new life that Christ brings. Identifying the changes and promises regarding the new birth God has completed in the client, while highlighting his or her new birth and new covenant relationship with God, makes these scriptures personal and applicable. This exercise intends to help the client in four areas:

1. It will guide the client in forming a philosophy of life or "worldview." Like a compass, a correct worldview provides direction for navigation through the decisions of everyday life. Simply stated, a worldview is one's practical philosophy of living. It influences how the client perceives the world and directs his or her choices. If the client understands who he or she is in Christ, and his or her true current spiritual reality, this will help develop a worldview that will aid the client in finding direction and purpose in life; it will also help him or her to negotiate the host of twists and turns life brings.
2. This exercise is a growth-shaping catalyst for godly change. Knowing the changes God says are possible, to the believer, is a motivator for this kind of transformation and can sustain a life-changing faith. God's kindness and love are what changes lives.

The Christian Therapist's Notebook

doi:10.1300/5334_02

3. If the client becomes well acquainted with the scriptures, he or she can recall these verses in times of trouble. When trials come in the walk of faith, and trials will come, knowing God's Word can anchor the believer in the storm. The promises of God and the truth about His place in the life of the believer can be the difference between the sadness of a shipwrecked life and the joy of hanging ten on a big wave.
4. This exercise can aid in building the client's godly self-esteem and in elevating hope, by recognizing what God has already done for him or her. Encourage the client to take a second look at life and to see it as God sees it. We feel good about ourselves as Christians, not because of all the wonderful attributes we possess, but because God values us and has a wonderful plan for our lives.

Scripture clearly states that those who become Christians have become a new creation. This change is like the birth of a child; big changes have happened and big changes are on the way. Knowing what transformations God has already effected in the heart and life of the believer makes all the difference in the way each day is lived out, and in how each problem is faced.

Instructions

First, make sure the client has established a saving relationship with Christ. Many good people, even those who have attended church or have a strong connection with God have not come to the place where they have this type of a relationship. Rather than making the judgment yourself, have the client look at verses and scripture highlighting salvation (e.g., John 3:16; Romans 3:23). If the client is not sure or if he or she needs more information, refer to the handout at the end of this chapter: "Four Spiritual Laws." Make certain the client understands how to take this initial step of faith, and that the client is secure in where he or she stands with God before using the New Creation exercise.

After having made certain the client has placed his or her faith in Christ, introduce the Christogram handout by discussing with the client his or her life and how it can be different with Christ. Often, it will be easy for the client to articulate emotional changes; however, articulating changes in beliefs, attitudes, and philosophy may take more time. For these, there needs to be scriptural input and greater understanding. Such changes come only as the client grows and gains spiritual maturity.

Next, take out an example of a Christogram. Use the completed handout at the end of the chapter, a handout that another client has volunteered, or one you have put together yourself. Hand the client the finished Christogram and have him or her look at a few of the verses that comprise the picture of what Christ promised to do in the life of the believer. Think together about what might be the central message of each verse. Make sure the client has a good understanding of what the chosen verses truly mean or promise. Look up one or two of the scriptures to see the context. The context will provide a greater understanding of what each verse is trying to communicate. The therapist teaches the client to learn skills, so take time to encourage the client to go at his or her own pace.

Next, lead the client to think of the implication of each verse and to describe how it applies to everyday life. Ask the question, "What would change in a person's life if he or she understood the meaning of this verse and applied it?" Let the client articulate several ways life would be different. Determine whether the client can then see how understanding the message of the chosen verse would influence him or her personally.

After the client has a good understanding of what the complete product is to look like, hand the client a blank Christogram handout and ask him or her to begin to make one to keep. At this point, check to see if the client has a Bible, preferably a version that is easy for him or her to read and understand. If the client is familiar with scripture and has a Bible, he or she may do much of this unaided. However, to be sure, provide the client with a list of verses that highlight his or her new creation status. If the client is unable to grasp the nature of this exercise, take him or her through the Four Spiritual Laws handout first.

Encourage the client to borrow verses from the model Christogram you handed him or her earlier. Optimistically, some of the verses you have reviewed have been important enough to include. In any case, encourage the client to be actively involved in the process.

Make sure to have the client begin with verses that are important to him or her, verses that touch issues he or she struggles with or that seem particularly salient. Make sure this is not merely an intellectual exercise. Try to have the client involved in picking the verses, interpreting the verses, and applying the verses. Encourage him or her to own each verse.

If possible, have the client hang the Christogram in a place where it will continually remind him or her of the reality that, in Christ, he or she is a new creation.

Vignette

Three years ago, Ron had gone into recovery following a seven-year span during which he abused both marijuana and alcohol. Following treatment, he attended Alcoholics Anonymous (AA) and Narcotics Anonymous (NA). When his sponsor suggested that he attend church as a way of connecting with his higher power, Ron agreed. He became a regular attendee at St. Marks Church of God. In the next year, he made a public commitment to Christ and became a member of that church.

Ron had come to therapy with many questions. Some of these questions were about life in general; others specifically concerned his beliefs and his struggle to grow as a Christian. Since the birth of his second child a year ago, he often found himself brooding, anxious, and occasionally depressed. He also complained that lately he found himself struggling with his faith and losing motivation in his recovery program.

Miguel, Ron's counselor, began the session by suggesting that they work together on an exercise that might help him to examine his faith more closely. Miguel had listened to Ron talk about his faith, but he took some time to read John 3:16 and Romans 6:23 to make sure Ron was comfortable with this initial step of faith. Ron enthusiastically told Miguel about coming to Christ and his attempts to grow as a Christian. The two talked for a while about what Ron hoped for in his spiritual life.

Miguel then asked Ron if he would like to complete an exercise that would lead him to think more clearly about the changes in his life. With Ron's assent, Miguel handed him a completed copy of the Christogram handout. "This will give you an idea of what yours might look like when we are done," said Miguel.

Picking 1 Corinthians 6:19-20 (NIV), Miguel took a Bible and read, "'Do you not know that your body is a temple of the Holy Spirit, who is in you, whom you have received from God? You are not your own; you were bought at a price. Therefore, honor God with your body.'" Miguel explained the context of the verse and its relation to some of the issues Ron was facing. "In verse 12 of the same chapter, it says, 'Everything is permissible for me, but I will not be mastered by anything.'" Ron and Miguel talked about this verse, about the choices Ron had made in the past, and about the better choices he was trying to make now.

Ron then looked at several other verses in the completed Christogram until Miguel was sure Ron knew how to complete the handout. Miguel also made sure Ron had a Bible at home that he could read and use to find verses. Then, giving Ron a new uncompleted copy of the Christogram, along with the completed model Christogram, Miguel closed the session in prayer, asking God to guide Ron in the coming week.

The next week, Ron returned to therapy with the Christogram half completed. Ron had chosen verses that had forgiveness as a theme and those which centered on what was possible with faith.

When asked about this, he explained that at times he would get down, thinking about all of the mistakes he had made in his life. "Over and over again, I need to remind myself I am not perfect, just forgiven." Ron went on to explain how this focus on forgiveness helped him to rethink his world.

Miguel then asked about the verses dealing with faith. "I struggle with thinking I will not make it, so I am tempted just to give up and drink or get high." Ron said, "Since the birth of my daughter, I have worried about money and wondered if I should stay at my job or try to find another one. I know God has helped me in the past before, but it is so easy to worry." Miguel then asked Ron to read some of the verses he had chosen regarding faith. The two then talked about what this kind of faith would look and feel like and how it would change Ron's life.

In the next two sessions, Miguel worked with Ron to complete the Christogram, including verses focusing on the victory God promises and the strength that faith in Christ can bring. Ron began to attend a few church-related twelve-step groups again and appeared to regain his stride. He even took the step of becoming a sponsor for a new young man in the recovery group.

It was also during this time that Ron decided to apply for a supervisor's position at work. Although he did not get that position, he did accept a similar position at another company later that year. Ron came to a clearer understanding of what Christ had done for him and began to live more in that reality.

Ron hung his Christogram on the refrigerator at home, as a reminder of all he now has as a Christian.

Suggestions for Follow-Up

In the following weeks after introducing this exercise, check in with the client and note the progress he or she has made. As with most therapy, the client will value what you value, so make sure you give adequate attention to this important exercise.

This exercise can form the foundation for a new understanding of things that have already happened spiritually. The concept of being a new creation in Christ is a foundational idea for spiritual growth and development. It would be hard to spend too much time on this key area.

Contraindications

This exercise is contraindicated if the client has never come to a personal relationship with God through Jesus Christ. Moreover, put this exercise to the side when the client has more immediate issues of safety, action, or obedience.

In addition, compartmentalization for some people is quite easy. Like water off a duck's back, sometimes the material covered seems to have no effect. If this is the case, simplify the session by going back to a more basic understanding of the new birth, focusing on faith, obedience, and truth.

Resources for Professionals

Clinton, T., and Ohschlager, G. (2002). *Competent Christian counseling.* Colorado Springs, CO: WaterBrook Press.

Collins, G. (1993). *The biblical basis of Christian counseling for people helpers.* Colorado Springs, CO: NavPress.

McGee, R. (1998). *Search for significance.* Nashville, TN: Word Publishing.

Pratt, M. (2004). *When my faith feels shallow: Pursuing the depths of God.* Birmingham, AL: New Hope Publishers.

Resources for Clients

Gunderson, G. (2003). *Biblical antidotes to life's toxins.* Peabody, MA: Hendrickson Publishers, Inc.
McGee, R. (1998). *Search for significance.* Nashville, TN: Word Publishing.
Moore, B. (2000). *Breaking free: Making liberty in life a reality in Christ.* Nashville, TN: Broadman and Holman Publishers.
Moore, B. (2000). *Breaking free from spiritual strongholds: Praying God's word.* Nashville, TN: Broadman and Holman Publishers.
Moore, B. (2004). *Believing God.* Nashville, TN: Broadman and Holman Publishers.
Morris, J. (2003). *From worry to worship: A 30-day guide to overcoming inferiority.* Birmingham, AL: New Hope Publishers.
Payne, A. (2002). *You may lose your balance, but you can fall into grace: Finding spiritual Renewal in life's quirky moments.* Birmingham, AL: New Hope Publishers.
Warren, R. (2002). *The purpose-driven life: What on earth am I here for?* Grand Rapids, MI: Zondervan.
Yancey, P. (1997). *What's so amazing about grace?* Grand Rapids, MI: Zondervan Publishing House.

Related Scriptures

> For in Christ all the fullness of the Deity lives in bodily form, and you have been given fullness in Christ. (Colossians 2:9, 10a NIV)

> But because of his great love for us, God, who is rich in mercy, made us alive with Christ even when we were dead. (Ephesians 2:4, 5 NIV)

> Therefore there is no condemnation for those who are in Christ Jesus. (Romans 8:1 NIV)

Christogram

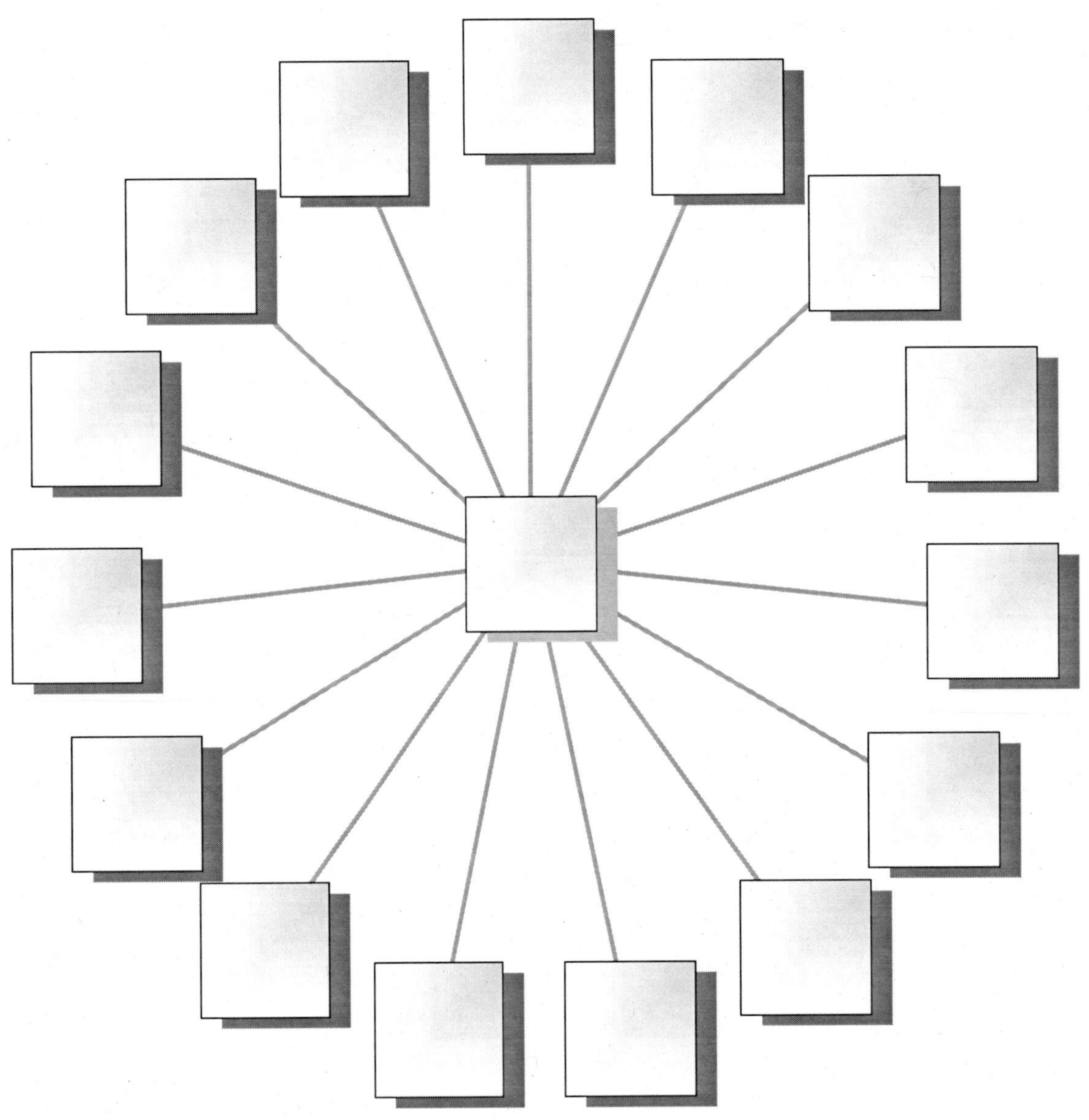

If anyone is in Christ, they are a new creation.

2 Corinthians 5:17 (NIV)

Model Christogram

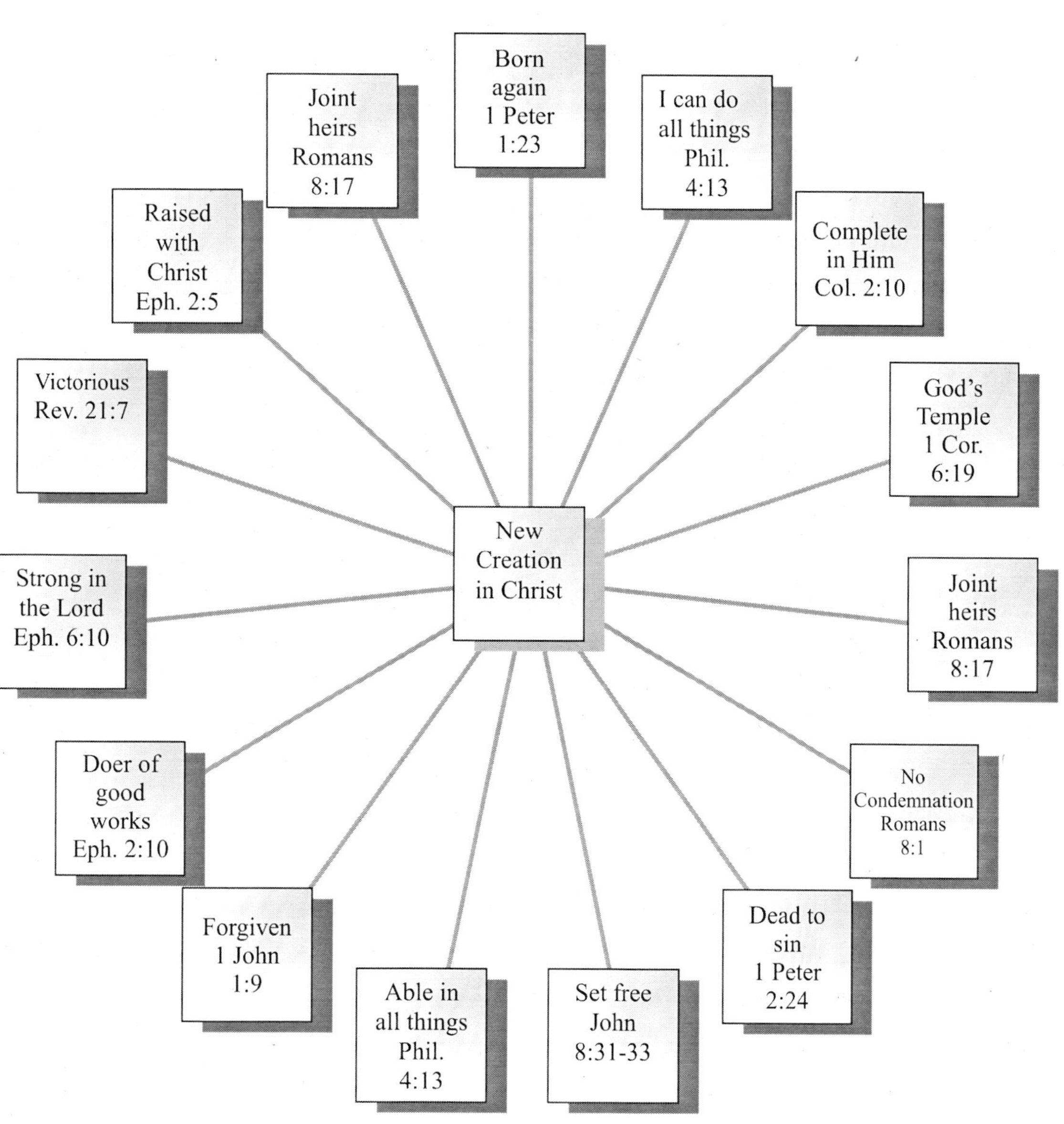

The Four Spiritual Laws

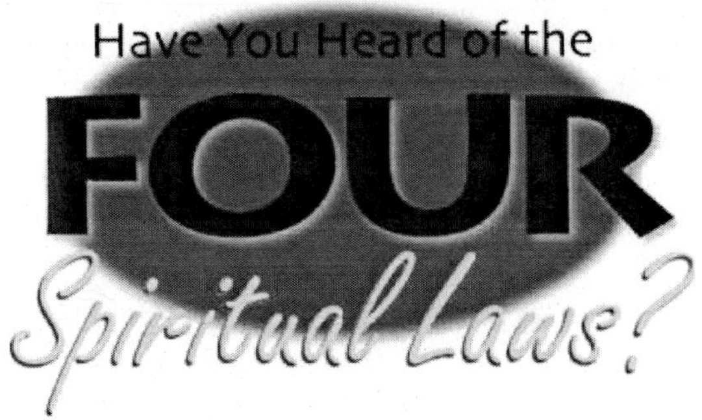

Just as there are physical laws that govern the physical universe, so are there spiritual laws which govern your relationship with God.

God **LOVES** you and offers a wonderful **PLAN** for your life.

God's Love
"God so loved the world that He gave His one and only Son, that whoever believes in Him shall not perish, but have eternal life" (John 3:16 NIV).

God's Plan
[Christ speaking] "I came that they might have life, and might have it abundantly" [that it might be full and meaningful] (John 10:10).

Why is it that most people are not experiencing the abundant life? Because . . .

Man is **SINFUL** and **SEPARATED** from God. Therefore, he cannot know and experience God's love and plan for his life.

Man Is Sinful
"All have sinned and fall short of the glory of God" (Romans 3:23).

Man was created to have fellowship with God; but, because of his stubborn self-will, he chose to go his own independent way, and fellowship with God was broken. This self-will, characterized by an attitude of active rebellion or passive indifference, is an evidence of what the Bible calls sin.

Man Is Separated
"The wages of sin is death" [spiritual separation from God] (Romans 6:23).

This diagram illustrates that God is holy and man is sinful. A great gulf separates the two. The arrows illustrate that man is continually trying to reach God and the abundant life through his own efforts, such as a good life, philosophy, or religion—but he inevitably fails.

The third law explains the only way to bridge this gulf . . .

Jesus Christ is God's **ONLY** provision for man's sin. Through Him you can know and experience God's love and plan for your life.

He Died in Our Place
"God demonstrates His own love toward us, in that while we were yet sinners, Christ died for us" (Romans 5:8).

He Rose from the Dead
"Christ died for our sins. . . . He was buried. . . . He was raised on the third day, according to the Scriptures. . . . He appeared to Peter, then to the twelve. After that He appeared to more than five hundred" (1 Corinthians 15:3-6).

He Is the Only Way to God
"Jesus said to him, 'I am the way, and the truth, and the life; no one comes to the Father, but through Me'" (John 14:6).

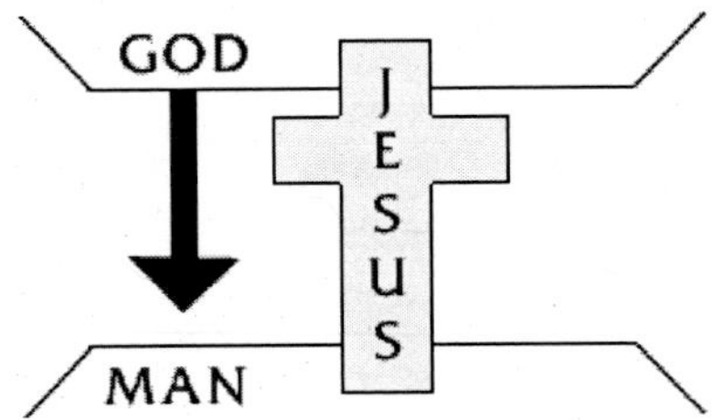

This diagram illustrates that God has bridged the gulf which separates us from Him by sending His Son, Jesus Christ, to die on the cross in our place to pay the penalty for our sins.

It is not enough just to know these three laws. . .

We must individually **RECEIVE** Jesus Christ as Savior and Lord; then we can know and experience God's love and plan for our lives.

We Must Receive Christ
"As many as received Him, to them He gave the right to become children of God, even to those who believe in His name" (John 1:12).

We Receive Christ Through Faith
"By grace you have been saved through faith; and that not of yourselves, it is the gift of God; not as a result of works, that no one should boast" (Ephesians 2:8,9).

When We Receive Christ, We Experience a New Birth
(Read John 3:1-8.)

We Receive Christ by Personal Invitation
[Christ speaking] "Behold, I stand at the door and knock; if any one hears My voice and opens the door, I will come in to him" (Revelation 3:20).

Receiving Christ involves turning to God from self (repentance) and trusting Christ to come into our lives to forgive our sins and to make us what He wants us to be. Just to agree **intellectually** that Jesus Christ is the Son of God and that He died on the cross for our sins is not enough. Nor is it enough to have an **emotional** experience. We receive Jesus Christ by **faith**, as an act of the **will**.

These two circles represent two kinds of lives:

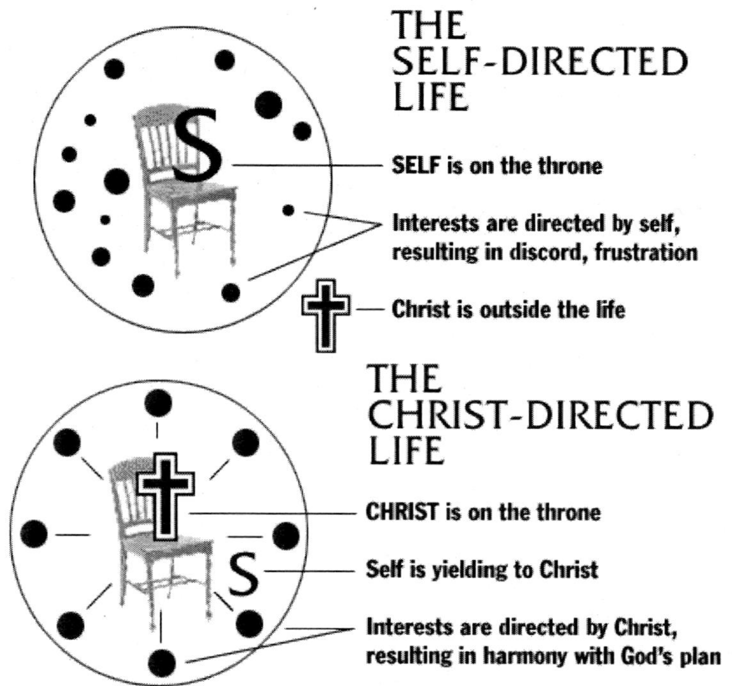

Which circle best describes your life?
Which circle would you like to have represent your life?

The following explains how you can receive Christ:

You Can Receive Christ Right Now by Faith Through Prayer

(Prayer is talking to God)

God knows your heart and is not so concerned with your words as He is with the attitude of your heart. The following is a suggested prayer:

> *Lord Jesus, I need You. Thank You for dying on the cross for my sins. I open the door of my life and receive You as my Savior and Lord. Thank You for forgiving my sins and giving me eternal life. Take control of the throne of my life. Make me the kind of person You want me to be.*

Does this prayer express the desire of your heart?

If it does, I invite you to pray this prayer right now, and Christ will come into your life, as He promised.

– 2 –

Snapshots

Philip J. Henry
Gene A. Sale

Guiding Scripture

The past was written to teach us.

Romans 15:4 (NIV)

Type of Contribution: Exercise, Handout/Homework

Objective

The client will be able to conceptualize his or her experiences by exploring and understanding his or her primary relational history through identifying situations and individuals having had either a negative or a positive effect on the client. This will help reveal repetitive patterns of behavior in multiple relationships, aid in identifying the relational and emotional needs that repeatedly appear in the life of the client, and highlight areas of strength to use in relational growth and development.

The client may also identify possible relational areas where repetitious negative patterns have caused him or her to feel stuck and nonproductive. In some cases, he or she no longer feels the hope that change is possible in certain areas of his or her life.

Rationale for Use

Experiences have a powerful influence on the present and future. Scripture suggests that experiences can teach about life and instruct how to live successfully. Each individual has a past full of wisdom; providing that person takes the time and has the tools to understand the events, the responses to the events, and how the events compose who the individual becomes. This exercise will assist clients in developing a retrospective perception that enables the client to see how he or she understood the event at the time and how he or she perceives it now.

By considering what he or she has been looking for in relationships and what he or she has received in relationships, the client will understand his or her own perspective that has affected and still does affect his or her life. This exercise, then, allows the client to see the ways individual needs and history have intertwined to produce the current pattern of acting and thinking.

The Christian Therapist's Notebook

doi:10.1300/5334_03

Instructions

The "Snapshots" exercise is interactive. Have the client fill out the handout while in session or assign it as homework, and then review it together. The goal is not the completion of the handout but the development of a skill set that will enable the client to make sense of his or her actions and reactions. This takes time and patience, as there is a natural resistance to doing new things; however, if the client will do the work, many good changes will emerge.

Talk with the client about his or her history of relationships and see if the client is open to exploring how those primary relationships have affected him or her. Take the Snapshots handout and begin with the person column. Ask the client to start with parents or guardians or the earliest relationships that he or she can remember. Once the client selects a person, begin to choose several events that are snapshots of his or her interactions with that person. Ask him or her to tell you about these events as if you were looking at a photograph. The client may be able to visualize these situations in his or her mind because these are usually emotion-packed events that seem to be encoded more consistently and completely by the developing brain.

Explain the exercise and help the client understand how to proceed by asking him or her to give you one example. Take the example all the way through, from the past event to the present perception of the event. See whether the client can discover patterns of things he or she was looking for or what he or she received. Ask him or her to examine these patterns and the results that have emerged in his or her thinking.

Ask the client whether there are any perceptions or thinking that he or she would like to change or think should change. If the client is open and has a spiritual foundation, ask him or her to look at spiritual events or notable moments that occurred in his or her relationship with God. You may want to complete the exercise with God as the person in the "person" column to see how the client's relationship with God has developed.

Vignette

Darryl is a thirty-year-old insurance sales representative. He is single and lives by himself in a comfortable apartment. He presented with symptoms of clinical depression and was referred by his medical doctor for counseling to complement the antidepressant medication he had been prescribed.

Darryl feels rather isolated and detached from friends, family, and co-workers. He states that he would like to be married and have a family, but he has never found the right person with whom to share his life. He is especially disappointed with his friendships. Though he knows a number of people, he feels he can get only so close before he loses interest in the relationship. This is true for both his female and male friendships. Darryl was in what he called a "serious relationship" with a young woman for a couple of years. Finally, she gave him the ultimatum: she was interested in a life partner; if he did not see the relationship going in that direction, she would just as soon end it. When he hesitated, she ended the relationship.

At this time he began taking inventory of his relationships and determined that he was not "connected" at a deep level with anyone in his life. Though he had received Christ as a child, Darryl feels now as if he is not particularly close to God. He attends church weekly, as a Christian duty, not because it is particularly meaningful to him.

I asked Darryl if he would consider doing the Snapshots exercise to examine his more significant relationships. He readily agreed, and the following were some of the results of the exercise.

Snapshot #1

PERSON: Father.

EVENT: My father was in the Navy. I recall, at age eight, standing next to my father's ship before he left on a six-month deployment. Though I felt proud, I also was sad, and everyone around me was crying.

WHAT YOU WANTED: A strong emotional connection with my father. I wanted to be with him.

WHAT YOU GOT: A kind but distant relationship.

RESULT: We were never close.

WHAT YOU THOUGHT ABOUT IT THEN: I thought that was just what dads do: they go away to provide for their families.

WHAT I THINK ABOUT IT NOW: I struggle with getting too close because I do not know how to do that.

Snapshot #2

PERSON: Mother.

EVENT: My eleventh birthday party.

WHAT YOU WANTED: My mother's undivided attention.

WHAT YOU GOT: She was busy attending to my younger sister, who was causing problems all through my party.

RESULT: I want to be special.

WHAT YOU THOUGHT ABOUT IT THEN: Angry with my sister for acting out.

WHAT YOU THINK ABOUT IT NOW: Angry with my mother for not giving me more attention.

Snapshot #3

PERSON: Friend, Steve.

EVENT: Saying good-bye before one of our five moves in twelve years.

WHAT YOU WANTED: I wanted to stay good friends with him.

WHAT YOU GOT: We lost touch not long after I moved, and I never heard from him again.

WHAT YOU THOUGHT ABOUT IT THEN: I hated saying good-bye to my friends.

WHAT YOU THINK ABOUT IT NOW: Getting close to someone is painful because one day you will leave.

After exploring several other significant relationships, the obvious pattern emerged of estrangement and feelings of abandonment. Darryl would get only so close to a person and withdraw because this was uncharted territory for him that would create a significant degree of anxiety. The way he coped with the anxiety was to create what was normal to him, rejection. He would scan the horizons of his relationships, waiting for the rejection to come. If the rejection did not come, he would create situations in which he would withdraw to alleviate the anxiety.

When the pattern repeated, his anxiety temporarily abated, but each time, Darryl would slip further into depression. Now in his thirties, he began feeling hopeless that he would ever find true intimacy in a relationship.

This pattern was also true in Darryl's relationship with God. We discussed how one's God-concept usually seems based on earlier relationships with their earthly father and how it is usually erroneous. In Darryl's case, lack of intimacy with his earthly father created a lack of intimacy with his Heavenly Father.

As Darryl began substituting his erroneous thoughts about God with biblical truths about God, he slowly began growing in this most important relationship. Darryl began to see that God's unconditional love could flow through him.

Suggestions for Follow-Up

Use the exercise as a guide for therapy, outlining the areas and relationships that might be the focus of therapy, and highlighting the people and events that have been major factors in the life of the client. This exercise can also help the client see how his or her perceptions and cognitions in therapy have positively evolved because of accomplished therapeutic goals.

The therapist can use this exercise as a baseline for understanding the genetic, cognitive, and emotional thinking of the client. It can also help the client, if he or she struggles with negative behavior patterns, to know it could be due to his or her friendships or family of origin.

Contraindications

This exercise is contraindicated when the current problem is not seemingly related to a life cycle event, or if the client does not believe that past unresolved events affect present and future behaviors.

It is also contraindicated when clients cannot remember the past because of repressed traumatic memories, or when communicating the events brings on symptoms of post-traumatic stress disorder (PTSD).

Resources for Professionals

Anderson, N. (2003). *Discipleship counseling*. Ventura, CA: Regal Books.
Flather, D. (1995). *The resource guide for Christian counselors*. Grand Rapids, MI: Baker Books.
Gunderson, G. (2003). *Biblical antidotes to life's toxins*. Peabody, MA: Hendrickson Publishers, Inc.

Resources for Clients

Bright, B. (1995). *How you can be filled with the Holy Spirit*. Orlando, FL: New Life Publications.
Crabb, L. (1988). *Inside out*. Colorado Springs, CO: NavPress.
Faulkner, P. (1996). *Making things right when things go wrong*. West Monroe, LA: Howard Publishing Co., Inc.
Jeremiah, D. (2000). *When your world falls apart*. Nashville, TN: W. Publishing Group, a division of Thomas Nelson, Inc.
Peale, N. (1994). *Help yourself with God's help*. Pawling, NY: Peale Center for Christian Living.
Phillips, B. (2001). *Getting off the emotional roller coaster (42 days to feeling great!)*. Eugene, OR: Harvest House Publishers.
Warren, R. (2002). *The purpose-driven life: What on Earth am I here for?* Grand Rapids, MI: Zondervan.

Related Scriptures

Wisdom is supreme; therefore get wisdom. Though it cost you all you have, get understanding. (Proverbs 4:7 NIV)

Does not wisdom call out? Does not understanding raise her voice? On the heights along the way, where the paths meet, she takes her stand; besides the gates to the city she cries aloud: "To you, O men, I call out; I raise my voice to all mankind. . . . Choose my instruction instead of silver, knowledge rather than choice gold, for wisdom is more precious than rubies, and nothing you desire can compare with her." (Proverbs 8:1-4, 10-11 NIV)

Consider it pure joy my brother, when you face trials of many kinds, because you know that the testing of your faith develops perseverance. Perseverance must finish its work so that you may be mature and complete, not lacking anything. If any of you lacks wisdom, he should ask God who gives generously to all without finding fault, and it will be given to him. (James 1: 2-5 NIV)

Snapshots

PERSON	EVENT	WHAT YOU WANTED	WHAT YOU GOT	RESULT	WHAT YOU THOUGHT ABOUT IT THEN	WHAT YOU THINK ABOUT IT NOW

Core Connections

Philip J. Henry

Guiding Scripture

Love the Lord your God with all your heart, with all your soul and with all your mind. Love your neighbor as yourself.

Matthew 22:37-39 (NIV)

Type of Contribution: Exercise, Handout

Objective

Positive core connections make up a significant part of a happy and healthy life. This exercise will allow the client to visualize the organization of his or her relational core connections and will help both the therapist and the client to accomplish the following:

1. Explore and understand the current relational world of the client.
2. Identify individuals who may cause barriers or links in the therapy process.
3. Help discover the client's relational patterns of interaction.
4. Identify closeness and distance of family of origin as well as other significant relationships.
5. Identify possible areas of trauma or areas where healing needs to occur.
6. Search for areas of relational growth and strength.
7. Examine where the client is in relationship to God.

Rationale for Use

The Bible tells us that relationships with God and with others are primary. These connections greatly affect both the thinking and the actions of the clients. They are necessary to a happy, healthy life. Jesus spoke of this in the Gospels when asked what the greatest commandment was. His answer: "Love the Lord your God with all your heart, with all your soul and with all your mind" and "Love your neighbor as yourself." Jesus is suggesting, if we put the correct priorities first, that is, really loving God and loving those around us, then the other parts of life will fall more easily into place and life is more likely to contain peace and joy.

Clients come seeking answers for problem issues in their lives. However, the core problems are often bigger than the presenting problems or the issues they would like to see solved. Take,

The Christian Therapist's Notebook

doi:10.1300/5334_04

for example, the heart patient who goes to the doctor wanting to cure a heart problem, only to discover that bigger issues must be addressed, and that other ways to address the problems do exist. Instead of a surgical quick fix, the doctor may prescribe a cessation of smoking, a change in diet, an increase in exercise, and/or a total change in lifestyle. For many clients, the problems for which they are seeking treatment relate to their personal relationships, those with God and with others.

Mixtures of positive and negative relationships have a tremendous influence on clients. Clients come to therapy with this set of complex relational patterns which are often fairly constant, but which are not acknowledged by or perhaps not even known to the clients; if they are known, clients often still are not aware of their implications.

This is particularly true of clients with personality disorders, who may feel as though life is falling apart, that people treat them unfairly all of the time, or that there is no reason for the way others act toward them. Such clients constantly feel like the victim or the scapegoat. Yet, what they fail to see is that others are reacting to them. Their actions, attitudes, and verbal comments often are the reasons others act toward them as they do; they become both actor and reactor in a circular process.

The "Core Connections" exercise allows clients to visualize how they have organized their relational core connections and will help therapists to explore and understand the current relational world of the clients. Talking with clients about the absence of relational connections in the inner circle of their lives is a good starting point for discussion.

This exercise helps identify individuals who may cause barriers or links in the therapy process, assists in discovering the client's patterns of interaction, and spots relational issues that remain concerning the family of origin along with other significant relationships. If areas where healing needs to occur or areas of trauma are identified, then the client and the therapist can address these concerns.

This exercise can also aid the therapist in the search for areas of relational growth the client has had in the past. It can also assist in identifying current relationships to use as established foundations upon which therapy can build.

Finally, this exercise can help the client to examine where he or she is in relationship to God. Since God is a person and the most important relationship anyone can have, understanding this spiritual relationship is vital for the client to create a happy and a healthy life.

Instructions

Talk with the client about the importance of relationships and get a sense of his or her awareness and ability to function in relationships. See if the client is open to exploring his or her core connections. This is a great exercise to begin therapy with because it gives a broad overview of where the client is in terms of his or her relationships, where he or she needs to go, and who may be of help in getting him or her there.

Hand the client the Core Connections handout and ask him or her to write the names of those people to whom he or she feels emotionally connected in each of the circles, adding also a word or two to describe each person. Help the client to understand how to proceed by asking him or her to give you one example. Suggest starting with the person to whom the client feels closest, writing his or her name in the innermost circle; the client can then work outward, adding names to each of the circles depending on the degree of closeness in these other relationships.

Encourage the client to be as open as possible. He or she should not spend too much time thinking about where each person goes or about the perfect word to describe a person. Also, observe and take note of any mixed feelings the client may express about these relationships. Emphasize honesty. Make sure the client puts each relationship in the appropriate circle; feelings of guilt or obligation should not guide the client on where to place a person.

Review the exercise with the client, taking time to note to whom he or she feels close and why. Observe where the client places the members of his or her family of origin and what words the client associates with them. This will give you an idea of the client's relationships in his or her early years and the conclusions he or she has reached about life.

Discuss the word or words the client has chosen for each of the individuals in the circles. Note what the inner circle of relationships is like for the client. Question him or her about this circle and ask how the circle is working: What did he or she hope for in each relationship? What has he or she received in each relationship? Moreover, how has the difference between these perceptions affected him or her? These are all great avenues to pursue while exploring the client's relational world.

Ask the client which circle God might go in. You might ask, "Since many people have a relationship with God, what circle would you place Him in right now?" Have the client choose various words to describe God or his or her relationship with Him. Talk with the client about how he or she came to this conclusion and help him or her to examine the truth and the implications of his or her beliefs.

Ask the client to think about change: What changes would he or she like to make to the relationships in the circles or to the words that describe the people in his or her life? Help the client to visualize how such changes will affect his or her life: Explore how the relationships may change and what might be reasonable steps to take to begin moving in a positive direction.

Take the time to pray with the client for the insight and the strength needed to remodel and change his or her relational world.

Vignette

Michael barged into the room like a whirlwind. "I am sorry I am late, but you should have given me better directions. The ones your secretary gave were awful. And your sign outside is too small. How is anyone supposed to see that from the road? You're lucky I made it here at all. And once I got inside the building, there were no directions to your office. You need an arrow or two to show people which way to go. It would have been helpful to know that I needed to eventually go upstairs to the second floor to get to this office." He paused for a moment.

"Are you always like this?" I asked. "Pretty much," he said and took a seat, leaning back and folding his hands behind his head.

My first thought was, "This man is obnoxious," and I visualized pushing him back down the stairs and watching him tumble repeatedly all the way down. Shaking off that mental image, I reminded myself that I was a therapist whose job is to be helpful. I thought, "If this is the way he interacts with strangers, what might his relationships with those who are close to him be like?" In all likelihood, they would not be good.

I handed the Core Connections handout to him along with a pen and a clipboard. "As a beginning exercise, I would like for us to examine your relationships with those around you," I said. Michael agreed, and I briefly explained that I wanted him to put names in the circles, starting with the inner circle and the names of those to whom he felt emotionally close.

"Where do I put the ones I hate?" he asked.

I explained that if he truly disliked them, then he should put them in an outside circle; however, if he disliked them but was still emotionally close to them, then he should put them in a closer circle and add a word or two to describe the friction in their relationship.

"Does my mother have to go in the closest circle?" he asked.

"You can put your mother wherever you want," I replied. I tried not to give too many instructions and encouraged Michael to get started. He worked feverishly for about ten minutes and then indicated that he was finished.

What was striking when I looked at his core connections was how few people were in his inner circle. I felt almost embarrassed to ask him about this, so I asked if he was sure that he was finished. He indicated that he had indeed completed the handout. From the lack of many close connections, I hypothesized that Michael might be lonely, perhaps very lonely. I thought it sad in a way. I also thought that maybe what I had already experienced with Michael might be one of the reasons his circles were so empty.

Looking more closely, I noticed that the first three circles contained only two names. One was his younger sister, who lived in another state, and to whom he had been close growing up. Under his sister's name, he had written the word "bossy" and the word "calm." I asked him about this relationship, and he told me that he talked with Judy about every other week, usually at his initiation. She would give him advice and never seemed too frustrated by anything. However, she had her own life, a husband, and three small children, so he tried not to call too often.

The second was his co-worker's name, under which he had written the words "smart" and "depressed." Robert, his co-worker, was into technology, and the two of them often discussed the latest computer updates and what they would have for lunch. Robert had times where he did seem to be seriously depressed, and during those times, Michael tried to avoid him because he too would begin to feel down, if he spent too much time listening to Robert.

When I asked Michael how he felt about having only two names in the first three circles, he replied that he did not know many people whom he trusted or who understood him. He said he felt it took quite a while to get to know him because he was more complicated than many other people were, and acquaintances did not want to take the time and energy to know him. He also told me that he could quickly size up people and tell them how to make their lives better, but they never seemed to listen, and so he stopped talking to them.

In the fourth circle, he had added a couple from his church who invited him over for lunch occasionally and two friends he had retained from college. In the fifth circle, he had written "mother," and under it, the words "mean" and "critical." "Well," I thought to myself, "this explains a lot."

Michael sighed deeply and explained that his father had passed away three years ago, and that he often had to care for his mother, but she did little to encourage their relationship. She was not happy with his choice of career, she nagged him about getting a girlfriend, she was not happy with his caregiving, or with anything he tried to do for her or to give her. Yet he felt obligated to help her, and so he did.

We talked about this relationship for a while, and I asked him what effect his mother had on him. He told me she prevented his involvement with other people because she required a great deal of his time. In addition, he was able to articulate that he had picked up some of her traits. I asked him if he believed he made others feel the way he felt with his mother. He admitted that he often became irritated due to others' incompetence and that it was easy to become critical. He said he did not want to be critical and actively tried to be more positive with people.When asked if that was working, he replied that he would do well for a while, but then would get tired or not think about it and say something "stupid."

I asked him if he was ever lonely. He reported that he was not lonely at work, but that on the nights and on the long weekends, he did feel a great deal of loneliness. I suspected that the criticism kept him from feeling so needy, lonely, and vulnerable; I made a note to talk with him about this in a later session.

After we had worked through the exercise to the last circle, which contained the names of his mechanic and a neighbor, I asked Michael in what circle he would place God and what words he would use to describe Him. Michael conveyed that he attended church on a weekly basis and talked of other religious duties, such as serving as a deacon for two rotations. I tried to refocus his attention by asking the question again.

"I would say that he would be pretty far out in the circles," Michael finally replied. I asked what words he would use to describe God. He thought for a moment and then said "judging" and "hard to please." "I think that God expects us to be perfect, doesn't he?" Michael asked.

We talked about this perception of God, where it had come from and how we see God through parent-colored glasses. We talked about what he wanted in a relationship with others and what he wanted from God. I found myself liking Michael once he let himself and others act without criticism. Time ran out. Michael thanked me for the session, said that he had a lot to think about, and made an appointment for the next week.

I knew, given his critical nature, that next week he would be upset about something, but I was thankful that he had begun to look at his core relationships and to imagine how it would be to have a different relationship with God and with others.

Suggestions for Follow-Up

The proximity or nonexistence of key relationships sheds some light on the client's beliefs, motivations, and emotions. The way the client perceives the given relationship may also affect his or her behavior in either a negative or a positive manner. If a client views a key person as distant, this perception may provide a beginning point for a discussion on how this relational core connection is affecting his or her current life.

People with eating disorders, addictions, and other mental disorders often lack the skills to relate at a core level or their close relationships are codependent in nature, with enablers having a negative rather than a positive influence. Twelve-step and other Christian support groups can provide new connections that aid in growth.

This exercise can also show the client's reliance on God or the lack of this relationship. Despite the differences or similarities in relational patterns, feedback from the Core Connections exercise shows the therapist the roles that family, friends, and God play in the cognitive belief system of the client.

This exercise can then serve as a tool for the therapist to compare the client's relationship growth before and during therapy. If therapy is going positively, there should be a corresponding change in the relationships when written on paper.

Contraindications

This exercise is contraindicated when the presenting problem is acute or a distinctly internal psychopathology or if the client lacks the most basic relational skills. In those cases, the exercise would merely be confusing or perhaps cause the client to feel or think more negatively.

Resources for Professionals

Clinton, T., and Ohlschlager, G. (2002). *Competent Christian counseling.* Colorado Springs, CO: Water Brook Press.

Collins, G. (2001).*The biblical basis of Christian counseling for people helpers.* Colorado, Springs, CO: NavPress.

Meir, P., and Wise, R. (2003). *Crazy makers.* Nashville, TN: Thomas Nelson.

Resources for Clients

Arterburn, S. (1995). *Addicted to love, understanding dependencies of the heart: Romance, relationships and sex.* Ventura, CA: Vine Books.

Carter, L. (2000). *People pleasers.* Nashville, TN: Broadman and Holman.

Carter, L., and Minirth, M. (1995). *The freedom from depression workbook.* Nashville, TN: Thomas Nelson.
Carter, L., and Minirth, M. (1997). *The choosing to forgive workbook.* Nashville, TN: Thomas Nelson.
Cloud, H., and Townsend, J. (1995). *Boundaries.* Grand Rapids, MI: Zondervan Bible Publishers.
Robinson, J. (1996). *Knowing God as father.* Ft. Worth, TX: Life Outreach International.
Springle, P. (1991). *Rapha's twelve step program for overcoming co-dependency.* Dallas, TX: Rapha Publishing/Word, Inc.
Virkler, H. (1992). *Broken Promises.* Dallas, TX: Word Publishing.
Warren, R. (2002). *The purpose driven life.* Grand Rapids, MI: Zondervan Bible Publishers.
Wright, H. (1994). *So you're getting married.* Grand Rapids, MI: Baker Books.

Related Scriptures

My command is this: Love each other as I have loved you. Greater love has no one than this, that he lay down his life for his friends. (John 15:12-13 NIV)

But if we walk in the light, as He is in the light, we have fellowship with one another, and the blood of Jesus, His Son, purifies us from all sin. (1 John 1:7 NIV)

I appeal to you, brothers, in the name of our Lord Jesus Christ, that all of you agree with one another so that there may be no divisions among you and that you may be perfectly united in mind and thought. (1 Corinthians 1:10 NIV)

Consequently, you are no longer foreigners and aliens, but fellow citizens with God's people and members of God's household. (Ephesians 2:19 NIV)

Core Connections

1. In each circle, list the people to whom you feel emotionally closest. Start with those closest to you in the inner circles and work out to the most distant.
2. You can put more than one person in each circle.
3. List one or two words next to each name that describes the person best.

– 4 –

Temptation Judo

Philip J. Henry
Gene A. Sale

Guiding Scripture

No temptation has seized you except what is common to man. And God is faithful; He will not let you be tempted beyond what you can bear. But when you are tempted, He will also provide a way out so that you can stand up under it.

1 Corinthians 10:13 (NIV)

Type of Contribution: Exercise, Handout

Objective

Trying to fight a temptation without meeting the underlying need is like trying to breathe under water. At some point, it will be time to rise to the surface for air. Helping a client discover the connection between his or her temptation and his or her need, while uncovering God's promise of escape, is that breath of air.

Rationale for Use

The purpose of this exercise is to achieve the following:

1. Explore and understand the connections among the situations, thoughts, and needs that make up temptations in the life of the client.
2. Identify the most common situations and needs in the life of the client.
3. Help the client problem-solve his or her emotional, relational, or physical needs in a more positive manner.
4. Identify God as a source of strength in times of temptation.
5. Learn how to connect with God's provision during times of need.
6. Identify possible situations and needs where temptation has led to a stronghold (area of defeat) in the client's life.
7. Search for new ways to think about temptation that can positively alter the core of those cognitions.

The Christian Therapist's Notebook

doi:10.1300/5334_05

Instructions

Talk with the client about the reality of temptations; see if the client is open to exploring the connections between temptations and needs in his or her life. Then have the client choose one situation in which he or she was tempted, encouraging him or her to pick one that was significantly difficult.

Give the client the "Temptation Judo" handout and ask him or her to be as open as possible when writing down the situation in which he or she was tempted. Try to avoid conveying judgment and creating feelings of unhealthy guilt. Real guilt will lead to repentance (change of mind), which is the goal of the exercise. Judgment and unhealthy guilt do not make for positive problem solving.

Identify the thought that ran through the client's head during the situation. Describe this as his or her "internal talk." Instruct the client to write down the "internal talk." If the client is unable to do this, identify what he or she might be telling himself or herself and verbalize a few of the choices he or she might face. Have the client choose the one that comes closest to his or her thinking. After doing this several times, the client will get better at identifying his or her own thought processes in these situations.

Once the thought is captured and articulated, move on to the next step: see if the client can identify the need that provided the motivation for the temptation. If he or she cannot find the need, go back and identify several situations and their accompanying thought processes. This will usually be enough of a prompt, allowing a pattern to emerge that points to one or more strong needs. If he or she is unclear of the thought processes behind some situations, the client can be instructed to think about it during the time until the next visit, to see if any clarity comes.

See if the client can begin to problem-solve ways of meeting the need or needs identified that do not perpetuate the problem. Brainstorm with him or her about meeting this need, encouraging the client to go beyond where he or she has been, not ruling any thoughts out initially. Some of these may be outside of what he or she feels comfortable with, and this is okay. Solutions are not meant to be found outside of growth. In addition, people often avoid longer-term goals, and this may be an area in which the client can achieve better understanding of the direction his or her life should take, and what God is calling him or her to do. It may also begin to signify where he or she can make wise, thoughtful choices and alter his or her negative behavior patterns.

Make sure to identify God as someone who understands and cares. He has promised to provide a way of escape, so have the client ask Him to make that evident. If the client desires or is willing to pray, this might be a good way to end the session.

Finally, be careful not to overwhelm the client, and to slow down if the client becomes overly anxious or appears pressured to come up with answers.

Vignette

Randy, a forty-two-year-old male, is a loving husband and father. He is active in his church and serves as a deacon. Randy is seeking counseling because of a continual problem he has that surfaces when he is driving: Randy gets very angry. When someone ahead of him is going too slowly or is talking on the cell phone and not paying attention to his or her driving, Randy becomes more than indignant—he flies into a rage. This usually mild-mannered and considerate person becomes someone else. He pounds the steering wheel and shouts curses, his face turns red, and his heart pounds in his chest. His own words are, "I'm out of control."

He admits that when he calms down, he feels embarrassed, especially if one of his children or his wife is in the car when it happens. One time, this happened on the way to church, and the car Randy was raging at turned into the church parking lot right in front of him. With his wife's support and encouragement, he is seeking counseling, as he seems unable to overcome the rage on his own.

The counselor encourages Randy to consider a possible connection between his road rage and some particular need in his life. Though he is a little skeptical, Randy agrees to consider that possibility. The counselor shows Randy the Temptation Judo handout and offers to go through the first line during the session.

At the counselor's request, Randy describes a specific incident when he was driving and lost his temper. He is then encouraged to think about his "internal talk." He describes this as telling himself that the other driver is being personally disrespectful of him and keeping him from being on time for his appointment.

After some discussion, Randy is able to identify two needs that relate to his internal talk. First, he recognizes his need to feel respected as a person. He is able to see that he may be overpersonalizing the incident, as the driver with whom he is angry does not even know him. Second, he sees the other driver's actions as keeping him from a desired goal, being on time. The counselor helps Randy see that each of these needs includes an implied threat to his self-esteem. The belief is that if a person disrespects me, he or she is worthy of punishment and if a person causes me not to meet my goals, he or she is worthy of punishment.

As an alternative way to meet the need, Randy is encouraged to consider feeling good about himself by being gracious and forgiving. Though he lost sight of it many times while driving, Randy genuinely wants to live a life that is pleasing to God. The counselor encourages Randy to consider a different approach when he feels anger emerging within him.

At these times, Randy is encouraged to focus on his "need" to honor God and to recite James 1:20 (NIV): "For man's anger does not bring about the righteous life that God requires." He is also encouraged to consider the active role of forgiveness in the Lord's Prayer in Matthew 6:12 (NIV): "Forgive us our debts, as we also have forgiven our debtors." He is also given an assignment—to study the parable of the unmerciful servant in Matthew 18:21-35 (NIV) and describe how this might relate to his situation.

Randy is encouraged to administer grace and forgiveness to himself for past and future incidents in which he may fall short of his goal of pleasing God in every situation.

Suggestions for Follow-Up

Have the client memorize the Guiding Scripture:

> No temptation has seized you except what is common to man. And God is faithful; He will not let you be tempted beyond what you can bear. But when you are tempted, He will also provide a way out so that you can stand up under it. (1 Corinthians 10:13 NIV)

Contraindications

This exercise should not be used with clients who are excessively impulsive or have any degree of obsession in thinking. Working through this activity with such a client might increase the likelihood that the client might become fixated on the topic and unable to disengage or find appropriate distance. With too many details he or she might be motivated to impulsively engage in the negative behaviors that were discussed.

Resources for Professionals

Anderson, N., Zeuhlke, T., and Zeuhke J. (2000). *Christ centered therapy*. Grand Rapids, MI: Zondervan Publishing House.

Crabb, L. (1988). *Inside out*. Colorado Springs, CO: NavPress.
Laaser, M. (2004). *Healing the wounds of sexual addiction.* Grand Rapids, MI: Zondervan Publishing House.

Resources for Clients

McGee, R. (1998). *Search for significance.* Nashville, TN: Word Publishing.
Means, P. (2002). *Men's secret wars.* Grand Rapids, MI: Baker Books.
Miller, J. (1991). *A hunger for healing.* New York: HarperCollins Publishers.
Mylander, C. (1986). *Running the red lights.* Ventura, CA: Regal Books.
Payne, A. (2002). *You may lose your balance, but you can fall into grace: Finding spiritual renewal in life's quirky moments.* Birmingham, AL: New Hope Publishers.
Rockwood, E. (1999). *When prayers are not answered.* Peabody, MA: Hendrickson Publishers, Inc.
Thurman, C. (1991). *Lies we believe workbook.* Nashville, TN: Thomas Nelson Publishers.
Why Wait? (2000). *Why wait?: 24 reasons to wait until marriage to have sex* [pamphlet]. Torrance, CA: Rose Publishing.
Yancey, P. (1997). *What's so amazing about grace?* Grand Rapids, MI: Zondervan Publishing House.

Related Scriptures

I have hidden your word in my heart that I might not sin against you. (Psalm 119:11 NIV)

When tempted, no one should say, "God is tempting me." For God can not be tempted by evil, nor does he tempt anyone; but each one is tempted when, by his one evil desire, he is dragged away and enticed. Then, after desire has conceived, it gives birth to sin; and sin when it is full-grown gives birth to death. (James 1:13-15 NIV)

Therefore, since we have a great high priest who has gone through the heavens, Jesus the Son of God, let us hold firmly to the faith we possess. For we do not have a high priest who is unable to sympathize with our weaknesses, but we have one who has been temped in every way, just as we are—yet without sin. Let us then approach the throne of grace with confidence, so that we may receive mercy and find grace to help us in our time of need. (Hebrews 4:14-16 NIV)

Because he himself suffered when he was tempted, he is able to help those who are being tempted. (Hebrews 2:18 NIV)

Temptation Judo

Situation	Thought	Need	Alternative way to meet need
1.			
2.			
3.			
4.			
5.			
6.			
7.			
8.			
9.			
10.			

No temptation has seized you except what is common to man. And God is faithful;
He will not let you be tempted beyond what you can bear. But when you are tempted,
He will provide a way out so that you can stand up under it.

1 Corinthians 10:13 (NIV)

– 5 –

Broken Mirrors

Lori Marie Figueroa

Guiding Scripture

He heals the brokenhearted and binds up their wounds.

Psalm 147:3 (NIV)

Type of Contribution: Exercise, Handout/Homework

Objective

This exercise will help clients to identify unresolved issues that have negatively affected their self-image, by moving the client to achieve hope and direction through a personal relationship with God.

Rationale for Use

A client's self-perception affects his or her cognitive, physical, and spiritual being. When a client has unresolved issues, it distorts his or her perception of life. In other words, the reflection he or she sees in the mirror is incomplete. Christian therapists need to convey to clients that God openly welcomes the brokenhearted. When addressing the unmet needs of client, counselors must convey God as a platform of hope, and seek to help the client identify and address unresolved issues in his or her life in order for true inner healing to occur.

The therapist should explore and gain an understanding of how the client perceives himself or herself. Through the analogy of a mirror, the therapist can ask the client to describe what he or she sees and what thoughts come to mind when looking at his or her reflection. Next, the client needs to acknowledge the individual people and situations that have negatively influenced his or her perception of self. This will help determine areas of unforgiveness that are impeding emotional, mental, or spiritual development.

Share scripture with the client as he or she begins to identify God as a source of hope in times of trouble. A client who has experienced physical or emotional pain needs a spiritual guide who can help him or her look at his or her reflection in a new, positive way. Words of inspiration can serve to encourage the client and lead to continuous healing. When Jesus' disciples abandoned Him at a crucial point in His life, Jesus asked them if they thought He should abandon them as well. Peter quickly replied, "To whom would we go? You alone have the words of life" (John 6:66-68 KJV).

The Christian Therapist's Notebook

doi:10.1300/5334_06

As hurting clients seek counsel, the model of Jesus is a great example for Christian therapists to follow. Jesus never promised one's life to be perfect and void of pain. On the other hand, Jesus Christ's goal was to demonstrate, through His life and words, how a character transformation provides meaning and joy in the midst of life's uncertainties. This adjustment leads to a change of heart in reaction to people and situations. This is more than simply forgiveness; it is a complete mind-set revival. As a client strives to react in a Christ-like manner, he or she will experience a peace that can protect him or her in times of pain. The client should also learn to turn to God in times of need and to develop healthy support systems with family members and/or friends.

Instructions

Ask the client to describe his or her reflection in the mirror. Determine if the client is open to exploring how situations and people may have affected his or her self-perception. Next, explain the goal of the exercise. Help the client understand how to proceed by asking him or her to give you one example of a situation that negatively affected his or her life. Have the client list events or people from childhood that affected him or her in a negative way. Amend the exercise to fit the needs of the given client.

In the second session, have the client continue listing events or people through the next stages of his or her life span. Explore reasons why any issues have been left unresolved: How did the mirror break? Some examples of unresolved issues may include divorce, childhood sexual abuse and abandonment, loss of a career, abortion, trauma, death, or even eating disorders. Work together with the client to look at the causes and effects of the issues. An important area to look at may be forgiveness. The client may need to learn to forgive another person, himself or herself, or even God.

In a future session, compare the initial cognitions with the new cognitions created because of the client's awareness of the issues. Have the client analyze the reflection as he or she sees it now. As a final step, therapists can share scriptures depicting God healing wounds and gluing each broken piece of the mirror back together. God can make him or her complete again. The client must understand that this newfound healing in Christ does not prevent any unexpected hurts from reoccurring. However, it does give a guide to the way he or she can respond and to whom he or she can turn in times of need.

Vignette

Dwight is a forty-five-year-old, single, Caucasian male who works as a mechanic at a local car dealership. His parents claim to be Christians, but they attend church only on Christmas and Easter. As a child, Dwight went each year to a Christian summer camp where he learned about God. However, he felt as if the reality of Christ did not apply to him. He loves his job of twenty years because it gives him an opportunity to fix things. He also feels at peace at work because he is able to spend most of his time alone.

Considering himself a loner, Dwight spent most of his weekends drinking at a local bar. Dwight admits to having an occasional one-night stand. However, he has no desire for a personal, long-term relationship or companionship. His relationships are short-term and of an unattached sexual nature.

Dwight is an only child. His parents have both been doctors at a prestigious local hospital since his childhood. He recalls, at a young age, reading books in the hospital lobby while his parents worked. He would walk around the hospital and look at children who were dying in the cancer ward. He would see some of them surrounded by family members. He confessed that he secretly wished the diagnosis of a disease on himself so his parents would acknowledge his existence.

At the age of eighteen, Dwight fell in love with the girl next door. She was upbeat and energetic. She made him feel loved and special. He spent every day following her around. At first, she seemed to look forward to his visits and gifts. However, within months, she began avoiding him. She ended their relationship when she left for college on the West Coast. He considered moving from the East Coast to follow her. However, once at college, she quickly began dating. She wrote him a letter saying she was engaged to the "man of her dreams." Dwight was deeply hurt.

Dwight started fixing cars for his neighbors. This led him to a job as a mechanic at a local car dealership. While at work, the wife of one of his customers began flirting with him. He ignored her at first. However, one late evening at work, he gave in to temptation. He had an affair with the woman. His customer confronted Dwight's supervisor about the affair. Since Dwight had always been a loyal employee, he received only a verbal warning. The Employee Assistance Program (EAP) mandated him to seek counseling, providing for three sessions.

Dwight was silent during the first therapy session. He simply nodded and refused to provide any personal information. He maintained distance from the therapist. He crossed his arms and looked at his watch throughout the session. The therapist gave Dwight homework to bring to the next session, asking him to describe his reflection as he saw it in a mirror. The therapist encouraged Dwight to explore how situations and people may have affected the way he perceived himself. Next, the therapist explained the goal of the exercise.

When Dwight went home that evening, he sat in front of the television; his mind was distracted. He looked at the mirror from afar with a smirk. However, curiosity led him to stand in front of the mirror. At first he thought, "All I see is me." The longer he stood there, though, the more aware he became of many details. He noticed a scar on his face, causing him to remember how he ran outside his home crying when he received "the letter" from his ex-girlfriend, tripping over a branch and falling into a rose bush. One of the thorns penetrated his face. Rather than attempting to ease the pain, he did not even bother to clean the wound. On a piece of paper, he described himself as a "scarred man." He saved this for his next session.

During the second session, the therapist asked Dwight if he had completed the homework. Dwight nodded and handed over the piece of paper. Dwight received the "Broken Mirror" handout and filled in the pieces with adjectives depicting his reflection. He wrote words such as unlovable, scarred, sad, mad, unworthy, and lonely. While they looked at the reflection, the therapist explained that they did not see a "scarred man," but instead someone who had been deeply hurt. The therapist showed a genuine desire to help Dwight achieve hope. Dwight was overwhelmed with the therapist's sincerity. He opened up and began sharing aspects of his childhood, including details of how he got the scar. With tears in his eyes, Dwight described how he felt broken. The therapist spent most of the session actively listening. The session ended when the therapist gave Dwight a homework assignment to look up Jeremiah 29:11 in a Bible.

By the third session, Dwight felt a remedial rapport with the therapist, who was now able to identify the unresolved issues that had negatively affected Dwight's self-image and led him to reject meaningful relationships. The therapist read aloud: "'For I know the plans, I have for you,' declares the Lord, 'plans to prosper and not to harm you, plans for hope and a future'" (Jeremiah 29:11 KJV). Dwight was unclear how that scripture personally applied to his life. He felt harm and pain consuming most of his life. Through open-ended questions, the therapist was able to help Dwight search deeper.

Learning from Jesus' example, how He reacted when others hurt Him, Dwight began to acknowledge there might be other ways of reacting to people and situations. He also finally realized he was lovable, despite his past hurts. He admitted the desire for a personal relationship with a woman but feared getting hurt again. He was also open to learning more about achieving a personal relationship with God. Since this was his last mandated session, he asked the therapist if he could pay out of pocket and continue the sessions on a monthly basis until he felt better. The therapist agreed.

Suggestions for Follow-Up

This exercise helps the therapist focus on areas negatively affecting the client's cognitions. As a result, clients can acknowledge that through God they are made perfect. During the process, it is important for the therapist to address important issues, such as unforgiveness, that may have hindered the client's spiritual or emotional growth.

Regardless of a client's poor self-image, this exercise provides therapists with a way to understand why the client has that perception. A suggestion for follow-up can be the establishment of clear therapeutic goals based on the client's answers. These answers may provide insight on how to renew the client's cognition in a positive manner. It is important for Christian therapists to seek God's wisdom continually through prayer while they explore the client's responses. As therapy progresses and inner healing takes place, a reissue of the exercise may show fewer broken pieces, and thereby offer the client encouragement, as evidence he or she is moving forward in a positive way.

Contraindications

Since this exercise focuses on internal perceptions, it is contraindicated when the presenting problem relates to external factors beyond the client's control. In addition, if the client has had a negative experience related to a mirror, another method of reflection should be used.

Resources for Professionals

Anderson, N.T. (2003). *Discipleship counseling*. Ventura, CA: Regal Books.
Anderson, N.T., Zuehlke, T.E., and Zuehlke, J.S. (2000). *Christ centered therapy*. Grand Rapids, MI: Zondervan Publishing House.
Huggins, K.D. (2003). *Friendship counseling*. Colorado Springs, CO: NavPress.

Resources for Clients

Crabb, L. (2001). *Shattered dreams*. Colorado Springs, CO: Waterbrook Press.
Edwards, D. (2001). *Revolution within*. Colorado Springs, CO: Waterbrook Press.
Smalley, G. (2004). *The DNA of relationships*. Wheaton, IL: Tyndale House Publishers, Inc.

Related Scriptures

> See now that I myself am He. And there is no God besides Me: I put to death and I bring to life; I have wounded and I will heal. (Deuteronomy 32:39 NIV)

> He sent forth His word and healed them; He rescued them from the grave. (Psalm 107:20 NIV)

But He was wounded for our transgressions. He was bruised for our inequities. The chastisement for our peace was upon Him. And by His stripes we are healed. (Isaiah 53:5 KJV)

My son, give attention to my words; Incline your ear to my sayings. Do not let them depart from your eyes; Keep them in the midst of your heart; for they are life to those who find them. And health to all their flesh. (Proverbs 4:20-22 KJV)

For I know the plans, I have for you," declares the Lord, "plans to prosper and not to harm you, plans for hope and a future." (Jeremiah 29:11 KJV)

Broken Mirror

Unemployed

Unforgiven

Divorced

Overweight

Adulterer

Sexually Abused

– 6 –

The Book of My Life

Lori Marie Figueroa

Guiding Scripture

Oh, that my words were recorded, that they were written on a scroll,
that they were inscribed with an iron tool on lead,
or engraved in rock forever!

Job 19:23-24 (NIV)

Type of Contribution: Exercise, Handout/Homework

Objective

The objective of this exercise is to help clients in therapy identify situations and/or people who have had a positive or negative impact on their lives, while also assisting clients in acknowledging that God has a plan for their lives.

Rationale for Use

Compare a client's life to a book. A book's foreword may include the way key people in the client's life perceive him or her. The table of contents may include key events that occurred throughout his or her life. The introduction may include his or her childhood or family history. Chapter 1 may contain the client's early childhood. The last chapter may either set forth the client's current stage of life or describe how he or she hopes his or her life would end. Looking at his or her personal book from beginning to end can help the client carefully examine his or her life and acknowledge the personal, physical, emotional, or spiritual growth in any given area.

In the Bible, Job expressed a desire to leave a legacy of his life. He understood that his triumphs and his trials were equally important. God has carefully planned every event and detail of the client's life. It is important to show the client God's presence throughout his or her life. Therapists can be the catalyst for clients to take a closer look at their past, present, and hopes for the future. This exercise can help therapists see if any inconsistencies exist within their clients' cognitions. It can also help identify possible areas of their clients' lives where growth has not occurred and aid in determining the people and/or situations that have hindered such growth. A book format can help clients see the value of their lives. Such a comparison can remind clients that their lives, in the same manner, can positively affect others.

The Christian Therapist's Notebook

doi:10.1300/5334_07

Instructions

Using the "The Life of . . ." handout at the end of the chapter, explain to the client that his or her life can be described as a book. Ask the client to write the book of his or her life, beginning with his or her childhood and including key people as well as key events. The chapters may be detailed or simply in outline form, whichever the client prefers. Suggest that the client work on two chapters at a time as homework, allowing the client to divide his or her life into phases as he or she sees fit. Discuss the chapters the client has written in each following session. However, let the client determine the pace. Certain clients may become stuck on a particular chapter. For example, clients may have experienced some type of abuse as a child, great difficulty in school, a traumatic event as a young adult, or a divorce as an adult. They likely will write about these types of experiences in greater detail and want to discuss this part of their history more expansively. In this way, let the clients lead you to the needed areas of discussion and resolution without bogging down completely and never moving beyond the particular event or phase.

Next, ask the client to explore the feelings experienced as he or she wrote the chapters of his or her life. Explore any events that have been left unresolved and are negatively affecting his or her life. Work together with the client to look at solutions. One possible area to evaluate is forgiveness.

In a following session, compare the beginning cognitions with the new cognitions created because of the client's awareness of the issues. Have the client write chapters on his or her expectations and/or hopes for the next ten years of his or her life. Discuss what changes need to occur for the client to obtain the desired outcome.

For the client who does not like to write, suggest drawing pictures on the back of the page. He or she may choose to write key words with the pictures. Remember that the goal is not to rush through the book. The goal should be to gain an understanding of key events in the client's life and to recognize how these events have affected his or her cognitions. As an important final step, use real examples from the client's story to show God's presence and hand throughout the stages of his or her life.

Vignette

Juan is a Hispanic, twenty-nine-year-old male. His parents immigrated to the United States from Argentina. He grew up in a happy home with loving parents and two younger sisters. Juan had been a believer since childhood. He often felt that he could see the hand of God working in his life. However, he more often felt the opposite. His best friend, Felipe, recently died in a car accident involving a drunk driver who had hit him. Juan could not understand why Felipe, a good-hearted person and believer in God, had died, while the guilty party lived. To confound the matter further, Juan was taking classes at a public community college with professors who did not share his Christian worldview.

He decided to go to church to find some answers. Although some of the members seemed sincere in their desire to comfort him, others scolded him for his lack of faith. Disappointed with this church, Juan went to yet another church. The new church offered a Counseling Center that was free to members. Since Juan was skeptical, the pastor agreed to allow him to attend three sessions at no cost. Although Juan wondered how the counselor could put his doubts to rest, he decided that time would be his only loss if the sessions did not ease his concerns.

During the first session, the therapist smiled at Juan as if greeting an old friend. Juan explained his doubts and anger toward God. The therapist listened and asked many open-ended questions. Juan was amazed at how the therapist did not try to impose his own personal faith or beliefs in God on him. To the contrary, the therapist emphasized Juan's individuality by ending the session with discussion of "The Book of Juan's Life." The therapist asked Juan to begin his story with his childhood, including key people and events. Juan agreed to work on two chapters at a time as homework. He was on spring break from school and had plenty of time to brainstorm and write. Before he knew it, he was already on Chapter 5, in which he described his teenage years, which was when he had met Felipe. He started crying and could not write anymore.

In the second session, Juan discussed the chapters he had written. He smiled as he described the first four chapters, in which he had detailed the challenges his family had overcome when they had moved to the United States. He proudly explained how his little sisters had looked up to him during this time. When he reached Chapter 5, however, he became silent. After some time, Juan shouted, "Why did God take him?!" The therapist asked him to describe Felipe and to explain what had occurred. Juan explained how much he missed his friend and how angry he was at God for taking Felipe away. The therapist was empathetic, nonjudgmental, and supportive, confirming for Juan that his feelings were common to the natural process of grieving. Juan was relieved to discover that grief is a process, and that he did not have to ignore or condemn his feelings. The therapist encouraged Juan to attend a weekly group session on bereavement, "Death Without a Notice."

During the third session, Juan explained how helpful the group sessions were to him. Writing his "autobiography" could also help Juan realize afresh that God was always by his side. Juan agreed to complete this assignment as well. At this point, he had already become a member of the church and was entitled to biweekly counseling sessions. The therapist asked Juan to explore the feelings he experienced as he wrote and read the chapters of his life. The therapist encouraged Juan to explore why he had never made peace with the drunk driver who had killed his friend. The therapist used scripture to help Juan look at the area of forgiveness. Juan took the bold step of writing a letter to the man who had taken the life of his best friend; the letter clearly portrayed his hurt and anger but ended with an expression of his forgiveness. He finally understood that he had to forgive this man for what he had done, just as Jesus had forgiven Juan's many sins throughout his life, such as idolatry toward women, dishonesty, selfishness, and lack of self-control.

In a following session, the therapist compared Juan's beginning cognitions with the new cognitions created out of Juan's growing awareness of the issues. After Juan completed the final chapter of his life, the therapist asked him to project where he saw himself in ten years. The therapist discussed what changes needed to occur for Juan to obtain the desired outcome for his life. As an important final step, the therapist used real examples from Juan's story to show God's presence and hand throughout the stages of his life. This served to reinforce Juan's sense of the leading of the Holy Spirit. Juan built new friendships with others at his new church who shared his same doubts and fears. He also began to initiate a new personal relationship with God by reading his Bible and praying to God on a daily basis.

Suggestions for Follow-Up

The Book of My Life exercise can positively influence the way a client continues to look at his or her life. Many clients spend too much time focusing on the past. God clearly desires His children to savor every moment of this present life. Therapists can encourage clients to pursue the spiritual discipline of prayer through meditation to provide peace in their lives and to solidify their personal relationships. Because the future is unknown, although it is beneficial for clients to set goals and acknowledge their hopes and dreams, therapists must also help them to accept those times when events do not turn out as expected.

The Book of My Life exercise also provides therapists with a way to understand clients' self-perceptions. Therapists can establish therapeutic goals based on the clients' answers. These answers may provide some insights into how to renew clients' cognitions in a positive manner. As therapy progresses and inner healing takes place, revisiting this exercise may reveal fewer broken narratives. Therapists may also find it helpful to refer back to the clients' books when clients are unsure of their progress.

Contraindications

The "Book of My Life" exercise is contraindicated when the client does not acknowledge a key event or is dishonest about any given stage of his or her life. In addition, a client who is depressed may focus on negative events and even become suicidal as he or she reaches the final chapters of his or her life.

Resources for Professionals

Anderson, N.T. (2003). *Praying by the Power of the Holy Spirit.* Eugene, OR: Harvest House.
Anderson, N.T., Zuehlke, T.E., and Zuehlke, J.S. (2000). *Christ centered therapy.* Grand Rapids, MI: Zondervan Publishing House.
Huggins, K.D. (2003). *Friendship counseling.* Colorado Springs, CO: NavPress.
Lewis, C. (1996). *The collected works of C.S. Lewis.* New York: Inspirational Press.
Zimmerman, J., and Dickerson, V. (1996). *If problems talked: Narrative therapy in action.* New York: Guilford Press.

Resources for Clients

Anderson, N.T. (2000). *Victory over darkness.* Ventura, CA: Regal Books.
Anderson, N.T. (2001). *Who am I in Christ?* Ventura, CA: Regal Books.
Crabb, L. (2001). *Shattered* dreams. Colorado Springs, CO: Waterbrook Press.
Edwards, D. (2001). *Revolution within.* Colorado Springs, CO: Waterbrook Press.
Kushner, H. (1981). *When bad things happen to good people.* New York: Avon Books.
Lewis, C.S. (2001). *Mere Christianity.* San Francisco, CA: HarperCollins.
Maxwell, J. (2000). *Failing forward.* Nashville, TN: Thomas Nelson Publishers.
Smalley, G. (2004). *The DNA of relationships.* Wheaton, IL: Tyndale House Publisher, Inc.
Warren, R. (2002). *The purpose driven life.* Grand Rapids, MI: Zondervan Publishing.

Related Scriptures

O Lord my God, I called to you for help and you healed me. (Psalm 30:2 NIV)

Forgive as the Lord forgave you. (Colossians 3:13b NIV)

We live by faith, not by sight. (2 Corinthians 5:7 NIV)

He heals the brokenhearted and binds up their wounds. (Psalm 147:3 NIV)

"For I know the plans I have for you," declares the Lord, "plans to prosper you and not to harm you, plans to give you hope and a future." (Jeremiah 29:11 NIV)

. . . you are in Christ Jesus, who has became for us wisdom from God . . . (1 Corinthians 1:30 NIV)

Blessed are the poor in spirit. (Matthew 5:3a NIV)

For the word of God is living and active. (Hebrews 4:12 NIV)

. . . but your grief will turn to joy. (John 16:20 NIV)

Be merciful to those who doubt. (Jude 1:22 NIV)

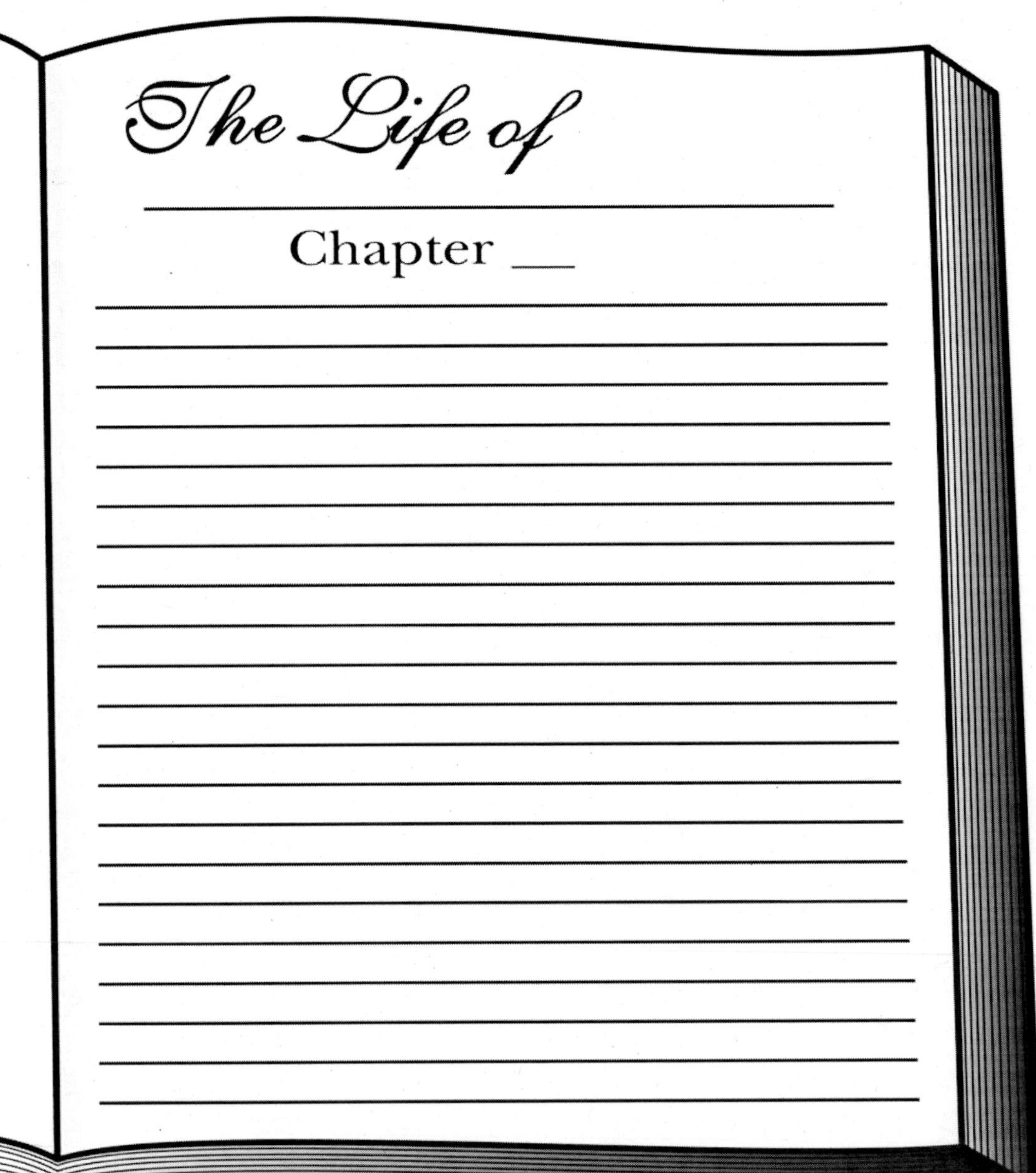

Oh, that my words were recorded,
that they were written on a scroll,
that they were inscribed with an iron tool on lead,
or engraved in rock forever!

Job 19:23-24 (NIV)

– 7 –

Tearing Down Strongholds

Philip J. Henry
Gene A. Sale

Guiding Scripture

The weapons we fight with are not weapons of the world.
On the contrary, they have divine power to demolish strongholds.

2 Corinthians 10:4 (NIV)

Type of Contribution: Exercise, Handout

Objective

The objective of this exercise is to enable the client to identify the strongholds in his or her life, to renounce these strongholds, and to ask God for His help in overcoming them. This will assist the client in beginning to take action toward living a more holy life. The biblical term for this process is *repentance.*

Rationale for Use

Christian therapy not only allows personal insight and a better understanding of ourselves but also involves obedience—repentance that moves the believer more in line with God's will. This allows God's power to work in the person's life, to bring about changes that he or she cannot make alone.

Many people hesitate to bring their failures and sins to God, the one who cares and who can help. Strongholds are the weak areas of life that God does not control. As a result, His peace and guidance are not present.

Instructions

Introduce the subject of strongholds and give biblical examples to help illustrate the main points, such as Jacob, who was scheming and manipulative, or Samson, who was overcome with lust, and so on. Also, explore personal and family histories, identifying obvious strongholds present in the family's background.

Talk with the client about the importance of tearing down strongholds and making Jesus Lord over every area of his or her life. Explain the "Tearing Down Strongholds" exercise and the significance of identifying how he or she is resisting God's will in his or her life. Help the client un-

The Christian Therapist's Notebook

doi:10.1300/5334_08

derstand how to proceed by giving an example of how this works in your life or in the life of another individual. Again, the Bible is full of examples of both strongholds and the effects the strongholds have on individual lives and families.

Ask the client to identify several strongholds in his or her life and to choose one he or she would like to identify and address first. Emphasize the importance of honesty in detailing these strongholds, but be alert to unspoken signs that the client is feeling overwhelmed or engaging in self-destructive or blaming behaviors. If such signs are present, identify these behaviors for the client and attempt work on these areas immediately. The first line of defense for defeating the stronghold is tackling any misplaced guilt and shame.

Using the "Tearing Down Strongholds" handout, ask the client to identify the components of his or her stronghold. Identify the action, the belief, the thought, and the desire that form this stronghold. Assist the client in asking God to help him or her with the separate components that make up this stronghold. Finally, have the client identify a real step he or she will take to deal with this problem area. For example, the client could attend an accountability group or ask God for help to begin the process of healing. Help to broaden the client's thinking about how his or her life would be different, how his or her thought patterns and corresponding behaviors would change, if he or she were successful in defeating this stronghold.

Vignette

Connie is a forty-seven-year-old divorcée with two college-age children from her thirteen-year marriage that ended fourteen years ago. Since her children went away to college three years ago, she has reportedly experienced mild to moderate depression. She is currently working two jobs just to make ends meet. She attends church weekly but reports that she does not feel truly connected to the large evangelical church, though she finds the worship services uplifting.

Connie, who has been a believer in Christ since she was a child, greatly values her relationship with God, but even in this relationship, she reports feeling disconnected and somewhat distant. She knows God loves her, but her feelings of closeness and intimacy with God have abated.

Connie describes one thing as characterizing this time in her life: isolation. She realizes that her isolation from friends, family, and the church probably lies at the heart of her depression, but she does not seem to have the time or energy to take the initiative to get involved with people; she feels as though no one will identify with her based on her experience. As she considers the future, she sees nothing but further loneliness and isolation.

When the counselor introduced the subject of strongholds to Connie, she responded positively and seemed interested to consider how they may contribute to her current situation. The counselor shared the biblical example of Elijah and his sense of isolation that created feelings of depression and how the Lord ministered to him (see 1 Kings 19).

Connie was able to identify several strongholds in her life associated with guilt and shame; she examined areas of her life, such as her divorce and her feelings of inadequacy in maintaining relationships, to her lack of belief that God will meet her relational needs. She decided to focus on the stronghold of isolation in her life.

Using the Tearing Down Strongholds handout, the counselor helped Connie determine the thoughts and desires that were creating her basic beliefs, under which she was functioning spiritually and relationally in terms of her isolation. Connie's basic desire was to have relationships in which she can love and feel loved in return. Her basic thoughts involved thinking that she needed others in her life to feel fulfilled. From these thoughts and desires came the belief that she will never feel fulfilled as a person because she is stuck in a situation where she cannot develop close relationships. The actions stemming from this belief produce her "stuckness": Connie abandoned any attempts to develop close relationships because of the stronghold that suggests she will never be able to develop close relationships again. She stopped initiating new relationships with others and began accepting her unhappiness as inevitable.

The counselor pointed out that Connie's basic desire and thoughts are indeed accurate. However, the conclusion she drew from her circumstances and her belief that she will never feel fulfilled because she cannot develop close relationships is erroneous. The counselor challenged this belief by asking Connie what evidence she has that the belief is true. The counselor also challenged Connie's "all or nothing" thinking regarding developing relationships; that is, the counselor challenged the belief that Connie needs to have a number of close relationships or no relationships at all.

After Connie agreed to modify her belief that she cannot ever develop relationships again by instead taking an incremental approach to relationship development, the counselor encouraged Connie to ask for God's help in changing her lifestyle to allow the development of relationships.

Connie agreed to change her actions in relation to her church attendance. Instead of going to the larger worship service on Sunday mornings, she agreed to participate in a small group meeting sponsored by the church and to take the steps necessary to establish relationships within that group.

The counselor worked with Connie during the next several sessions on incrementally implementing a plan for getting to know the people in her small group. She volunteered to e-mail prayer requests mentioned in the group to the group members so they can pray for one another during the week. She worked with the group leaders in planning a social event for the group, and, gradually, Connie began to establish connections with the people in her small group.

Progressively, as Connie became more relationally connected to the group, her depression began to abate. Feeling less depressed, she seemed to have more energy to spend on activities in her small group and she gradually began attending the larger worship service again. This time, the service seemed more meaningful, as she visited and sat with people from her small group during the worship service. The content of the small group Bible study has encouraged Connie to look at her relationship with God in a new way. She believes she is growing spiritually again.

Suggestions for Follow-Up

The Tearing Down Strongholds exercise depends on where the client is at in his or her walk with the Lord and on his or her stage of spiritual maturity. For some, the issue is a lack of knowledge and growth. For these clients, take time to provide scripture examples and information about the basics of living the Christian life as God intended.

For other, more spiritually mature Christians, the issue is not knowledge based but motivation based. That is, the problem is within the heart. For these clients, spend time on the desire-related issues of the strongholds. Leaving this first love (Revelation 2:4) always results in a return to bondage of some type.

Note: This is a good time to pray with and for the client. This will help the client feel connected to God and provide him or her with a model of what steps to follow to overcome this stronghold in his or her life.

Contraindications

This exercise may be contraindicated if the client is not stable enough to be fully engaged in the therapy process. Physical and mental stability is necessary before any spiritual battle should be fought. Jesus gave instructions to consider whether one can win before one undertakes any battle (Luke 14:31). If the client is not strong or stable enough to engage in spiritual warfare, take steps to train him or her in this area before attempting to bring about significant change.

Resources for Professionals

Anderson, N. (2000). *The bondage breaker.* Eugene, OR: Harvest House Publishers.

Brandt, H., and Skinner, K. (1997). *Heart of the problem.* Nashville, TN: Broadman and Holman Publishers.

Bubek, M. (1984). *Overcoming the adversary.* Chicago, IL: Moody Press.

Wagner, C. (1988). *The third wave of the Holy Spirit.* Ann Arbor, MI: Vine.

White, T. (1990). *The believer's guide to spiritual warfare.* Ann Arbor, MI: Vine.

Resources for Clients

Anderson, N. (2000). *The bondage breakers study guide.* Eugene, OR: Harvest House Publishers.

Carlson, D. (2000). *Overcoming hurts and anger.* Eugene, OR: Harvest House Publishers.

Kok, E. (2002). *A woman who hurts: A God who heals.* Birmingham, AL: New Hope Publishers.

McDonald, J. (2000). *I really want to change . . . So, help me God.* Chicago, IL: Moody Publishing.

Mintle, L. (2002). *Breaking free from anorexia and bulimia.* Lake Mary, FL: Charisma House.

Mintle, L. (2002). *Breaking free from depression.* Lake Mary, FL: Charisma House.

Mintle, L. (2002). *Breaking free from negative self-image.* Lake Mary, FL: Charisma House.

Mintle, L. (2002). *Compulsive overeating.* Lake Mary, FL: Charisma House.

Moore, B. (2000). *Breaking free: Making liberty in life a reality in Christ.* Nashville, TN: Broadman and Holman Publishers.

Moore, B. (2000). *Breaking free from spiritual strongholds: Praying God's word.* Nashville, TN: Broadman and Holman Publishers.

Related Scriptures

> The weapons we fight with are not weapons of the world. On the contrary, they have divine power to demolish strongholds. We demolish arguments and every pretension that sets itself up against the knowledge of God, and we take captive every thought to make it obedient to Christ. (2 Corinthians 10:4-5 NIV)

> Finally, be strong in the Lord and in his mighty power. Put on the full armor of God so that you can take your stand against the devil's schemes. For our struggle is not against flesh and blood, but against the rulers, against the authorities, against the powers of this dark world and against the spiritual forces of evil in the heavenly realms. Therefore put on the full armor of God, so that when the day of evil comes, you may be able to stand your ground, and after you have done everything, to stand. (Ephesians 6:10-13 NIV)

> Stand firm then, with the belt of truth buckled around your waist, with the breastplate of righteousness in place, and with your feet fitted with the readiness that comes from the gospel of peace. In addition to all this, take up the shield of faith, with which you can extinguish all the flaming arrows of the evil one. Take the helmet of salvation and the sword of the Spirit, which is the word of God. (Ephesians 6:14-17 NIV)

> Simon Peter answered, "You are the Christ, the Son of the living God." Jesus replied, "Blessed are you Simon son of Jonah, for this was not revealed to you by man, but by my Father in heaven. And I tell you that you are Peter, and on this rock I will build my church, and the gates of Hades will not overcome it." (Matthew 16:16-18 NIV)

Tearing Down Strongholds

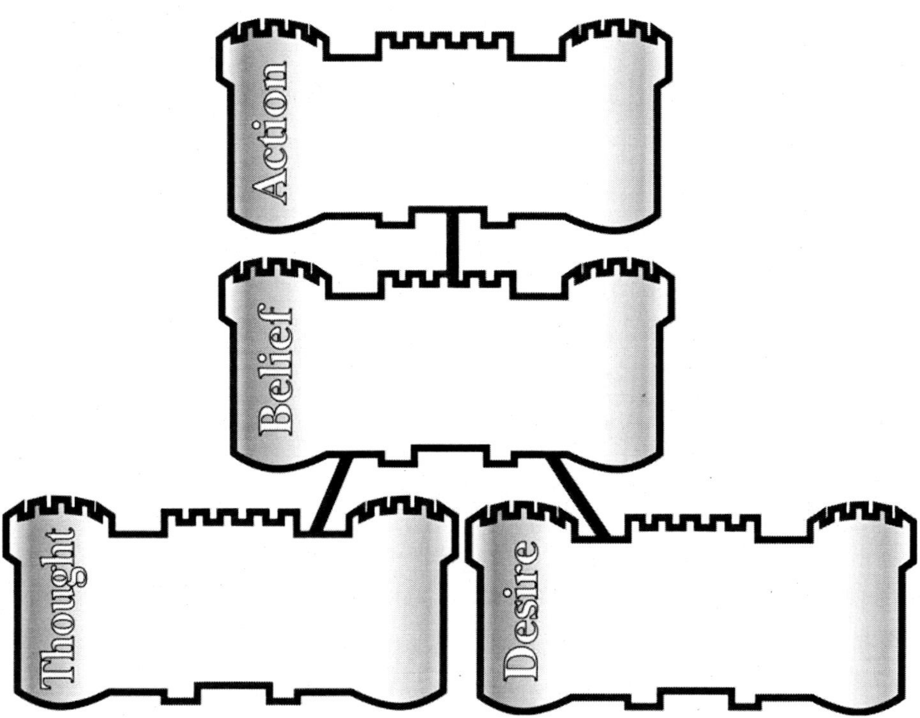

What I'm ready to renounce…

I will ask God to help…

I will start by…

The weapons we fight with are not weapons of the world.
On the contrary, they have divine power to demolish strongholds.

2 Corinthians 10:4 (NIV)

– 8 –

Cross over to the Other Side

Lori Marie Figueroa
Philip J. Henry

Guiding Scripture

Multitudes, multitudes in the valley of decision!

Joel 3:14 (NIV)

Type of Contribution: Exercise, Handout

Objective

The objective of this exercise is to help clients acknowledge the consequences a recurring fantasy can have on their relationship with God, their family life, their job, their academic performance, their nocturnal patterns, their relationships, and their daily lives.

Rationale for Use

Clients seeking therapy may be aware of the strong role a recurring fantasy has in their lives. The sinful nature of human beings can distort their cognitions and affect their emotions. Clients may have fantasies about engaging in a sinful activity. In other words, they may begin to believe "the grass is greener on the other side." Use the "Cross over to the Other Side" exercise to assist clients in following through with their fantasies on paper to see the consequences in reality.

Many times, fantasies become a safe haven for clients to ponder, "What if?" However, from the beginning of time, the Bible shows the consequences of giving in to sin. God gave Adam and Eve a paradise to commune with Him. Yet, that was not enough. They gave in to the temptation of tasting the "grass on the other side." As a result, they endured unnecessary suffering.

This exercise can be extremely beneficial in addressing the issue of adultery with a client who has mentally committed this sin and is considering making the fantasy a reality. Since fantasies tend to focus on the positive, a reality check can open the client's eyes. Clients must realize a consequence occurs as the result of every decision they make. Although consequences can be either positive or negative, they still have an effect, not only on the clients, but also on the people indirectly connected to the clients' decisions. For example, the decision to have an affair with a co-worker can have a direct impact on a client's children, spouse, or boss and even on his or her job performance. Most important, this outward decision to commit a sin can affect the client's personal relationship with God; it can also prevent the client from achieving God's plan for his or her life.

The Christian Therapist's Notebook

doi:10.1300/5334_09

Christian therapists can show clients God's view on sin through scripture and through historical events depicted throughout the Bible. This can help clients visualize the causes and effects of sin throughout generations. Scripture can also illuminate the concept of "free will": God gives people free will to make decisions, but people must seek God's wisdom before making those decisions. Understanding this truth is important to resisting the temptations faced each day to make selfish choices that meet the desires of the flesh.

Next, therapists must determine the unmet needs in clients' lives that cause them to pursue fantasies. Examples of unmet needs include a desire for respect, a desire for quality time, a desire for physical touch, or a desire for healthy communication. Spouses seeking individual therapy should be encouraged to pursue marital therapy, if the issue leading them to therapy is a direct result of an unmet need in the marriage. As Christian counselors, God expects us to seek His wisdom as we help couples rekindle, rather than dissolve, the sacrament of marriage.

Through cognitive therapy, therapists can help clients reevaluate cognitions concealing the reality of a situation. Begin the evaluation by reassessing any seemingly pleasurable feelings associated with the fantasies. Christian clients can be encouraged to examine how sin separates the mind, heart, and soul from God, who has a purpose for their lives. Clients must learn that God's purpose is not one of merely immediate gratification, but one of *eternal* fulfillment.

Finally, while looking at the entire picture, therapists must help their clients answer what solution-focused therapy calls the "miracle question," namely, "What if?" Using the miracle question, clients can begin to acknowledge their ultimate goals. Once these goals are established, therapists can help clients set realistic expectations in their personal, professional, and spiritual lives.

Instructions

Using "The Other Side" handout, ask the client to describe his or her fantasy. Clearly explain that fulfillment of the fantasy designates that he or she has made a decision to cross over an imaginary bridge to another side. Have the client then identify specific details of his or her life that would change if he or she decided to succumb to the fantasy. Next, have the client make a list of the consequences, including people harmed, if he or she fulfilled the fantasy. It is important for the client to list the specific names of the people who would be affected by the decision to fulfill the fantasy. In other words, have the client answer the question, "What if I acted on this fantasy?"

To assist the client in completing the handout, use open-ended questions, as opposed to leading questions, so the client carefully considers the outcomes of following through with the decision at hand. Have the client read each consequence and the name of each person aloud when the list is completed. Ask the client to explore the feelings experienced as he or she wrote and read aloud the consequences and the list of names. Finally, ask the client to consider this question: "Have your thoughts on the fantasy changed after looking at the consequences?" Discuss the cost of the fantasy in both personal and spiritual terms.

Explore the client's unmet need. Work together with the client to look for godly ways to meet this need. Seek wisdom from the Bible as you provide biblical examples of people who suffered from following a fantasy, as opposed to following God's perfect will for their lives.

Vignette

Ralph is a fifty-five-year-old, married, African-American male who works as the vice president of an advertising firm. He has been married to Stephanie for twenty years. He was brought up Baptist, and he attends church every Sunday with his wife and two children. He has been fantasizing about pursuing a sexual relationship with his thirty-year-old secretary, Rachel. Ralph enjoys working overtime, as it allows him an opportunity to spend more time with Rachel. Although he has not confessed his fantasy to anyone, he thinks the feelings of attraction are mutual.

Ralph is the middle sibling in a family of three children. Although he always felt loved by his family, he describes feelings of neglect in comparison to his older and younger brothers. Ralph dreams at night about being romantically involved with his secretary. He also confesses to visualizing his secretary's face while having sex with his wife. He describes experiencing mixed feelings of both guilt and pleasure.

When Ralph first met Stephanie in college, he immediately felt attracted to her. They started their relationship as friends. He loved spending time with her, and he admired her ambitious nature. They dated for about two years, and during this time, Stephanie was always there to provide words of encouragement. They engaged in premarital sex, a memory he recalls with a smile, and once this had occurred, Ralph realized that Stephanie could possibly become his lifetime partner. Soon after, he proposed. Before long, the honeymoon phase of their marriage ended, and things began to change. Stephanie became pregnant with their first child. Their sex life changed from a frequency of every other day to once a week, even after the child was born. When Stephanie became pregnant with their second child, their sex life changed again—to only once a month—always planned and never spontaneous. Ralph felt that Stephanie placed the children's needs first; in other words, he felt neglected. This opened the door to unresolved feelings of neglect from his childhood that began to resurface in his adult life.

Years later, their marriage continued to revolve around the children, church, and his job. Although Ralph was proud of his children, he felt empty. After fifteen years of marriage, his eyes began to wander. He began secretly having an emotional affair on the Internet that seemed to fulfill his need for words of reassurance. At times, these communications contained sexual overtones.

Soon after this cyber-affair, Ralph began developing a friendship with his secretary, Rachel. A young, beautiful, vibrant woman who treated him with respect, she always had a kind word to say to him. They began meeting for lunch, and, before long, Ralph began working overtime with her. They would order dinner and chat in his office for hours. Rachel seemed to love being with him, and he began feeling attractive and appreciated again.

Ralph met with a male friend and colleague, Joseph, and shared the feelings he was having toward his secretary. Ralph told Joseph that he had decided he was ready to move to the next level with Rachel. At this point, his sexual attraction to her was extremely strong, and he found himself daydreaming about her at work, which affected his job performance. Joseph advised him to seek marital therapy. At first, Ralph was resistant, but after a day of contemplation and prayer, he agreed to attend individual therapy.

Ralph was nervous during the first therapy session. He described his job; he explained how his performance and ability to concentrate had declined over the past weeks. The therapist probed for information through open-ended questions, asking Ralph to describe his personal life. Ralph explained how he felt trapped in a marriage without love or sex, for the sake of his children, and quickly shifted to his ideal relationship, the one with his secretary. The therapist listened as Ralph described his thoughts and feelings and then asked Ralph the miracle question: "What if?" This was the beginning step toward Ralph acknowledging his ultimate goal.

The therapist gave Ralph an assignment not to remain alone with Rachel until their next session. He was advised to call his wife if he was ever alone with his secretary. At first, Ralph smirked at the suggestion, but he was curious to see whether he would be able to follow through with this seemingly simple task, so he agreed.

During their second session, the therapist further probed Ralph's relationship with his wife and children. Ralph described how much he enjoyed spending time with his children. He began comparing his wife to his secretary and explained how he wished Stephanie were more like

Rachel. He explained that he had completed the previous session's assignment with a great deal of difficulty. He was somewhat angry because his secretary had seemed to notice the change. He described a sexual dream he had had about Rachel. He explained how he felt disconnected from God. Despite his feelings of guilt, he seemed drawn toward thoughts of a future with his secretary. The Christian therapist encouraged Ralph to seek God's wisdom and strength through prayer. The therapist explained how an outward decision to commit a sin could affect a personal relationship with God; it can also prevent achieving God's plan for one's life. Ralph listened with tears in his eyes but remained silent. The assignment not to remain alone with his secretary was extended until their next session.

By the third session, Ralph was ready for the "Cross over to the Other Side" exercise. Ralph described the fantasy of having sex with his secretary. He provided further details of a desire to divorce his wife and date his secretary. As he completed the exercise, the therapist explained to Ralph that if he followed through with the fantasy, he would have made a decision to cross over an imaginary bridge to another side. Ralph was encouraged to identify and write down specific details of how his life would change if he made the decision to follow through with the fantasy.

Next, Ralph made a list of the consequences that would result from his decision, including the specific people who would be harmed, if he followed through with the fantasy. He listed his wife, parents, friends, co-workers, and boss, and with tears in his eyes, he also wrote down the names of his children. The therapist asked open-ended questions to help Ralph carefully consider the outcomes of following through with the decision at hand.

Ralph read each consequence and the name of each person aloud. The therapist asked Ralph to explore the feelings he experienced as he wrote and read over the consequences and the list of people who could be harmed. The therapist asked Ralph whether his thoughts about his fantasy had changed after examining the consequences, and the two of them discussed the personal and spiritual effects of the consequences of the fantasy. The therapist shared some scripture: "No test or temptation that comes your way is beyond the course of what others have had to face. All you need to remember is that God will never let you down; he'll never let you be pushed past your limit; he'll always be there to help you come through it" (1 Corinthians 10:13 MSG).

Ralph began setting clear boundaries with his secretary. He and Stephanie also attended a marriage retreat at their church. He scheduled weekly lunch dates with Stephanie, as well as with his children. He continued to seek God's wisdom through prayer. He began building a strong support system through church. He asked Joseph to hold him accountable for his actions and words. Shortly thereafter, his secretary resigned.

Suggestions for Follow-Up

Months later, follow up by looking at the previously unmet needs to determine whether those needs have been met. The therapist should ask the client to look at the fantasy again to see if its appeal remains. If the client still prefers the fantasy to reality, the therapist should revisit the exercise, focusing on that specific unmet need. Finally, ask the client how God has helped him or her to overcome the obsession with the sinful fantasy.

Contraindications

This exercise is contraindicated if, after exploring the consequences of the fantasy, the client believes that it is nonetheless worth pursuing. If euphoric recall (remembering only the good parts) occurs, the therapist may need to utilize another technique beneficial to the unique needs of the given client. In addition, the exercise may have less value for a client with a limited understanding of man's sinful nature and the need for reliance on God and God's will in his or her life.

Resources for Professionals

Begg, A. (2002). *Lasting love: How to avoid marital failure.* Chicago, IL: Moody Publishers.

Dobson, J. (1996). *Love must be tough: New hope for marriages in crisis.* Nashville, TN: W. Publishing Group.

Harley, W.F. (2001). *His needs, her needs: Building an affair-proof marriage.* Grand Rapids, MI: Revell Books.

Pittman, F. (1990). *Private lies: Infidelity and the betrayal of intimacy.* New York: W.W. Norton and Company.

Resources for Clients

Carder, D. (1992). *Torn asunder: Recovering from extramarital affairs.* Chicago, IL: Moody Publishers.

Hall, L. (1998). *An affair of the mind: One woman's courageous battle to salvage her family from the devastation of pornography.* Colorado Springs, CO: Focus on the Family Publishing.

Leman, K. (2000). *Sex begins in the kitchen: Because love is an all-day affair.* Grand Rapids, MI: Revell Books.

Reccord, B. (2002). *Beneath the surface: Steering clear of the dangers that could leave you shipwrecked.* Nashville, TN: Broadman and Holman Publishers.

Virkler, H. (1992). *Broken promises: Healing and preventing affairs in Christian marriages.* Nashville, TN: W. Publishing Group.

Related Scriptures

> No temptation has seized you except what is common to man. And God is faithful; he will not let you be tempted beyond what you can bear. But when you are tempted, he will also provide a way out so that you can stand up under it. (1 Corinthians 10:13 NIV)

> Watch and pray so that you will not fall into temptation. The spirit is willing, but the body is weak. (Matthew 26:41NIV)

> Marriage should be honored by all, and the marriage bed kept pure, for God will judge the adulterer and all the sexually immoral. (Hebrews 13:4 NIV)

> The body is not meant for sexual immorality, but for the Lord, and the Lord for the body. (1 Corinthians 6:13b NIV)

> Therefore honor God with your body. (1 Corinthians 6:20b NIV)

> . . . at the beginning the Creator made them male and female, and said, "For this reason a man will leave his father and mother and be united to his wife, and the two will become one flesh." So they are no longer two, but one. Therefore what God has joined together, let man not separate. (Matthew 19:4-6 NIV)

> The Lord God said, "It is not good for the man to be alone. I will make a helper suitable for him." (Genesis 2:18 NIV)

> For he will command his angels concerning you to guard you in all your ways. (Psalm 91:11 NIV)

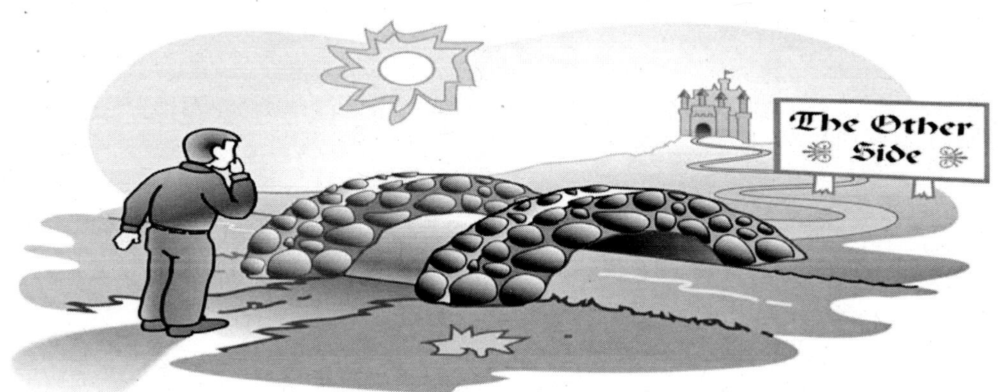

Fantasy	*Things that would change if Fantasy was fulfilled*	*List of people harmed if Fantasy was fulfilled*

– 9 –

Run the Race

Lori Marie Figueroa
Philip J. Henry

Guiding Scripture

. . . let us run with perseverance the race marked out for us.

Hebrews 12:1 (NIV)

Type of Contribution: Exercise, Handout/Homework

Objective

This exercise will help bring focus to clients with generalized anxiety disorder by allowing them to gain a sense of peace and begin to understand God's purpose for their lives through the use of cognitive therapy.

Rationale for Use

Generalized anxiety disorder (GAD) does not discriminate based on gender, income, or marital status (Rych and Sanderson, 2004). The lifetime prevalence of this disorder is approximately 4 to 6 percent in the general population and is more common in women than in men. Although maladaptive schemas may trigger the cause, genetic predisposition or life circumstances, within or beyond control, and a lack of focus or purpose can also exacerbate qualms. Clients may feel overwhelmed as they fulfill numerous tasks on a daily basis. Unable to prioritize events and people, these feelings of anxiety intensify.

According to the DSM-IV, which provides criteria by which one can properly diagnose GAD, worry and other associated symptoms must be present for at least six months and must adversely affect the patient's life (e.g., the patient misses workdays or cannot maintain daily responsibilities). Clients with GAD may experience irritability, fatigue, restlessness, insomnia, distorted cognitive processes, poor concentration, unrealistic assessment of problems, poor coping strategies, and/or poor problem-solving skills.

In a spiritual sense, clients with GAD have no clear direction. This lack of focus contributes to feelings of hopelessness and a sense of chaos. Despite their ability to multitask, a feeling of lack of control will remain. GAD clouds clients' vision, thereby creating an inability to see God's purpose for their lives. The "Run the Race" exercise helps clients reevaluate core beliefs and create a specific focus for their lives.

The Christian Therapist's Notebook

doi:10.1300/5334_10

Prioritizing their lives can be difficult because clients may be apprehensive about changing routines. However, Christian counselors can encourage clients to concentrate by seeking God's will for their lives and removing any unnecessary areas that are creating stress. Accepting God has a specific purpose for their lives can reduce clients' anxiety and bring about peace.

Next, clients must learn how to prioritize events and people. As clients realizes that they do not need to worry about pleasing others, they can stop behaving in ways that do not support the goals they have chosen to focus on, which are emotional stability and peace.

Instructions

Talk with the client about his or her daily routine. Determine whether routine tasks serve a specific purpose. Help the client acknowledge and eliminate unnecessary tasks. Find out when feelings of anxiety began. Listen carefully as the client mentions any key past events that may have caused these feelings of anxiety. Also, look for any repetitive patterns in the client's life; have the client describe excessive worries. Clients may acknowledge factors creating their stress but not know how to remove these stressors from their routine.

Compare the client's life to running a race. Have the client list reasons *why* he or she is running; examples of this may be fear of losing a job or disappointing someone. Next, have the client list *what* he or she is running from. This question may remain unanswered if the client is unsure of how to respond. Through open-ended questions, counselors can reveal areas of concern that clients can acknowledge and list when ready.

For Christian clients, it is helpful to meditate on whether or not they are seeking God's will as they run. Most clients experiencing GAD will realize they are not trusting or relying on God in their lives. Consider addressing this issue when reminding them that God's plan provides peace and leaves no room for worrying.

Next, it is important for the client to reflect on where he or she is running. A commonality of clients with GAD is a lack of focus or direction. Through reflective-listening techniques, the counselor can help the client write down one or two specific goals for his or her future. The client can be encouraged to reflect on the goals in relation to God's will for his or her life.

Finally, it is important to inquire about relationships in the client's life. If the client is part of an enmeshed, disengaged, or dysfunctional family, he or she may feel alone, without a trustworthy support system. Unhealthy friendships or a lack of social relationships can cause the client to experience anxiety. A careful exploration of positive and/or negative relationships can help the client work on deficient areas or positive existing areas of support.

Working through the "Run the Race" handout may require more than one session. Consider using the handout as a homework assignment so that the client reflects on areas discussed in therapy. Be patient while the client tries to focus on specific areas, one at a time. Realize that, for the client to stop worrying, he or she must have faith that God will provide what is needed. Faith is not an easy concept for the client with GAD to grasp, but faith will develop as the client learns to rely on God through prayer and mediation. Remind the client of Jeremiah 29:11 as a source of hope in his or her life.

Vignette

Mary is a thirty-five-year-old, married, Caucasian female who works as an administrative assistant at a prestigious bank. She was raised Catholic but has not attended church since she started working at the bank. She feels overwhelmed between work and her personal life. She worries excessively about everything—things left undone and time constraints. Before she started working at the bank, Mary was at peace with her life. Her focus was on decorating her home and helping her husband with his painting business. She and her husband even attended church groups on Wednesday and Sunday nights.

Mary was the oldest sibling in a family of five children. Since both of her parents worked outside the home, she was responsible for cooking meals, cleaning the house, and caring for her brothers and sisters. Sundays at church seemed to be the only time her family spent together. She felt close to God when at church but distant during the week. She also remembers having had difficulty sleeping, as she worried about all of the tasks awaiting her the next day. Mary felt lonely and lacked solid relationships with family members.

When she got married, she experienced a new sense of freedom. Her husband did not make her feel obligated to serve him in any way. He seemed content just to have her close. As a stay-at-home wife, she was happy decorating and taking care of the house. However, after a month of this, she became bored. She applied at a bank and soon began the life of a professional. Her husband supported her decision.

Weeks after beginning the job at the bank, Mary found herself completing the tasks of others in addition to those officially part of her own job description. Her boss, as well as her co-workers, acknowledged her effectiveness and gave her extra duties. One night at home, she began feeling anxious. Six months later, she found herself still worrying excessively. Concerned about his wife's emotional well-being, the husband encouraged her to seek counseling.

Mary was very talkative during her first therapy session. She described her intense, demanding job and named this as her primary reason for feeling stressed. The therapist encouraged her to explain how she balanced her work life and home life. Mary explained that she did not feel that there was an existing balance between the two. Her job had become her priority and consumed most of her energy. The therapist coached Mary as she decided whether each task of her daily work life met a specific purpose. Mary was able to acknowledge and eliminate two unnecessary job-related tasks. This was a positive step; Mary felt a small sense of relief.

During the second session, the therapist used open-ended questions to find out when Mary's feelings of anxiety had begun. Mary explained how she had never learned to delegate tasks but instead tried to meet everyone's needs herself. Her role in her family of origin was the "other mom," and as she described her current job-related duties, she saw a correlation between her job at the bank and the role she had held in her family of origin. For the duration of this session, the therapist and Mary discussed her relationship with God. She admitted that she had allowed her job to overshadow all other aspects of her life, including impeding her spiritual growth.

By the third session, Mary felt a curative rapport with the therapist. The therapist was able to determine the root of her anxiety disorder through sharing the Run the Race handout with Mary. Through open-ended questions, the therapist guided Mary in answering each question. As she completed the handout, Mary began questioning her past behavior as well as her current direction. She seemed ready to begin setting goals and to gain clarity about what was important in her life.

In the first box of the "Run the Race!" handout, Mary answered the question with the same question: "Why *am* I running?" She began questioning why she seemed unable to enjoy a peaceful life without chaos. The therapist was able to use this opportunity to explore the desire for a "worry-free" life by having Mary describe times in her life when she had felt at peace. The therapist also probed to see whether any negative cognitions were interfering with Mary's desire for peace. Mary admitted she had thoughts of guilt that consumed her when she was pursuing something for her own benefit, instead of the benefit of someone else; she replaced these thoughts with positive cognitions.

Subsequent sessions revealed a need for clear direction in Mary's life. With a new sense of hope, Mary was willing to work with the therapist to outline specific goals and means of attaining each objective. She received assignments that supported those goals. One of the assignments included confronting co-workers and refusing to accept tasks outside of her official duties. At first, Mary was afraid to do this, but she built up enough confidence to complete the task successfully. As she completed the entire handout, she realized the need for a renewed relationship with God. She began attending her church group again and establishing healthy friendships.

Suggestions for Follow-Up

After four sessions, again have the client complete the same handout as homework. Compare the new answers with those obtained in the first session. Positively affirm any progress made. Discuss how a reliance on God has influenced the client's "race."

Contraindications

The "Run the Race" exercise is contraindicated when the source of the anxiety is a general medical condition that may require medication, or if the client has a substance abuse problem, which is necessary to address before therapy proceeds.

Resources for Professionals

Beck, A., and Emery, G. (1985). *Anxiety disorders and phobias: A cognitive perspective.* New York: Basic.

Rych, J., and Sanderson, W. (2004). *Treating generalized anxiety disorder: Evidence based strategies, tools and techniques.* New York: Guilford.

White, J. (1999). *Overcoming generalized anxiety disorder: A relaxation, cognitive restructuring and exposure based protocol for the treatment of GAD.* Oakland, CA: New Harbinger.

Resources for Clients

Mintle, L. (2002). *Breaking free from a negative self image.* Lake Mary, FL: Charisma House.

Wright, H. (1998). *Winning over your emotions.* Eugene, OR: Harvest House Publishers.

Related Scriptures

> Cast all your anxiety on Him because He cares for you. (1 Peter 5:7 NIV)
>
> When anxiety was great within me, your consolation brought joy to my soul. (Psalm 94:19 NIV)
>
> Who of you by worrying can add a single hour to his life? (Matthew 6:27 NIV)
>
> Therefore do not worry about tomorrow, for tomorrow will worry about itself. Each day has enough trouble of its own. (Matthew 6:34 NIV)

. . . let us run with perseverance the race. . .

Hebrews 12:1 (NIV)

Why am I running?

What am I running from?

Where am I running?

Who is running with me?

How am I seeking God's will as I run?

– 10 –

Getting It in Gear

Philip J. Henry

Guiding Scripture

. . . faith by itself, if it is not accompanied by action, is dead.

James 2:17 (NIV)

Type of Contribution: Exercise, Handout

Objective

The objective of this exercise is to identify key areas where the client's faith needs to be put into action by discovering the thoughts, behaviors, or actions that need to be changed for this to happen. If successful, the client should be able to conceptualize, visually and cognitively, the progress necessary for change to occur and to record transformation of key behaviors and auxiliary behaviors to determine progress toward the desired goal(s).

Rationale for Use

Changing any habit or behavior is always difficult. It has been said that the "road to hell is paved with good intentions," and that may be so. Failure is infectious; when failure to change recurs, the client can begin to believe nothing will ever be different. Many people live life close to a "living hell" primarily because they never move beyond the wishing and wanting stage of change to the *doing* stage; therefore, they miss what God has in store for them.

Often, good intentions and a true desire to change do exist, but change does not occur. Why is this? Because faith begins with some movement, it requires action to achieve results. Even if the person has an understanding of God and recognizes His plan, that does not necessarily mean his or her life will have the joy and peace Jesus promised. The doing part of faith is necessary for this. In Matthew 7, Jesus compares those who do what He says to a wise man who builds his house on a rock. This house survives even the toughest storm. However, those who *hear* but choose not to *do* are like those who build their house on sand. The storm also comes to this house, but unlike the house on the rock, the one on sand does not endure.

Starting a new behavior or ending an old one is difficult because behaviors connect to so many other pieces of life. These pieces, if not considered in the overall change, block the initial motivation and movement of change; they grind the gears of progress to a halt.

The "Getting It in Gear" exercise allows the client to visualize the connection the desired change has with other key behaviors. Consider this practice in the initial steps of any positive

The Christian Therapist's Notebook

doi:10.1300/5334_11

change. An active, life-changing faith is one that not only changes one's behavior but also infuses and generates freshness into many areas of an individual's life. This, then, makes the faith come alive.

Instructions

Talk with the client about the most important issue he or she wishes to address. This can be either a negative behavior to eliminate or a positive behavior to begin. Make sure to take sufficient time to understand the issue at hand and why it is important to the client. Often, the presenting issue in counseling is not the "real" issue the client seeks to address.

Explain the exercise and help the client understand how to proceed by asking him or her to name aspects of life he or she would like to change, and then work with the client to refine the list to just one primary issue. If he or she chooses more than one, have the client choose which issue to address first. Using the "Getting It in Gear" handout, put this desired change in the centermost gear. Ask the client to think about what other behaviors, situations, relationships, thoughts, or attitudes he or she would need to modify for this change to be successful. Focus first on the behaviors, and move on to the other influences only after addressing several behaviors. Put these other behaviors and secondary factors around the center gear.

Ask the client, "If you were to begin to change one of these behaviors, where would you start?" Breaking down change to a tangible, bite-size portion in this way is important. Often, clients are stuck because they do not know where to start. Most change is front-end loaded. This means that most of the physical, emotional, and physical energy is necessary in the initial phase in order to make any change happen. Think small, measurable, and concrete goals when working in these initial stages.

If the person is ready to commit to change, get a solid commitment for change in one or more of the identified areas. Tell the client that he or she will be accountable to you.

As a final step, ask, "With what gears do you feel you need God's help the most in order to move?" Discuss this and make sure the client understands his or her responsibility in the process. Emphasize that God will not be responsible for the work He has equipped and enabled him or her to do. If the client is comfortable, have the client pray for God's help in making this change in his or her life. Make sure, though, that this is a request for help, not an avoidance of responsibility.

Vignette

"It seems like I never get anything done," Bob reported as the session began. Bob had been thinking about making changes in his life since he first became a Christian several years ago, but he never seemed to make it happen. He wanted to lose weight and get in shape; he had plans to return to school and finish his degree; he wanted to pray more, to fix up his house, to—you name it, and Bob wanted to change it. However, change did not come easily to Bob. Dr. Goss, his counselor, thought for a moment about Bob's comment and said, "I have an exercise here that might help you focus on what you need to change and help you move in that direction."

Dr. Goss took out the "Getting It in Gear" handout and said, "Before I begin to work with you on this exercise, I need to know what you really want to change. What is it you truly desire to change in your life? Where do you feel God is leading you to do things differently?" Bob began to list the things he wished were different in his life. Dr. Goss worked with him, helping him articulate his thoughts. When they had reviewed all of the areas Bob wanted to change, Dr. Goss said, "If you had to choose just one area to change, what would that area be?" Bob struggled with this question, and for five minutes, he talked about his growing faith in God and about his possibilities. Finally, Bob said, "More than anything, I would like to return to school and finish my degree. I know God has gifted me in that area, but I don't seem to be able to take the time to actually do what I know I should."

When he was sure this was, in fact, what Bob really wanted to pursue, Dr. Goss gave Bob the handout and asked him to put "finish my degree" in the middle gear. Dr. Goss explained that other steps were necessary for the "finish my degree" gear to turn: "Each of these gears connected to the 'finish my degree' gear is as important as choosing the initial gear because they make the middle gear go around. This is the *doing* part of faith, and it takes just as much faith to do the little things as the big."

"What would be the first thing you would need to do in order to begin this process?" Dr. Goss asked. Bob indicated that he would need to make an appointment with an advisor at the college to see how many credits he currently had and what was necessary to finish the requirements of the degree. Dr. Goss instructed Bob to write "appointment with advisor" on a gear next to the gear labeled "finish my degree." Dr. Goss explained to Bob that this next step is the most important because this step is where the action really begins. He then held Bob accountable by asking him to pick a date for completion of this step. Bob wrote a date one week from the current date on the gear labeled "appointment with advisor." "I will check with you at our next meeting to see if you have completed this task. Are you sure you want to do this, and are you sure you can do it in the time you have suggested?" Dr. Goss asked. Bob replied that he believed there would be sufficient time for him to complete this task.

Moving on to another gear, Bob put "reapply to college." "I will need to reapply to college," Bob reported. "I have been gone for more than five years. I don't think I will need to redo everything, but I will need to update my application." In another gear, he put "sign up for courses," and in another, "apply for loans." "Get books" followed this and, finally, "attend the first class."

Dr. Goss again emphasized how much of the effort behind getting the degree is merely starting up the gears. "By the time you attend class, you're halfway through," he joked with Bob. Dr. Goss made a copy of the plan and put one of the copies in Bob's file. As the session ended, Dr. Goss prayed that God would grant Bob wisdom and strength to become the person God wanted him to be. Bob left the session, walking happily out of the office.

The next week, Dr. Goss checked Bob's success in meeting with an advisor. Although he had not met with the advisor, he had made an appointment for the upcoming Wednesday. He eventually did follow through, meeting with his advisor and filling out an enrollment application. Throughout the next several months, Bob faithfully took the steps he considered necessary to move toward completing his degree. With each movement toward his goal, a second benefit was recognized: Bob reported that he felt more positive and confident, and he began eating better and taking the time to exercise. His outlook seemed to change as he moved toward this goal that he had previously all but given up on completing. After reducing his sessions to once a month, Bob completed his therapy. Fifteen months later, Dr. Goss received a graduation announcement from Bob that contained a personal note, thanking Dr. Goss for the wise counsel and guidance in helping him to accomplish a piece of what God had in mind for his life.

Suggestions for Follow-Up

In the following weeks after the client completes the handout, see whether there has been any progress in getting the targeted gears moving toward the client's commitment to change. If the client had made a commitment but no change occurred, find out why. Keep the client accountable; do not be passive about this. Clients expect to be challenged, and being overly agreeable when they have not done what they have agreed to is not helpful.

If change has occurred in key areas, even if the changes are small, highlight these and use the Getting It in Gear handout to track the client's behaviors in upcoming weeks. Be encouraging of any progress. Even a little progress may be more than the client has managed to make for months, or even years. Keep encouraging and tracking the one or two behaviors the client has committed to change and problem-solve with him or her should difficulties arise. Like coaching, change requires encouraging, teaching, and guiding.

Contraindications

If the client cannot choose one behavior or even identify one behavior to change, he or she is probably not ready to change or may need a simpler exercise. Also, watch that the key areas chosen belong to the client and are not the therapist's personal preferences. Clients often desire to please; however, if they are not invested in the plan, they will not follow through with the work.

Resources for Professionals

Adams, J.E. (1986). *The Christian counselor's manual.* Grand Rapids, MI: Zondervan Bible Publishers.

Collins, G. (1993). *The biblical basis of Christian counseling for people helpers.* Colorado Springs, CO: NavPress.

Patton, J. (1993). *Pastoral care in context: An introduction to pastoral care.* Louisville, KY: Westminster/John Knox Press.

Runcorn, D. (2003). *Choice, desire and the will of God: What more do you want?* Peabody, MA: Hendrickson Publishers, Inc.

Resources for Clients

Anderson, N., and Miller, R. (2002). *Getting anger under control.* Eugene, OR: Harvest House Publishers.

Dobson, J. (1999). *Love must be tough.* Nashville, TN: W Publishing Group.

Faulkner, P. (1996). *Making things right when things go wrong.* West Monroe, LA: Howard Publishing Company, Inc.

Lockley, J. (2002). *The practical workbook for the depressed Christian.* England: Authentic Lifestyles.

Maxwell, J. (2000). *Body and soul: Walking with God to total health.* Birmingham, AL: New Hope Publishers.

Morris, J. (2003). *From worry to worship: A 30-day guide to overcoming inferiority.* Birmingham, AL: New Hope Publishers.

Phillips, B. (2001). *Getting off the emotional roller coaster [42 days to feeling great!].* Eugene, OR: Harvest House Publishers.

Schuller, R. (1988). *Success is never ending.* Nashville, TN: Thomas Nelson.

Tadlock, J. (2003). *When it's rush hour all day long: Finding peace in a hurry-sick world.* Birmingham, AL: New Hope Publishers.

Related Scriptures

> And God is able to make all grace abound to you, so that in all things at all times, having all that you need, you will abound in every good work. (2 Corinthians 9:8 NIV)
>
> Trust in the LORD and do good; dwell in the land and enjoy safe pasture. (Psalm 37:3 NIV)
>
> Because the Sovereign LORD helps me, I will not be disgraced. Therefore have I set my face like a flint, and I know I will not be put to shame. (Isaiah 50:7 NIV)

So do not fear, for I am with you; do not be dismayed, for I am your God. I will strengthen you and help you; I will uphold you with my righteous right hand. (Isaiah 41:10 NIV)

Model Prayer

Lord, thank you for loving _______. Help [him or her] to begin the steps [he or she] needs to take to experience the life that you have planned for [him or her]. May [he or she] follow Jesus who was obedient to you in even the small things so that [he or she] may experience the joyful life that he offers. In his name, I ask this. Amen.

Getting It in Gear

1. In the middle of the center gear, list one thing you would like to change.
2. In each gear around the center gear, list the things you would have to change if you were successfully going to move the center gear.

. . . faith by itself if it is not accompanied by action is dead.

James 2:17 (NIV)

– 11 –

Bad Dog–Good Dog

Steven T. Zombory
Philip J. Henry

Guiding Scripture

. . . whatever is true, whatever is noble, whatever is right, whatever is pure, whatever is lovely, whatever is admirable—if anything is excellent or praiseworthy—think about such things.

Philippians 4:8 (NIV)

Type of Contribution: Exercise, Handouts/Homework

Objective

This exercise will assist in encouraging clients to consider how they feed the good and bad sides of themselves, resulting in insight into the triggers of negative behaviors and leading to the insight and motivation necessary to begin the process of positive change.

This exercise will do the following:

1. Explore the client's current environment in terms of positive and negative reinforcers.
2. Identify situations and individuals who have had negative and positive effects on the client and provide an understanding of how the client conceptualizes these experiences.
3. Identify where repetitious negative choices have caused the client to feel stuck and nonproductive.
4. Aid the client in identifying seemingly neutral decisions that have either a negative or a positive effect.
5. Encourage the client to take responsibility for his or her choices and begin to take control of his or her life.
6. Uncover repeated areas of learning and coping to use in building relational growth and areas of strength.

Rationale for Use

At times, a client is so entrenched in destructive patterns fed by his or her culture and environment that positive change is extremely difficult or nearly impossible. In these cases, a large part of the problem lies in the ideas the client may have in his or her mind that may actually prevent

The Christian Therapist's Notebook

doi:10.1300/5334_12

the growth, creative thinking, and cultivation of faith necessary to provide a foundation for building positive change.

The Bible admonishes the believer to consider what occupies his or her mind and environment. This is common sense. The friends, interests, entertainment, possessions, and other things people spend the most time with and surround themselves with will naturally interest and capture them. If a person desires to have the "good" side win, he or she must use scripture, his or her will, and positive choices to move in that direction.

The same is true for the client. He or she will become good or bad, positive or negative, based on what he or she feeds himself or herself. Many problems and issues, even those of a serious nature, disappear as the correct habits develop.

In reaching for new goals, prior to undertaking any new significant endeavor, begin by surrounding each decision with the positive thoughts and beliefs that make the accomplishment possible. Feeding on God's promises, what He says about His creation, and looking at examples of positive role models are all part of the process. This will motivate the client to go beyond where he or she is and reach for all that God has for him or her. Correct input is the key for successful output.

Instructions

Talk with the client about the inner struggle between good and bad. Start with Romans 7:14-25, using Paul's discussion of his internal struggle. The Apostle Paul wants to do the good but does not do it. The bad that he does not want to do, he ends up doing. Make sure to normalize this struggle. Romans 3:23 says that we all sin. There is a balance to be struck here. The client with false guilt sees so much wrong that he or she has no idea where to begin and feels overwhelmed, and another client may not see much wrong with anything he or she does. The latter may need to inspect his or her conscience and learn to distinguish between right and wrong thinking.

Compare this struggle to two dogs that fight for dominance. Tell the client that the dog he or she feeds the most grows stronger and bigger and wins the fight. Ask the client if he or she would like to examine what feeds the good dog and what feeds the bad dog in the struggle.

Begin with the "bad dog" column on the handout at the end of the chapter. Ask the client to list those things which he or she thinks contribute to the problem or encourage negative or ungodly thinking. Carefully and thoughtfully, let the client discover the connection his or her thoughts and feelings have with the choices he or she makes. Assigning this as homework will allow the client time to think about what feeds these negative behaviors and thoughts. Be careful not to agree with the client too quickly or to let him or her off too easily. Real remorse leads to repentance and freedom.

Make sure not to blame the client; just examine. It is not the therapist's work to convict. Let the Holy Spirit have space to work. Do instruct and challenge though, when it is necessary.

Next, move on to the "good dog" column of the handout; examine what feeds the client's positive behaviors and thoughts. If possible, take the same amount of time on this as on the negatives. Clients are not usually good at finding what makes the good dog grow. Often, clients complete this section while coming up with excuses for why they cannot move in the positive direction. Again, give the Lord space to speak, and give the client the silence to hear what the Holy Spirit is trying to say. It will take persistence to stay with finding what causes the good to grow in the client's life.

Ask the client what changes, if any, he or she would like to make, and have him or her make a firm commitment to make those changes. Have the client choose what needs to go and what should replace it.

Together complete the "Building for Successful Change Contract," including what he or she will commit to change, and ask the client to sign and date the contract. The therapist can then sign as a witness to the commitments.

Vignette

Jan introduced herself as a new Christian and a recent graduate of college who was working as a server, waiting for the right job to come along, all while trying to rebuild her life after breaking up with a boyfriend she had lived with for over two years. Jan hoped that she would "not make the same mistakes twice." "I know I did many things wrong," she said. "I guess we were too young and immature. I thought we were going to get married," she added, "but those hormones got going, and, well, you know, I loved him." I nodded, recognizing the power of hormones and love, and she smiled. She thought counseling could help her gain perspective and smooth out the rough spots in her life.

When we talked about what she wanted to accomplish in therapy, Jan was all over the place. She wanted to focus on her career. She wanted to grow as a Christian. She wanted to become more mature and learn to make better choices. She told me about a new man she had met and asked what I thought about her dating someone who did not share her faith. She stated that she wanted a stable, sane life but admitted that she was not living a lifestyle conducive to reaching that goal; she had almost moved in with another man, whom she barely knew, the week before.

I suggested that we look at what the Bible said about her struggle to do the right thing. I had her read Romans 7:14-25. After reading this passage, she agreed that she had many of the same struggles described in the verses. "I want to do the good, but I don't end up doing it, so the bad is what I usually end up with," she said.

I told Jan that life was like two dogs fighting. "Which one wins?" I asked. "I guess whatever one I want to," she replied. I agreed with this but also began telling her the story of a man who had two dogs that he would take to town. Not having television or other sources of entertainment in those days, the townspeople would gather around and bet on the two dogs. The man always knew how to set the odds—which dog would win—even though the dogs were very evenly matched. One day, he told a friend the secret: "The dog I want to win gets the best food, while the dog I want to lose gets locked up and barely fed at all. By the end of the week, I know which dog will win."

I suggested that although the situation might not be that clear-cut for her, it would be helpful to examine what she was figuratively feeding herself. She agreed, and we began looking at what she fed the bad part of herself. "Well," she said, "I do have some friends I like to party with." I asked her what "party" meant, and she said, "You know, drinking at clubs. That's how I met Grant." Grant was her ex-boyfriend with whom she had recently had the breakup. "I think I do drink a little too much at times. I know it's not the best. I get a little carried away at times." She then explained how she had lived a promiscuous lifestyle before making her commitment to Christ and how she, at times, was tempted to return to this lifestyle. She complained that she did not like being by herself and got bored easily.

The next thing she listed under "bad dog" was the name "Linda." "Linda is a good friend of mine, but she is not good for me. Linda drinks too much and uses drugs. She always wants me to come with her to meet some guy she knows, and they all end up being losers." She talked about Linda leading her into several situations that were questionable and that scared her. Next, she listed her job. "It is more of a bar than a restaurant. I like it because it is easy and it is good money, but I don't like the way I am treated, the atmosphere, or the feeling that there is something better for me," she said. "I know that if I stay there I am wasting my time."

The next few "bad dog" items took a while for Jan to pinpoint. "I guess I watch too much TV," she finally said. "I watch all of those reality programs, even though I know they are just a waste of time." Then it appeared as if a lightbulb had gone on in her head, and she added "Brian" to the list. She told me that she had been talking to him again, even though she knew he was not right for her; there was no one else, so she had gone on one or two dates with him and had even let him stay over at her place one night.

Next, she listed three other men whom she was somewhat interested in dating. "These are not the right men for me, but they are the ones I pick and who always pick me." As we talked, she began to understand how her need for male companionship moved her to make wrong choices—a good therapeutic interaction.

She seemed to become stuck at this point, so I asked Jan to continue considering more of what fed the bad dog for homework and suggested that we turn to thinking of what fed her good side.

Jan told me that she had become a Christian three months ago through her friend Phyllis. "When I am with her I feel good and I feel like I am getting somewhere. Through Phyllis's influence, I even attended Bible study a few times and really enjoyed it. I felt closer to God and I could think clearly about life." We listed "spending time with Phyllis" and "attending Bible study" in the "good dog" column. Jan said her New Year's resolution was a commitment to go to her Bible study for two months.

Next, she mentioned music. "I just had a birthday, and one of my Bible study members gave me this Christian CD that I have been playing on the way to work. It really does help me focus for the day, and I find myself praying that God would guide me during the day. I would like to find more music like this," she said. She mentioned that she had heard of a Christian bookstore that had many choices of CDs. She also mentioned that she was a reader and had heard that there were quite a few Christian books she might be interested in reading. "I would like to read something on dating," she said. She asked me if I knew of any books, and I wrote down a few titles I thought she might find interesting and that fit her particular situation.

The next week, we completed the Bad Dog–Good Dog exercise, and I asked her to consider making a commitment to eliminate some of the negative "food" and to add some positive "food." Jan asked if she could think about this because right now she really needed to talk to me about Brian. He had called again, and she was unsure of what to do. We talked about Brian for the rest of that session and again in the following session.

About a month later, she came into our session and reported that she was ready for her life to change. She had given notice at work, she had been attending Bible study with Phyllis, and she had broken it off with Brian. She also said that she was ready to commit to eliminating several of her negatives and to adding several of the positives.

Although this may appear to be a simple exercise, for Jan, it made a world of difference. She has a new job, is actively involved in her church, attends Bible study with Phyllis, and is happier and more in control of life than ever before.

Suggestions for Follow-Up

Once the client has identified the things that feed the good side of him or her, work with the client to come up with a plan that will help him or her be more accountable, not only to himself of herself, but also to you as the counselor. There is a tension here. On the one hand, the client is the only one who really can monitor the input of his or her life, so he or she must take responsibility. On the other hand, it is helpful for the counselor to encourage and check in with the client about progress in this area.

Creating a contract indicating what the client will agree to both in the beginning and at the conclusion of therapy is a good way to track the progress of the client. Be sure to include dates and deadlines, if these are appropriate.

Contraindications

This exercise should not be used if the client is highly resistant and would be opposed to considering his or her positive and negative personal life inputs.

Resources for Professionals

Anderson, N., Zuehlke, J., and Zuehlke, T. (2000). *Christ centered therapy.* Grand Rapids, MI: Zondervan Publishing House.

Collins, G. (2001). *The biblical basis of Christian counseling for people helpers.* Colorado, Springs, CO: NavPress.

Laaser, M. (2004). *Healing the wounds of sexual addiction.* Grand Rapids, MI: Zondervan Publishing House.

Resources for Clients

Bright, B. (1995). *How you can be filled with the Holy Spirit.* Orlando, FL: New Life Publications.

Miller, J. (1991). *A hunger for healing.* New York: HarperCollins Publishers.

Petersen, R., and Whiteman, T. (1997). *Fresh start: Eight principles for starting over when a relationship doesn't work.* Wheaton, IL: Tyndale House Publishers.

Schuller, R. (1985). *The be happy attitude.* Waco, TX: Word Books.

Swenson, R. (1999). *The overload syndrome: Learning to live within your limits.* Colorado Springs, CO: NavPress.

Walker, S. (2001). *Driven no more: Finding contentment by letting go.* Minneapolis, MN: Augsburg Fortress Publishers.

Ward, R. (1984). *Self-esteem gift from God.* Grand Rapids, MI: Baker Book House.

Warren, R. (2002). *The purpose driven life.* Grand Rapids, MI: Zondervan Publishing House.

Related Scriptures

> If any of you lacks wisdom, he should ask God, who gives generously to all without finding fault, and it will be given to him. (James 1:5 NIV)

> Do not be anxious about anything, but in everything by prayer and petition, with thanksgiving, present your requests to God. And the peace of God, which transcends all understanding, will guard your hearts and your minds in Christ Jesus. (Philippians 4:6-7 NIV)

> Trust in the LORD with all your heart and lean not on your own understanding; in all your ways acknowledge Him, and He will make your paths straight. (Proverbs 3:5-6 NIV)

> So I say, live by the Spirit, and you will not gratify the desires of the sinful nature. For the sinful nature desires what is contrary to the Spirit, and the Spirit what is contrary to the sinful nature. They are in conflict with each other, so that you do not do what you want. But if you are led by the Spirit, you are not under law. . . . Those who belong to Christ Jesus have crucified the sinful nature with its passions and desires. Since we live by the Spirit, let us keep in step with the Spirit. (Galatians 5:16-17, 24-25 NIV)

Bad Dog—Good Dog

In the chart below, list the things that help you move toward negative thinking or actions and the things that cause you to move in a positive direction.

1.	
2.	
3.	
4.	
5.	
6.	
7.	
8.	
9.	
10.	

. . . whatever is true, whatever is noble, whatever is right, whatever is pure, whatever is lovely, whatever is admirable—if anything is excellent or praiseworthy—think about such things.

Philippians 4:8 (NIV)

BUILDING FOR SUCCESSFUL CHANGE CONTRACT

This ___________ day of ___________________,

I, ____,

commit to eliminating these activities from my life

____

____

____

____

____

____

____

____

____

____

and adding

____

____

____

____

____

____

____

I humbly ask for God's help in creating a positive life where I can grow.

____

Client Date

____

Counselor Date

– 12 –

It Was Wrong

David R. Miller
Philip J. Henry

Guiding Scripture

Have mercy on us, O LORD, have mercy on us, for we have endured much contempt.

Psalm 123:3 (NIV)

Type of Contribution: Exercise, Handout

Objective

Abuse has a way of choking off the voice of the abused. The pain and frustration experienced by a victim of abuse multiplies over the years that the secret remains hidden. No trauma is more hurtful than that which occurs in the safest environment, the home, and no trauma is more deeply felt than when the abuser is one of the trusted, "inner circle" of one's family. Our ministry as Christian counselors will undoubtedly bring us into contact with people asking for help to find the voice inside of them that is crying out for release and justice. We serve God by helping to find that voice.

Rationale for Use

In his book *Man's Search for Meaning,* Victor Frankl, a psychiatrist and Holocaust survivor, offered the profound truth that "abnormal behavior in response to an abnormal situation is normal." As we counsel the physically, sexually, emotionally, or spiritually abused, we must be aware that abuse survivors sometimes react irrationally to the pain, which may add to the confusion that has caused them to seek our counsel.

Christian counselors are conduits, or pipelines, for God's grace and mercy to hurting people of any age, sex, background, or present situation. We must, if we are to help, put our personal feelings aside and focus on the needs of our clients. We may hear things from abuse survivors we would rather not hear, but we must hear them if we are to help. Above all, the client must feel safe with you, the counselor. Your client will need to express the pain, shame, and embarrassment he or she has been feeling and is still experiencing. The client will need to feel that you are listening without judging him or her or evaluating his or her responses to the violations experienced, perhaps many years earlier.

Abuse survivors will not forget their abuse, and they are unlikely to get to the point of recovery where they can live their lives without feeling any residual damage. God is a God of forgive-

The Christian Therapist's Notebook

doi:10.1300/5334_13

ness and recovery, but scars remain in most cases. As you help your client explore the painful experiences that brought him or her to counseling, encourage reliance on God for wisdom in dealing with a history of abuse, as well as patience and trust in the Lord while the healing process takes place.

As you get to know your client, begin building a mental "life map" for him or her that will help both of you understand what counseling can accomplish. You will need to learn about the present state of your client's life. Is he or she living successfully now? If your client is an adult, is he or she happily married? If there are children, how does your client feel about being a parent? If your client is a professed Christian, what is his or her relationship with God like? If the abuse was sexual, what is your client's sexual life like? If the abuser is still in the client's life (e.g., a family member), how does he or she relate to that person now? What kind of self-blaming messages (e.g., "It was wrong for me to give in so easily") do you hear from your client? Where is the anger located inside your client? Where is the fear located, and how is it expressed?

Above all else, as you listen and learn, model God's love and gentleness with your client. Many abuse survivors have led damaged and inadequate lives because of the early hurt they experienced. If your client is a female who was abused as a child, she will likely have had more than one marriage by the time she comes to counseling. She may be sexually unresponsive to her present husband and morally strict and legalistic with her children. Your client may have a secret substance abuse issue that will need to be confessed and addressed, but model God's grace, love, and nonjudgmental acceptance as you learn about these issues. You are God's instrument of recovery with this person.

Instructions

As you begin the counseling process, remember to focus on two essential counselor qualities, nonjudgmental listening and complete confidentiality. As you listen to the story of your client's abuse, you will probably doubt the truthfulness of parts of the story. This is normal because time changes memories, and sometimes memories adjust to meet the client's emotional needs. For example, a sexual abuse survivor will inevitably feel some level of guilt and responsibility for what happened and now may adjust his or her memories of the event to fit this need to feel responsible. Do not challenge the client's statements! Ask open-ended questions (e.g., "How did that make you feel?"), and be patient in waiting for your client to come to the needed realizations. Remember, "talking out" various incidents seems to help clients the most.

Spend some time explaining your commitment to confidentiality. If you are a church-based Christian counselor, take care to promise that you will not tell your client's story to anyone in the church. A church-based counselor needs to work out an agreement with the pastor ahead of time that confidentiality is necessary. Tell your client, in no uncertain terms, that you will not discuss his or her issues or story with anyone else—not the pastor, not your own spouse or friends, no one at all. Remember too that confidentiality requirements continue even after the counseling terminates.

As you get to know your client in the first session or two, it is acceptable to ask a number of background questions. You will need to know the details of the story, while remembering that some or many details become skewed over time. You need to learn about the type of abuse (physical, sexual, emotional, etc.), who the perpetrator was, how many times the abuse occurred, and the span of time when the abuse occurred (e.g., between the ages of six and ten). Find out whether the perpetrator is still alive and in the client's life (e.g., a parent or other relative), how your client feels when he or she is around that person now, and how your client handles this challenging experience.

Encourage your client to bring in photographs of himself or herself at the time when the abuse occurred. Family pictures can be emotionally evocative and can help bring long-suppressed emotions to the surface. A word of caution on expressed emotions may be helpful: It is *not* your job simply to make the client feel better. Many times, a client must temporarily feel worse before beginning to feel better. When tears, angry outbursts, or sadness are expressed by your client, let those emotions run their course. *Do not rescue the person!* Your client needs to express the emotions he or she is feeling, and you need to get out of the way and let the pain be expressed so that healing may proceed.

Once the client is comfortable discussing the abuse with you and has begun to work through some of the accompanying emotions, it is important to make sure that the client knows that he or she is not to blame and that the abuser was wrong. At this point, you may bring out the handout "It Was Wrong" to work through with the client. Let the client fill in the squares with his or her own words and take plenty of time talking through each section. Because self-blame is often very ingrained in abuse survivors, you may very well have to reinforce these principles over and over, either through talking or through repeating the completion of the actual handout.

Ask your client to tell you how God fits into this picture of abuse, and do not be surprised if God is presented as an ambivalent or even negative figure in the client's story. A client may ask, "How could God have let that happen to me?" The client is not really seeking an answer, however, but simply voicing what has in all probability been a long-held question the client has been too embarrassed to ask anyone else. If your client is a child or teenager, be very careful about how you raise the issue of God's protection. A counselor may be tempted to say, "You don't have to worry anymore. God will protect you from further harm." This could lead to the client rejoining with, "Well, why didn't God protect me the first time?" You will not be able to answer that question for your client, so beware of making any promises.

As you move through the counseling process, encourage the client to think about these major points regarding recovery. You will need to emphasize that any abuse survivor is unlikely to get to a point in recovery where the abuse ceases to bother him or her at all. Another important point is, if the abuser is still alive and in the client's life, the client should not expect to be able to relate to the abuser as if the abuse had never happened. This is unrealistic and should not be a goal of counseling. Another point to stress is that forgiveness does not erase memories, and even though your client may have forgiven the abuser, that abuser will always be a negative element in your client's life.

Use biblical resources to help your client. A number of excellent recovery books can be found in any comprehensive Christian bookstore, a few of which are included in the reference lists at the end of this chapter. Personal journaling can also help your client process memories and feelings surrounding the abuse. Support groups for abuse survivors may also be present in the area for your client to access. Above all, encourage your client to continue to walk close to God. He or she needs to stay in church, attend available Bible study groups, and participate in prayer groups and mission outreaches because helping others is one of the keys to abuse recovery. Assure your client of your continued support and confidentiality and encourage him or her to return to talk whenever necessary. Moreover, do not forget that you, as the counselor, need to be patient.

Vignette

Joan was, at the time of our meeting, in her early fifties and single. Joan had a college education and held a high-prestige position at a large insurance agency in our city. She told me that she was responsible for about 200 people. She had been with this company since graduating from college, felt very secure, and believed she was a well-liked person at the company. Joan was a member of the church to which my wife and I belonged, and, to be honest, I had always assumed that Joan was probably divorced because she was always alone in church and belonged to the women's Bible study group.

However, Joan was not divorced. Though attractive, well educated, and socially adept, she had never married nor did she have any children. As we began the counseling process, she shared with me that, although she dated "sometimes," she had never been able to connect with a man and had just about given up on the idea of marriage. She claimed that marriage seemed to be "not in the cards" for her, but she was happy with her job and her group of friends. Joan seemed to be a committed Christian, and I had no reason to doubt that her walk with the Lord was anything but good.

In our first session, after discussing my role as church counselor and issues of confidentiality, I asked Joan why she had come in for counseling. Her response surprised me. I had expected to hear about depression, loneliness, financial insecurities, and searching for God's guidance to be the top issues on her mind, but, once again, I was wrong. Joan wanted to talk about her elderly father, long widowed and living in a retirement village not too distant from our city. Joan shared with me that she was primarily responsible for the care of her father, and while she had two sisters, they lived quite a distance away and could visit only occasionally. Joan was the primary caregiver for her father, who was becoming increasingly frail and who had expressed a desire to move in with her. She was more than a little ambivalent about this and asked me what I thought she should do. Was she, according to the Bible, required to "honor" her father by agreeing with his wish to live with her?

I sensed that there was more to the story than what she was sharing, and I mentioned this to Joan by saying, "It sounds to me as if you are uncertain about how to handle this decision, Joan, but is there more to this? Is there something else I should know in order to help you?" She replied, "Dr. Miller, I am an abuse survivor and my abuser is my father, the person we have been talking about, the one who now wants me to allow him to move in with me. Do you see my predicament? No one at the church knows this, and I would be so embarrassed if anyone found out. You see, that is why I cannot just simply agree to let my father come live with me. I do not trust him even now, and I could not bear the thought of us living together. I don't know what to do!"

Our first session ended with my encouraging Joan to visit the local Christian bookstore, to pick out one or two books from the list I provided, to read and discuss during our next session. I encouraged Joan to resist the persuasion of others in this matter and to listen to the quiet leadership of the Holy Spirit on this important issue. I asked Joan if she would like us to spend some time in prayer, and she tearfully nodded in agreement. I prayed aloud and Joan, overtaken by weeping at this point, was unable to pray audibly. We ended the session. Joan agreed to pray about this every time she could find an undisturbed moment, to search her Bible, and to read the books I had recommended before our next session. Joan left the session seeming encouraged.

Our second session began with a discussion about some of Joan's reading and moved on to a discussion of several very relevant questions. Joan had been thinking a lot about the command to honor her parents. Due to the severity of the situation with her father, I suggested we think about Proverbs 20:7 (NIV): "The righteous man leads a blameless life; blessed are his children after him." I asked Joan an obvious question to help her become more aware of what the true issues are: Had her father led a righteous and blameless life? Of course not! Might Joan then, I asked, be exempt from the command to honor her father? We also looked at Mark 13:12 (NIV) and the words of Jesus, describing the dark days leading up to the rapture: "Brother will betray brother . . . , and a father his child." I asked Joan to think about whether her father had betrayed her and her sisters, as well as the Lord, in the incestuous sexual sins he had perpetrated against his immediate family and the larger family of God. Could it be, I asked, that her father had surrendered his fatherly position the moment he had betrayed his daughter?

I then moved our discussion to the fact that her father had been wrong in what he did and that what he did was wrong. Through open-ended questions, I tried to determine whether Joan was shouldering any part of the blame for the abuse. I took out the It Was Wrong handout and put it on the desk between us. I asked Joan to review it and together we worked through filling in the situation that was wrong, why it was wrong, the effects, and what could be done now. I had Joan write on the handout in her own words but helped her identify what she was thinking and feeling.

The second session ended with Joan agreeing to consider prayerfully what we had explored in this session. I assigned Joan a homework project that included writing her father a letter, explaining in detail her reasons for not allowing him to come to live with her. I politely asked her not to pull any punches and to be as candid and honest with him as she could. Joan was not going to mail the letter, at least not at this point in her therapy, but I thought it would be helpful if she could put her thoughts down on paper. She was going to speak with her sisters by phone in the next day or two to see if they had been thinking about this issue as well. We prayed and then Joan left the office.

We spent our next several sessions exploring Joan's evolving thinking on the issue of honoring a dishonorable parent. She shared her letter with me, and we discussed it point by point to see if Joan was, in any way, still denying the seriousness of what her father had done to her. She was slowly reaching the conclusion that God would not want her to place herself in the position of being a victim again. Joan also seemed to be more comfortable with the fact that she was not the sole potential caregiver for her father, and that she had every right to be assertive with her sisters and expect them to share the burden of any care provided. We also explored the issue that her father, apparently a weak Christian, if a Christian at all, would himself be better off not being in a situation where he could be tempted to sin again. I very carefully impressed upon Joan that she and her sisters were in no way responsible for what their father had done to them, and that he alone bore the guilt for his own sinful behavior.

Joan made good progress in therapy, and by the end of the eleventh session, she was confident in her God-provided strength, now insisting that her father was not going to move in with her and that, if necessary, the three sisters and their families would work together to financially provide for nursing home care for their father. Joan was encouraged to deal with her father in whatever way she felt led by the Holy Spirit. She could face him with his unconfessed sin, or she could leave it alone. Now, in her early fifties, she felt able to get on with her life, as she phrased it. Joan told me that what had helped her the most was having a Christian counselor who would listen to what she considered an "embarrassing" past without judging her or making hasty recommendations to do this or that. Joan needed to talk without feeling criticized or judged. She told me she had just about given up on talking to "church people" because she had had prior experiences with pastors and others that had not gone well. She was so relieved that God had brought into her life a Christian counselor who did not criticize, correct, judge, or preach to her in the counseling sessions.

Suggestions for Follow-Up

Joan was encouraged to keep the letter she had written to her father and add to it as additional thoughts came to her mind. She was also encouraged to rebuild her relationships with her sisters so that, as the time for providing care for their father arrived, they would be prepared. Joan agreed to continue reading Christian spiritual growth books for women and abuse survivors and to stay in touch with me as much as she needed. She planned to continue being involved in church and the women's Bible study group and was even willing to take more of a leadership role in these activities than she had in the past.

I was impressed with Joan's dedication to progress. She needed to hear herself express her feelings, and she needed to weep and become angry at times; it was my job to avoid interfering with the work of the Holy Spirit, working through me in our counseling sessions. For successful counseling, you must listen without criticizing or correcting, avoid preaching or teaching, and acknowledge that the only expert on your client's life is God and the client, not you, the counselor.

Contraindications

A wise counselor once said, "Do not unzip what you may not be able to zip back up." Be careful to allow enough time to complete the counseling process. Counseling an abuse survivor like Joan can be a time-consuming and long-term project. I had to make room in my counseling schedule for Joan to return once a month or so for years after the working portion of our counseling terminated. This comes under the headings of both follow-up and long-term support.

Suicide and other self-injurious behaviors are always risks with an abuse survivor. Competent Christian counselors need to be alert to any of the signs of depression and potential suicidal ideation from such a client. I gave Joan my home phone number and permission, in an emergency, to call me. We discussed the emergencies that could occur, and self-destructive thinking topped the list. Joan knew I would be willing to get her into a hospital for treatment if her depression went out of control, which it thankfully did not.

Consider giving a referral to a support group. Joan attended an abused women's support group at one of the larger churches in town and found that to be of great help. A good counselor will be aware of the referral possibilities available in the local community.

Resources for Professionals

Kok, E. (2002). *A woman who hurts, a God who heals: Discovering unconditional love.* Birmingham, AL: New Hope Publishers.

Kollar, C.A. (1997). *Solution-focused pastoral counseling.* Grand Rapids, MI: Zondervan Publishing House.

Resources for Clients

Carlson, D. (2000). *Overcoming hurts and anger.* Eugene, OR: Harvest House Publishers.

Hawkins, D. (2004). *When pleasing others is hurting you.* Eugene, OR: Harvest House Publishers.

Horton, A.L., and Williamson, J.A. (1988). *Abuse and religion: When praying isn't enough.* Lexington, MA: Lexington Books.

Related Scriptures

> I the Lord search the heart and examine the mind, to reward a man according to his conduct, according to what his deeds deserve. (Jeremiah 17:10 NIV)

> Do not repay evil with evil or insult with insult, but with blessing, because to this you were called so that you may inherit a blessing. (1 Peter 3:9 NIV)

> And if anyone causes one of these little ones who believe in me to sin, it would be better for him to be thrown into the sea with a large millstone around his neck. (Mark 9:42 NIV)

It was WRONG.

SITUATION that was wrong	WHY it was wrong	The Effects	What can be done now

– 13 –

Bowing Down

Philip J. Henry

Guiding Scripture

Flee from sexual immorality. . . . Do you not know that your body is a temple of the Holy Spirit, who is in you, whom you have received from God? You are not your own; you were bought at a price. Therefore honor God with your body.

1 Corinthians 6:18a, 19-20 (NIV)

Type of Contribution: Exercise, Handouts/Homework

Objective

The goal of this exercise is to restore healthy relationships with God and others by helping the client to achieve the following:

1. Understand the connection between emotional pain and his or her problematic sexual behaviors.
2. Identify individuals who hurt him or her or have been hurt by his or her actions.
3. Identify the memories, situations, and images that trigger problematic sexual behaviors.
4. Understand that sexual problems are common and that there is hope through a relationship with God.
5. Explore the meaning he or she has taken from past sexual problems.
6. Be receptive to receiving help from God in times of need.
7. Begin to understand how Christ views what the client has lost as a result of sexual acting out, and how God can be a resource during troubled times.
8. Take the steps necessary to make a firm commitment to bow down to God and resist the devil.

Rationale for Use

Everyone worships something. People may not physically bow down or pledge allegiance to anything, but most organize their lives around those things which they worship. These things or behaviors become the centerpieces in their lives. This is true for counselors, and it is certainly true for clients as well.

Sexual immorality, while a common life organizer or object of worship, has the potential to be a harsh master. There are many examples of those who have bowed down and let sexual appetite

The Christian Therapist's Notebook

doi:10.1300/5334_14

become their master. Even the strong can succumb to this tyrant. Samson, a biblical figure with incredible strength, allowed his passions to lead his decisions, and this resulted in a tragic life. His pursuit of sexual appetite led him to lose his natural God-given ability, his sight, and, finally, his life. Sadly, this has happened to countless men and women throughout history.

The Bible clearly states that, in the end, this type of behavior or pursuit always brings pain because it seats sexuality in the place of God, and because many types of sexuality devalue people, reducing them to objects. If these two important relationships are out of balance, then nothing flows correctly.

Often, this sexual acting out or imbalance grows out of some type of past hurt or abuse, whether sexual or otherwise. Out-of-control sexual behavior may simply be the best answer individuals have found to the question of pain in their lives. Unfortunately, this is like digging a hole—the more progress made, the deeper the individual goes. Short-term solutions to avoid pain end up causing more pain, and on and on it goes.

Thankfully, there are many biblical examples of sexual restoration and healing. Anyone can be freed from the tyranny of sexual expression gone wild, as well as from the pain and brokenness that typify this lifestyle. The purpose of this exercise is to help the client explore areas of sexual brokenness and mistakes and come to terms with both the pain and the guilt of the related behaviors, thoughts, and actions. This is often a long process, as guilt and pain must be confronted repeatedly, like the peeling away of the layers of an onion.

If the love of God is allowed to enter the picture, rather than running from God when the client encounters a difficult sexual issue, pain, or temptation, running to God becomes the better solution. Only through God's help will a client experience true positive sexuality, a restored balance in life, and the proper placement of sex as servant rather than master.

Finally, if therapy is to be a success in this area, the client must make a commitment to decide what or who will be the master of his or her life, or the one to whom he or she will choose to bow down or submit. Helping the client to see the results of his or her choices and aiding the client to draw near to God can result in him or her taking an initial step toward victory in this area.

Instructions

Before beginning this exercise, the therapist should take a moment to make sure personal boundaries are clear regarding his or her own sexual issues. Problems relating to sex are usually complicated and difficult to discuss. The therapist should make sure that his or her heart and mind are in a good place before working on these issues with others.

Using the "Bowing Down" handout, talk with the client about his or her sexual behavior. Lead him or her in discussing the memories, guilt, shame, and secrets that surround the behavior. Be aware of physical implications, emotional pain, and spiritual warfare. One of the best ways to get comfortable talking about sexual issues in a clear and candid way is to practice asking the questions.

Encourage the client to be as open as possible, but avoid being pushy or judgmental. Use the handout as a concrete object that can center and refocus the discussion. Help the client to see clearly that secrets keep him or her sick, and that opening up and talking, or perhaps confessing, is the path to peace. Let the client take as long as he or she wants to tell his or her story fully.

Find out what specific sexual memories or behaviors are most troubling. This will usually take several sessions. Like peeling an onion, the layers come off one by one until the truth becomes more visible. Encourage the client to reveal any secrets or other issues he or she has failed to mention so that together you can get to the truth. The client may not be lying about the issues, but instead he or she may be holding back information until there is enough trust in the therapist to continue; a primary concern may be whether the therapist can handle the client's secrets gently and professionally.

If a history of sexual abuse is present, make sure to stabilize the client before proceeding to anything else. At a minimum, make sure that the client is not experiencing any flashbacks or that discussing the abuse is not causing him or her an inordinate amount of anxiety. The safety of the client is a priority. However, if the client is an adult, do not automatically jump on the abuse as if the abuse is the only important issue the client possesses. He or she may have other sexual issues to address or, at least, bring to your attention. Also, make sure not to head off into too many directions at once. Be clear about what therapy will accomplish. Hosts of other issues often accompany sexual issues.

Feelings of guilt will often be a part of sexual confessions. Let the client explore his or her own guilt. Do not let the client off the hook too easily. Let the client work through what he or she is feeling, and do not rescue him or her from these feelings; doing so may shortcut the client's motivation to change.

If the client has a sexual addiction, encourage him or her to explore the associated emotional pain and inquire how that pain became sexually connected. Tie the pain the client feels with the release of acting out sexually and let him or her come to terms with the implications. Allow the client to list the negatives and positives of the addiction. It is essential to replace the perceived positives with more positive actions, while using the negatives as fuel for change.

Explore with the client how he or she views God and what God thinks of him or her. Let the client express his or her emotions toward God. Sexual acting out often takes the place of honest emotions, so you may witness tears, anger, depression, withdrawal, or any number of distracting or avoiding behaviors. See if the client is able to identify the losses brought about by his or her actions. See if he or she can take responsibility for those actions and their consequences. This is not as easy as it sounds; the denial can run deep.

Use biblical examples of sexual misconduct and healing to offer a balanced picture. The Bible provides many examples, from incest to infidelity. Make sure to communicate the grace, forgiveness, and love of God. The client is exposing a very vulnerable part of his or her life. Be firm, clear, and gentle.

If appropriate, provide referrals to support groups and information on other resources when needed. Twelve-step recovery groups for sexual addiction, Loveaholics and Sexaholics Anonymous, sexual abuse recovery support groups, and a host of other groups, such as Celebrate Recovery, may be supportive adjuncts to the therapy process.

Vignette

As Martin entered the counseling office, he looked as if he had just stepped off the pages of *GQ* magazine. With his slicked-back dark hair, his expensive Italian dark blue suit, bold matching tie, and shiny black loafers, he was the picture of sartorial splendor. Martin was a Christian, a church member, a very successful real estate attorney, and a sexual addict.

After looking at the intake sheet, I began to talk with Martin about his sexual problems. Although Martin was still married, things were, as Martin put it, "not going well." This may have been the understatement of the year. His marital relationship was extremely tense and very hostile; the two were on the verge of a separation.

A little over five years prior, Martin had begun spending an increasing amount of time viewing pornography online. At first, it was just a way for him to relax after work, to find some release from the tension, but soon it became a substitute for many things in his life. His viewing frequency had gone up and down previously, but now he was spending many hours a week on this endeavor, and the time spent seemed to be increasing. In addition, his wife had discovered that he had begun visiting sexually explicit chat rooms online, and participating in the discussions, when she noticed a $500 charge from one of these services on their Visa bill. Martin also had been to several massage parlors and, on occasion, had cruised the bars or clubs hoping to find willing sexual partners.

Surprisingly, Martin continued to be active in his church and shared almost all of these facts with his wife. She had been supportive and forgiving at first. However, Martin was not able to stop these behaviors, even though he had promised to, and he confessed the more grievous sins almost as soon as he repeated them. Each time, Martin would be contrite and would seek to return to his wife's favor. This happened repeatedly until Sharon gave him the ultimatum to go to counseling "or else." Thus, here he was, compliant but resistant.

Taking out the "Bowing Down" handout, I asked Martin if he would be willing to complete an exercise about his sexual difficulties to discern how these difficulties had taken control of his life. Martin agreed, and I began by asking him about some of his first memories of sexuality. He reported that his parents had never talked about sex while he was growing up. He recalled that his mother had caught him masturbating once while looking at the magazines his father had kept in the basement, but no one had talked about it. He reported that he had felt very upset and filled with shame as she had lectured him. We labeled this event "caught by mother" and placed it under the "memories and shame" category of the handout. His father had never talked to him about that incident or about sex in general. Consequently, almost all of the sexual education Martin had received at home was shame producing.

Another sexual memory that Martin shared involved when, as a fifteen-year-old, he and an older cousin had became sexually involved at a Thanksgiving Day celebration at his grandparents' house. The advances had surprised Martin, and while he had not actively sought her, he had not and did not consider her to have been abusive. We labeled this "Thanksgiving day incident" and placed it under the "secrets" category of the handout, since Martin had never before shared that event with anyone. Martin talked about how that event had triggered his desire for sexual experimentation. Although this relationship had not continued, it had triggered something in Martin that he still wanted to repeat.

Martin had not been athletic. Although he had been mature for his age when in school, he still had been painfully shy, not a great student, and prone to feeling alienated from the other students. Sexual experiences had become for him a way to hide some of the loneliness and failure and to help him fit in. This in turn had led to multiple relationships in high school, lasting from a single evening to several months. During this time, he also had moved from occasionally watching pornography to a steady diet of X-rated videos.

As our session continued, I let Martin lead the discussion as he talked about his memories. I then asked Martin to discuss the shame he had regarding sexuality. Much of what I had heard already from him indirectly indicated that he was experiencing an overwhelming sense of guilt, but I wanted to see if he could identify this himself and was curious about what exactly made him feel guilty.

"I guess the problem with Barbara was the worst," he said. Barbara is the wife of Martin's best friend, Bert. Martin had tried to seduce Barbara without success. Bert found out, and that led to a violent confrontation between the two friends. Even after this, Martin still tried to contact Barbara. He reported that he felt like a loser pursuing a relationship that was going nowhere, but he had lost all sense of self-control.

I asked Martin to take the "Bowing Down" handout home and to think about other secrets he was keeping, what he thought about God, what God thought about sex, and the losses that had resulted from Martin's out-of-control sexual behavior. We prayed together, and Martin urgently reported that he truly wanted to change.

In the following weeks, Martin and I continued to talk about his sex life using the "Bowing Down" handout as a guide, and we investigated the things he had given up in order to please this demanding sex-god inside him. It was during this time that Sharon left him. Although she had left before for a day or two, this time she moved in with her sister and obtained a divorce attorney. To Martin, this was like a pitcher of ice water in the face. He was shocked, to say the least. He showed emotion for the first time in therapy and cried, even though he tried with all of his might to regain control.

In the following sessions, we talked about how he had served his sexual pleasure and where the pleasure had taken him. He listed "my life," "my friend Bert," "several important jobs and contacts," "my self-respect," "my marriage," and several other items as things he had lost already or was in the process of losing.

Martin reported that he had always viewed God as a distant, uncaring God who would possibly forgive when he did something wrong. However, although he was certain that God did love him, he also believed that God did not like him and had given up on him. In his time of need, he often turned to God and found comfort and support. Increasingly, he felt more connected to God and made an appointment to talk with his minister about his relationship with God and becoming more involved in the church. At one session, Martin reported that he wanted to worship God and had recommitted his life to God. I led him in a prayer affirming this, and we tried to map out steps to help him achieve success in keeping that promise.

Martin began to attend a support group for sexual addiction and met others there who struggled and were lonely, just as he was. I encouraged Martin to read several books on sexual addiction, and he began to educate himself on the subject. In a few months, Martin was able to get almost all of his sexual acting out under control, and he began to live a more balanced, fulfilled life.

Unfortunately, this story does not have a completely happy ending. Sharon did divorce Martin. Once she had left, she refused to come to therapy or meet with him under any circumstances. Nevertheless, Martin did not falter. He took this as a wake-up call and continued attending his counseling sessions, his support group meetings, and his church. As of now, he continues to bow down before the true God, the Maker of heaven and earth.

Suggestions for Follow-Up

This exercise depends on the willingness of the client to address the presenting sexual issues with candor, as well as his or her willingness to obey God.

As with spiritual strongholds, the problem here is often with the heart. Clients with sexual problems may have made commitments in the past but did not follow through with them. For some, the battle against lust is lost because they have tremendous guilt or just lose heart. For these clients, take time to provide scripture and information about the basics of the Christian life and spiritual warfare.

Included as part of this exercise is the handout "How You Can Be Filled with the Holy Spirit: Transferable Concepts," by Bill Bright. This handout can be used to further the client's understanding of what it means to surrender all areas of his or her life to God's control.

Note: This is a good time to pray with and for the client. Praying for the client's protection, wisdom, and strength should always be a priority.

Contraindications

This exercise may be contraindicated if the client is not willing to examine the areas of sexual immorality or is minimizing or otherwise deceptive concerning his or her activities and attitudes. In these cases, the counselor should have the client work on another issue that might prove to be an easier task or suggest that the client return to counseling when he or she is ready to be more open.

Resources for Professionals

Anderson, N. (2000). *The bondage breaker.* Eugene, OR: Harvest House.
Langberg, D. (1997). *Counseling survivors of sexual abuse.* Wheaton, IL: Tyndale House Publishers, Inc.
Whitehead, B. (2003). *Craving for love.* Grand Rapids, MI: Kregel Publications.
Whiteman, T., and Petersen, R. (1994). *Love gone wrong: What to do when you are attracted to the wrong person over and over.* Nashville, TN: Thomas Nelson Publishers.

Resources for Clients

Anderson, N. (2000). *Steps to freedom in Christ.* Ventura, CA: Gospel Light Publications.
Arterburn, S. (1995). *Addicted to love—Understanding dependencies of the heart: Romance, relationships and sex.* Ventura, CA: Vine Books.
Arterburn, S., Stoeker, F., and Yokey, M. (2000). *Every man's battle: Winning the war on sexual temptation one victory at a time.* Nashville, TN: Waterbrook Press.
Curtis, B., and Eldridge, J. (1997). *The sacred romance: Growing closer to the heart of God.* Nashville, TN: Thomas Nelson Publishers.
Laaser, M. (2004). *Healing the wounds of sexual addiction.* Grand Rapids, MI: Zondervan.
Langberg, D. (1999). *On the threshold of hope: Opening the door to healing for the survivors of sexual abuse.* Wheaton, IL: Tyndale House Publishers.
Means, P. (1999). *Men's secret wars.* Old Tappan, NJ: Fleming H. Revell Company.
Mylander, C. (1986). *Running the red lights.* Ventura, CA: Regal Books.

Related Scriptures

> It is obvious what kind of life develops out of trying to get your own way all the time: repetitive, loveless, cheap sex, a stinking accumulation of mental and emotional garbage; frenzied and joyless grabs for happiness; trinket gods; magic-show religion; paranoid loneliness; cutthroat competition; all-consuming-yet-never-satisfied wants; a brutal temper; an impotence to love or be loved; divided homes and divided lives; small-minded and lopsided pursuits; the vicious habit of depersonalizing everyone into a rival; uncontrolled and uncontrollable addictions; ugly parodies of community. I could go on.
>
> This isn't the first time I have warned you, you know. If you use your freedom this way, you will not inherit God's kingdom.
>
> But what happens when we live God's way? He brings gifts into our lives, much the same way that fruit appears in an orchard—things like affection for others, exuberance about life, and serenity. We develop a willingness to stick with things, a sense of compassion in the heart, and a conviction that a basic holiness permeates things and people. We find ourselves involved in loyal commitments, not needing to force our way in life, able to marshal and direct our energies wisely. (Galatians 5:19-23 MSG)

> So I say, live by the Spirit, and you will not gratify the desires of the sinful nature. For the sinful nature desires what is contrary to the Spirit, and the Spirit what is contrary to the sinful nature. They are in conflict with each other, so that you do not do what you want. But if you are led by the Spirit, you are not under law. The acts of the sinful nature are obvious: sexual immorality, impurity and debauchery; idolatry and witchcraft; hatred, discord, jealousy, fits of rage, selfish ambition, dissensions, factions, and envy; drunkenness, orgies, and the like. I warn you, as I did before, that those who live like this will not inherit the kingdom of God. But the fruit of the Spirit is love, joy, peace, patience, kindness, good-

ness, faithfulness, gentleness, and self-control. Against such things there is no law. (Galatians 5:16-23 NIV)

"Everything is permissible for me"—but not everything is beneficial. "Everything is permissible for me"–but I will not be mastered by anything. "Food for the stomach and the stomach for food"—but God will destroy them both. The body is not meant for sexual immorality, but for the Lord, and the Lord for the body. (1 Corinthians 6:12-14 NIV)

Bowing Down

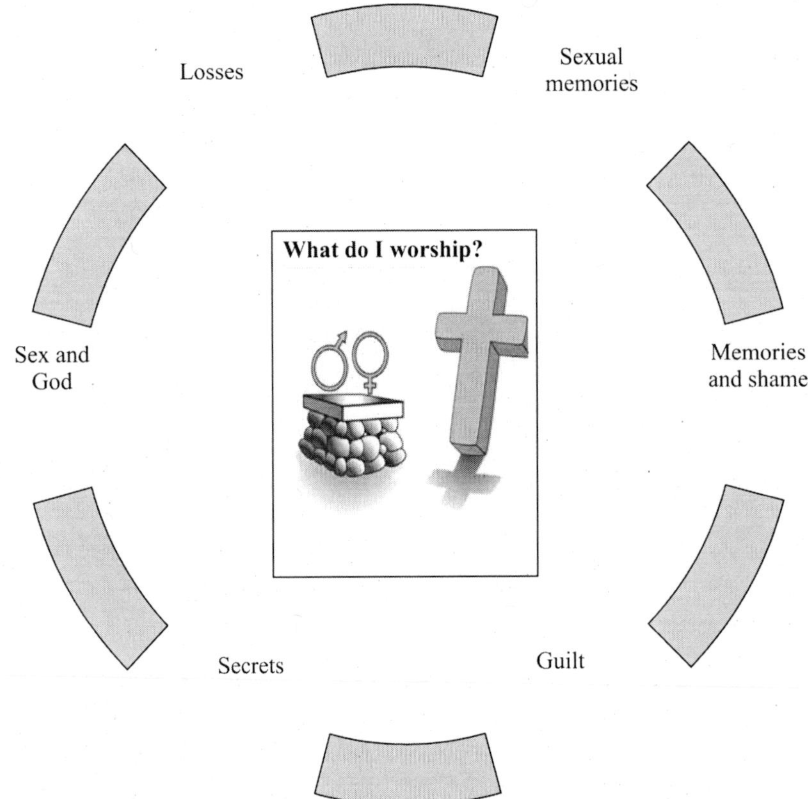

Flee from sexual immorality. . . . Do you not know that your body is a temple of the Holy Spirit, who is in you, whom you have received from God? You are not your own; you were bought at a price. Therefore honor God with your body.

1 Corinthians 6:18a, 19-20 (NIV)

How You Can Be Filled with the Holy Spirit: Transferable Concepts

Every Day can be an Exciting Adventure for the Christian

who knows the reality of being filled with the Holy Spirit and who lives constantly, moment by moment, under His gracious direction.

The Bible tells us that there are three kinds of people.

1. Natural Man

(One who has not received Christ)

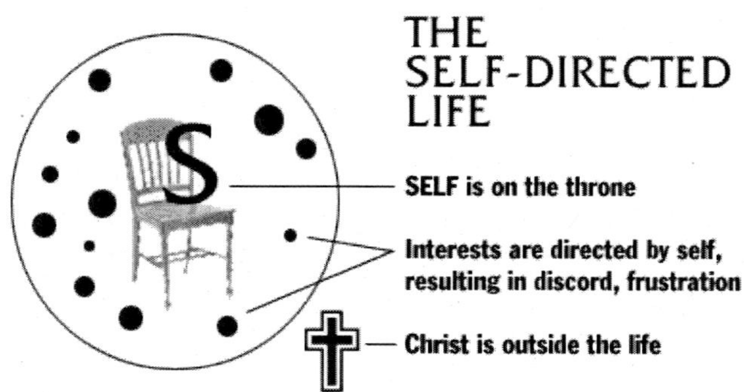

"A natural man does not accept the things of the Spirit of God; for they are foolishness to him, and he cannot understand them, because they are spiritually appraised" (1 Corinthians 2:14).

2. Spiritual Man

(One who is directed and empowered by the Holy Spirit)

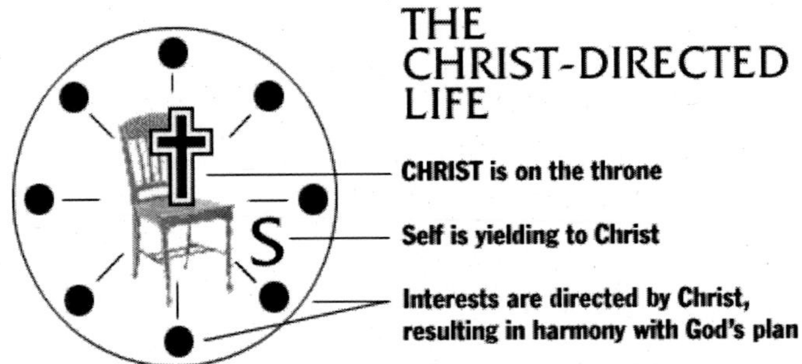

"He who is spiritual appraises all things. . . . We have the mind of Christ" (1 Corinthians 2:15).

3. Carnal Man

(One who has received Christ, but who lives in defeat because he is trying to live the Christian life in his own strength)

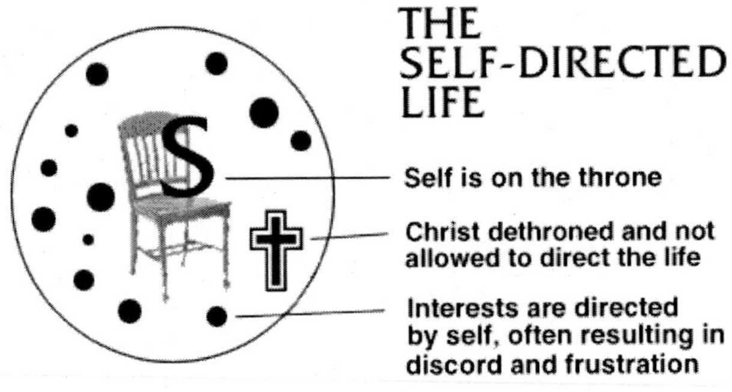

"And I brethren, could not speak to you as to spiritual men, but as to carnal men, as to babes in Christ. I gave you milk to drink, not solid food; for you were not yet able to receive it. Indeed, even now you are not yet able, for you are still carnal. For since there is jealousy and strife among you, are you not fleshy, and are you not walking like mere men?" (1 Corinthians 3:1-3).

God Has Provided for Us an Abundant and Fruitful Christian Life

"Jesus said, 'I came that they might have life, and might have it abundantly'" (John 10:10).

"I am the vine, you are the branches; he who abides in Me, and I in him, he bears much fruit; for apart from Me you can do nothing" (John 15:5).

"But the fruit of the spirit is love, joy, peace, patience, kindness, goodness, faithfulness, gentleness, self-control; against such things there is no law" (Galatians 5:22-23).

"But you shall receive power when the Holy Spirit has come upon you; and shall be My witnesses both in Jerusalem, and in all Judea and Samaria, and even to the remotest part of the earth" (Acts 1:8).

The Spiritual Man—Some spiritual traits which result from trusting God:

Christ–centered
Empowered by the Holy Spirit
Introduces others to Christ
Effective prayer life
Understands God's Word
Trusts God
Obeys God

Love
Joy
Peace
Patience
Kindness
Faithfulness
Goodness

The degree to which these traits are manifested in the life depends upon the extent to which the Christian trusts the Lord with every detail of his life, and upon his maturity in Christ. One who is only beginning to understand the ministry of the Holy Spirit should not be discouraged if he is not as fruitful as more mature Christians who have known and experienced this truth for a longer period.

Why is it that most Christians are not experiencing the abundant life?

Carnal Christians Cannot Experience the Abundant and Fruitful Christian Life

The carnal man trusts in his own efforts to live the Christian life:

1. He is either uninformed about, or has forgotten, God's love, forgiveness, and power (Romans 5:8-10; Hebrews 10:1-25; 1 John 1; 2:1-3; 2 Peter 1:9; Acts 1:8).
2. He has an up-and-down spiritual experience.
3. He cannot understand himself—he wants to do what is right, but cannot.
4. He fails to draw upon the power of the Holy Spirit to live the Christian life.

(1 Corinthians 3:1-3; Romans 7:15-24; 8:7; Galatians 5:16-18)

The Carnal Man—Some or all of the following traits may characterize the Christian who does not fully trust God:

(The individual who professes to be a Christian but who continues to practice sin should realize that he may not be a Christian at all, according to 1 John 2:3; 3:6, 9; Ephesians 5:5).

The third truth gives us the only solution to this problem. . .

Jesus Promised the Abundant and Fruitful Life as the Result of Being Filled (Directed and Empowered) by the Holy Spirit

The Spirit-filled life is the Christ-directed life by which Christ lives His life in and through us in the power of the Holy Spirit (John 15).

1. One becomes a Christian through the ministry of the Holy Spirit, according to John 3:1-8. From the moment of spiritual birth, the Christian is indwelt by the Holy Spirit at all times (John 1:12; Colossians 2:9-10; John 14:16-17). **Though all Christians are indwelt by the Holy Spirit, not all Christians are filled (directed and empowered) by the Holy Spirit.**
2. The Holy Spirit is the source of the overflowing life (John 7:37-39).
3. The Holy Spirit came to glorify Christ (John 16:1-15). When one is filled with the Holy Spirit, he is a true disciple of Christ.
4. In His last command before His ascension, Christ promised the power of the Holy Spirit to enable us to be witnesses for Him (Acts 1:1-9).

How, then, can one be filled with the Holy Spirit?

We are Filled by the Holy Spirit by Faith; Then We Can Experience the Abundant and Fruitful Life Which Christ Promised to Each Christian.

You can appropriate the filling of the Holy Spirit **right now** if you:

1. Sincerely desire to be directed and empowered by the Holy Spirit (Matthew 5:6; John 7:37-39).
2. Confess your sins.
   By **faith** thank God that He **has** forgiven all of your sins—past, present and future—because Christ died for you (Colossians 2:13-15; 1 John 1; 2:1-3; Hebrews 10:1-17).
3. Present every area of your life to God (Romans 12:1-2).
4. By **faith** claim the fullness of the Holy Spirit, according to:
   1. **His Command**—Be filled with the Spirit. "And do not get drunk with wine, for that is dissipation, but be filled with the Spirit" (Ephesians 5:18).
   2. **His Promise**—He will always answer when we pray according to His will. "And this is the confidence which we have before Him, that, if we ask anything according to His will, He hears us. And if we know that He hears us in whatever we ask, we know that we have the requests which we have asked of Him" (1 John 5:14-15).

Faith can be expressed through prayer . . .

How to Pray in Faith to be Filled with the Holy Spirit

We are filled with the Holy Spirit by **faith** alone. However, true prayer is one way of expressing your faith. The following is a suggested prayer:

> Dear Father, I need You. I acknowledge that I have been directing my own life and that, as a result, I have sinned against You. I thank You that You have forgiven my sins through Christ's death on the cross for me. I now invite Christ to again take His place on the throne of my life. Fill me with the Holy Spirit as You **commanded** me to be filled, and as You **promised** in Your Word that You would do if I asked in faith. I now thank You for directing my life and for filling me with the Holy Spirit.

Does this prayer express the desire of your heart? If so, bow in prayer and trust God to fill you with the Holy Spirit **right now**.

How to Know That You are Filled (Directed and Empowered) with the Holy Spirit

Did you ask God to fill you with the Holy Spirit? Do you know that you are now filled with the Holy Spirit? On what authority? (On the trustworthiness of God Himself and His Word: Hebrews 11:6; Romans 14:22-23.)

Do not depend upon feelings. The promise of God's Word, not our feelings, is our authority. The Christian lives by faith (trust) in the trustworthiness of God Himself and His Word. This train diagram illustrates the relationship between **fact** (God and His Word), **faith** (our trust in God and His Word), and **feeling** (the result of our faith and obedience) (John 14:21).

The train will run with or without the caboose. However, it would be futile to attempt to pull the train by the caboose. In the same way, we, as Christians, do not depend upon feelings or emotions, but we place our faith (trust) in the trustworthiness of God and the promises of His Word.

How to Walk in the Spirit

Faith (trust in God and in His promises) is the only means by which a Christian can live the Spirit-directed life. As you continue to trust Christ moment by moment:

1. Your life will demonstrate more and more of the fruit of the Spirit (Galatians 5:22-23) and will be more and more conformed to the image of Christ (Romans 12:2; 2 Corinthians 3:18).
2. Your prayer life and study of God's Word will become more meaningful.
3. You will experience His power in witnessing (Acts 1:8).
4. You will be prepared for spiritual conflict against the world (1 John 2:15-17); against the flesh (Galatians 5:16-17); and against Satan (1 Peter 5:7-9; Ephesians 6:10-13).
5. You will experience His power to resist temptation and sin (1 Corinthians 10:13; Philippians 4:13; Ephesians 1:19-23; 2 Timothy 1:7; Romans 6:1-16).

Spiritual Breathing

By faith you can continue to experience God's love and forgiveness.

If you become aware of an area of your life (an attitude or an action) that is displeasing to the Lord, even though you are walking with Him and sincerely desiring to serve Him, simply thank God that He has forgiven your sins—past, present and future—on the basis of Christ's death on the cross. Claim His love and forgiveness by faith and continue to have fellowship with Him.

If you retake the throne of your life through sin—a definite act of disobedience—breathe spiritually.

Spiritual breathing (exhaling the impure and inhaling the pure) is an exercise in faith that enables you to continue to experience God's love and forgiveness.

1. **Exhale**—confess your sin—agree with God concerning your sin and thank Him for His forgiveness of it, according to 1 John 1:9 and Hebrews 10:1-25. Confession involves repentance—a change in attitude and action.
2. **Inhale**—surrender the control of your life to Christ, and appropriate (receive) the fullness of the Holy Spirit by faith. Trust that He now directs and empowers you; according to the **command** of Ephesians 5:18, and the **promise** of 1 John 5:14-15.

– 14 –

Panic Breaker

Philip J. Henry

Guiding Scripture

So do not fear, for I am with you; do not be dismayed,
for I am your God. I will strengthen you and help you;
I will uphold you with my righteous right hand.

Isaiah 41:10 (NIV)

Type of Contribution: Exercise, Handout

Objective

Facilitating the client's search for the root of his or her fear by acknowledging when the panic begins to arise and noting the accompanying thoughts will encourage the client to understand what the thoughts mean. Therefore, this will allow the client to uncover his or her philosophical and spiritual roots and identify scriptures that provide insight and support. Finally, the client is encouraged to recognize that God is love and that His perfect love casts out all fear.

Rationale for Use

Fear is a natural, God-given emotion. In the right circumstances, it can correctly warn us to take precautions that can keep us from harm or even death. Panic, however, is an abnormal fear when no real danger is present or an exaggerated response to a possible fear. Clients are often unaware of the underlying thoughts that accompany their panic. Unfortunately, if these thoughts are not exposed and changed, the thinking will carry on, and the panic will continue to reoccur. This pattern of irrational fear is not a part of the life of peace and joy that God desires for us.

One of the best ways to change thinking is to allow scripture to provide balance to a mind that has run amok. Repeatedly comparing thoughts with scripture effectively brings about correction to problematic thought patterns.

Ultimately, it is not merely a matter of maintaining thought control; it is also a case of connecting with a "mind changer." God is the real source of reassurance and peace in the midst of trouble. Helping the client actively connect with God in times of trouble is the keystone of this exercise.

The Christian Therapist's Notebook

doi:10.1300/5334_15

Instructions

Begin by helping the client to connect with God, thereby gaining His assistance, wisdom, and strength to defeat the negative pattern controlling the client's life. This is not a minor point. Often, the root of fear will be difficult to detect, and the power to overcome the fear is equally difficult to obtain.

Using the handout at the end of the chapter, help the client to identify the most common situations and thoughts leading him or her to feelings of panic. Explain how unhealthy thoughts connect to the feelings of panic and how changing the thoughts will lessen or eliminate the panic.

Once these situations and thoughts are identified, the client can then be encouraged, slowly, to uncover the meaning of the fearful thoughts. To aid in this task, ask the client to begin keeping a journal. Have the client write about the times and thoughts that accompany his or her panic attacks. Explore with the client how the thoughts and conclusions associated with the panic have developed throughout his or her life.

Look for conclusions or meanings tied to common thoughts of fear and unbelief, such as the following:

- I must be in control or things will be out of control.
- I can't trust God to handle this for me.
- I am the only one I can trust.
- I will never be free of this panic.
- It will happen again.
- There is no escape; I will keep having this trouble.
- I'm on my own.
- There is no one to help me.
- God doesn't care enough to help.

The meanings and/or conclusions of the client can then be uncovered, examined, and compared with the promises of scripture. The counselor can assist the client in understanding the connection between the negative situations, thoughts, and meanings that breed panic in his or her life.

Assist the client in changing thinking patterns by helping him or her to find scripture verses promising God's protection and peace or confronting the distorted meanings the client has developed from his or her history and faulty thinking. Make sure these verses speak specifically to the client. If he or she cannot find any meaning in the verses, or the verses are not personal and relevant, there will be no change of heart. The client may wish to pray using the verses or promises found in scripture, which may lead his or her thoughts to form conclusions different from those created by the panic-driven meanings. Use the verses to draw new conclusions about the client's life, such as the following:

- God is in control.
- I will defeat this problem.
- God will never leave me nor forsake me.
- I can do all things through Christ who strengthens me.
- God does care and can help.
- I am okay with God.
- When I am afraid, I will trust in Him.
- The Lord is my strength and my salvation.

Discuss these new conclusions with the client to see if he or she can embrace the concepts. If the client's conclusions and thoughts change, then he or she will be well on the way to becoming panic free.

Vignette

Maria, a thirty-one-year-old, Hispanic mother of three and a third grade elementary teacher, had begun having panic attacks nine months after the birth of her third child. At these times, she would begin breathing rapidly, which caused her to feel light-headed and, as she had reported to her husband, as if she were going to die. As time went on, these attacks gained in strength, and shortly before entering therapy, she began having one to two episodes a day. Although she usually managed to keep them from becoming full-blown panic attacks, she found herself frequently exhausted and troubled by the effort. Maria's husband and minister encouraged her to seek help. Being a Christian, Maria sought out a Christian counselor. It was important to Maria that her counselor understood her Puerto Rican heritage and was accepting of her faith.

After listening to her and acquiring general information for about half of a session, the counselor asked if Maria would be willing to try an exercise that might aid her in controlling her panic. Maria was indeed willing, so the counselor used the "Panic Breaker" handout to explain how her thoughts were tied to her feelings of panic and losing control.

As Maria and her counselor worked through the handout, it became apparent that most of Maria's panic occurred when she was headed home from work or when she was at work and thought of all she had to do when she got home. Thoughts such as "I will never be able to do it" and "I don't have enough time" began her thinking process, and then she quickly moved on to other broader thoughts, such as "I must be in control or things will be out of control."

As she discussed this pattern with her counselor, two meanings continued to emerge. The first was "I can't trust God to handle this for me." Although Maria was not saying this or thinking this specifically, when she stopped to put her separate thoughts together, this was the underlying message that was revealed. The second message was "God doesn't care enough to help me; I am the only one I can trust."

When she discussed these meanings with her counselor, Maria became noticeably embarrassed. She reported that this was not what she wanted to think or what she wanted to believe, but early in her life, there had been occasions when she felt God had let her down. One of these occasions was the death of her father when she was twelve years old. Now when she thought about other difficult situations, her faith was not strong enough to help her stay positive.

During her second and third sessions, Maria, with her counselor's help, continued to monitor her panic attacks. She was quite dutiful about writing down the situation and her thoughts prior to and during the panic attacks. She was beginning to see that many of the thoughts had the same root that led to doubting God's care for her and her ability to trust God.

As the two worked together, Maria seemed to gain confidence that she could both monitor and, at times, prevent her panic attacks. She began to feel that she was gaining control over her life again, and that God was helping her put her life back together. The counselor suggested she read and memorize Hebrews 13:5b (NIV): "Never will I leave you; never will I forsake you." The counselor also gave Maria a list of scripture verses that focused on God helping and not leaving.

Over the next eight weeks, Maria's faith grew, and she found herself experiencing fewer episodes of panic. She also made some sensible changes in her schedule. She asked her mother-in-law and closest friends to help with the children, so she could now take more time to rest and exercise. She began to recognize that the entire world did not rest on her shoulders and that she could trust God and ask others for help.

After twelve weeks, Maria reduced her therapy sessions to once a month. Four months later, she completed therapy.

Suggestions for Follow-Up

Situations that appear to be triggers for panic need to be monitored over time, so this exercise requires weekly review. First, the counselor should lead the client to see how his or her history has reinforced the thinking and and the meanings drawn from this thinking. Second, the counselor should help the client to explore the inconsistencies between what he or she purports to believe and how he or she acts.

Encourage the client to memorize Philippians 4:6-7 (NIV): "Do not be anxious about anything, but in everything, by prayer and petition, with thanksgiving, present your requests to God. And the peace of God, which transcends all understanding, will guard your hearts and your minds in Christ Jesus."

Contraindications

This exercise is contraindicated when the client's panic attacks are extreme. If the client has severe attacks, he or she may initially need medication or instruction on how to manage the attacks physically as an initial step toward symptom reduction.

Resources for Professionals

Springle, P. (1990). *Rapha's 12-step program for overcoming codependency.* Dallas, TX: Rapha Publishing/Word, Inc.

Warren, R., and Baker, J. (1998). *Celebrate recovery.* Grand Rapids, MI: Zondervan Publishing House.

Wright, H. (2003). *The new guide to crisis and trauma counseling.* Ventura, CA: Regal Books.

Resources for Clients

Haggai, J. (2001). *How to win over worry.* Eugene, OR: Harvest House Publishers.

Mintle, L. (2002). *Breaking free from stress.* Lake Mary, FL: Charisma House.

Morris, J. (2003). *From worry to worship: A 30-day guide to overcoming inferiority.* Birmingham, AL: New Hope Publishers.

Phillips, B. (2001). *Getting off the emotional roller coaster [42 days to feeling great!].* Eugene, OR: Harvest House Publishers.

Williams, D. (2004). *If God is in control, why do I have a headache?* Birmingham, AL: New Hope Publishers.

Related Scriptures

> Never will I leave you; never will I forsake you. (Hebrews 13:5b NIV)
>
> Do not be anxious about anything, but in everything, by prayer and petition, with thanksgiving, present your requests to God. And the peace of God, which transcends all understanding, will guard your hearts and your minds in Christ Jesus. (Philippians 4:6-7 NIV)
>
> I can do everything through him who gives me strength. (Philippians 4:13 NIV)

Panic Breaker

Time and situation:	Panic thought:	The meaning or conclusion about the panic:	New thought, conclusion, or scripture:
1.			
2.			
3.			
4.			
5.			

Do not be anxious about anything, but in everything, by prayer and petition, with thanksgiving, present your requests to God. And the peace of God, which transcends all understanding, will guard your hearts and minds in Christ Jesus.

Philippians 4:6-7 (NIV)

– 15 –

Where Was God?

Steven T. Zombory
Philip J. Henry

Guiding Scripture

My God, my God, why have you forsaken me?

Matthew 27:46b (NIV)

Type of Contribution: Exercise, Handout

Objective

Facing difficult life circumstances often evokes a wide range of emotions and raises a number of important questions concerning the nature of God and the Christian faith. Dealing with adversity in a redemptive manner requires the client to honestly address and resolve emotions, such as anger and doubt; rethink unrealistic expectations regarding the nature and character of God and His purposes for allowing suffering in the client's life; cultivate a biblically based understanding of God; and enlist the comfort and support of other members of the body of Christ while working through issues of grief and loss.

Rationale for Use

Even the most faithful people ask, "Where was God?" when bad things happen. A painful experience or series of difficult circumstances can test the faith of even the most dedicated believer. In this context, the client may desire to remain faithful, sustain hope, and deepen his or her understanding of who God is and how He operates in the world. The client may even reaffirm his or her commitment to the promises of God by continuing to believe in the possibility of a positive outcome and maintain the disciplines of regular scripture reading and prayer in the face of a difficult trial. However, the Bible clearly teaches that the world is fallen and imperfect, and that fact requires the client to come to terms with the painful reality that life may not always turn out the way he or she had hoped it would.

Trust is often damaged or even shattered when expectations of how God should respond in a given situation do not match the actual circumstances and personal experiences. The client may expect God to do one thing when, to his or her surprise, He does something else. This leads the client to question his or her beliefs about the character of God and may cause him or her to wonder whether his or her thoughts about God are, in fact, true. Since trust is the foundation of any intimate relationship, a lack of trust in God deeply affects how the client interacts with Him.

The Christian Therapist's Notebook

doi:10.1300/5334_16

It limits the client's willingness to pursue a deeper relationship with Him and hinders his or her ability to receive the strength and grace He provides for the client to deal effectively with adversity.

This exercise examines the impact that painful life experiences have on the client's sense of connectedness to God. It provides a safe way for him or her to identify, express, process, and resolve the grief, frustration, and anger that often accompany difficult circumstances, particularly those involving past abuse and loss. It may also help the client understand how situations have shaped his or her feelings and attitudes about God's nature and character. Working through this exercise in a spirit of honesty can pinpoint misconceptions and unrealistic expectations the client may hold regarding how God should operate in the world. It may encourage the client to dialogue with God as he or she navigates through the painful questions and emotions inherent in the grieving process.

This exercise can also help the therapist to identify the people or situations that frequently grieve the client, the underlying feelings that accompany this grief, the patterns of sorrow that are unique to the client, and the possible areas where healing needs to occur.

Instructions

Building rapport through communicating that difficult questions and negative emotions can be expressed and addressed within the context of therapy is the important first step that helps the client confront his or her grief and loss. Adopting a critical or judgmental stance that conveys that the client's spiritual doubts are inappropriate and a sign of weak faith will almost certainly sabotage the therapeutic alliance. Be intentional about connecting with the client relationally.

Normalize the emotions that come with grief or trauma and assure the client that it is normal and human to wonder about God's purposes in the midst of suffering. Then, ask the client to identify a difficult time in his or her own life that caused him or her to question the presence and power of God because He appeared to be absent when he or she needed Him. The difficult situation that the client describes may very well be the reason he or she has sought counseling. When you have given the client plenty of time and space to relay the challenge facing him or her, take out the "Where Was God?!" handout. Have the client write a description of the difficult situation.

Once the client describes the situation, ask him or her to identify and list the various emotions that surface, the feelings that accompany the situation in which he or she finds himself or herself. Pay particular attention to feelings accompanying grief or trauma and explore them if it is appropriate to do so. Next, help the client write in what that emotion communicates to him or her about his or her understanding of God. In other words, what does the actual situation and the emotional responses generated convey to the client about God's character or about His love and care for him or her?

As a final step, challenge the client to consider the possibility that negative feelings toward God may be the consequence of unrealistic expectations he or she adopted at some earlier point in time or of a misunderstanding of biblical teaching about what God is like. Begin to explore an alternative view of God based on biblical examples, rather than on evidence gathered from negative life experiences and difficult circumstances. Then help the client to write down the truth about the situation he or she is facing.

Vignette

Margaret is a thirty-nine-year-old, married, Caucasian female with two young children. She and her husband are committed Christians who have been actively involved in the life and ministry of their local church for several years. Margaret appreciates the many blessings she has enjoyed in the past and has maintained a deep commitment to her relationship with God. A series of difficult life circumstances, however, has recently caused her to question her faith and to doubt truths she once accepted without hesitation.

Margaret decided to enter therapy for help with feelings of depression and anxiety related to her life circumstances. Approximately one year ago, her mother experienced a sudden heart attack and passed away before the medical team arrived at her home. Then, Margaret's husband, who always prided himself on his strong work ethic, unexpectedly lost his job eight months ago when his company downsized. As a result, he could no longer afford medical insurance for his family. The financial pressures associated with raising a family were mounting daily. To make matters worse, Margaret had been feeling fatigued and listless during the past few months but had attributed it to the stress of her current situation. She finally went to see a doctor when her exhaustion became debilitating and was stunned when she was diagnosed with an advanced stage of breast cancer.

Margaret had always believed firmly in God's love and goodness, but this string of adversities had deeply shaken her faith. She had operated under the assumption that as long as she obeyed God, tithed regularly, practiced her daily devotions, and served in the church, God would reward her faithfulness by protecting her and her family from harm. However, life was not cooperating with her expectations, and Margaret found herself battling a wide range of strong emotions that included anger, sadness, frustration, hopelessness, fear, and despair. She had even begun to wonder whether it was possible or even desirable to maintain belief in a loving God when faced with such inexplicable suffering.

When Margaret began therapy, she had difficulty admitting the intensity of her negative emotions toward God because she viewed them as indications of a weak faith. "If I could only just believe God more," she would often say, "I wouldn't be struggling with these feelings." Rather than challenge these statements directly, the therapist concentrated, first, on building a relationship of empathy and trust with Margaret. The therapist gave Margaret the freedom to explore and verbalize the nature and reasons for her spiritual struggles at her own pace. Over the next several sessions, the intensity of her negative emotions lessened, as Margaret expressed her fears, doubts, and concerns, and she began to wonder how she might respond to her circumstances in a more adaptive manner.

During the fifth session, having established a strong working relationship with the client, the therapist took out the Where Was God handout and asked Margaret to complete it as they talked together. The therapist had Margaret list each difficult situation that was confronting her. Beside each, the therapist had Margaret list her feelings about the situation. Next, the therapist had Margaret write what the hard circumstance means about God, in her opinion. The therapist then used the handout as a springboard to begin challenging some of Margaret's basic operating assumptions about God and life. The therapist focused particularly on Margaret's assertion that spiritual faithfulness would insulate her from the harsh realities of life in a fallen world. The therapist shared a number of different examples from the scriptures of godly men and women who had suffered a wide variety of hardships while they were serving God. Margaret commented that she had not thought about the spiritual life from that perspective before and agreed to read those passages as part of a homework assignment. The therapist encouraged her to begin looking carefully at biblical teachings regarding the nature of God and the purpose of suffering. The therapist stressed that a proper understanding of who God is and how He operates in the world needed to rest on the truths revealed in God's word, rather than on personal interpretations of life circumstances. As the session was nearing the end, the therapist had Margaret complete the remainder of the handout, writing in what she was beginning to see was the truth about the situation and God.

For the remainder of the session, Margaret and her therapist brainstormed together to identify potential sources of social, emotional, financial, and spiritual support that she and her family could enlist for assistance with her own personal needs as well as the needs of her family. They then formulated a plan that detailed the specific steps Margaret could take to make her needs known to others.

Suggestions for Follow-Up

After identifying a key situation that the client is grieving over, let him or her talk about it as needed. Because grief has its own pace and flow, the client should be given space to wrestle with and work through the emotional and spiritual implications of his or her loss and its impact on his or her relationship with God.

Resist the temptation to defend God and His actions. He is sovereign, which means that He has a specific purpose for all the things He allows in life. God's thoughts and ways, however, are often mysterious and incomprehensible. Focus all efforts on helping the client sort through the feelings toward God that his or her life circumstances are generating. Examine the misconceptions and unrealistic expectations he or she has adopted regarding the spiritual life and encourage him or her to develop an understanding of God that is drawn from the scriptures rather than from life experiences. Relevant Bible passages, recorded sermon series, and thoughtful books that honestly examine issues and questions related to grief and suffering can facilitate healing, spiritual growth, and a restored confidence in God's goodness and grace. Reading or memorizing scripture that reinforces His love and sovereign purposes for His people, even in and through personal suffering, is a good place to start. God's truth, as revealed in His word, must ultimately replace misconceptions that have developed from negative life experiences.

Support groups focusing on particular issues, such as grief and loss, sexual abuse, and substance abuse may also be helpful in addition to individual therapy. Sharing personal struggles with the body of Christ is essential to the process of growth because one receives comfort, strength, and a biblical perspective within the context of the spiritual family. Building supportive and intimate connections with others who suffer in similar ways can be a particular source of encouragement, as group members work together to encourage mutual healing and maturity.

Contraindications

Watch for signs of depression and complications associated with grief. If signs of major depression or excessive grief arise, consider an intervention that matches the severity of the client's symptoms.

Resources for Professionals

Allender, D. (1990). *The wounded heart: Hope for adult victims of childhood sexual abuse.* Colorado Springs, CO: NavPress.

Crabb, L. (2001). *Shattered dreams: God's unexpected pathway to joy.* Colorado Springs, CO: Waterbrook Press.

VanVonderen, J. (1995). *When God's people let you down: How to rise above the hurts that often occur within the church.* Minneapolis, MN: Bethany House.

Resources for Clients

Nouwen, H. (2001). *Turn my mourning into dancing: Finding hope in hard times.* Nashville, TN: W. Publishing Group.

Stanley, C. (1989). *How to handle adversity.* Nashville, TN: Thomas Nelson.

Stanley, C. (1997). *The blessings of brokenness: Why God allows us to go through hard times.* Grand Rapids, MI: Zondervan.

Youssef, M. (1998). *If God is in control, why is my life such a mess? Experiencing God's sovereignty during dark and difficult days.* Nashville, TN: Thomas Nelson.

Related Scriptures

No, in all these things we are more than conquerors through him who loved us. For I am convinced that neither death nor life, neither angels nor demons, neither the present nor the future, nor any powers, neither height nor depth, nor anything else in all creation, will be able to separate us from the love of God that is in Christ Jesus our Lord. (Romans 8:37-39 NIV)

Therefore we do not lose heart. Though outwardly we are wasting away, yet inwardly we are being renewed day by day. For our light and momentary troubles are achieving for us an eternal glory that far outweighs them all. (2 Corinthians 4:16-17 NIV)

I have told you these things, so that in me you may have peace. In this world you will have trouble. But take heart! I have overcome the world. (John 16:33 NIV)

Where was God?!

SITUATION	ACCOMPANYING FEELING	WHAT THAT MEANT OR MEANS TO ME ABOUT GOD	THE TRUTH ABOUT THE SITUATION

Faith is trusting in the character of God when the world gives you reason not to trust.

– 16 –

The Why's of Weight

Philip J. Henry

Guiding Scripture

So whether you eat or drink or whatever you do, do it all for the glory of God.

1 Corinthians 10:31 (NIV)

Type of Contribution: Exercise, Handout

Objective

Bringing about change in a client's unhealthy relationship with food involves at least three steps. First, the client must identify the areas of his or her life connected with the issue of food. Second, the client must identify the needs that food is meeting in his or her life. Finally, the therapist must help the client discern where to begin addressing the particular food issue and how to access God's help and strength.

Rationale for Use

Eating problems and controlling weight are complicated issues because many other factors and concerns are often involved, including genetic factors, body type, nutrition, and metabolism, as well as gender issues, family history, eating and exercise patterns, and emotional concerns. Often, these issues directly connect to the food or eating disorder, which makes any real progress challenging.

The core of food-related issues, spiritually speaking, is that food displaces God in the central place of the person's life. Food, rather than God, becomes the center. Food, whether in the context of an eating disorder or simply eating too much or not enough, becomes the focus or prime motivation of the client. This exercise helps the client explore the place of food in his or her life and highlights key areas where food initially began to meet his or her needs.

Resolution of food-related issues is not easy, but scripture helps us to understand that the ultimate goal for the client is God's glory. If we can help our clients adopt this goal, at least three things will happen.

First, the process of putting God back in the center will allow the client to align his or her purposes with the purposes of God. As a result, he or she will have God's support, His strength, and the ability to call on Him in times of stress and trouble. This will help the client begin to meet the needs the eating disorder is currently meeting and help him or her regulate the emotions that

The Christian Therapist's Notebook

doi:10.1300/5334_16

seem to churn under the surface. Moving from a food-focused to a God-focused life leads to emotional stability and peace.

Second, God can begin to help the client see new possibilities in his or her life, possibilities that were present before but were invisible as long as food captured his or her attention. As the client begins to see the key areas in his or her life that connect to food and the needs in those areas, he or she can begin to think about other ways to meet these needs.

Finally, putting God and His glory at the center of life allows the client to take risks and engage in new activities. These new grace-filled activities lead the client toward positively and healthily gaining what the eating disorder previously provided. Through this process, the therapist and the client develop a roadmap of the journey leading to healthy eating and a healthy lifestyle.

Instructions

Take some time to talk with the client about his or her understanding of the role that food plays in his or her life. Find out to what extent the client's relationship with food is causing a problem and when food-related habits and behaviors initially began. The client will likely see this as an expected part of therapy and be anxious to tell his or her individual history.

Do not be surprised if these issues accompany intense emotions. Many people have feelings of worthlessness and/or low self-esteem connected to their weight or with issues relating to food. Validate the feelings that arise whenever possible, while having the client tell you what he or she is feeling. Food, for many people, is a type of drug that hides emotions. Even in the first session, the expression and tolerance of emotions, particularly negative ones, should be both encouraged and modeled.

The client may also explore his or her perception of God and God's thoughts. This will give you a sense of how to approach the client spiritually. Often, there is a disconnection between the client's beliefs (or what the client says he or she believes) and his or her thoughts and actions. Make a note concerning issues you will want to revisit later to explore more thoroughly.

Once the client has a sense of being heard, show the client the "The Why's of Weight" handout and help him or her identify areas connected with the current eating patterns or issues. Possible areas may be depression, loneliness, or staying at home excessively. Write these areas in the blank circles on the handout. While the client may have already mentioned these in his or her narrative, having the client return to the areas helps will give you time for further exploration and analysis.

As you work through the handout, explore the ways each area connects with the client's eating habits. One way to help the client discover areas that connect with food is to ask the client how his or her life would be different if there was not an issue with food to consider. If he or she is overweight or obese, ask the client to think about how his or her life would change if he or she weighed less. How would that alter the areas connected with food? How would his or her spiritual life change? How would God think of him or her differently? Emphasize honesty.

If needed, help the client brainstorm what activities he or she emotionally connects with food. One method of doing this is to ask the client what would be different if he or she lost the weight and were the "perfect size," or if the problem with food ended. This will give you an idea of the role food plays in the client's life.

If the client begins to have trouble working through the handout or identifying areas he or she connects with food, you may want to utilize the following miniexercise. Have the client put his or her weight at the top of a blank sheet of paper or on the back of the handout. Using intervals of two or five pounds make a chart that goes from the client's current weight down to his or her desired weight. Then, ask the client to close his or her eyes and tell you how he or she feels at each weight. This should give you some idea of the thinking that blocks him or her in the quest to lose weight. If he or she becomes overwhelmed during this process, stop immediately and return to the handout. If this happens, you will have an idea of the pace at which the client can proceed in therapy.

Once you believe the client has exhausted the areas of his or her life that are connected with the food issue, have him or her write a word or phrase under each of the circles describing the need being met by the food. This part of the process may take time for the client to complete, but identifying these needs is essential. Validate those needs and talk through each one with the client. Next, talk with the client about alternative ways to meet these needs that are currently being met by food. Ask, "What other ways could this need be met?"

Working through this handout may take several sessions and may act as a guide for the overall treatment of the client. Take time to let the client emotionally and cognitively process the connections that are emerging.

When the client has completed the initial handout, help him or her identify one area he or she is willing to change. Complete this process by asking him or her to identify which areas would be the hardest to change and which would be a little easier. Ask the client if any of the areas seem easier to change than others. Begin with the area he or she feels is the easiest to change. Remember that food problems are tough and the urge to quit is almost universal for those who try to make changes. Start slowly by working on the easiest issue and provide constant and consistent support to the client. Even small changes may be the best progress he or she has made in years.

Review the handout to see whether the client has written a spiritual issue in any of the circles. If so, explore this with the client to see how it connects with his or her relationship with God. If no spiritually related issue arises, ask the client to explain how his or her relationship with God would need to change if success was going to occur with his or her food problem. Often, one necessary move is to take food out of the middle circle and put God at the center of his or her life. This needs to occur not only in word but also in deed. Help the client develop small steps that would include God in his or her life. Having the client read scripture and pray can be a great start. Having the client journal may have the added benefit of externalizing his or her thoughts and feelings, allowing him or her the perspective to see patterns and gain wisdom. If the client is comfortable, pray for and with him or her. Be very aware of family and religious histories, which might block spiritual support and thus turn it into a negative experience.

Work with the client at the pace he or she chooses. Give him or her readings and tapes to reinforce the work done in sessions. Suggest appropriate support groups that are available. Talk with the client about what he or she may have experienced or learned in the support group and tie the Why's of Weight handout to support group work whenever possible. This will help to create a network for success.

Vignette

Sarah, a single, twenty-nine-year-old, Caucasian female, works as an elementary school teacher. She is a committed Christian who regularly attends church, loves her job, and is positive about most aspects of her life. However, for the past seven years, Sarah has been gaining weight and struggling with issues relating to food. Although at various times she has lost some of the weight by dieting and exercising, Sarah feels she is getting too heavy. Currently, she is about sixty to seventy-five pounds overweight. More recently, her eating has become increasingly compulsive and out of control.

Sarah grew up in a home where she was "the baby" of the family. As is commonly seen in parental interactions with youngest children, Sarah's mother and father gave her almost anything she wanted. Her family regularly attended church, and Sarah finds memories of her church to be pleasant ones. She says she felt close to God many times as a child and teenager and was active in church events until she went to college. Her parents were loving and somewhat overprotective. The family owned a deli where both her mother and father worked, so some of Sarah's earliest memories connect with her parents giving and nurturing her with food. Now, Sarah finds a compulsion to eat when she feels stressed or begins thinking about how alone she feels.

Sarah binges at times, especially when she feels more depressed and is unable to cope with life or with her feelings. Most of these intense feelings come when she thinks about the lack of a significant relationship in her life. For much of her week, Sarah is alone. Although she sees co-workers at her job and congregation members at her church, very little of her personal life is shared with anyone. Because of her weight, she has avoided social situations that might prove to be embarrassing. Loneliness seems to fill her life.

When she began therapy, Sarah had little insight about the part that food played in her life, and little knowledge about where to start to change her long-standing eating patterns. She knew she felt depressed and had a problem with weight and overeating, but the urge to engage in compulsive eating seemed just to come on her at times, with little or no warning. Several weeks before coming to therapy, the binging increased to the point where she felt she was losing control.

In her first session, Sarah felt uncomfortable and found it embarrassing to share her feelings regarding the issue of weight and overeating. As a Christian, she felt she should be able to give the problem to God or pray about it and be successful. Her failure made her feel that she not only had a problem with food but also was a "bad Christian."

By the third session, the therapist had enough information to gain an understanding of the scope of the problem and to connect with Sarah to the point where she was more comfortable talking about herself. The therapist then began to work with her using the the Why's of Weight handout by asking Sarah to begin to think about the areas of her life that connected to her overeating. The therapist said, "I want to have you begin a worksheet that will help us work together to understand the role that food plays in your life." This was said in a way that was geared toward finding information rather than provoking guilt.

Although Sarah was a little apprehensive, she was willing to try this. The therapist suggested that they do one or two of the circles in the office, and then she could complete the rest of the handout at home.

In the first circle, Sarah identified that her depression was connected with her eating. She noted, in times of sadness, she was more inclined to think about or focus on food. The two needs the food was meeting were the need for a reward and the need for something to change her mood when she was feeling depressed. In the second circle, Sarah wrote loneliness. She said that food provided a friend when no one else was there, and when she thought about her lack of male relationships, food helped her get over the feeling that no one cared. At home, Sarah identified more of the reasons behind her emotional connection with food. She found her uncomfortable thoughts concerning her own body, her lack of success at various activities, her poor family connections, her lack of exercise, and her lack of growth as a Christian were all connection points or triggers for her binging.

In subsequent sessions, Sarah identified other reasons for her food obsessions and realized that food had become the central part of her life. She looked to food to help her cope, to provide comfort, to be her friend, and she was even willing to put other important activities aside to pursue her eating. In one session, she announced that she realized that food had taken the place of God and other people in her life. She ended that session by praying with her counselor and asking God to help her put food in its proper place in her life. She reported later that this was the first time in years she had allowed herself to become hopeful that she would make progress with this problem.

In the next session, the therapist encouraged Sarah to think about how she could change her connections with food. Sarah was asked to use the same handout to rate how easy or difficult it would be to change each factor connected to her overeating. Sarah felt that the depression would be the hardest to conquer, while the loneliness might be easier because there might be something she could do to eliminate or lessen those feelings.

After talking for some time about the way that food helped her with loneliness and the need for connection, Sarah and her therapist brainstormed how to meet this need. Together they formed a plan that would involve Sarah attending an Overeaters Anonymous meeting. This went well, as Sarah became connected with others who were struggling with similar issues. Three months later, Sarah joined a Bible study at her church that provided the much-needed friendships. Circle by circle, Sarah began to address her connection with food and to meet the real need that food met in her life in a more positive and biblical way.

Suggestions for Follow-Up

For this exercise to work, the counselor must work with the client both to coach the client and to hold him or her accountable. The counselor must realize that many clients struggling with weight and food addiction issues feel overtaken by a sense of hopelessness and at times self-pity. A family physician, dietician, group therapist, or, at times, a marriage and family therapist can provide support and additional help for clients.

It is important as a counselor to be firm but loving. One way to do this is to have the client choose a direction and then accept no excuse for noncompletion of the suggested task. This ability to see even a small amount of movement can motivate clients and create momentum for other changes. Spiritual, physical, and emotional growth takes time, so be patient and supportive.

Contraindication

Therapists should always recommend that a client consult a physician before undertaking any major weight loss or weight change program. Therapists may also want to recommend that the client consult a dietician and locate a support group. Scripture suggests that there is success in a multitude of counselors (Proverbs 15:22).

Resources for Professionals

Christian, S. (1986). *A very private matter of anorexia nervosa.* Grand Rapids, MI: Zondervan.
Jantz, G. (1995). *Hope, help and healing for eating disorders.* Cork, Ireland: Bradshaw Books.
May, G. (1988). *Addiction and grace.* New York: HarperCollins.
McDonald, J. (2000). *I really want to change . . . So, help me God.* Chicago, IL: Moody Publishing.
McGee, R., and Mountcastle, W. (1991). *Rapha's 12-step program for overcoming eating disorders* (a Rapha recovery book). Nashville, TN: Thomas Nelson.

Resources for Clients

Alcorn, N. (2003). *Mercy for eating disorders: True stories of hope and real answers for healing and freedom.* Tulsa, OK: Harrison House.
Minrith, F., Meir, P., Hemfelt, R., Sneed, S., and Hawkins, D. (1990). *Love hunger: Recovery from food addiction.* New York: Ballantine Books.
Minrith, F., Meir, P., Hemfelt, R., and Sneed, S. (1991). *Love hunger: Weight-loss workbook.* Nashville, TN: Thomas Nelson.
Mintle, L. (2002). *Breaking free from compulsive overeating.* Lake Mary, FL: Charisma House.
Remuda Ranch: http://www.remuda-ranch.com.
Roth, G. (1989). *Why weight: A guide to ending compulsive eating.* New York: Penguin Books.

Vredevelt, P., Newman, D., Beverly, H., and Minrith, F. (1992). *The thin disguise: Understanding and overcoming anorexia and bulimia.* Nashville, TN: Thomas Nelson.

Related Scriptures

Oh God, you are my God, earnestly I seek you; my soul thirsts for you, my body longs for you, in a dry and weary land where there is no water. (Psalm 63:1 NIV)

Do not work for food that spoils, but for food that endures to eternal life, which the Son of Man will give you. (John 6:27 NIV)

Therefore I tell you, do not worry about your life, what you will eat or drink; or about your body, what you will wear. Is not life more than food, and the body more important than clothes? (Matthew 6: 25 NIV)

The Why's of Weight

1. In each circle, list the areas of your life that are connected with food. Start with those emotionally important to you.
2. Under each identified area, put one or two words that identify the need that is being met by the food.
3. If you were going to change one of these connected areas, which would be the easiest? Which would be the hardest?
4. Identify where you might start and what that might look like.

– 17 –

I Miss . . .

Philip J. Henry

Guiding Scripture

Jesus wept.

John 11:35 (NIV)

Type of Contribution: Exercise, Handout/Homework

Objective

This exercise will help the client cope with loss or grief, leading him or her to healing from the initial and continued aspects of what he or she misses, enabling the client to come to terms with the pain in his or her life. Actively seeking and accepting help from God aids this process.

Rationale for Use

Sometimes life hurts. The Bible makes it clear that we live in a fallen world. Therefore, many aspects of life bring us pain. Although a number of examples exist, death and loss are two primary losses we experience in life. Grief is a response to loss that is natural and yet unnatural—natural because it is a part of life as we know it, but unnatural because it was not present in God's original plan. Therefore, it does not fit.

This exercise will help the client explore his or her loss, not merely in terms of something that is gone, but also as something that he or she continues to miss. In death, for example, one must cope with not just the physical loss of the person but also the continued loss of the relationship with that person. Other losses, such as a decline in physical health, the end of a marriage, the loss of a job, or moving, also take their toll. However, the continuing changes are often the most difficult for clients.

Specifically, the exercise will help the client do the following:

1. Explore the emotion that accompanies his or her loss.
2. Understand the connection between the original loss and the emotional pain that continues.
3. Identify the memories, situations, and images that trigger feelings of loss and cause the most hurt.
4. Express the feelings of grief in a safe, non injurious manner.
5. Explore what meaning he or she has taken from the loss.

The Christian Therapist's Notebook

doi:10.1300/5334_18

6. Encourage the client to receive help from God in times of need.
7. Begin to understand how God views his or her loss and tap into how God can be a resource during troubled times.
8. Search for ways to think about the loss, forming the basis of recovery.

Instructions

Talk with the client about what has happened to him or her. Let the client take as long as he or she wants to explain what led up to the loss, how the loss happened, and what the results have been in his or her life. Let the client tell his or her story. Find out specifically what memories or images repeatedly cause hurt. Respect the pain the client may bring and give it the space this kind of wound demands. Recognize that what has happened is significant and communicate this to the client in every way available to you.

At times, guilt will be a part of this. Let the client explore his or her genuine guilt and let him or her separate it from false, unrealistic guilt. Do not let the client off the hook too early. Allow him or her to sort out and own the feelings he or she is experiencing.

Encourage the client to explore the current effects of his or her loss. Again, let him or her take time to come to terms with the loss, intellectually and emotionally. If the client is tearful, cries, or moans, do not intervene; it is good for the client to see that he or she can talk openly with you, that you can handle his or her pain and will help carry the load he or she has to bear.

Explore how the client's views of the world and God have changed because of the loss. Allow the client to express anger, frustration, or any other emotion toward God or others. Such expression generally takes one of two forms. The client may either bottle it up and suffer quietly, or the client may rage at others or the world in general. A combination of the two reactions is also common.

As the client shares, try to understand how he or she understands or has found meaning from the experience and help him or her work to discover this. Although the client may not articulate this directly, you can infer this from his or her attitudes, values, and patterns of thinking.

Identify God as someone who understands and cares; however, do not interfere with the client's articulating of his or her feelings about the loss in relationship to God. Clearly convey your tolerance of his or her pain and feelings.

Use the Psalms to show that a person may express strong emotion to God and about God. Psalm 22 is a good example of this kind of a Psalm. Christ repeated a messianic Psalm on the cross. There are many other examples to choose from, so use a variety or let the client find one that speaks to him or her personally.

Vignette

Mary was the epitome of a grief-stricken client. She sat on the edge of the couch and cried—sobbed actually. She sucked in great gasps of air, and although she tried to speak, her words would not come, as she again gave into the grief cries of her heart. Mary's husband of twenty-eight years had died six months before from a massive heart attack. He was one of those "no exercise, smoking, extra meat and potatoes" people who ate too much and exercised too little. Now, Mary faced a world by herself.

In three earlier sessions, Sue, a counselor on staff at her church, had listened to Mary as she recounted her experience of her husband's death. Mary vividly reported coming home and finding David on the floor in the living room near his favorite chair, her vain attempts to rouse him, the 911 call, the ambulance, the emergency room, and then the doctor telling her, "I am sorry, ma'am, but, he didn't make it." She also described the funeral, as well as her choices and confusion about what to do about everything—a million little decisions to be made at a time when she was barely able to think.

From talking in previous sessions with Mary, Sue was aware that some of the initial grief and shock had passed. Mary was doing much better, although at times, like today, the grief would come over her and it seemed to be just as painful as when it first happened. However, these times now seemed to be less frequent and shorter in duration.

Mary now must live a life without David, and she was missing him very much. When Mary regained her composure, Sue asked Mary if she would like to organize her thoughts and feelings about what had happened and what she was experiencing. Mary agreed: "I would like to think a little clearer," she said.

Sue, Mary's counselor, took a copy of the "I Miss . . ." handout and sat next to her, so the two of them could look at the handout together. "I would like you to help me see snapshots of things you remember about David." Mary thought for a minute and then said, "One of the things I remember is being at home and hearing a honk outside and knowing that David would be home in a second. He always lightly tapped the horn twice as he came into the driveway. Then he would come in, hug me, and give me a kiss on the cheek, and we would eat and share our days' experiences together." Sue wrote a summary of what Mary had said in the first two columns of the handout. "When do you think of this or miss him the most?" Sue asked. Mary thought for a moment. "In the evening, after I come home from work. I go into the kitchen, and it's just me. I feel so alone in that house, and it is so big and empty now." She began to cry.

Sue let Mary have space to experience her feelings, and when Mary signaled she was ready to go on, Sue asked her what being in the kitchen alone in the evening meant to her now. At first, Mary seemed confused by the question and said that it did not mean anything. Then, after sitting silently, she replied, "I guess I wish I wasn't there or I could go somewhere else, or I feel afraid I will be alone for the rest of my life." As Sue guided the conversation, Mary was able to articulate that she was very afraid of a future without her husband and was depressed about the idea of spending the rest of her life alone. Sue guided her gently through the assumptions she had developed since her husband's death, listening and supporting.

Sue then asked Mary about how her spiritual life had been affected by her husband's death. Mary replied that she had always attended church and thought she was close to God, but David's death had led her to question much of what she thought she believed. "I am mad sometimes at God and want to yell at Him; other times I feel closer to God than I have ever felt before in my life. Both of these feelings can happen on the same day." Sue tried to assure Mary that these feelings were very normal and that God could handle her strong feelings and questions.

Sue read to Mary: "My God, my God why have you forsaken me? Why are you so far from saving me, so far from the words of my groaning? Oh my God, I cry out by day, but you do not answer, by night, and am not silent" (Psalm 22:1-2 NIV). Listening to the reading of Psalm 22, Mary realized that Jesus had spoken some of these words from the cross. Mary and Sue talked about how Jesus had handled this difficult situation, and of His great love for both of them.

Sue asked Mary to take the handout home, to notice other times when she experienced grief, and to organize her thoughts by writing them down on the handout. The next week, Mary shared other parts of her life that felt empty to her. "I feel like there is a hole in my life that cannot be filled," she said. Mary kept sharing, and Sue kept listening and supporting. Mary also found some Psalms that spoke to her and wrote some of the verses on note cards. Sue suggested that Mary treat these verses as prayers if the verses reflected the true feelings of her heart.

Mary's process of understanding the losses in her life continued for several months. It was an up-and-down process, with Mary seeming to move three steps forward only to fall two steps back. With the help of her counselor, Sue, and a grief support group, Mary began to function more normally. Her sleeping and eating patterns returned to normal, and she began attending church again and visiting her daughters.

At the anniversary of Mary's husband's death, Sue was there with Mary to help her face the waves of grief that returned and threatened to drown her. Mary did not drown but, instead, continued to make progress in taking back her life. Sixteen months after her husband's death, Mary discontinued therapy. She still considers Sue to be one of God's greatest gifts to her.

Suggestions for Follow-Up

Use the Psalms as examples of honest pain and real dialogue with God in times of loss. In time, help the client find new ways to meet the needs left unmet by the loss. The therapeutic process often will take months, perhaps years, to address all the areas of loss in a client's life.

Contraindications

If the client's skills for daily functioning (hygiene, sleep, eating) have not returned, discontinue exploring loss until some level of stabilization has occurred. If extreme depression, self-injury, suicidal ideation, or other complications of grief should arise, consider a referral for a complete medical and psychiatric interview. The use of medication or other psychological interventions may be necessary for a period of time.

Resources for Professionals

Lester, A. (2003). *The angry Christian: A theology for care and counseling.* Louisville, KY: Westminster John Knox Press.
Wright, H. (2003). *The new guide to crisis and trauma counseling.* Ventura, CA: Regal Books.
Wright, N. (1998). *Winning over your emotions.* Eugene, OR: Harvest House Publishers.

Resources for Clients

Crabb, L. (2001). *Shattered dreams.* Colorado Springs, CO: WaterBrook Press.
Davis, V. (1994). *Let me grieve but not forever: A journey out of the darkness of loss.* Nashville, TN: W. Publishing Group, a division of Thomas Nelson Publishers, Inc.
Eareckson Tada, J. (1997). *When God weeps.* Grand Rapids, MI: Zondervan Bible Publishers.
Jeremiah, D. (2000). *When your world falls apart.* Nashville, TN: W. Publishing Group, a division of Thomas Nelson Publishers, Inc.
Kok, E. (2002). *A woman who hurts, a God who heals: Discovering unconditional love.* Birmingham, AL: New Hope Publishers.
Rhea, C. (2003). *When grief is your constant companion: God's grace for a woman's heartache.* Birmingham, AL: New Hope Publishers.
Rockwood, E. (1999). *When prayers are not answered.* Peabody, MA: Hendrickson Publishers, Inc.

Related Scriptures

> But I call to God, and the LORD saves me. Evening, morning and noon I cry out in distress, and he hears my voice. (Psalm 55:16 NIV)

> My God, my God why have you forsaken me? Why are you so far from saving me, so far from the words of my groaning? O my God, I cry out by day, but you do not answer, by night, and am not silent. Yet you are enthroned as the Holy One; you are the praise of Israel. In you our fathers put their trust; they trusted and you delivered them. They cried to you and were saved; in you they trusted and were not disappointed. (Psalm 22:1-5 NIV)

Answer me when I call to you, O my righteous God. Give me relief from my distress; be merciful and hear my prayer. (Psalm 4:1 NIV)

Lord, you have assigned me my portion and my cup; you have made my lot secure. The boundary lines have fallen for me in pleasant places; surely I have a delightful inheritance. I will praise the Lord, who counsels me; even at night my heart instructs me. I have set the Lord always before me. Because he is at my right hand, I will not be shaken. (Psalm 16:5-8 NIV)

For he must reign until he has put all his enemies under his feet. The last enemy to be destroyed is death. (1 Corinthians 15:25-26 NIV)

But I will tell you something wonderful, a mystery I'll probably never understand. We're not all going to die—but we are all going to be changed. You hear a blast to end all blasts from a trumpet, and in the time that you look up and blink your eyes—it's over. On signal from that trumpet from heaven, the dead will be up and out of their graves, beyond the reach of death, never to die again. At the same moment and in the same way, we'll all be changed. In the resurrection scheme of things, this has to happen: everything perishable taken off the shelves and replaced by the imperishable, this mortal replaced by the immortal. Then the saying will come true:

Death swallowed by triumphant Life!
Who got the last word, oh, Death?
Oh, Death, who's afraid of you now?

It was sin that made death so frightening and law-code guilt that gave sin its leverage, its destructive power. But now in a single victorious stroke of Life, all three—sin, guilt, death—are gone, the gift of the Master, Jesus, Christ. Thank God! (1 Corinthians 15:51-57 MSG)

I Miss…

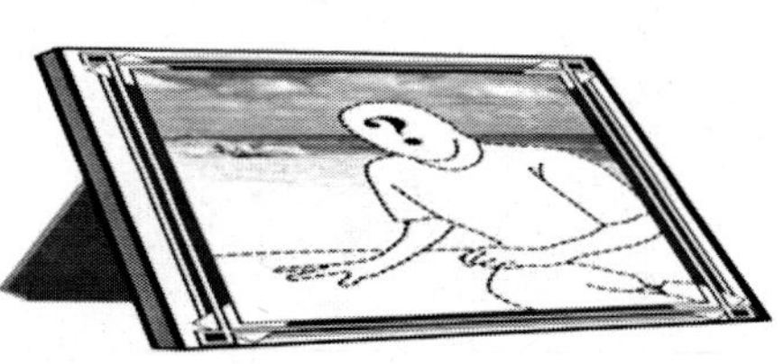

What I remember	What I miss (specifically)	When I miss it	What it means to me
1.			
2.			
3.			
4.			

– 18 –

Unmanageable

Philip J. Henry

Guiding Scripture

. . . When I want to do good, evil is right there with me. . . . Who will rescue me . . . ?

Romans 7:21, 24 (NIV)

Type of Contribution: Exercise, Handout

Objective

The goal of this exercise is to encourage the client to examine areas of his or her life that have become unmanageable, due to alcohol/drug abuse or other addictive behaviors or actions, and to realize that these things are unmanageable. This is the first step toward a sane, stable, and fulfilling lifestyle, and it opens the door toward connecting with God, a power that can assist in restoring sanity.

Rationale for Use

The word *unmanageable* is not just a term of jargon used by those in the substance abuse treatment field. It is the reality of clients in the throws of an addiction. More than anything, this unmanageability is the result of denial, which creates an inability to see reality. For the substance abuser, denial hides the fact that he or she is powerless and that, given enough time, the abuser will destroy his or her life.

Denial allows the addict to be comfortable with the continued use of substances because it provides a guard against any negative thinking regarding the consequences of his or her using. Like bars on a cage, denial locks the user into a lifestyle that, for many, is a "living hell."

One may say that denial stands for this:

Don't
Even
k**N**ow
I
Am
Lying

The Christian Therapist's Notebook

doi:10.1300/5334_19

Under the power of an addiction, the addict lies to himself or herself, first saying that the addiction is not a problem. This lie leads to more lies (e.g., I can stop anytime; I'll quit tomorrow) that are then told to others and then to God. The result of these lies is to create distance in the addict's relationships with self, others, and God and keeps honesty and intimacy at bay. With help, this exercise will encourage the client to examine his or her life, to explore the areas that have become unmanageable. Then the client can decide if he or she needs to change and can strategize where to begin this process.

Often, the addicted client shows great ambivalence. On the one hand, the addicted client knows things have not been going well. On the other, it seems too difficult to face the issues and change. As the addiction grows, the addict's lies grow to include lying to others to maintain the habit and to minimize any problems. When this happens, the sick, unmanageable side of life spreads like an infection, while the healthy, balanced, manageable part of life shrinks. The addict's life begins to fall apart little by little. Nevertheless, the addicted client experiences fear of the unknown and fear of change. Therefore, the client keeps repeating a behavior even though it does not work. The result is an unmanageable life.

This exercise seeks ultimately to identify the effects of drugs or alcohol abuse in a clear and concrete way. The goal is to begin to chip away at the client's denial and to let the client discover what areas of his or her life have become unmanageable. Writing down these areas externalizes them and helps the client gain perspective in his or her life. After uncovering these uncontrollable areas, the client can then consider the implications of each area. Explore these areas of unmanageability by finding out how and why they began and where they might inevitably lead if the same behaviors persist.

This exercise also seeks to help the client see his or her powerlessness over his or her addiction. Wanting, wishing or dreaming hard enough does not produce change. The addict knows much about how life should be but is unable to live by this knowledge. Recognizing how unmanageable life is flows naturally into this question: "How can life be sane again?"

The client can use this exercise to explore the emotional loss that occurs when admitting that his or her life has become out of control, and this exercise will facilitate in identifying the memories, situations, and images that trigger and have contributed to the unmanageability of his or her life.

Finally, the client will begin to see God, not as an enemy, but as a helper and friend, someone who can see through the craziness of his or her life and help restore sanity. Asking God for direction in knowing where to start and for the power to complete the change process is the real key for successful recovery.

Instructions

Clients who abuse alcohol or drugs are notoriously manipulative and deceptive. Be aware of this factor when beginning this exercise with a client. Specifically, do not fall prey to promises, excuses, blaming, minimizing, or other defense mechanisms commonly seen in those suffering from addiction. On point here, although an exaggeration, is this joke: "How can you tell when addicts are lying?" Answer: "Their lips are moving." Clearly focus on the client's behavior and the consequences he or she is facing. Also, stay away from talking about others and the part others play in the client's problem.

Talk with the client about the aspects of his or her life that are out of control or about areas that have been difficult to manage. Find out specifics. Often, clients will minimize, rationalize, intellectualize, distract, or use any of a variety of other techniques to avoid facing the truth. Be firm, very firm, but be kind as well.

Often, guilt will play a part in the client's unwillingness to be honest. Encourage him or her to deal with the guilt later. Remember that the individual is powerless when in the throws of an addiction, so blaming is nonproductive. Identify how the addiction is making his or her life unmanageable. Repeatedly tie his or her use of alcohol and drugs to the unmanageability, while incorporating as many illustrations as possible. If possible, let him or her take the lead once the process has begun. If the client is not ready to admit things are very unmanageable, let the exercise go to the level he or she is ready to see and acknowledge. Do not force this. This is the incomplete connection, and it will take time.

Pray for and with your client, if he or she is willing. Spiritual insight is necessary to break denial. Encourage him or her to explore the current effects of his or her unmanageable behavior. Let the client take his or her time to come to terms with the losses that have resulted from this behavior.

Explore the client's view of God. Often, it is the client's view of God that may block the path to receiving help from Him. Let him or her express anger, frustration, or any other emotion toward God concerning his or her struggles that led to the addictive behavior. Identify God as someone who understands and cares. However, do not push this if he or she is not ready. Patience is important. A twelve-step program or Christian drug and alcohol program is a necessary adjunct to any psychotherapy for alcohol or substance abuse. This can be a good beginning, providing the client is willing to explore this option.

Vignette

One evening, I encountered a thirty-one-year-old man, with long, sandy blond hair, who had come to therapy at the request of his wife. The client was an occasional church attendee, a carpenter-contractor, a father of two beautiful daughters, ages four and five, and a cocaine addict and alcoholic.

When asked about why he was there, Jack smiled broadly and said, "I have come to pay the piper." When the counselor asked what he meant by that, Jack explained that he had been having a "little fun," and now he has to pay for it by being good and coming to therapy. Jack said that he did not want to be in trouble with his wife and wanted to sleep at home. He had been in the "doghouse" for some time, so he thought that coming to counseling might help. He readily admitted to using both alcohol and, on occasion, cocaine. However, Jack quickly added that it had been several weeks since he had used crack.

As he talked, it became clear that Jack had grown up in a very religious home. As he talked about his family of origin, his mood became suddenly somber. He was an only child. He related that his father had been a pastor for years before leaving the ministry and becoming an insurance agent. His mother also had been quite devout in her faith and had worked in the local Christian school that he had attended.

From an early age though, Jack had had his own ideas about life and what he wanted from it. He had been constantly bored in classes and would become a distraction, interrupting, getting out of his seat, and refusing to be quiet, even after having been threatened with serious consequences. In addition, Jack had a learning disability, which had made it difficult for him to do math work of any kind. As a result, he and his parents had spent hours working on arithmetic with little success. Unfortunately, the Christian school had seemed to equate the ability to compute math with godliness, so Jack had felt not only like a failure much of the time in class but also like a "bad person." His demeanor became even darker as he spoke of his struggles in middle school with his parents and teachers.

Jack reported that this friction had continued until high school, when he had convinced his parents that the local public school had more to offer him, so he had headed off to public school to attend special education classes. The first couple of years had seemed to go better, but then Jack began hanging around with a group of students who used pot and alcohol. This continued until the end of high school, when his alcohol abuse became very consistent.

After high school, Jack managed to land a construction job with one of his uncles. Jack seemed to excel at this type of work, and he quickly became a regular member of the construction crew. After a few years, he moved into an apartment with some friends and his alcohol use increased dramatically. Nonetheless, he did manage to show up for work. Later he began using cocaine again. At times, he would binge; this was usually on the weekend, once he had received his paycheck.

He then met Laura, and it was love at first sight. He met her at a bar that he and some of his friends frequented after work. She was smitten with him, and within six months, they were married. "Now I have two daughters and a mortgage, and that's pretty much it," Jack said and sat back, smiling broadly.

When asked if there was anything bothering him about his alcohol and crack use, Jack replied, "Sure, I have been in some trouble, but things are still under control. I go to church, and I work." At this point, I asked Jack if he was willing to take a look at what difficulties his alcohol and crack use had caused in his life. Jack replied quickly that he would be glad to discuss that.

Taking the "What Has Become Unmanageable?" handout, I said to Jack, "I am going to let you identify areas of your life in which your alcohol or drug use has been a problem. I handed Jack the handout and a pen. Can you think of any trouble your use has caused?" "Well," Jack said, shrugging his shoulders, "I am in trouble with my wife." He wrote "Laura" in the first circle. He went on to describe how his relationship with his wife had deteriorated as his use increased. He even shared that he had some fear that, if he continued to use, his relationship might not last. He talked for a while about incidents where he knew the addiction had led him to make big mistakes. He ended with admitting that he had roughly grabbed and shoved his wife one night in an angry exchange of words.

When asked to name another problem area that was unmanageable, Jack mentioned his trouble with the law; he wrote "DUI" in the next circle. He described the arrest and the court scene, the loss of his license, and the money that he had spent to hire a lawyer. He also mentioned a drunk and disorderly charge he had received after a heated discussion during a football game at his favorite watering hole, and several near escapes when he had drugs in the car and thought the police would stop him.

In the next circle, Jack wrote "work." He reported that, after working for his uncle for years, his uncle had fired him two years ago. Since then, he had picked up construction jobs here and there, but he did not have a steady job now, as he had previously. He mentioned that he had not spoken to his uncle since the firing and avoided family gatherings, as he feared that they would all preach at him.

"Money" went into the next circle, and Jack spoke openly about his financial crises. His drugs and drinking had eaten his savings, and he was just barely making it month to month.

As we went circle by circle through the handout, Jack connected emotionally with the process. What originally had been an appointment to fulfill and a duty to his wife has transformed into an exercise at examining his life.

"Depressed" he wrote in another circle. At one point, he stopped and said, "I want things to be different, but I don't really know where to begin." I did not comment but let him continue with the exercise.

Near the end of the session, I suggested that he think about the problems his drinking had caused his wife and two daughters. "I know it's not right," he said. "I don't want my kids to drink, and I hate to think of my family remembering me as I am." At this point, Jack became noticeably shaken. He looked at the floor for several minutes and seemed to will his emotions to stay in check. "I don't know where to begin," he said after the silence.

After talking for some time about the unmanageability of his life and how he was truly powerless, Jack began to see that he needed help. Jack agreed to undergo an evaluation at a local drug and alcohol facility.

Suggestions for Follow-Up

Denial is an extremely tough defense to break down. A client may know the truth, and yet, so often, he or she finds it consistently difficult to admit incapability at running his or her life and at delivering self.

Real faith does not develop overnight. Coming back to the same issues repeatedly seems to be a waste of time. However, the reality that life has become unmanageable is the only one of the twelve steps that must be present during every step of recovery. Only through a daily realization of our own emptiness, that is, an understanding that our lives are unmanageable and we are unable to govern ourselves, can we ask God to fill us and help us to change (see Matthew 5:3-4).

Contraindications

This exercise is contraindicated when the client needs detoxification or inpatient treatment for his or her addiction. To break through the denial, the client must engage in the therapeutic process at his or her current level of motivation and understanding. Use this exercise in the initial stages of treatment, when the client has returned to pretreatment thinking or when the client has relapsed.

Resources for Professionals

Johnson Institute (1987). *How to use intervention in your private practice.* Minneapolis, MN: Johnson Institute Books.

May, G. (1988). *Addiction and grace.* New York: HarperCollins.

McDonald, J. (2000). *I really want to change . . . So, help me God.* Chicago, IL: Moody Publishing.

Miller, W., and Rollnick, S. (2002). *Motivational interviewing: Preparing people for change.* New York: The Guilford Press.

Morris, B. (1993). *The complete handbook for recovery ministry in the church.* Waco, TX: Thomas Nelson.

Springle, P. (1990). *Rapha's 12-step program for overcoming codependency.* Dallas, TX: Rapha Publishing/Word, Inc.

Warren, R., and Baker, J. (1998). *Celebrate recovery.* Grand Rapids, MI: Zondervan Publishing House.

Resources for Clients

Dunklin Memorial Camp (1991). *The family recovery process.* Okeechobee, FL: Dunklin Memorial Camp.

Dunklin Memorial Camp (1992). *Regeneration workbook.* Okeechobee, FL: Dunklin Memorial Camp.

Hirsh, S. (2003). *Women and addiction 1-2* [CD and cassette]. Colorado Springs, CO: Focus on the Family.

McGee, R., and McClesky D. (1994). *Conquering chemical dependency: A Christ-centered 12-step process.* Nashville, TN: LifeWay Press.

Parham, P. (1987). *Letting God: Christian meditations for recovery.* New York: HarperCollins.

Warren, R., and Baker, J. (1998). *Celebrate recovery.* Grand Rapids, MI: Zondervan Publishing House.

Warren, R., and Baker, J. (1998). *Taking an honest spiritual inventory.* Grand Rapids, MI: Zondervan Publishing House.

Related Scriptures

There is a way that seems right to a man, but in the end it leads to death. (Proverbs 14:12 NIV)

The fear of the Lord is the beginning of wisdom, and knowledge of the Holy One is understanding. (Proverbs 9:10 NIV)

Blessed are the poor in spirit, for theirs is the kingdom of heaven. Blessed are those who mourn, for they will be comforted. (Matthew 5:3-4 NIV)

What Has Become Unmanageable?

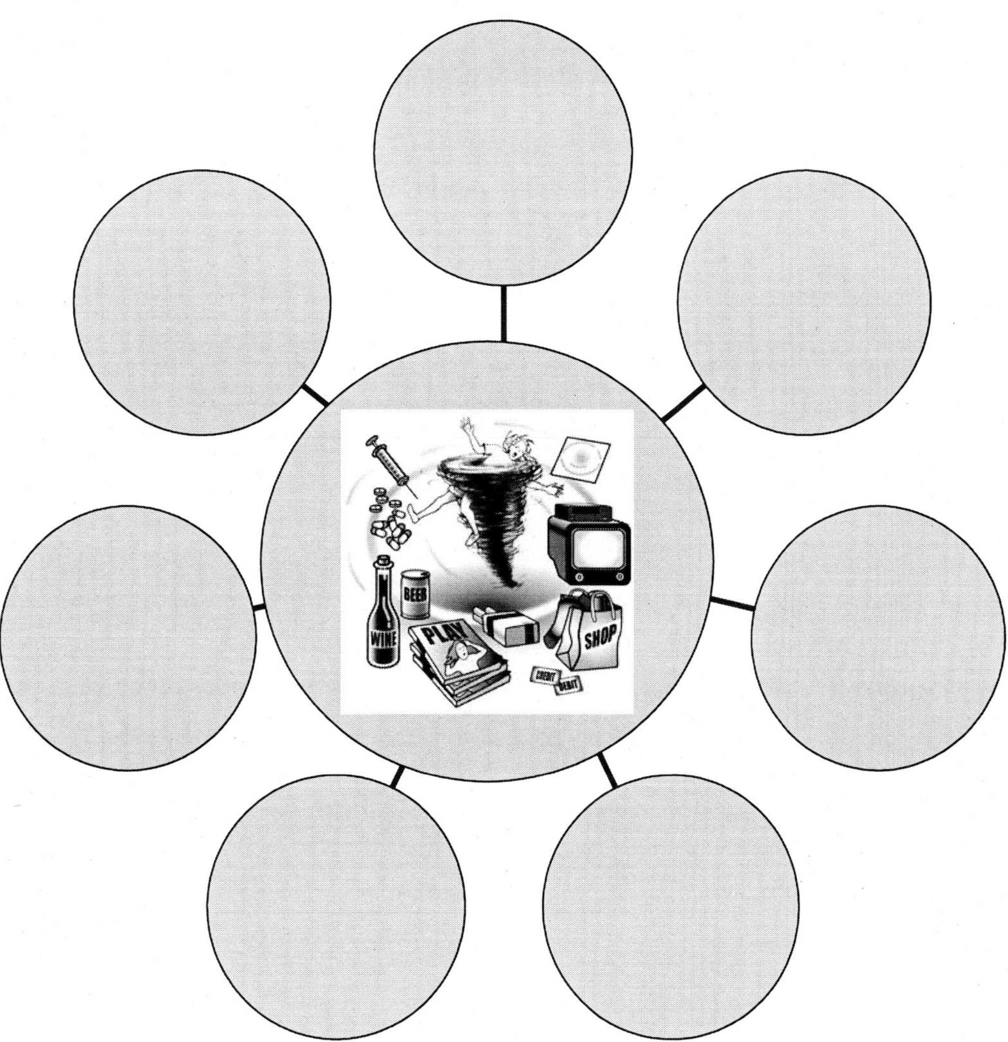

Identify areas of your life in which your alcohol or drug use has caused problems.

SECTION II:
HOMEWORK, HANDOUTS, AND ACTIVITIES FOR COUPLES AND FAMILIES

– 19 –

Complete or Compete

Judith T. Casey
Lori Marie Figueroa

Guiding Scripture

My lover is mine and I am his.

Song of Songs 2:16 (NIV)

Type of Contribution: Exercise, Handout

Objective

It is important for a couple to recognize that they are God's perfect gift for each other. It is also important for the couple to understand that it is God's intention for them to *complete* the other and not *compete* with the other. In so doing, they will realize the concept of God's meaning of "oneness."

Rationale for Use

When a couple is married, they promise before God to devote themselves to each other. These vows are more than just words. The devotion to which God calls the couple means lovingly sharing with each other through daily actions. The Song of Songs beautifully depicts the unification of souls that couples experience as they consummate their marriage. However, the marriage must be maintained beyond the marriage bed.

God never breaks His vows or promises, nor should married couples. Devotion includes loyalty and passion. An obligation, on the other hand, is a passionless responsibility that may not include loyalty. Married couples must constantly renew their devotion to God's sacrament of marriage and resist falling prey to society's portrayal of marriage as passé or temporary "until someone better comes along."

One way couples can recognize God's place in their marriage is to understand that their mates are a gift from God. When we choose a gift for someone we particularly love, we select it with care, taking into consideration the person's wants, needs, and ultimate desires. This is what God did when He created Adam and Eve, as described in Genesis 1 and 2. God formed Adam from the dust of the earth, but then decided that it was not good for man to be alone. He put Adam to sleep and created Eve from Adam. When Adam awakened from the "surgery," God presented Eve to him as His perfectly chosen gift. The two would now realize their completeness through the marriage relationship. The "two" became "one." In His wisdom and sovereignty, God in-

The Christian Therapist's Notebook

doi:10.1300/5334_20

tended for the couple to be together as life mates as His gift to each of them. Had He not intended for them to be together, He could have prevented the marriage. If either partner decides that his or her spouse "just is not the right one," then he or she draws God's integrity into question. With that in mind, as each partner receives God's gift, then the words that are used should be spoken with thought and consideration for building the marriage, rather than destroying the relationship.

Instructions

Make sure the couple understands that the following steps cannot/should not be rushed through in one session. It will take time for their marriage to improve.

1. Determine whether each partner recognizes his or her mate is God's personally selected gift for him or her. Use scripture and discussion of God's creation of marriage and His purposes for marriage.
2. Ask the couple to list areas in their marriage where they feel that they *complete* each other. In addition, ask the couple to identify the areas where they think they tend to *compete* with each other.
3. Spend time further discussing God's intentions for marriage and how husband and wife are to become one.
4. Address the role of sexual intimacy within the marriage in general, and then in their marriage in particular. Look at emotional, spiritual, and mental components as well as physical issues.
5. Identify areas within the marriage that either the husband or the wife views as an obligation rather than an opportunity to express devotion. Have the couple share their responses with each other. Encourage each partner to listen silently while the other expresses his or her perceptions and associated feelings.
6. Determine whether the husband and wife individually perceive their marriage as an opportunity for devotion (lovingly sharing) or as an obligation (mere responsibility and disconnected drudgery).
7. Help the couple modify their perceptions of obligation and drudgery through renewed thinking and, if necessary, changed behavior.
8. Help the couple understand that their choice of words in addressing each other affects how those words are received. Harsh words can have devastating effects on a spouse, as well as on the marriage.
9. Have the couple declare their love and devotion to each other in writing. A written love letter or a verbal or written contract vowing to love and be devoted to each other would be appropriate.
10. Guide the couple in prayer to thank God for His personally selected gift of their spouse and the added gift of their marriage. Together, ask God for a daily renewal in heart, soul, and mind. Ask Him to show them the beauty of their union as He intended it to be, allowing for an attitude of devotion.

Vignette

Bob and Betty came to the counselor after four months of marriage. Although they had dated for three years prior to the wedding and thought they knew each other fairly well, Bob and Betty were now convinced they had made a horrible mistake.

Before marriage, they had prepared themselves through premarital counseling, reading books, and asking questions of "seasoned" married couples. However, the two quickly discovered that some things could be learned only as the marriage experience was lived out on a day-to-day basis. They were totally shocked, frustrated, and ready to quit.

Betty was convinced that she had "married the wrong person." She further thought that, if they divorced while they were still young, maybe she could find the "right" person and, thereby, "find happiness."

Through the counseling process, including using the "Complete or Compete" handout in sessions over several weeks, Bob and Betty began to understand that God, in His providence, could have interrupted their wedding at any time prior to the actual ceremony had He not intended for them to be together. Recognizing that He did not do that, they began to act on the belief that they were God's perfect gift for each other. The change in thinking began a change in Bob and Betty's behavior toward each other. They began to appreciate each other, thereby releasing the other to act with devotion, rather than simply going through the motions of carrying out obligations with bitterness and anger. They were soon living with a sense of completing each other rather than competing with each other. This new mind-set brought new life into what had previously appeared to be a dead marriage.

Bob and Betty's original commitment for counseling was twelve weeks. At the end of that time, they committed to another twelve weeks. Now, two years later, Bob and Betty appreciate each other and love what God has done in their marriage. The two now work with other couples, sharing what they have learned and encouraging the other couples in God's plan for their marriages.

Suggestions for Follow-Up

This exercise can lead to enrichment of a Christian marriage that may be experiencing conflict due to the couple's preconceived beliefs, ideas, perceptions, and culture or an ignorance concerning God's intentions for the sacrament of marriage.

Therapists should review the responses again after several sessions to determine if the specific areas and the marriage in general have improved in terms of the concept of completion versus competition.

The couple will need to understand that it will take time and concerted effort for spiritual, emotional, and marital growth to occur.

Contraindications

This exercise is contraindicated when the couple did not marry in a church or do not perceive God as a factor in the marriage. It is also contraindicated when one of the partners is not in favor of including God in their marriage. Another contraindication may be if one partner is not in favor of completing a contract of any kind. A final contraindication may be a dysfunction that requires medical attention.

Resources for Professionals

Family Life Today: www.familylife.com.

Horn, W. (2004). Encouraging healthy marriages: Strengthening the American family. *Christian Counseling Today,* 12(1), 34-36.

Laaser, M., and Laaser, D. (2004). Recovering from infidelity. *Christian Counseling Today,* 12(1), 48-51.

Larson, P.J. (2004). Results for couples in crisis. *Christian Counseling Today,* 12(1), 72-73.

Lewis, R., and Boehi, D. (2001). *HomeBuilders couples series: Building teamwork in your marriage.* Little Rock, AR: Group Publishing, Inc.
McMahon, J., and McManus, M. (2004). The marriage savers movement. *Christian Counseling Today,* 12(1), 66-69.
Morris, S.H. (2004). Emotionally focused couples therapy. *Christian Counseling Today,* 12(1), 62-65.
Oliver, G.J., and Oliver, C.E. (2004). Marital anger and highly conflicted couples. *Christian Counseling Today,* 12(1), 56-58.
Parrott, L., and Parrott, L. (2004). When bad things happen to good marriages. *Christian Counseling Today,* 12(1), 38-40.
Rainey, D. (2000). *HomeBuilders couples series: Building your marriage.* Little Rock, AR: Group Publishing, Inc.
Rosberg, G., and Rosberg, B. (2004). Marriage as God intended: Theology is the real issue. *Christian Counseling Today,* 12(1), 71.
Rosberg, G., and Rosberg, B. (2004). Not on our watch! Divorce-proofing marriage. *Christian Counseling Today,* 12(1), 70-71.
Weber, C.H., and Hart, A. (2004). Depression in couples. *Christian Counseling Today,* 12(1), 42-45.

Resources for Clients

Chapman, G. (1995). *The five love languages: How to express heartfelt commitment to your mate.* Chicago, IL: Northfield.
Chapman, G. (1995). *Two tape series: The five love languages: How to express heartfelt commitment to your mate.* Chicago, IL: Northfield, Book Sounds.
Christenson, L. (1970). *The Christian family.* Minneapolis, MN: Bethany Fellowship.
Curtis, B., and Eldredge, J. (1997). *The sacred romance: Drawing closer to the heart of God.* Nashville, TN: Thomas Nelson.
Evans, J. (2003). *Audio series: Return to intimacy.* Amarillo, TX: Family and Marriage Today.
Family Life Today: www.familylife.com.
Rainey, D. (2003). *Staying close: Stopping the natural drift toward isolation in marriage.* Nashville, TN: Thomas Nelson.
Rainey, D., and Rainey, B. (1995). *The new building your mate's self-esteem,* Updated and expanded edition. Nashville, TN: Thomas Nelson.
Smalley, G. (1988). *If only he knew: What no woman can resist.* Grand Rapids, MI: Zondervan.

Related Scriptures

> Then God said, "Let us make man in our image, in our likeness, and let them rule over the fish of the sea and the birds of the air, over the livestock, over all the earth, and over all the creatures that move along the ground." So God created man in his own image, in the image of God he created him; male and female he created them. God blessed them and said to them, "Be fruitful and increase in number; fill the earth and subdue it. Rule over the fish of the sea and the birds of the air and over every living creature that moves on the ground." (Genesis 1:26-28 NIV)
>
> When the Lord God made the earth and the heavens—and no shrub of the field had yet appeared on the earth and no plant of the field had yet sprung up, for the Lord God had not sent rain on the earth and there was no man to work the ground, but streams came up from the earth and watered the whole surface of the ground—the Lord God formed the man from the dust of the ground and breathed into his nostrils the breath of life, and the man be-

came a living being. . . . The Lord God said, "It is not good for the man to be alone. I will make a helper suitable for him." Now the Lord God had formed out of the ground all the beasts of the field and all the birds of the air. He brought them to the man to see what he would name them; and whatever the man called each living creature, that was its name. So the man gave names to all the livestock, the birds of the air and all the beasts of the field. But for Adam no suitable helper was found. So the Lord God caused the man to fall into a deep sleep; and while he was sleeping, he took one of the man's ribs and closed up the place with flesh. Then the Lord God made a woman from the rib he had taken out of the man, and he brought her to the man. The man said, "This is now bone of my bones and flesh of my flesh; she shall be called 'woman,' for she was taken out of man." For this reason a man will leave his father and mother and be united to his wife, and they will become one flesh. (Genesis 2:4-7, 18-24 NIV)

My lover is mine and I am his. (Song of Songs 2:16 NIV)

Complete or Compete

Directions: Fill in the charts below as indicated by the column heading of each.

*Ways I **Complete** My Spouse*	*Ways My Spouse **Completes** Me*

*Ways I Think I **Compete** with My Spouse*	*Ways I think My Spouse **Competes** with Me*

My lover is mine and I am his.
Song of Songs (Song of Solomon) 2:16 (NIV)

– 20 –

The Beauty of a Butterfly

Lori Marie Figueroa

Guiding Scripture

It was majestic in beauty, with its spreading bough. . .

Ezekiel 31:7 (NIV)

Type of Contribution: Exercise, Handout

Objective

This exercise will help couples in therapy acknowledge opportunities for growth in their marriage by looking at God's intention for marriage as demonstrated in the Bible.

Rationale for Use

This exercise is helpful for couples within their first five years of marriage who have difficulty accepting challenging times. When a couple is dating, feelings of "butterflies in their stomachs" is a common description to illustrate the passion and new love in the air. The expectations each partner brings as he or she walks down the aisle can be similar but often are just as unique as each individual is. The idea of spending the rest of their lives together is majestic. Visions of butterflies freely flying through gardens symbolize a perception of love in its purest form.

God shows us how love conquers all through various relationships in the Bible. This exercise strives to show couples that relationships endure a process of transformation as the couple reveals themselves and begins to understand each other. Couples should be helped to see difficult times as opportunities for growth in their relationship. Therapists should also encourage couples to look for the beauty in their marriage, even during challenging times. Even Adam and Eve, the first recorded couple in the Bible, remained side by side even after they sinned. The Bible never states that their lives were perfect after they wed. In fact, it was after they were united that they both sinned. However, through parenthood and other challenging events their marriage still remained.

Christian therapists can show couples how God has a plan for their lives as two individuals who have become a couple. A person can learn to maintain his or her individual personality while embracing the union in marriage. Therapists can share how God's plan for marriage involves a process of transformation. At this point, couples can begin to identify areas of successful growth, while trusting in God for wisdom toward addressing areas that seem to be stagnant.

The Christian Therapist's Notebook

doi:10.1300/5334_21

Therapists can also use this exercise to address any unhealthy communication patterns. Role-plays are effective tools to teach couples healthy communication patterns.

Instructions

After talking generally with the couple about what brought them to counseling and where they are in their marriage relationship, ask the couple to think of their marriage as a journey of transformation, showing them the "Journey of Transformation" handout at the end of the chapter. Discuss with them how a butterfly begins as a simple caterpillar, and through proper nourishment and time, God turns this wormlike larva into a beautiful butterfly. This process of transformation is part of God's plan for the couple's lives. Next, have the couple mentally review their marriage from their first date through the present, and help them list areas where *growth* has occurred, both individually and as a couple.

Next, have the couple reflect and list on the handout periods of *stagnation* where no growth seemed to take place. Ask each partner to express to the other any concerns or specific examples he or she remembers during this period of stagnation. Encourage the partner who is practicing reflective listening to paraphrase what he or she has heard before expressing his or her viewpoints. Use this as an opportunity to assess communication styles and struggles. Take time to address these in the context of working through the handout.

Using the analogy of a butterfly, ask the couple to smile as they write down the many *times of beauty* shared in their marriage. You may want to duplicate the handout and have the couple do this part individually. Once they have completed filling in the last section, have each spouse share his or her list with the other. Compare any similarities and acknowledge any differences. Help them to celebrate the times of beauty they have experienced together.

Give the couple a mutual homework assignment to find and read areas of the Bible that show God's intention in His creation of marriage. Instruct the couple to look at the role of different characters in the Bible, from Adam and Eve in Genesis to married characters in the New Testament. Couples such as Jacob and Rachel (see Genesis 29:9-29) show the persistence in a relationship as Jacob worked fourteen years for the woman he loved. Isaac and Rebekah (see Genesis 24:10-28, 54-67) display a biblical account of love at first sight. Another couple who remained side by side through challenging times were Abraham and Sarah.

Encourage the couple to maintain dialogue regarding areas of growth, stagnation, and beauty in the lives of these biblical characters. Have the couple compare the journeys of the characters to their own journey. Encourage them to pray together as a couple for unity during challenging times and for appreciation in times of beauty.

Vignette

Susan, a Caucasian, forty-year-old female, and Jason, a Caucasian, forty-one-year-old male, sought marital therapy because of what they considered to be a boring, unfulfilling marriage. When asked what brought them to counseling, Susan complained about her husband, Jason, withdrawing to his computer every evening after dinner. The therapist helped her to verbalize to Jason how that made her feel—angry, hurt, and ignored. Next, Jason was asked how he felt. The therapist helped Jason open up and Jason began talking about growing up in a family where he was criticized and never able to meet his parents' expectations. The therapist helped him bring this around to his response to Susan's nightly complaints. He revealed that her complaints made him angry and want to stay away from her. Though Jason had not realized it himself, through the therapist's questions, he was led to the discovery that Susan's demands and unhappiness with him brought up the same feelings he associated with his parents. As a result, the more

Susan whined, the more he withdrew. The therapist helped them to see that they were stuck in a "dance," doing the same things but growing further apart.

The therapist took out the "Journey of Transformation" handout and showed it to Susan and Jason. He then led the couple to think about their marriage as a journey of transformation. They talked together about marriage being a process that includes times of growth, times of seeming stagnation, and times of beauty, and that no couple shares only times of beauty without the growth and even stagnation. The therapist compared a marriage to the formation of a butterfly, beginning as a caterpillar and finally becoming a beautiful butterfly, with a larval stage in between. The therapist helped Susan and Jason see that too often couples find themselves in the larval stage and give up on the marriage, just when it is on the verge of reaching the butterfly stage. Susan and Jason were asked to think back on their relationship from the time of courtship and list together on the handout the areas or times when they had *grown,* either individually or as a couple.

At first, Susan and Jason tried to say they had not grown at all. Pressed a bit, however, they slowly began to verbalize small ways that they had grown. Susan listed that she had grown in the area of self-discipline, and Jason agreed. Jason shared that he thought he had become more responsible in handling their finances and chores around the home, and Susan agreed. Then, as they looked back on their marriage and talked about the early years, they realized that, in fact, they were more thoughtful of each other. Jason had learned to call Susan during the day or when he was going to be late coming home from work, and Susan had learned to give Jason some undivided attention when he arrived home from work. Susan was able to verbalize that perhaps her growth in this area made her more resentful of Jason's withdrawal after dinner most evenings. They also agreed that they had grown in the area of their finances, adopting a budget and working together to open and regularly contribute to a savings account, and in putting each other before the demands of their respective families.

Next, the therapist asked Susan and Jason to reflect on and list periods or areas of *stagnation* in their relationship, areas where perhaps no growth had taken place or where they felt "stuck." Susan and Jason both wondered aloud if they were presently in a time of stagnation. Each of them relayed that they felt stuck in their present interactions and unable to break out of the tension and conflict that they were experiencing. The therapist asked both partners to again express to each other the way that they were feeling. Jason practiced reflective listening and paraphrasing after Susan stated voicing her concerns and observations. Susan, in turn, listened and summarized after Jason shared his list of concerns. As the therapist encouraged them to look behind their anger to see what other emotions and feelings may be causing the anger, Susan shared that she felt empty inside. She began to realize that she was looking to Jason to fill the emptiness and meet all her needs. Jason shared that he felt inadequate to make Susan happy and felt that nothing he could do would be good enough for her. As a result, he shared, he had stopped trying. He acknowledged that her disapproval felt like his parents' disapproval, and so he just wanted to avoid it. The therapist asked each of them to agree to take one step toward the other in the following week. Susan agreed not to harangue Jason about spending time with her after dinner; instead, she decided to join an exercise class meeting on Tuesday and Thursday nights with her friend from work. Jason agreed to limit his computer time to one hour or while Susan was attending her class. They both agreed to plan a fun night out on Friday night to begin renewing the good times they had had together in the past.

Continuing with the analogy of a butterfly, the therapist then asked Jason and Susan to list on the handout the *times of beauty* they had shared in their marriage. Again, they were somewhat slow to acknowledge the positive aspects of their relationship. The therapist persisted, however, and allowed silence until they began to think and remember. Slowly, they created quite a list of beautiful times they had shared, including their wedding, the day they had been baptized together, the first night in the new home they had purchased three years before, Jason's support of

Susan when her father passed away, spending the day at the beach with their nephews, and Jason's graduation from his master's degree program when he had given Susan the diploma for typing all his papers. Through this part of the exercise, Susan and Jason began to relax and to smile, remembering the good times they had shared and what they appreciated about each other. The therapist encouraged them to take the handout home and to continue to add to the list.

Suggestions for Follow-Up

Guide the couple as they celebrate times of beauty they have shared and mutually develop solutions and action plans for any areas of stagnation within the marriage. Revisit the exercise months later to see whether any areas require growth or have changed in positive way.

Contraindications

This exercise is contraindicated if either member of the couple has experienced infidelity or unresolved childhood trauma that is negatively affecting their marriage and impeding their growth. These must be addressed first in the therapy, whether individually or as a couple. Another contraindication may be the presence of unspoken sexual problems in the marriage that have affected the couple's communication.

Resources for Professionals

Beck, A. (1988). *Love is never enough. How couples can overcome misunderstandings, resolve conflicts, and solve relationship problems through cognitive therapy.* New York: Harper and Row.

Burt, M., and Burt, R. (1996). *Stepfamilies: The step by step model of brief therapy.* New York: Brunner/Mazel.

Chapman, G. *The five love languages: How to express heartfelt commitment to your mate.* Chicago, IL: Moody Publishing.

Christensen, A., and Jacobson, N. (1999). *Reconcilable differences.* New York: Guilford.

Datillio, F., and Padesky, C. (1990). *Cognitive therapy with couples.* Sarasota, FL: Professional Resource Press.

Gurman, A., and Jacobson, N. (Eds.) (2002). *Clinical handbook of couple therapy,* Second edition. New York: Guilford.

Hudson, P.O., and O'Hanlon, W.H. (1991). *Rewriting love stories: Brief marital therapy.* New York: Norton.

Jacobson, N., and Christensen, A. (1998). *Acceptance and change in couple therapy: A therapist's guide to transforming relationships.* New York: Norton.

Luquet, W. (1996). *Short-term couples therapy: The imago model in action.* Sarasota, FL: Professional Resource Press.

Markman, H., Stanley, S., and Blumberg, S. (1997). *Fighting for your marriage: Positive steps for preventing divorce and preserving a lasting love.* San Francisco, CA: Jossey-Bass.

Miller, S., Miller, P., Nunnally, E., and Wackman, D. (1991). *Talking and listening together.* Littleton, CO: Interpersonal Communications Programs.

Oliver, G. (Ed.) (1999). *Trust builders: True stories of marriages strengthened by trials.* Ann Arbor, MI: Vine Books.

Waite, L.J., and Gallagher, M. (2000). *The case for marriage: Why married people are happier, healthier, and better off financially.* New York: Doubleday.

Walsh, F. (Ed.) (1999). *Spiritual resources in family therapy.* New York: Guilford.

Worthington, E. (1993). *Hope for troubled marriages: Overcoming common problems and major conflicts.* Downers Grove, IL: InterVarsity Press.
Worthington, E., and McMurry, D. (1994). *Marriage conflicts: A short-term structured method.* Grand Rapids, MI: Baker.
Wright, H. Norman (1995). *Marriage counseling: A practical guide for pastors and counselors.* Ventura, CA: Regal.
www.aamft.org. American Association of Marriage and Family Therapists. The largest association of marriage and family therapists; historically has often been neutral about whether therapists should take a positive stance for promoting marital reconciliation.
www.afa.net. American Family Association. An organization that provides strong advocacy for traditional family values.
www.couplecommunication.com. Interpersonal Communication Programs, Inc., Sherrod and Phyllis Miller. This organization produces Couple Communication I and II.
www.frc.org. Family Research Council. Provides excellent profamily articles and research monographs.
www.lifeinnovations.com. Life Innovations, Inc. Publishers of PREPARE/ENRICH and many other marriage-strengthening materials.
www.ncfr.org. National Council on Family Relations. An organization designed to promote family well-being; among other things, this organization produces the *Journal of Marriage and Family and Family Relations.*
www.nire.org. National Institute of Relationship Enhancement. Provides professional training in Bernard Guerney's highly effective models of marriage and family enrichment.
www.smartmarriages.com. Smart Marriages, Inc. Excellent resource for marriage-strengthening articles, materials, and training.

Resources for Clients

Bodmer, J. (1999). *When love dies: How to save a hopeless marriage.* Nashville, TN: W. Publishing Group, a division of Thomas Nelson.
McManus, M. (1995). *Marriage savers: Helping your friends and family avoid divorce,* Revised edition. Grand Rapids, MI: Zondervan.
Page, S. (1997). *How one of you can bring the two of you together: Breakthrough strategies to resolve your conflicts and reignite your love.* New York: Broadway Books.
Robinson, J. (2000). *Communication miracles for couples: Easy and effective tools to create more love and less conflict.* York Beach, ME: Conari Press.
Young, E. (2004). *The ten commandments of marriage: The do's and don'ts of a lifelong covenant.* Chicago, IL: Moody Publishing.
www.family.org. Focus on the Family. Variety of excellent biblical resources for strengthening marriages and the family.

Related Scriptures

> If I speak in the tongues of men and of angels, but have not love, I am only a resounding gong or a clanging cymbal. If I have the gift of prophecy and can fathom all mysteries and all knowledge, and if I have a faith that can move mountains, but have not love, I am nothing. If I give all I possess to the poor and surrender my body to the flames, but have not love, I gain nothing. Love is patient, love is kind. It does not envy, it does not boast, it is not proud. It is not rude, it is not self-seeking, it is not easily angered, it keeps no record of wrongs. Love does not delight in evil but rejoices with the truth. It always protects, always trusts, always hopes, always perseveres. Love never fails. (1 Corinthians 13:1-8a NIV)

Wives, submit to your husbands as to the Lord. For the husband is the head of the wife as Christ is the head of the church, his body, of which he is the Savior. Now as the church submits to Christ, so also wives should submit to their husbands in everything. Husbands, love your wives, just as Christ loved the church and gave himself up for her to make her holy, cleansing her by the washing with water through the word, and to present her to himself as a radiant church, without stain or wrinkle or any other blemish, but holy and blameless. In this same way, husbands ought to love their wives as their own bodies. He who loves his wife loves himself. After all, no one ever hated his own body, but he feeds and cares for it, just as Christ does the church—for we are members of his body. "For this reason a man will leave his father and mother and be united to his wife, and the two will become one flesh." This is a profound mystery—but I am talking about Christ and the church. However, each one of you also must love his wife as he loves himself, and the wife must respect her husband. (Ephesians 5:22-33 NIV)

May the Lord make your love increase and overflow for each other. . . . (1 Thessalonians 3:12 NIV)

. . . love one another deeply, from the heart. (1 Peter 1:22 NIV)

. . . love one another, for love comes from God. (1 John 4:7 NIV)

Journey of Transformation

Times of growth

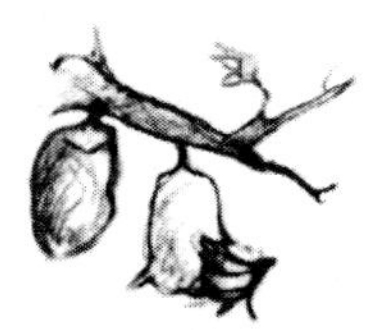

Times of stagnation

Times of beauty

– 21 –

Love Is . . .

David R. Miller
Philip J. Henry

Guiding Scripture

Love is patient, love is kind. It does not envy, it does not boast, it is not proud.
It is not rude, it is not self-seeking, it is not easily angered, it keeps no record of wrongs.
Love does not delight in evil but rejoices with the truth.
It always protects, always trusts, always hopes, always perseveres.
Love never fails.

1 Corinthians 13:4-8a (NIV)

Type of Contribution: Exercise, Handout

Objective

The world seems confused about love. A person can "love" his or her favorite musical group," and a person can "love" his or her home team and "hate" the opponent. A child can "love" chocolate ice cream, Christians "love" Jesus, and, yes, a person can "love" his or her new car. In a world turned upside down, it is important for Christians and Christian counselors to remain right side up on the subject of love. Love, in scripture, is a command, not an option. If a Christian is going to obey the Lord in the area of love, he or she must have a clear understanding of what love really is.

Rationale for Use

Christians should take the commands of God seriously. God gave a command, not a request, "to love our neighbors as our selves" and to love our spouses "as Christ loved the Church." Each person is here on earth because Christ showed the greatest type of love, to give one's life for another. Missing from any biblical description of love is romance—the emotional and passionate aspect of love, the longing for another person without whom one will surely die.

Certainly, Bible writers recognize romantic love, and the Bible contains many stories of great loves, both romantic and dutiful. David loved Bathsheba with a passionate love, and he loved his friend Jonathan with a brotherly love. The lives of Ruth, Boaz, and Naomi show many variations of a love story. The disciples loved Jesus, and he loved them in return. The sisters Mary and Martha loved Jesus and showed their platonic love for Him in different ways. Jesus loved his

The Christian Therapist's Notebook

doi:10.1300/5334_22

friend Lazarus enough to bring him back from the dead. Moreover, God loves so much that He gave up His only son to die for the sins of the world, and this is the greatest love of all.

It is vital to focus on biblical characteristics of love and to learn how those characteristics can produce immense changes in people. Some characteristics of love seem relatively easy to master ("love your children"), while others are more difficult ("love your enemies"). Love is developmental and needs nurturing if it is to grow. Love, as stated earlier, is a command rather than a suggestion or an option.

It is the ultimate goal for a believer to learn adequately, or to have his or her learning refreshed, about the role of love in a godly relationship, the purpose of which is to glorify God in every instance and activity. Once the client understands what love is and how it is supposed to work in his or her life, the differences become apparent. Believers in Christ have the ability to have their love needs met by God alone, even though He rarely asks for this level of commitment.

Instructions

The first session with the couple or the individual client is critical in setting the tone for success in marriage counseling. It is important to remember the significant elements of personal attitude and behavior which emanate from the chair of the counselor and which greatly influence how each client perceives the helping process. It may be a good idea to do a personal review of counseling skills, including empathy, rapport building, neutrality, transparency, genuineness, clarity, unconditional positive regard, the integration of Christian principles, and realistic optimism before counseling. Once the "precounseling check-off" is completed, counseling may begin.

The first session with the couple or individual will be primarily consumed by information gathering, initial relationship assessment, and relationship building. Share with the couple the usual course of counseling related to relationship issues. Clients can be very nervous about how long the process will take, how much personal information they might have to reveal, whether they can trust the counselor to maintain confidentiality, and what they might expect as a reasonable outcome of counseling. For example, marriage counseling involving a couple still living together usually takes from six to ten sessions. Offer a number as a general guideline because it helps clients relax, thus allowing the process to go more smoothly.

Listen carefully as each partner shares his or her perceptions and feelings. Be careful to avoid commenting or correcting at this early stage. The goal in the beginning is to gain insight into the relationship; accomplish this through attentive listening, not talking. If the information is not volunteered, ask each client about his or her Christian commitment, how Jesus Christ relates to his or her day-to-day life, what he or she believes God wants for him or her, and how seriously he or she takes God's word. Consider beginning this process by reading this exercises's Guiding Scripture to the couple, and then ask each of them to rate, on a scale of 1 to 10 (1 being lowest), how he or she believes their relationship measures up to that biblical standard of love. It will be important to note the inevitable variance between the estimates of each partner and the meaning behind these estimates. Tread slowly and gently here, as the couple may hear only the criticisms, which will shut down any further progress in counseling.

In preparation for the second session, ask the couple to list, privately and without discussion, the five strong points and five weak points of their marriage. Ask them to use the Guiding Scripture as a measuring device. As the second session gets under way, begin by asking the couple if they have done their homework, and, if so, whether they are ready to share their perceptions. At this point, expect some nervousness. The couple may not be accustomed to sharing their personal feelings with each other, especially when someone else is listening. Be prepared to deal with "I forgot" answers. If either the husband or the wife is not prepared, accept this as resistance to treatment but move the process forward despite that.

It is important to model good listening skills throughout the counseling sessions. Couples often claim the reason their relationships are in trouble is that their partners talk but do not listen. Model the correct listening skills with the couple while retraining them to listen to each other. Make sure that one partner is not answering or talking for the other. Watch for phrases such as, "He always thinks I'm more interested in the children than him," or "She is always too tired for sex." Gently stop such comments, turn to the other partner and say, using the previous example, "Your wife thinks that you think she cares more about the children than you. What do you think?" Do not let the couple interrupt each other. If this happens, stop the conversation and say, for example, "John, I can't help noticing that you aren't letting Sharon finish what she wants to say. Are you aware you are doing that?" Usually, gentle reminders combined with good role modeling greatly help the counseling process attain its goals.

The third and fourth sessions focus on analyzing in greater depth the characteristics of love that the couple studied in 1 Corinthians 13. Discuss which one of the characteristics God clearly sees as important is the easiest and which is the most difficult for each to master. Typically, the husband is often less patient than the wife is, and the wife tends to be the better "record keeper." The husband becomes angry more often, and the wife tends to feel hurt rather than angry. Both husbands and wives tend to feel less than perfect as sexual and romantic partners, and each spouse will feel that his or her physical self-image has declined with age. Discuss the issue that Bible passages, such as the Guiding Scripture, contain the goals for perfection, which the couple is not expected to attain perfectly. Remind the couple that the goal of Christian marriage counseling is to become as much like Christ as possible, even while recognizing that all human beings will fall short of the mark. We do the best we can while striving to become more mature.

In the fifth or sixth session, introduce the issue of forgiveness. Help the couple focus on "keeping no records" and persevering in their relationship. Remind them that forgetting past offenses is not the goal. Only God has the ability truly to forget past sin. Focus instead on forgiving with as much spiritual power as lies within each of the partners. The power of saying "I forgive you" goes well beyond the meaning of mere words. Forgiving and being forgiven are what matters. This is both a spiritual and a psychological process when one partner says he or she forgives the other. The spiritual component in saying "I forgive you" in front of one's partner and witness is much the same as going forward in church to ask for prayer or to recommit one's life to Christ. Words spoken publicly in the presence of witnesses tend to have more staying power than words spoken privately. The psychological element relates to cognitive dissonance, an uncomfortable mental state brought about by holding two or more opposing viewpoints on the same issue. Once a person has said, "I forgive you," this creates a mental state that supports the statement made. In other words, a statement said aloud is either truth or a lie. For most, the thought of being a liar is uncomfortable, and so a lie becomes difficult to voice. Therefore, it is much more beneficial to hold to the promise. Nevertheless, both the spiritual and psychological aspects of this process manifest in the person asking for or granting forgiveness orally, in front of a witness.

Once the counseling process begins to conclude, focus on the "Love is . . ." handout. Give each partner a copy of the list of what God says love is and ask the couple, individually and without discussing it, to place a "+" or a "–" to the left of each characteristic, indicating his or her perceptions about whether the other partner has improved, stayed the same, or declined during counseling. During the final session, discuss the list with the pluses and minuses, and explore the impact of any changes on the relationship. Remember, the Holy Spirit uses such counseling sessions to set a pattern of Spirit-led thinking and feeling that should help sustain the relationship for years to come. End the final session with prayer, emphasizing the positive aspects of change and to trust in God that the remaining unchanged issues will be resolved with His help.

Vignette

Adam and Jesse had been married less than a year when Adam called for a counseling appointment at our church's counseling center. This was Adam's first marriage and Jesse's second. Jesse had two daughters from a previous marriage that had ended when her husband, for reasons yet unclear, told her he did not want to be married anymore and could not take the responsibility of being a husband and a father. He would support his wife and daughters well, but he did not want to be with them anymore. Jesse's divorce had occurred about four years before she had agreed to marry Adam.

Adam and Jesse, and her girls, were fixtures at our church prior to their marriage. Adam was active in the men's ministry, Jesse was very involved with women's service activities, and the girls were well known as well-behaved, bright children who were involved in all the children's activities at the church. Most people in the church were not surprised to hear of their engagement and were happy for them. Therefore, it came as something of a surprise to me to see them in the counseling office within a year of their marriage.

The presenting problem, according to Adam, was that Jesse seemed never satisfied with his Christian leadership in the home, and she questioned the sincerity of his feelings for her. Jesse admitted to the suspicion that Adam might have married her for two self-serving reasons. First, she thought Adam might have asked her to marry him so that he could attain full status in the church as a married man with children who had, in effect, "rescued" them from single-parent status. Second, she worried that getting married was really a way to camouflage his lack of true Christian love, not just for her, but for everyone.

Adam agreed that he had heard all this before, but only since their marriage, not during their dating or engagement period. Adam seemed genuinely confused and hurt by Jesse's allegations. Adam saw himself as a reasonably good Christian with honest motives for marrying Jesse. He complained that no matter how he proclaimed his love for his new wife, and regardless of how well he behaved himself as a husband and stepfather, it was never good enough for Jesse. Adam and Jesse were equally confused, but about different things. Adam was confused that his motives and behavior were being misunderstood and rejected, and Jesse was confused about her doubts and suspicions in the face of her stated love for Adam. Clearing the smokescreen of confusion was what this couple needed.

While the first sessions focused on information gathering and rapport building, as homework for our second session, I asked them to give some thought to what love meant to each of them and perhaps to write down a few of their thoughts on the subject. I suggested they not share their ideas about the nature of love until they returned to the office next week. They agreed, and as an additional suggestion, I asked them to set aside thirty minutes a day just to sit quietly with each other. They were not to read anything more into this assignment than that I wanted them to be alone, with the television and other distractions turned off. They were to turn off the phone during this time, and the children, who were aged eight and six, were to be in their rooms playing and were not to interrupt their parents for any reason during this thirty-minute period. This time was not for sex or any other activity, except sitting together and perhaps talking, though talking was not required. Adam and Jesse agreed to try the assignment.

At the following counseling session, which took place the next week, Adam and Jesse reported that they had done their homework. Each had written his or her thoughts about love and reported that their "quiet times" together were proving helpful. They felt that their relationship had been renewed somewhat.

Jesse volunteered to share her thoughts about love and was able to go into some detail about what she expected of Adam in this area. Her comments seemed reasonable, and because I had known Adam fairly well before their marriage, I wondered silently if he was really unable to live up to her expectations. Adam, for his part, related love primarily to sexual fidelity, financial responsibility, and always being on Jesse's side, plus the emotional component. Again, I was interested because these areas were the very ones Jesse criticized in Adam. They agreed that parental love, as well as husband-wife love, involved putting Jesus first. Adam and Jesse agreed that Adam was "pretty good" about leading family devotions, praying at meals, and generally attending to the area of spiritual leadership, which was one of Jesse's areas of criticism. At this point, I decided to see Adam and Jesse in individual sessions, a practice that is very common in my counseling sessions. I had to find out what was really bothering Jesse about her new husband, so I suggested that she come in alone next week and then Adam could come in alone the following week.

The session with Jesse was both revealing and helpful to our counseling efforts. Jesse talked openly about her first marriage and shared how well she assumed things were going. It was clear that her first husband's demand for a divorce came as a total shock and was still on her mind these five or so years later. The problem was that Jesse's first husband had been a great Christian husband, just as she agreed Adam was, and that confused and frightened her. If she was so wrong the first time, what had she missed, and how could she prevent a reoccurrence of the same tragedy in her second marriage? It seemed her answer was to question and doubt Adam's motives, not because of anything he had done, but because of what her first husband had done. We talked this through, and Jesse slowly came to realize that she was working against her own interests with her doubts and criticisms of Adam. As the session ended, I asked Jesse to spend the next two weeks (I would see Adam alone next week) really thinking and praying about her own thoughts and expectations of her husband.

My session with Adam was designed to be supportive of his efforts to become the best husband he could. We talked about Jesse's concerns following the shock of her first divorce, and I suggested that her complaints and criticisms were not really aimed at him, though he may feel as if they were, but were really a remnant of the past trauma of her first divorce. We agreed that the best Adam could do was to be the best husband he could, under God's guidance. I stated my feeling that, by every objective measure, he was doing a good job as a new husband and stepfather. Such encouragement was important to Adam because, if he became discouraged in his efforts, he might come to feel that his marriage to Jesse was a mistake.

Our next session turned out to be our last. With both Jesse and Adam present, we went over the list of love attributes given in 1 Corinthians 13, using the "Love Is . . ." handout. We reviewed the checklist items one by one, with each partner stating how he or she felt the other partner manifested that love characteristic. Jesse agreed that Adam was patient and extremely kind, and he did not envy or behave jealously toward her. He did not boast about his own abilities; he was not too proud. He certainly was not rude or self-seeking; he kept his temper and did not seem to remember her failings. He told the truth without exception; he was protective of her and the children. He trusted her. He was optimistically hopeful, and she believed he would stay with her, and their relationship would persevere, as long as they lived. Adam possessed all the of characteristics and he was passionately and romantically interested in being with her whenever possible.

Yes, she agreed, this was love! Jesse had come to realize that the emotional damage done to her when her first husband abandoned her was the primary reason she had been so critical and judgmental of Adam. He was a good husband in all aspects, and he mirrored the qualities of love we had examined so carefully. Jesse accepted the idea that love is what love does, and Adam showed his love for her at every turn. Once again, the Bible acted as the open door to marriage fulfillment for a Christian couple. Once they stated their acceptance of God's word as true and everlasting, they could accept the next step of applying biblical principles to the problems of their marriage. Never had I felt such power of the Holy Spirit working through me than while helping this couple. What worked was counseling using the Bible as the base and final authority, which is what Christian counseling should always do.

Suggestions for Follow-Up

Exposure to God's word was what helped Jesse and Adam. As follow-up, they enrolled in the "newly married" class at their church and continued their high level of involvement in general Christian ministries. I also suggested they review 1 Corinthians 13 from time to time as a way of evaluating the continued progress of their marriage. Forgiveness certainly applied in this marriage, and I recommended that they continue to work on renewing their promises to forgive from time to time.

Contraindications

Some clients may be overwhelmed by the Guiding Scripture for this exercise. If this happens, break down the exercise into single steps to focus on just one of the characteristics of love at a time. Be alert for manipulation by one or both of the married clients, and if this happens, stop the couple's counseling and focus on the individual partner attempting manipulation. In addition, if physical or other forms of abuse are continuing to take place while the couple is in counseling, stop counseling until the abuse is addressed and stopped.

Resources for Professionals

Adams, J. (1986). *The biblical view of self-esteem, self-love and self image.* Eugene, OR: Harvest House Publishers.

Clarke, R. (1986). *Pastoral care of battered women.* Louisville, KY: Westminster John Knox Press.

Resources for Clients

Arterburn, S., and Felton, J. (1991). *Toxic faith: Understanding and overcoming religious addiction.* Nashville, TN: Thomas Nelson, Inc.

Hawkins, D., Hemfelt, R., Minirth, F., Meier, P., and Sneed, S. (1990). *Love hunger.* Nashville, TN: Thomas Nelson, Inc.

Nieder, J., and Thompson, T. (1991). *Forgive and love again.* Eugene, OR: Harvest House Publishers.

Related Scriptures

> My purpose is that they may be encouraged in heart and united in love, so that they may have the full riches of complete understanding, in order that they may know the mystery of God, namely, Christ, in whom are hidden all the treasures of wisdom and knowledge. (Colossians 2:2-3 NIV)

> Now that you have purified yourselves by obeying the truth so that you have sincere love for your brothers, love one another deeply, from the heart. (1 Peter 1:22 NIV)

> A man's wisdom gives him patience; it is to his glory to overlook an offense. (Proverbs 19:11 NIV)

> Be kind and compassionate to one another, forgiving each other, just as in Christ God forgave you. (Ephesians 4:32 NIV)

Model Prayer

Dear God, we know we are not capable of Godly love for each other without Your divine guidance. Please God, direct this believing couple as they build a marriage and a family that will please You. We know You only want the best for us and we trust in Your love and Your grace. We ask these things in Jesus' name. Amen.

+ or −	Love is patient
+ or −	Love is kind
+ or −	Love does not envy
+ or −	Love does not boast
+ or −	Love is not proud
+ or −	Love is not rude
+ or −	Love is not self-seeking
+ or −	Love is not easily angered
+ or −	Love keeps no record of wrongs
+ or −	Love does not delight in evil
+ or −	Love rejoices with the truth
+ or −	Love always protects
+ or −	Love always trusts
+ or −	Love always hopes
+ or −	Love always perseveres
+ or −	Love never fails

Love is patient, love is kind. It does not envy, it does not boast, it is not proud. It is not rude, it is not self-seeking, it is not easily angered, it keeps no record of wrongs. Love does not delight in evil but rejoices with the truth. It always protects, always trusts, always hopes, always perseveres. Love never fails.

1 Corinthians 13:4-8a (NIV)

– 22 –

A New Beginning: Premarital Counseling for the Second Marriage

David R. Miller

Guiding Scripture

If anyone does not provide for his relatives, and especially for his immediate family, he has denied the faith and is worse than an unbeliever.

1 Timothy 5:8 (NIV)

Type of Contribution: Exercise, Handout/Homework

Objective

Premarital counseling is always a good idea. However, it is never as critical as when the marriage is not the first for either spouse and there are children from the previous marriage(s) who will need to blend into the new home. God always wants the best for children, and the demands on men and women who already have children and are planning to remarry are great. Such couples need insight, understanding, information, and godly wisdom to help the reconstructed family be a success.

Rationale for Use

The guiding philosophy in premarital counseling is understanding that the vast majority of divorced people will remarry, and this includes Christian people no less than any other. Those of us who serve as counselors to the people of God, the followers of Jesus Christ, must recognize that some of the people we serve will remarry, and that those families will blend to become a new family, regardless of what others think might be the theologically correct thing to do. We must also consider, given the words of God about the protection and care of children (see Exodus 22:22-24; Job 29:12; Malachi 3:5), what God would want for those children. Would God want children to remain in a single-parent home when a two-parent home is available, awaiting only a remarriage? What would Jesus want us to do about the care of children? We do premarital counseling for second marriages simply because there is a need among God's people. We minister as the need arises.

The Christian Therapist's Notebook

doi:10.1300/5334_23

Instructions

An essential aspect of premarital counseling for second marriages is to have the full participation of both the parent with custody of the children and the soon-to-be stepparent. Participation by both sides of the proposed new family is so important that it is hard to overstate the case. You would be better off as a counselor to gently refuse to have a counseling session unless and until both partners can come in together. The reasoning is simple. If the one requesting counseling cannot get cooperation from his or her intended marriage partner, it means one of two things. First, it may mean that the one wanting the appointment has little influence with his or her intended spouse, and therefore the impending marriage is unequal and unbalanced to begin with and is likely to fail, regardless of the value of premarital counseling. The second meaning relates to the other partner, the one who will not come to counseling. We assume that a person has the greatest ability to influence his or her intended spouse just prior to the marriage. If the intended partner will not cooperate with the person's wishes now, he or she never will. Moreover, the benefits of premarital counseling become a distant, unachievable reality.

Thus, Christian counselors should gently but firmly insist that the counseling appointment wait until both partners are available and willing to be involved. This is an issue of professional judgment rather than personal preference. Therefore, wait until they both can come in together.

Let us assume that things have worked well and you have the couple with you in your office; one partner has children, and the other does not. Your goal as a Christian and as a counselor is to share information that will support the healthful development of the second marriage and stepfamily. However, before you can share relevant information, you have to listen and learn enough about the couple and any other individuals involved to know which issues are most relevant. You will want to ask gently the following questions of each member of the couple. You will ask these questions in the presence of both partners because you want to model openness; an added benefit is having each partner learn what he or she may have been reluctant to ask about before. It is amazing to me how many clients involved in premarital counseling are afraid to ask the most basic question, such as, "Why did your first marriage end?"

1. How long has it been since each of you divorced?
2. Have you shared the reasons for the end of your other marriage with each other?
3. What were those reasons?
4. Are your parents and other family members, including your children, in favor of your impending marriage?
5. What will be your living arrangements after the marriage?
6. You attend different churches now. How will you choose a church after the marriage?
7. Tell me about how you were involved in your family before the divorce.
8. What have you decided about prayer before meals and family devotions, and how often you will attend church?
9. Has child discipline been discussed? How have you decided to handle it?
10. How will you handle visits from the other children, your future spouse's children, who live with the other parent?
11. Are you in agreement on what you believe about God, Jesus, and the Church?
12. All couples argue. If you had to guess, what would you think your first argument would be about?
13. Have you truly said good-bye to the other marriage? How do you know?
14. What do you believe God expects from the new marriage and family?
15. How will you spend your leisure time? Have you thought about how vacation time would be used?

16. Have you discussed any family obligations that already exist or that may come up, for example, taking care of aging parents?
17. Talk to me about responsibility to each other. Have you discussed that you will always know where the other one is, or that either one of you will always call about being late?
18. Are there any existing loyalties that may interfere with your new marriage? For example, some parents are more loyal to their children than to their new partners, even though the children will eventually grow up and leave the home. Have you discussed that at all?
19. How sure are you that your partner prefers your company to that of anyone else? How do you know?
20. Are you sure that you are getting married for the right reasons? Could we talk about what those reasons might be?

It is surprising to learn how many Christian couples anticipating a second marriage have not discussed any of these important issues. I get the feeling at times that they think God will just magically take care of any problems that come up, even though they know that did not happen in their earlier marriages. So ask the difficult questions, knowing this may be the only time such important issues are raised by an outsider. I have found that couples tend to avoid asking the hard questions for fear of either alienating or offending their intended spouse. The Christian counseling office has to be that safe place where hard questions are raised and confronted, perhaps for the first and only time.

Vignette

Jeanette and Jim met at work. Jim was a sales and distribution manager for a medium-sized computer software company, and Jeanette was a mid-level programmer for the same company. Both were in their early thirties and had been with the company for between five and ten years, and both felt secure in their jobs and the skills they possessed. They met at a singles Bible study offered through a large Southern Baptist church in the city, and they had known each other and been dating for almost two years. Jim had never been married and had no children, while Jeanette had been married and divorced once and had one child, a son named Jeremy. Both Jeanette and Jim had solid Christian testimonies and everyone who knew them thought they made a great couple.

Our first appointment came at the recommendation of the leader of the Bible study class they attended together. After announcing the engagement and the congratulations were offered, the teacher took Jeanette and Jim aside after church one Sunday to talk to them about their need for premarital counseling, strictly as a preventative measure to help them get started correctly. Their teacher, himself a divorced and remarried man, knew the challenges of remarriage and being a stepparent. The teacher, as he shared with me by telephone, had some concerns about Jim's motivations for marriage and expectations of what it would be like afterward.

We spent the first session becoming acquainted, and the couple provided the necessary information for our standard intake forms, which are required of all new clients. I was careful, as always, to explain our appointment-scheduling arrangement, issues of privacy and confidentiality, how to contact me in a true emergency and what constituted an emergency, how we would end the counseling process, and how many sessions we would need.

As the intake process continued, I weaved in some of the questions mentioned earlier and noted their responses carefully. I learned that Jeanette's first marriage had been abusive, both physically and psychologically, with the first indicators of future abuse coming even while they were dating. It is worth considering the state of mind Jeanette had at that time and the reason why she tolerated the abuse, however unhappily, for as long as she did. Jeanette revealed that she had witnessed her mother being beaten, and that she had very little contact with either of her parents. Jeanette just could not feel comfortable around her father, and even though she was sure the abuse of her mother had stopped, Jeanette did not feel like she wanted to be in that environment.

Jim's background was very different. He was the only child of two schoolteachers who described his early years as pleasant, if a little boring. Jim's parents were solid Christians who held very conservative views on cultural offerings, such as movies and music. Jim clearly felt he had missed out on the fun when he was younger, believing as he did that there was nothing wrong with the things he had not been allowed to experience. Smiling, he said that was all in the past now, and he was on good terms with his parents. I asked about his relationship with his parents, and Jim proclaimed it to be good and healthy, if a little quiet and conservative. There had been no abuse of any kind, and Jim felt his parents were good to him still.

Our second session focused on the future. I wanted to learn about their expectations and hopes for their marriage, and what, if any, obstacles or detours they saw on the horizon. I again interwove some of the questions presented earlier, and I was particularly interested in Jim's feelings about becoming a father to Jeremy. Jeanette, I should add, was thoroughly pleased and hopeful about the stepfather Jim could be to her son. She felt that Jim was a good man in every way and would be a great role model for Jeremy and might balance out some of the negative and worldly influences from his absent father. Jeanette added that Jeremy and Jim seemed to get along well together, and she felt the transition to a stepfamily would be easy for all concerned. I wasn't so sure!

The third session continued with more background information related to Jeanette's and Jim's experiences growing up in their individual families. I had raised some of these issues before, but I was suspecting a problem on the horizon that I wanted to confront. I asked both of them to talk about their same-sex parents and whether they wanted to be the same kind of parents to Jeremy and other children that might come along later. Would Jeanette want to be like her mother? Why or why not? Would Jim want to be the same kind of father he saw in his family growing up? Why or why not? I knew the answers would be important to counseling, not only for my professional approach, but also for this couple to hear from each other on issues usually not discussed while dating and preparing for marriage.

We learned that Jim was expecting a more liberal Christian family than the one in which he was raised. He felt cheated by not having had the fun the other kids had, for no reason other than his father's strict interpretation of certain parts of the Bible. Jeanette, on the other hand, was going in the opposite direction. She grew up in a non-Christian environment that had been abusive, alcoholic, and often frightening because of the violence against her mother. Jeanette wanted to ensure that this would not happen in the new family they were creating, and she hoped that Jim would be the conservative father she had never known, either in her own father or in Jeremy's dad. It was clear that Jim was looking for a more relaxed Christian environment while Jeanette was hoping for a safer, more protective, and more conservative home. We had some work to do!

In preparation for our third session, I handed Jim and Jeanette the "Indispensable List" handout and asked them to make up a short list of five "indispensables." These would be qualities, attitudes, behaviors, or anything else either one *must* have if their marriage was to succeed. I offered some ideas to get them started, pulling from information I had learned in earlier sessions with other clients. Clients commonly say they need honesty, safety, security, faithfulness, financial security, love, sex (how frequent?), companionship, friendship, loyalty, spiritual leadership or spiritual submission, and fun. I explained to this couple that I would ask both of them to explain what they meant by the words or phrases they chose for the Indispensable List. For example, if Jim said he needed loyalty from Jeanette, how would he know he was getting it? If Jeanette said that she absolutely needed faithfulness from Jim, what would make her feel she was having this need met? What would Jim do or not do to cause Jeanette to believe he was being faithful? Even though these were just examples at the time, I was preparing them for a serious discussion of personal needs during our next session. I instructed them to prioritize the items on their lists, with the fifth item being the one that was the least important of the five and the item being the most important.

Our fourth session, as expected, focused on the Indispensable List. We began by starting at the bottom of each list, the number five item for each person, and then working our way up the list. My experience reveals that working through the list will take one or two sessions, this process should not be rushed. Be prepared to clarify the words or phrases your clients use and ask for examples if there is any doubt or confusion.

Jeanette's list went about as expected, with a normal amount of clarification, which seemed to be just what was necessary for Jim to understand her perspective. It was a different experience with Jim. Jim's second "indispensable" was that Jeanette's son, Jeremy, accepts him and loves him as a father. I asked for clarification of what Jim meant. He explained that he felt that, if he were to be Jeanette's husband and an equal partner in the new home they would establish, he would need to have Jeremy treat him as a father, call him by an appropriate term, such as "Dad," and accept correction and discipline by Jim when necessary.

I could tell from the expression on Jeanette's face that this was the first she had heard this from Jim. Jim continued his explanation by saying he had been talking to his former pastor and was impressed that God wanted him to assume immediate spiritual leadership in the home, and he did not see any reason this should not happen. Jeanette was clearly surprised by this revelation, and I could tell she did not know how to respond. She said to me later that, for the first time, she felt their upcoming marriage might be in danger. Jeanette knew that, although Jeremy liked Jim, it was too soon to expect him to accept Jim as the father figure in the home. In addition, if Jeremy told his biological father that such demands were being placed on him, the father would try to get custody away from Jeanette.

I asked Jim to come in alone for the next session. In preparation for the session, I asked Jim to pray and search his Bible for input on the issue of his assuming parental authority as a stepfather, to which he agreed. I was very sure he would not find biblical support for his position, and I believed as well that his prayers would help him to see the wisdom of putting the needs of Jeremy and Jeanette above his own.

I did not raise the issue right away in our session without Jeanette, choosing instead simply to talk with Jim, help him feel at ease, and hope he would feel I was on his side and the side of marital success. I asked Jim to talk a little more about his relationship with his father, which I knew was distant and unemotional. As we talked, I pointed out that Jim's childhood feelings of rejection could be reproduced in his future stepson, Jeremy, if he made demands on him that Jeremy was not emotionally prepared to fulfill. Just as Jim's father had rejected him by being distant and uninvolved in his life, so too could Jim convey the same message of rejection to Jeremy by moving too rapidly into the father and disciplinarian role. I suggested to Jim that he should focus on his marriage to Jeanette, for many reasons, including that Jeremy would be out of the house and on his own in ten or fewer years. "You are not marrying Jeremy," I told him, "and you may sabotage the very thing you care so much about if you go ahead and insist that your wishes and needs be seen as more important than those of Jeanette and Jeremy." We discussed "servant-leadership," a concept I knew Jim had been learning about in Bible study, and we discussed how to be a leader without become a dictator.

Jim responded better than I had expected, which raised my estimation of his spiritual maturity. I sensed a bit of relief in Jim, and I guessed that he had been feeling a lot of pressure from his former pastor and a few others to be more assertive in this soon-to-be marriage than he really felt was appropriate. I told him, and I would bring it up again when Jeanette was present, that he had every right to demand respect and obedience from Jeremy, but that the discipline of the boy had to be left to his mother, at least for two years after their marriage. I shared with Jim the research that reveals that moving to quickly into the disciplinarian role is the number one cause of divorce for second marriages involving children. I emphasized to Jim that he would never replace Jeremy's "real" father and he should not hope to do so. The best he could hope for would be that Jeremy would respect and like him, but there just was not enough time for a true parental relationship to develop between Jim and Jeremy. As long as Jeremy's biological father was in the picture, Jim would take a distant but friendly second place in Jeremy's life. Jim had a lot to think about before our next session with him and Jeanette, so we ended the session with a brief prayer for wisdom from God.

Our next session brought Jim and Jeanette back into the counseling office together. From their body language, I could tell it had been a good week. Jim had shared our last discussion with Jeanette, and they had talked it through. Jeanette shared her anxiety over Jim's expectations of her son and was greatly relieved when Jim left from our session with a change of heart in the matter. Jim talked about feeling his prayer for wisdom had been answered, at least partially, and he was going to be able to relax and let God work in Jeremy's heart in regard to his new stepfather. Jim stated that he was prepared to follow my suggestion to hold back on the discipline of Jeremy for at least the first two years of their new marriage, and under no circumstances would Jim resort to physical punishment of Jeremy.

We worked our way through the remaining items on their Indispensable List without encountering problems of much significance. It seemed to me that we had successfully dealt with the one major issue potentially hurting the upcoming marriage. This couple had a great deal working in their favor, not the least of which was their commitment to Jesus Christ. We all agreed that continued church attendance and involvement was of prime importance, and that they had the potential of becoming a beacon of God's grace and wisdom, as others observed them overcoming their personality and background differences to build a new family that would glorify God. We prayed together, asking God for continued wisdom and grace, and we could feel the presence of the Holy Spirit there in the office with us. We then terminated the formal sessions, with an invitation to return as needed or just to share an update. I promised Jim and Jeanette that my wife and I would attend their wedding, which we did. As far as I am aware, Jim , Jeanette, and Jeremy are doing great in their new family. Praise God!

Suggestions for Follow-Up

As we terminated our sessions, I suggested that Jeremy might need some help adjusting to his new family. If this happened to be the case, I would be happy to recommend a Christian counselor who specialized in children. I also expressed my appreciation for their sincere desire to serve God as a newly married couple and shared my willingness to help them in any way in the future. Jim and Jeanette agreed to keep me aware of how their lives were developing, but I also emphasized that I would seek them out for information. I suggested that they review their Indispensable List periodically and consider updating it every couple of years or so.

Contraindications

We cannot counsel an absent person, one who is not attending counseling sessions. The inability or refusal of one partner severely limits the ability of any counselor to help. A client may attend counseling sessions but be so oppositional that he or she works against progress in counseling. A person may have his or her own agenda and be unwilling to work cooperatively for the greater good of the couple or family. Moreover, if there is any kind of ongoing abuse, threat, or intimidation, counseling will have to stop until that issue is resolved satisfactorily.

Resource for Professionals

Visher, E.B., and Visher, J.S. (1988). *Old loyalties, new ties: Therapeutic strategies with stepfamilies.* New York: Brunner/Mazel Publishers.

Resources for Clients

Anderson, N.T., and Mylander, C. (1996). *The Christ-centered marriage: Discovering and enjoying your freedom in Christ together.* Ventura, CA: Regal Books.
Ferguson, D., Ferguson, T., Thurman, C., and Thurman, H. (1994). *Intimate encounters.* Nashville, TN: Thomas Nelson, Inc.
Parrott, L., and Parrott, L. (1995). *Becoming soul mates.* Grand Rapids, MI: Zondervan Publishing House.
Smalley, G. (1988). *Hidden keys of a loving lasting marriage.* Grand Rapids, MI: Zondervan Publishing House.

Related Scriptures

> Fix these words of mine in your hearts and minds; tie them as symbols on your hands and bind them on your foreheads. Teach them to your children, talking about them when you sit at home and when you walk along the road, when you lie down and when you get up. (Deuteronomy 11:18-19 NIV)

> He will turn the hearts of the fathers to their children, and the hearts of the children to their fathers . . . (Malachi 4:6 NIV)

> Now fear the Lord and serve him with all faithfulness. Throw away the gods your forefathers worshipped beyond the River and in Egypt, and serve the Lord. But if serving the Lord seems undesirable to you, then choose for yourselves this day whom you will serve, whether the gods your forefathers served beyond the River, or the gods of the Amorites, in whose land you are living. But as for me and my household, we will serve the Lord. (Joshua 24:14-15 NIV)

Indispensable List

List, in ascending order, the five most important things you absolutely <u>must</u> have if you are to remain in this marriage and have it be successful. If this is an upcoming marriage, list those things you <u>must</u> have in order for your marriage to be a success. The husband should do his list, and the wife hers. Do not share your lists until the counseling session. Remember; start with #5 as your <u>least</u> important item and move up to #1, which should be your <u>most</u> important item.

	Wife	**Husband**
#1	____________________	____________________
#2	____________________	____________________
#3	____________________	____________________
#4	____________________	____________________
#5	____________________	____________________

– 23 –

Nothing Like the Brady Bunch

Lori Marie Figueroa

Guiding Scripture

They will be divided, father against son and son against father, mother against daughter and daughter against mother . . .

Luke 12:53 (NIV)

Type of Contribution: Exercise, Handout

Objective

This exercise will help clients identify changes in roles, alliances, parental arrangements, household responsibilities, rules, expectations, and demands that have occurred because of a result of a blended family, while demonstrating that God is at the center of the new family.

Rationale for Use

On James Dobson's "Focus on the Family" Web site, author Rich Buhler contributed an article titled "Is it Really 50 Percent?" In this article, Buhler states that although many proclaim that 50 percent of all marriages end in divorce, the actual figure is not as alarming. Buhler shares researcher George Barna's most recent survey of Americans in 2001, which estimates that 34 percent of those who have ever been married have been divorced. However, because of this percentage, blended families are common. In fact, three out of every five families who visit a therapist will include children from previous relationships (Hart, 1996). This exercise shows that not all families have smooth transitions, as in the TV sitcom *Brady Bunch* popular decades ago. Even Christian families face challenges that seem insurmountable. Unresolved issues from previous relationships can breed seeds of unhappiness. These seeds can bear sour fruits in the lives of the children involved in the new blended family.

This exercise addresses the issue of blended families within Christian therapy. When two people fall in love and begin a new marriage, their challenge is to find a way for two unique individuals to coexist. If ex-spouses or children from a previous relationship are in the picture, the marriage inherits an additional set of challenges.

Feelings of guilt, shame, and despair can cause partners to hold back within the marriage, thus affecting the family as a whole. God's grace is the only solution to these unresolved feelings. However, some clients may be unaware at a conscious level of the existence of these feel-

The Christian Therapist's Notebook

doi:10.1300/5334_24

ings. Therefore, therapists can help such families understand the existing relationships among the family members and also how each one perceives the others.

Next, therapists must help the clients to see the blended family as a hopeful new beginning, full of expectations. Refer to Jeremiah 29:11 (NIV): "'For I know the plans, I have for you,' declares the Lord, 'plans to prosper you and not to harm you, plans to give you hope and a future.'" Family members can have the opportunity to express their heart's desires in regard to the new family. Such dreams can serve as a stepping stone, as the family sets goals of commitment, appreciation, affection, quality time, and coping mechanisms for unexpected challenging times.

Instructions

First, using the chapter handout, the therapist should ask each member of the family to fill in the squares with the members of the new blended family as he or she best sees fit. Give examples, such as "the blamer" or "the overachiever," for them to use in describing family members. Ask them to list one positive adjective for each member. Use the responses to define clearly the perceptions and expectations of all family members. Serve as a mediator as the family works together to define the new roles of each member.

Teach family members through scripture to see one another as a blessing, while accepting one another as unique individuals. It is important for clients to acknowledge and identify any feelings of loss experienced by any of the family members due to divorce or death. During the therapeutic sessions, clients should discuss how these unresolved feelings have affected the family as a whole.

This is a great opportunity to share 1 Corinthians 12 from the Bible:

> Now the body is not made up of one part but of many. If the foot should say, "Because I am not a hand, I do not belong to the body," it would not for that reason cease to be part of the body. And if the ear should say, "Because I am not an eye, I do not belong to the body," it would not for that reason cease to be part of the body. If the whole body were an eye, where would the sense of hearing be? If the whole body were an ear, where would the sense of smell be? But in fact God has arranged the parts in the body, every one of them, just as He wanted them to be. If they were all one part, where would the body be? As it is, there are many parts, but one body.
>
> The eye cannot say to the hand, "I don't need you!" And the head cannot say to the feet, "I don't need you!" On the contrary, those parts of the body that seem to be weaker are indispensable, and the parts that we think are less honorable we treat with special honor. And the parts that are unpresentable are treated with special modesty, while our presentable parts need no special treatment. But God has combined the members of the body and has given greater honor to the parts that lacked it, so that there should be no division in the body, but that its parts should have equal concern for each other. If one part suffers, every part suffers with it; if one part is honored, every part rejoices with it." (1 Corinthians 12:14-26 NIV)

This analogy of the body can show the family the value of each member and the importance of supporting family members in times of need.

New families should always encourage communication and prayer as they seek to build a spiritual household. Demonstrate for them the role that God plays as the Father, the center of the family, and the head of their household. They should learn to seek His wisdom first and not become overly enmeshed with any one family member. The family can also learn to overcome challenges through spiritual disciplines, such as meditation and scripture memorization.

Vignette

Nicole is a thirty-three-year-old, Hispanic female who works as a social worker. She has one biological son named Sergio. Her son's biological father lives in another state and has minimal contact through mail correspondence. They were never married. She has raised Sergio as a single mother for the past five years. She recently married Mario, a thirty-five-year-old Hispanic male who has two biological daughters, Julie and Lindsey. Mario works as a manager at an insurance agency. Mario is divorced and the biological mother of his daughters lives in another state and is remarried, with three children from her new spouse. She remains in contact with her daughters via phone and mail correspondence. Her daughters visit her every other Christmas holiday and during the summer. Mario has been raising his daughters alone for the past three years.

The parents of both Mario and Nicole are Christians and have been married for over thirty years. Mario and Nicole both come from large extended families whose members are very close, and both families remain connected by including the other in major family festivities.

Nicole and Mario have sought therapy because of a mutual concern over their new family unit affecting their children. They want to make sure the children have the opportunity to express their feelings or concerns in a nonthreatening environment. During the first session, the therapist asked the children to write down on a piece of paper who their mother was. The therapist advised them that they could write down anyone in the family; it did not necessarily have to be a biological parent. Interestingly enough, Sergio and Julie wrote down their biological mothers. However, Lindsey wrote down the name of her grandmother (Mario's mother). In a similar manner, they reviewed the other family roles. The family's homework assignment was to draw a family tree with their new family members in mind.

During the second session, the therapist asked each member to share his or her family tree. This was a great opportunity to compare how different family members perceived the family unit. This led to a discussion of why certain people were included or excluded from the individual's family tree. The siblings argued about the importance of certain family members. The therapist was able to teach the family the concept of active listening and healthy communication. The family then took the assignment home to draw one family tree together as homework.

By the third and final session, the family members seemed to appreciate one another better. The children shared the newly combined family tree with pride. The therapist even noticed how they sat closer to one another. Mario's daughters sat closer to Nicole, and Sergio embraced Mario. The therapist read Jeremiah 29:11 (NIV) aloud: "'For I know the plans, I have for you,' declares the Lord, 'plans to prosper you and not to harm you, plans to give you hope and a future.'" The therapist explained to the family that although the future would be challenging at times, God gave their family hope for a fulfilling future.

Sharing 1 Corinthians 12 from the Bible reminded the family of the value of each member and the importance of supporting family members in times of need. The therapist commended the family on their positive communication and prayer. The therapist reminded the family of the role God plays as the Father, in the center of the new family and as head of their household. They were encouraged to seek His wisdom first and not become overly enmeshed with any one family member. The family was also encouraged to overcome challenges through spiritual disciplines, such as meditation and scripture memorization.

Suggestions for Follow-Up

As therapy progresses, the exercise may be used to compare the family's perceptions of roles as well as any changed cognitions. Follow up the exercise by teaching the family to practice the spiritual disciplines of study and meditation. Through prayer and a reliance on God, the follow-up can show the family's progress and growth.

Contraindications

This exercise is contraindicated when any of the members of the family are not secure in their relationship with God. In addition, a contraindication may exist if the counselor has stereotypes about stepfamilies based on his or her own attitudes and belief systems. Another contraindication can be the lack of presence of one of the new members.

Resources for Professionals

Anderson, N.T., Zuehlke, T.E., and Zuehlke, J.S. (2000). *Christ centered therapy.* Grand Rapids, MI: Zondervan Publishing House.

Briesmeister, J.M., and Schaefer, C.E. (1989). *Handbook of parent training.* New York: John Wiley and Sons, Inc.

Goldenberg, I., and Goldenberg, H. (2000). *Family therapy: An overview.* Belmont, CA: Wadsworth/Thomas Learning.

Hart, A.D. (1996). *Helping children survive divorce: What to expect; How to help.* Nashville, TN: W Publishing Group, a division of Thomas Nelson Publishers, Inc.

Huggins, K.D. (2003). *Friendship counseling.* Colorado Springs, CO: NavPress.

Minuchin, S. (1993). *Family healing.* New York: The Free Press.

www.family.org. Focus on the Family. Variety of excellent biblical resources for strengthening marriages and the family.

Resources for Clients

Brandt, H.R., and Dowdy, H. (1978). *Building a Christian home.* Wheaton, IL: Victor Books.

Chapman, G., and Campbell, R. (1997). *The five love languages of children.* Chicago, IL: Moody Press.

Dobson, J., and Dobson, S. (2002). *A devotional night-light for parents.* Sisters, OR: Multnomah Publishers, Inc.

Laing, S., and Laing, G. (1994). *Raising awesome kids in troubled times.* Woburn, MA: DPI International, Inc.

Shelly, J.A. (1982). *The spiritual needs of children.* Downers Grove, IL: InterVarsity Press.

Smalley, G. (2004). *The DNA of relationships.* Wheaton, IL: Tyndale House Publishers, Inc.

Stinnett, N., Stinnett, N., Beam, J., and Beam, A. (1999). *Fantastic families.* Monroe, LA: Howard Publishing Co.

Vazquez, C.I. (2004). Parenting with pride Latino style. New York: HarperCollins Publishers.

www.family.org. Focus on the Family. Variety of excellent biblical resources for strengthening marriages and the family.

Related Scriptures

> "For I know the plans I have for you," declares the Lord, "plans to prosper you and not to harm you, plans to give you hope and a future." (Jeremiah 29:11 NIV)

> Honor your father and your mother, so that you may live long in the land the LORD your God is giving you. (Exodus 20:12 NIV)

These commandments that I give you today are to be upon your hearts. Impress them on your children. Talk about them when you sit at home and when you walk along the road, when you lie down and when you get up. Tie them as symbols on your hands and bind them on your foreheads. Write them on the doorframes of your houses and on your gates. (Deuteronomy 6:6-9 NIV)

O my people, hear my teaching; listen to the words of my mouth. I will open my mouth in parables, I will utter hidden things, things from of old—what we have heard and known, what our fathers have told us. We will not hide them from their children; we will tell the next generation the praiseworthy deeds of the LORD, his power, and the wonders he has done. He decreed statutes for Jacob and established the law in Israel, which he commanded our forefathers to teach their children, so the next generation would know them, even the children yet to be born, and they in turn would tell their children. Then they would put their trust in God and would not forget his deeds but would keep his commands. (Psalm 78:1-7 NIV)

But from everlasting to everlasting the Lord's love is with those who fear him, and his righteousness with their children's children—with those who keep his covenant and remember to obey his precepts. (Psalm 103:17 NIV)

Children's children are a crown to the aged, and parents are the pride of their children. (Proverbs 17:6 NIV)

Train a child in the way he should go, and when he is old he will not turn from it. (Proverbs 22:6 NIV)

Discipline your son, and he will give you peace; he will bring delight to your soul. (Proverbs 29:17 NIV)

See that you do not look down on one of these little ones. For I tell you that their angels in heaven always see the face of my Father in heaven. (Matthew 18:10 NIV)

Jesus said, "Let the little children come to me, and do not hinder them, for the kingdom of heaven belongs to such as these." (Matthew 19:14 NIV)

Children, obey your parents in the Lord, for this is right. "Honor your father and mother"—which is the first commandment with a promise—"that it may go well with you and that you may enjoy long life on the earth." Fathers, do not exasperate your children; instead, bring them up in the training and instruction of the Lord. (Ephesians 6:1-4 NIV)

If anyone does not provide for his relatives, and especially for his immediate family, he has denied the faith and is worse than an unbeliever. (1 Timothy 5:8 NIV)

THE
BRAYDIE
BUNCH
THE
BUNCH

– 24 –

Control

David R. Miller
Philip J. Henry

Guiding Scripture

Who of you by worrying can add a single hour to his life?
. . . But seek first His kingdom and His righteousness, and all these things will be given to you as well. Therefore do not worry about tomorrow, for tomorrow will worry about itself. Each day has enough trouble of its own.

Matthew 6:27, 33-34 (NIV)

Type of Contribution: Exercise, Handouts/Homework

Objective

No person is more frustrated and unhappy than when trying to control the uncontrollable. Control of the world, in general, and family, in particular, is a most fruitless and futile thing to attempt. Yet, at times, exerting control seems the most natural thing in the world to do. We care, so we want to influence. We love, so we want the best for those closest to us. For many Christians, to care is to exercise beneficent control, but we need remember that trying to control others is a worldly, rather than a spiritual, pursuit. We are not in control of others, and we delude ourselves in thinking and believing we are. God will take care of all of our tomorrows—a lesson slowly and painfully learned by most.

Rationale for Use

Anxiety hurts! Worry is a psychologically, sometimes physically dangerous and damaging mental activity. Our loving Father cautions believers to let Him take care of the future, which is under His control alone. God loves us and wants us to be relatively pain and worry free, if we will only heed the cautions and instructions He provides. We hurt ourselves and disappoint God when we try to control the uncontrollable, rather than trusting in His love and care for the future.

The core of addressing anxiety- and worry-related problems lies in placing oneself on a par with God. At some level, anxious and worried believers are accepting the proposition that "I have to do what God cannot do. I have no confidence that God is really in charge of my future. Therefore, I must be worried and anxious about the future and work to control all the elements I can." The irrationality of such thinking has apparently escaped the person seeking to control what no human being can possibly control, that is, one's future. People who are "control freaks"

The Christian Therapist's Notebook

doi:10.1300/5334_25

are frightened and anxious and believe that they are doing the best they can, even though that "best" will never be good enough. The realization of this impossibility is what drives people to control all they can, while fearing failure in the very attempt.

Counselors seek to help a control-driven person for several important reasons. First, control is always anxiety based and anxiety can make a person sick. People who are anxious and fearful (these feelings usually coexist, even if not admitted to by clients) tend to experience physical symptoms, including shortness of breath, rapid or irregular heartbeat, trembling or shaking, sweating, choking sensations, nausea and other forms of abdominal problems, numbness in the extremities, a feeling of just not being themselves, hot flashes or chills, and a worry that they are losing control and maybe even going insane. While we all may experience some of these symptoms in situations of high anxiety, the controlling person feels anxious all the time, and so the symptoms are not relieved as the situation changes, as is true for others.

Assisting the client burdened with the need to control involves opening up his or her awareness to what lies behind the feelings and behaviors that are causing him or her distress. For believers and nonbelievers alike, awareness of control motivation involves recognizing that they really do believe, at some level, that they have the power to control future events and the people involved, and, therefore, they must do everything they can to control and direct the path the future will take.

When confronted with the certainty that they want to be God (or whatever higher power a nonbeliever may construct), expect clients to modify their behavior and adjust their thinking to be more reality based. This will not be an easy or brief process in most cases. Typically, people who are controlling have been that way for most of their lives, with worry, anxiety, and frustration becoming their constant companions. People who are controlling have often failed and are therefore angry and frustrated with their incompetence as controllers. Jobs have been lost and marriages ended because the controllers would not stop trying to achieve control, even though their previous attempts have failed. This can become a self-perpetuating agony for clients, who will benefit from your guidance on escaping such a negative cycle.

Instructions

The first step, as always, is to become familiar with your client's general background. This includes childhood experiences (control issues often have their genesis here), family background, favorite and worst memories, adolescent experiences, and adult history, especially as related to manifestations of control. It may be helpful to ask the following questions:

1. Did your mother or father suffer from anxiety, excessive worry, or a need to control as you were growing up?
2. Did your parents encourage you and your siblings to explore the world outside the family? Alternatively, were they fearful of what might happen if you did?
3. Do you remember your parents being excessively interested in what you were thinking, doing, or feeling?
4. Was one or both of your parents known as a perfectionist?
5. As a child, do you remember feeling as if unreasonable demands were being placed on you?
6. Did your parents react negatively to the expression of emotions, such as anger, sadness, disappointment, or joy?
7. What do you remember about your sense of your "role" in the family?
8. Do you feel as though you grew up feeling insecure in any way?
9. How was God involved in your family of origin? Was God a distant deity, a watchful but critical presence, or a loving and forgiving Father?
10. What impact does your childhood have on your being here in counseling?

Once you have asked these questions, while carefully and gently exploring your client's responses, you can begin to formulate your thinking on what factors might be involved in the development of a controlling nature by your client. Be careful to be tentative as you make suggestions to your client as to why he or she is the way he or she is. Be reluctant to begin interpretation too early in the process because there is much more to learn, and only time and careful listening will fill in the blanks. If you want to make suggestions to encourage your client to keep working, phrase your statements along these lines: "I want to emphasize that what I am about to say may easily be incorrect. We have only just begun the counseling process, and I have much more to learn about you. But as you asked, one possibility is . . ." Phrasing your thinking tentatively allows your client to accept or reject your suggestions without feeling as if he or she is contradicting you or disagreeing with what you have suggested.

Next, move on to exploring the actual personal controlling behaviors. What has your client been doing or saying that causes others to be concerned that he or she is excessively controlling. Focus here on the deed rather than the thought. True, we act on what we think, but your client will probably find it easier to identify and talk about the behaviors first, and moving on to the thought process later. For example, controlling people may behave in ways others would consider perfectionistic—never satisfied no matter how much effort people invest into a project or activity. Another example could be forcing a spouse or children to do work repeatedly until it is done perfectly, such as having to wash the dishes repeatedly until they are "spotless," or spending hours and hours on a trivial homework exercise because of "sloppy writing." Controlling people may have trouble at work getting assignments done because each project develops so slowly to ensure perfection. At this point, focus on the behavior, rather than the thinking, to ensure that you, the counselor, understand just how your client's control issues have gotten him or her into trouble.

Once you have a grasp on the behavior, move onto goals. You probably will be three or four sessions into the counseling process at this point, and you should be confident that you know the client well and have developed the beginnings of a good empathic relationship. Goals should be wide ranging and individual, but most will tend to revolve around the issues of perfectionism, a strong need for social approval, and a desire to be in charge.

Controlling and perfectionistic people tend to have unrealistically high expectations about themselves and others. When anything goes wrong, they become excessively disappointed and discouraged and engage in the "blame game," targeting themselves, others, or both. Along with this, controlling clients tend to focus on the smaller mistakes of life and have a difficult time getting over a past error in judgment or a social gaff. They tend to ruminate on past mistakes and can easily provide you with a long list of all of their mistakes and blunders. These clients talk much about the "shoulds," "oughts," and "musts" of their lives, rather than truly seeking perfection for its own sake. These people are so afraid of failing that they focus on the potential negative aspects of every situation and challenge. When a new opportunity presents itself, the perfectionist says, "Now, how can I blow this one?" rather than "How can I succeed?"

The need for social approval tends to be a strong motivation for controlling people. As you listen to your client talk about his or her problem with being controlling, ask yourself this question: "Who is doing the evaluating of this person?" For example, perhaps your male client consumes his life with proving to his children that he is not only a good father but also a great father, in fact one of the world's best all-time dads. Or, as you deal with that female client who is excessively thin but still dieting, think about whom she is trying to please. As you work with the depressed teenage boy who made a suicide gesture after failing to make the varsity football squad, ask, "Who is he afraid of disappointing?" Sadly, perfectionistic parents all too often produce children with a similar mind-set and the pain that comes with it. We tend to find families where issues of control are common, and then other families where such issues are noticeably absent.

Some controlling clients simply have an excessively strong need to know and control the future. Often, such needs follow some traumatic event, such as a serious automobile accident, a sudden death of a loved one or close friend, or a more widespread tragedy, such as a hurricane. Such events tend to threaten the sense of security most people have under normal circumstances, which tends to continue uninterrupted unless or until a traumatic event occurs. Others may have personality issues that cause them to feel frightened and insecure as a matter of course, not needing a traumatic event to create the fear and insecurity. Use the "Let Go and Let God" handouts at the end of this chapter to help your client make his or her control issues more concrete. As homework, ask your client to take the time to cut out and paste images of his or her control targets onto the blank handout provided, to bring in for the next session.

Remember to let the client control the rate of counseling, but you should control the overall structure. Naturally, controlling clients will try to control the counseling sessions just as they attempt to control all other aspects of life. You are God's representative in the counseling office, and you will help your client surrender control to God by first accepting the professional control you exercise over the sessions. Emphasize through your comments and suggestions that you are a Christian who accepts God's control over your life and feel free, if appropriate, to give personal examples to encourage your client's progress.

Vignette

Christian legalism is the raising of personal preferences to the level of spiritual commands. Legalistic Christians tend to believe they possess the absolute truth on living spiritually, and even insight into the gray areas of life that are not specifically addressed in the Bible. They see these arenas of life as somehow open and available to them to regulate as they choose. Legalists tend to be controlling to a fault, while also professing belief in the indwelling power of the Holy Spirit. They tend to behave as though they know the perfect mind of Christ and can never be wrong as long as they stay close to God. As an example, consider Rusty and his family, a group of believers almost destroyed by a controlling, legalistic father.

At the time I knew him, Rusty was the part-time pastor of a small fundamental Bible church in a rural area outside Roanoke, Virginia. Rusty was a graduate of the Bible Institute connected to the large Christian university where I taught at the time. The Bible Institute is a two-year program for men called to the pastorate but who have family obligations precluding a four-year college or seminary program. Graduates of this program tend to make strong pastors firmly committed to the Word of God. Rusty had taken the pastorate of the church immediately upon graduating from the Bible Institute; he was well on his way to building the church membership back up to its former numbers and ministry. Rusty and his wife, Patricia, were parents to two boys, Alex, age thirteen, and Paul, age seventeen. Alex and Paul attended the Christian school also connected to the university, which housed the Bible Institute. We all knew one another to some extent, and our acquaintance was what led this couple to come see me at the counseling center.

My appointment calendar simply stated that Rusty and Patricia were coming to talk about their oldest son, Paul, a senior at our Christian high school. One of the more exciting aspects of Christian counseling is rarely knowing what to expect from a new counseling appointment. If you are like most counselors, you will find anticipation of the challenge God is bringing to you to be one of the most rewarding aspects of your ministry. I certainly did not know what was coming when anticipating my first session with Rusty and Patricia, but I sure found out in a hurry!

Rusty's anger and frustration showed all over his face when he came in that first day. This father and pastor was very much a "regular guy" in most areas, including his personality. He was down-to-earth with no pretensions. What you saw was pretty much what you got, and I got both barrels! Rusty was furious that his older son, Paul, could have the impudence to refuse to obey and follow his father's plans for his future. Paul, it turned out, wanted to go into the military after high school instead of attending the Bible Institute. Rusty was determined that Paul would have the advantages that he had missed. He could not comprehend why his son would choose a path other than what his parents wanted for him. He was confused and angry and felt like a failure as a father, even though both Paul and his younger brother, Alex, were great students and very well thought of by everyone.

Where then was this perceived failure? Paul planned to enter the military, which would provide him with a free college education, which in turn would provide him with a career path within the military system. Paul was not being rebellious, in my opinion, by differing from his parents in the view of the path his life should take. Rusty shared with me that he was not able to talk to Paul about this without becoming angry with him. He stated more than once that Paul was choosing to go outside the "sphere of protection" God provides for those who follow parental guidance, and this was the cause of his frustration. Rusty and, to a lesser extent Patricia, believed that children should always follow parental guidance no matter what the age or circumstances; the only time children should choose for themselves was when their parents are deceased or unable to communicate. Rusty was quick to cite Old Testament passages he saw as supporting his power as father and Paul's error in choosing to do otherwise. Our first session ended with Rusty and his wife agreeing to return for a second visit and to seek parenting examples in the New Testament for discussion during the next session.

The second session with Rusty and Patricia revealed that Paul had shown no willingness to give in and change his plans, and that Rusty had been unable to find specific examples of parenting in the New Testament, especially as they might apply to the situation facing his family. We talked for a little while about why that might be and examined the possibility that God just might have a life plan for Paul different from what his parents wished. We discussed trusting God for all things, even the lives and direction of grown children. We explored how God had worked in the lives of Rusty and of Patricia, leading up to salvation, the call to the pastorate, and, now, the decisions Paul was making. We further examined the possibility that Rusty was usurping the role of the indwelling Holy Spirit in his son's life and discussed whether he was aware that he might be doing this. He admitted that he was not, but Patricia quietly said that she thought Rusty was being too controlling with Paul.

Our third session followed a visit Rusty had made to the dean of the Bible Institute, a man I knew well, and who did not hold the same strict interpretation of the parental role in choosing life plans for grown children. I sensed a change in Rusty. He was more calm and at ease than I had ever seen him. When I asked what had been going on, he quickly and happily responded that it had been such a relief to learn that God really was in charge of *all* aspects of his life and the life of his family. He had decided that the best he could do, under God, was to advise and pray for his children and then trust in God to direct them.

Rusty claimed that he did not want to be so strict with Paul but felt that such intervention was what God expected of a father. Patricia seemed very pleased and commented that things had been much better at home. I suggested to them that they might be surprised at the eventual decision Paul would make, knowing that many children and young adults make decisions in line with parental expectations once the pressure to agree is off. Young adults, we decided, needed to feel responsible for their own decisions, and they could be expected to resist excessive pressure to conform to parental desires.

I wish I could take credit for the change in Rusty. I knew in my heart that God had used the dean and me to help Rusty biblically align his thoughts and prayers in a more Holy Spirit–focused way. We talked about the joys of *really* trusting God, especially when we parents know in our hearts that we cannot be in total control as our children grow to maturity. They really needed to "let go and let God," and once they had taken this step, their problem melted away. Of course, Rusty and Patricia would still experience anxiety and concern as their sons created lives of their own, but as Christian parents, they could do only their best and then step back to watch God work in their children's lives. We ended the final session by reading aloud together Matthew 6:33 (NIV): "But seek first His kingdom and His righteousness, and all these things will be given to you as well. Therefore do not worry about tomorrow."

Suggestions for Follow-Up

Issues of control may be deeply rooted in the psyche and personality of your client. If the behavior is pervasive and debilitating, you may want to explore the genesis of the need to control, an exploration that may prove time-consuming and difficult. The need to control often stems from a childhood or other previous life experience involving a sense of threat by the unknown. Many Christians believe that perfect obedience to God (impossible, of course) will reveal God's perfect will, not only for oneself but also for others. This is often an arrogant and power-driven conviction that can ruin a family or a relationship.

Patience and occasional follow-up are recommended with a formerly controlling client. As with other addictive behaviors, surrendering control is not easy or quick. Trusting in God is the only solution.

Contraindications

Sadly, the need to control can be a symptom of depression and helplessness. Make sure you are "beginning at the beginning" with your client and resist drawing a client into intense counseling for a problem that is, in fact, secondary to another.

Resources for Professionals

Collins, G. (1993). *The biblical basis of Christian counseling for people helpers.* Colorado Springs, CO: NavPress.

Flather, D. (1995). *The resource guide for Christian counselors.* Grand Rapids, MI: Baker Books.

Resources for Clients

Haggai, J. (2004). *How to win over worry.* Eugene, OR: Harvest House Publishers.

Jeremiah, D. (2000). *When your world falls apart.* Nashville, TN: W. Publishing Group, a division of Thomas Nelson, Inc.

Morris, J. (2003). *From worry to worship: A 30-day guide to overcoming inferiority.* Birmingham, AL: New Hope Publishers.

Related Scripture

> I keep asking that the God of our Lord Jesus Christ, the glorious Father, may give you the Spirit of wisdom and revelation, so that you may know him better. (Ephesians 1:17 NIV)
>
> And do not grieve the Holy Spirit of God, with whom you were sealed for the day of redemption. (Ephesians 4:30 NIV)
>
> But we ought always to thank God for you, brothers loved by the Lord, because from the beginning God chose you to be saved through the sanctifying work of the Spirit and through belief in the truth. (2 Thessalonians 2:13 NIV)

Let Go and Let God!

Sample Handout:

Let Go and Let God!

– 25 –

Parenting After Divorce

David R. Miller
Lori Marie Figueroa

Guiding Scripture

By wisdom a house is built, and through understanding it is established; through knowledge its rooms are filled with rare and beautiful treasures.

Proverbs 24:3-4 (NIV)

Type of Contribution: Exercise, Handout

Objective

Only the stress a parent feels when a child is seriously ill or dies exceeds the stress that parents feel after divorce. Typically, following divorce, one parent is awarded primary custody and the other parent, now called the absent parent, is allowed to have visitation and is required to provide some measure of financial child support. Sound divorce research clearly indicates that the single, custodial parent needs many kinds of support and encouragement to maintain a good home for the children. This often includes counseling. Single parents ask for counseling primarily for child management and discipline concerns, but also for addressing feelings of loneliness and isolation.

Divorced families are calling on Christian counselors to provide counseling that will lead to more effective parenting by the single parent as well as improved development and adaptation by the children. This is a very serious counseling responsibility, and counselors should not agree to engage in such counseling unless they are prepared professionally and spiritually to be involved for the long term. Once a counseling relationship is established, counselors can expect to remain involved with these families long after the weekly work of counseling concludes. Counselors can expect to receive phone calls and return visits for months, even years, as the children grow and the lives of the family members change. Counseling single parents is unlike any other form of helping. If counselors accept this responsibility, they should see themselves as the helping arm of God administering grace, love, and support to these parents and families.

Rationale for Use

Christians are as likely to feel confused about the place of God in the divorce tragedy as would anyone else. As with any traumatic event, people ask why, even when not truly expect-

The Christian Therapist's Notebook

doi:10.1300/5334_26

ing an answer. They ask, not out of disbelief, but because of being human and unable to do anything else.

This is where Christian counseling comes in. Important truths, shared in an empathic and caring way, if the parents are willing, will help resolve uncertainties and bring the postdivorce family into an even closer and more beneficial walk with the Lord. Christian counselors are conduits for God's grace to hurting people, and few hurt more deeply than the newly divorced Christian single parent.

Instructions

First, the responsibility of parents to build a home for their children is not dependent upon marital status. While God provides special protection for "the fatherless," the biblical duties assigned to parents are not reduced for the divorced parent. Consider the promise found in Psalm 10:14 (NIV): "But you, O God, do see trouble and grief; you consider it to take it in hand. The victim commits himself to you; you are the helper of the fatherless." These ancient words show the commonality of disruption to the family. In biblical times, one can only imagine how many mothers died in childbirth and how many fathers died prematurely due to wars and accidents, as well as the general shortened life span due to inadequate hygiene and poor medical care. Surely, numerous single-parent homes existed in biblical times, and yet we see no special exception for the struggling parent. It is as if God is saying, "I will help you, but what I expect from you as a parent is not changed because your marital status has been altered."

God provides protection and prayer access, but He does not do the parenting. While Christians can rely on the guidance of the Holy Spirit when in need of direction and on the promise of answered prayer when they need support, all parents must do the best job of parenting possible. God empathizes with the fears and anxieties of single parents, but He does not remove them from the situation. Single parents may feel like quitting, but they must remember this: "No temptation has seized you except what is common to man. And God is faithful; he will not let you be tempted beyond what you can bear. But when you are tempted, he will also provide a way out so that you can stand up under it" (1 Corinthians 10:13 [NIV]).

While God does not exempt single parents from responsibility, neither does He restrict His blessings to single-parent families. A family headed by one parent has equal status in God's eyes. In human terms, when one parent leaves the home, the parental wisdom reduces to half. However, the guidance from the Holy Spirit is not reduced by any circumstances short of spiritual rebellion. The single mother or father with custody may rest assured that God is still God no matter what the circumstances and that, while most humans may feel out of touch with God at times, He is never out of touch with His creation.

A third and very important point in this discussion relates to the nature and makeup of the "traditional" family. While it seems clear from scripture that God intends a family to begin when a male and a female unite in godly marriage, later to produce children, it is also clear that the Bible does not reveal much at all about what a typical or normal family should look like. The Bible reveals next to nothing about the family of Peter or John or Paul. Can a family with live-in relatives, such as cousins, aunts, or grandparents, still consider themselves a family? As a marriage matures and children grow and exit the home to start their own families, are the parents still a family when it's only them at home? Is a stepfamily still a family? Consider all the stepfamilies that must have existed in biblical times, with premature death and other health problems commonly taking parents from their children. God simply does not provide a specific picture of a traditional family.

The Bible describes the family in terms of what it does rather than what it is. The Bible provides precious little detail about "ideal" family makeup but offers much about what a family should do. The mind-set to instill in clients who are single parents is that they are not, repeat not, fundamentally different from any other parent. More stress, less support, more hours working, and fewer hours playing make up the short-term lot that befalls single parents. Nevertheless, from God's perspective, single parents differ only in their circumstances, not in their position or status in the kingdom of God. The church should hold Christian single parents in the same high regard as any other parent. Single parents are likely to be, along with their children, the victims of someone else's sin and not their own. The church must be sensitive to special needs and opportunities for service to single-parent families, but the church should treat such families no differently than any other "nontraditional" family created by the death of a parent or other special circumstances beyond their control.

When counseling single parents, the stories of their lives and marriages are very important. Listen carefully and patiently to the stories that unfold. Be prepared for tears and expressions of anger, confusion, and questions without answers. Christians who have experienced the departure of a spouse, for any reason, are likely to manifest symptoms similar to those of post-traumatic stress disorder (PTSD). These symptoms include insomnia, flashbacks to either good or bad events, dreams with a desertion theme, fears and anxieties about their ability to survive this terriblelife event, anxiety caused by coming into contact with elements of the previous life, such as church, neighborhood, in-laws, visitation by ex-spouse, and many others.

Single parents often feel that no one in their families or social circles understands how they really feel. As a counselor to such parents, you need to provide as much empathic understanding as possible. The issue of self-blame will come up in counseling and needs gentle and compassionate confrontation. Much spiritual and psychological damage can result from unmanaged self-blame following a divorce. Christian counselors help by asking gentle, open-ended questions to aid the single parent in dealing with self-blame. Consider the following examples:

> "Joan, I hear you saying that the affair your husband had, which led to the divorce, was partly your fault. Are you saying that you had the power to control your husband's feelings for that other woman?"
>
> "Sounds like you blame yourself for your husband beating you. You mentioned that if you did not have dinner ready exactly on time, your husband would become enraged and get violent with you. Are you saying that if you did everything perfectly, your marriage would still be intact?"
>
> "You have mentioned how much you have changed physically in the years since your marriage and that if you were more attractive and younger, your husband wouldn't have had to look elsewhere. I guess that means your husband looks just as young and attractive as when you were married. Is that right? And do you mean that your husband's behavior is understandable and acceptable because you are not twenty-two anymore?"
>
> "Julie, you feel like a failure because your marriage ended, and you also feel that God let you down by not healing your marriage. However, your husband declared himself homosexual, correct? Is that not the reason he abandoned you and the children? The Bible clearly teaches that one person is not responsible for the sinful actions of another. God didn't let you down, your husband did, and even though God did not heal your marriage, He can surely heal you and the children."

Counselor responses such as these might seem somewhat blunt and confrontational, but at times in the counseling process, a counselor must bring the client to the point of facing reality. Confront in love and under the guidance of the Holy Spirit, but continue to do much more than "just" listen.

Five Important Self-Help Actions for the Single Parent

This brief listing of behaviors, actions, and attitudes, if employed, can greatly help a single parent with custody maintain a godly home for self and children.

1. *Take care of yourself.* Consider this statement: "If Momma ain't happy, ain't nobody happy!" Of course, no one can simply remove the pain and sadness that divorce causes, and happiness will not be common in the first months postdivorce, but single parents must know that their attitudes and feelings have great impact on the children. For example, a mother may find the need to set aside personal time to relax, get some exercise, go to a movie or out to dinner with friends, anything to break the pattern or worry and stress that tends to follow a divorce. Even if this means hiring a babysitter or asking a family member to assist with child care, a mother's state of mind is too important to the children's welfare to allow her to slip into depression and anxiety. Attending church is another way single parents can take care of themselves. The command not to "forsake" church applies to all but is especially important for stressed-out and worried single parents.
2. *Avoid extremes.* The tendency for many new single parents is to slide to one extreme or the other in terms of child care and management. Single moms often become either total pushovers who give in to every whine and demand from the children or drill sergeants who tolerate no childish behavior and rule with an iron hand. Balance is the key to successful single parenting, and extremes are usually a fear reaction by parents. When this form of extreme reaction is developing, it is time to confront the client gently about parenting issues.
3. *Resist isolation.* Even a divorce that is unavoidable due to abuse, desertion, or criminal behavior carries with it unpleasant consequences. Christian single parents tend to feel embarrassed and guilty after their divorce, despite the misbehavior of the other spouse. Feeling guilty and embarrassed, single parents tend to isolate themselves from family and friends at a time when they need more support than ever before. They stop attending church. They refuse invitations to go out for an evening with friends. Choir members leave the choir. Sunday school teachers give up their classes. AWANA leaders resign. As a counselor, encourage your client to maintain helpful relationships as an adjunct to the counseling you are providing. One or two hours a week with a counselor is no substitute for church and an active social life.
4. *Access recovery resources.* Excellent books and videos for single parents are available at any moderate to large Christian bookstore. Larger churches may sponsor weekend workshops for single parents. Of course, solid Christian counseling is a primary resource for divorce recovery. Caution the client considering such resources that no person, no matter how well educated, can possibly be an expert on his or her family. The best anyone can do is offer suggestions that have helped many families, with the provision that one size does not fit all when it comes to parenting. Be sure to caution the single-parent client that the expert he or she is listening to or reading is communicating in helpful generalities that may not be appropriate for his or her situation.
5. *Let God teach you what you need to learn from this experience.* Becoming angry with God is an understandable reaction to divorce but it is also unproductive. God has a plan for the client's life; the client must have faith that, no matter how dark the days following separation and divorce, God will bring the client through them successfully. Clients should be encouraged to take psychoactive medicines carefully, if at all. Sometimes, medicating away the fear and anxiety just prolongs the recovery time.

Note: Encourage the client to use the "Single-Parent Review" handout at the end of this chapter to help the client place events and feelings into a godly perspective.

Vignette

The Christian university where Linda and I taught employed both Bob and Terry. Bob was director of maintenance for the university and Terry worked in the office of the registrar. They had two children, Amy, age thirteen, and Bobby, age ten. All seemed well with this family, at least on the outside. My wife and I knew Terry better than we knew her husband, Bob. As teachers, we visited the registrar's office on a regular basis, but we rarely saw Bob. We knew from conversations that this couple had married young, prior to their conversion to Christianity. They appeared to be dedicated Christians who worked hard at being Christians and good parents for their children. All we knew about this family was positive.

In my office at the university counseling center, I received a call from Terry. As I returned her call, I assumed she had a concern about one of the children. As a child, adolescent, and family therapist, I found that most of my contacts, such as the one from Terry, involved children as their focus, but not this time. Terry was in tears and said that she needed to see me right away, if possible. As was customary for employees of the university, I made immediate arrangements for her.

Terry came in later that same day, still in tears, and told me that Bob had confessed to a longstanding affair with another woman, which had produced a child. Bob had asked for a divorce and had already begun to move out of his present home and in with his new love interest. The children had not been told yet, but Terry was sure they must suspect what was happening. This had unraveled all within the past twenty-four hours. Terry was crushed!

I listened to her story and tried to empathize with the grief and sadness she was facing; mostly I just let her talk. Tears flowed. Anger flamed. Questions were asked that could not be answered, and God was doubted. I listened without much comment but with much interest and concern. I could sense only a little of what this Christian wife and mother was feeling, but I knew that, right now, in the early phase of counseling, I could help the most by saying the least.

On a practical level, Terry was secure with her job at the university, and she felt that she would probably be able to remain in the family home because it was mostly paid off, due to a family legacy received some years earlier. The children were doing well in the Christian school connected to the university, and Terry felt sure that neither would want to move out to be with their father. Bob's job was apparently very demanding and had kept him away or on call for much of the time they had been at the university. In other words, according to Terry, the children really had not seen much of their father for the past few years. Only now was Terry realizing that perhaps all the time Bob said he was working, he had really been with the other woman. More tears! Though I doubted that Terry heard me, I mentioned that Bob could lose his job over this once word reached the leadership of the university. She showed no reaction.

We scheduled a second appointment later that same week. We discussed the fluidity of the situation, and I reminded Terry that things could change rapidly one way or another in just a few days. We prayed; rather, I prayed while Terry wept, and we ended the first session. I recommended that Terry tell the children what had happened, but she should avoid saying anything negative about Bob. I wanted her to remember that, just in case there was reconciliation, she did not want to put negative images into the children's heads, images that could never be removed once in place.

By the time our second counseling session took place, Bob had moved out and the children had been told. Terry showed fewer tears but more anger, which was expected. I encouraged her to keep expressing herself, and I reminded her that she was completely safe and free from judgment in my office. The few comments I made were either to keep Terry talking or to remind her that I was 100 percent on her side in this matter. No matter what Bob might say about his reasons for the affair, he alone was responsible for the terrible thing he had done to his wife and children.

Terry asked whether I thought the children needed to see a counselor as well. I responded, "Not yet," and suggested she wait until the situation had settled down a little. Of course, if she saw any worrisome signs in either of the children, we would arrange for counseling right away. I told Terry that, because I was her counselor, it would be better for the children, when the time was right, to see another person in the counseling center. I would arrange that at that time. She seemed relieved that her children appeared to be coping better than she had expected, but I reminded her that these were early days yet, and we needed to remain watchful with the children.

Our third session revealed more anger but also more optimism from Terry about her chances of surviving the apparently impending divorce. Bob had not been back to the home since his initial leaving, but he had called the children once or twice on the phone. Amy, the thirteen-year-old, had refused to talk to her father, but Bobby had seemed okay taking his calls. As is very typical with oldest daughters, Amy was firmly on her mother's side in this tragedy, and I encouraged Terry to be patient with Amy and not make any demands on her to accept contact from her father. We discussed at length the issue that Bob, by his immorality and abandonment of the family, had surrendered all his rights as husband and father. He should consider anything positive he received from Terry or the children as a gift and not something he had a right to have. I encouraged Terry to talk to Amy about being respectful of her father, even while she was distancing herself from him. No, Amy did not "owe" her father respect, but this is what God would want from her anyway.

By the time our fourth session began, Terry was beginning to adapt very slowly to her changed status. She was seeing herself differently, but not quite ready to see herself as a potentially "single" person. She was a little more accustomed to being without a husband and doing more things on her own. To her credit, she had continued to attend and be involved in her church. Even though the children initially resisted, Terry insisted that they continue with their youth and children's activities at church. Terry had talked to her pastor and to each child's youth leader about the change in their family. This was a wise decision on Terry's part and indicated to me that she was making a good adjustment to the change in the family. She shared that she had had no contact with Bob since the day he left, but that Bob had been putting money in their joint account, which relieved her. I continued to listen and support without making many suggestions.

Our sessions continued, and the children began a counseling relationship with another counselor in our counseling center. Gradually, Terry's session changed from one per week to one every other week. This was her choice, but I saw enough improvement over the months of counseling that I did not feel the need to object. Over the course of our time with each other, I saw Terry maintain her role as mother and add to that role the one of primary and sole caretaker. This was a good indicator of how she was doing, and I was pleased to see her progress.

Throughout the counseling process, I offered insights and comments related to how God might be working in her life and the lives of her children, as well as providing parenting information on such subjects as discipline, chores, school, and contact with the children's father. At the time of our last formal counseling session, Amy, then fourteen, had agreed to go with Bobby to visit their father as long as she did not have to meet his "girlfriend," to which their father agreed. Bobby seemed to be adjusting well, as long as he did not have to lose his father completely. As always, I left future sessions up to Terry, but I let her know that I was convinced she had done a great job of adapting to such a terrible situation. She committed to remaining in church and not letting Bob's behavior destroy her Christian testimony. Overall, this family did an excellent job of dealing with the sin of their father.

The situation of Terry, Bob, and their children is a reminder that bad things can and do happen to good people. In no sense did Terry or the children deserve what happened to them. The bad stuff was all Bob and no one else, period. Terry needed compassionate support and good, solid, Bible-based information that would help her to move through the process of change; this she received from others and me. She was wise and strong and insisted on being treated like the solid Christian woman she was, regardless of the failure of her husband. All the while, her church family continued to support her and the children. They will never be the same after the divorce, but, in some sense, they might be better for seeing the way God protected them and provided for them during the darkest days they had ever known.

Suggestions for Follow-Up

Follow-up in cases of divorce involves offering availability through phone contacts and offers of emergency counseling sessions, as needed. Because my wife and I were members of Terry's church, it was relatively easy to see how they were doing, while not being intrusive or curious.

Contraindications

Suicidal and self-destructive behaviors are always a risk when a family is going through a traumatic experience such as divorce. If others observe or report any such behaviors, take proper action. Such action might involve consulting other family members, recommending hospitalization, or referral for medical intervention such as antianxiety medications. While none of these options was needed for Terry and her children, the possibility always exists.

Resources for Professionals

Miller, D.R. (1994). *Counseling families after divorce.* Dallas, TX: Word, Inc.
Popenoe, D. (1996). *Life without father.* New York: The Free Press.

Resources for Clients

Cloninger, C. (2000). *When the glass slipper doesn't fit.* Birmingham, AL: New Hope Publishers.
Sweet, R. (2003). *A woman's guide to healing the heartbreak of divorce.* Peabody, MA: Hendrickson Publishers, Inc.
Visher, E.B. and Visher, J.S. (1991). *How to win as a step-family.* New York: Brunner/Mazel Publishers.

Related Scripture

> For the eyes of the Lord range throughout the earth to strengthen those whose hearts are fully committed to him. (2 Chronicles 16:9a NIV)

> The eyes of the Lord are on the righteous and his ears are attentive to their cry; the face of the Lord is against them those who do evil, to cut off the memory of them from the earth. The righteous cry out, and the Lord hears them; he delivers them from all their troubles. The Lord is close to the brokenhearted and saves those who are crushed in spirit. (Psalm 34:15-18 NIV)

> Be careful to obey all these regulations I am giving you, so that it may always go well with you and your children after you, because you will be doing what is good and right in the eyes of the Lord your God. (Deuteronomy 12:28 NIV)

Single Parent Review Sheet

My personal, God-given, strengths are:

1.

2.

3.

4.

5.

The strengths of my children and my extended family are:

1.

2.

3.

4.

5.

Some of the things God may want me to learn from this experience are:

1.

2.

3.

4.

5.

The five most important things I need to pray about are:

1.

2.

3.

4.

5.

– 26 –

The Broken Bough

David R. Miller

Guiding Scripture

But if anyone causes one of these little ones who believe in me to sin,
it would be better for him to have a large millstone hung around his neck
and to be drowned in the depths of the sea.

Matthew 18:6 (NIV)

Rock-a-bye, baby, in the treetop,
When the wind blows, the cradle will rock,
When the bough breaks, the cradle will fall,
And down will come baby, cradle and all.

Anonymous nursery rhyme

Type of Contribution: Exercise, Handout

Objective

Divorce has become the broken bough in the lives of today's children. Divorce brings children crashing down into a changed world beyond fixing. Children fear abandonment more than injury or death. A certain level of mental, emotional, and spiritual maturity must exist in a child or adolescent to enable a grasp of such concepts as death and serious injury, but every child knows what it feels like to be lost. Every child has had the experience of feeling separated from a parent, even if only for a moment, and every child understands the sense of being lost. Children fear monsters less than losing a mother or father and death less than separation from parents. To a child, having parents divorce compares to the feeling of being lost.

When parental divorce enters the life of a child, everything changes. In spite of reassurances from loving and concerned parents, the child will feel abandoned by the absent parent and may feel betrayed by the parent who stays at home. Among adults surveyed about their worst memory from childhood, those whose parents had divorced overwhelmingly chose that event as the worst, while adults from intact families offered a wide range of other traumatic events as the most difficult of their lives (Hodges, 1986).

The Christian Therapist's Notebook

doi:10.1300/5334_27

Rationale for Use

James, the half-brother of Jesus, emphasized an important element of Christianity when he said, "Religion that God our Father accepts as pure and faultless is this: to look after orphans and widows in his or her distress and to keep oneself from being polluted by the world" (James 1:27 NIV). A concern for the fatherless is as old as recorded history and was a very important principle of Christian life in the early church.

In present-day America, approximately half of all children will spend some part of their birth-to-age-eighteen years living with just one parent, and in more than 95 percent of such situations, the single parent will be the mother. If the church family is to be of aid to "the fatherless," it needs to be aware of the problems that are all too common in single-parent families (Hodges, 1986).

Christian counselors are called on to recognize that in some instances divorce is the only solution, such as in cases involving sexual perversion, child or spousal abuse, criminality, or untreated addictions. While it is fair to say that no divorce pleases God and that people should do all that is possible to help to heal a struggling marriage, the reality is that people in postdivorce families seek out counselors for help. It does little good to rail against the evils of divorce. People call on counselors to help identify and facilitate their transition to a better place in life.

Of single-parent boys and girls, only one in three averaged monthly contact with the absent parent, and just one in six saw his or her absent parent once a week or more. The sad fact is that fewer than 50 percent of all children of divorce saw their absent parent even once in the previous twelve months (Hodges, 1986). One can only imagine the emotional upheaval experienced by children who are essentially abandoned by a parent. Father loss particularly affects boys, who, in effect, are left to grow up without a male role model to emulate.

Divorce and parent absence greatly affect children's education. For example, 38 percent of elementary age single-parent children were low academic achievers, compared to 24 percent low achievers for children from intact families. In high school, 34 percent of single-parent children were low achievers, compared to 23 percent of teenagers from intact families. Single-parent children and teenagers are also more likely to be late or truant and to face school disciplinary measures at a much higher rate. Three times as many single-parent children and teenagers face expulsion from school, compared to those with two parents at home, and these adolescents are twice as likely to drop out of school (Hodges, 1986). Clearly, counselors are going to have many parents coming for help with their misbehaving or underachieving children and teens.

God has success rather than failure in mind for families. The writer of Proverbs summed up God's expectations well when he wrote, "By wisdom a house is built, and by understanding it is established, and by knowledge the rooms are filled with all precious and pleasant riches" (Proverbs 24:3-4 NIV).

Single-parent homes deprive children of the wisdom of two parents. Two parents are clearly better than one when it comes to leading a family. Emotional support is often more limited in the family of the absent parent. Grandparents, for example, often become less involved with the children over time. The absence of one parent may hinder sex role development in the same-gender child. Adolescent discipline at home tends to become a greater concern in single-parent families. Children may experience stress and worry about the safety of the custodial parent and may refuse to go to school or day care after a divorce or separation. The custodial parent will probably have less time to spend with children due to the need to manage the home alone, and children may not be able to participate in sports and other after-school activities because of the need to be at home. Decreased parental attention may lead to excessive exposure to television and participation in other activities that parents would not allow if present in the home. Counselors face no shortage of issues to confront when counseling children from single-parent families.

Instructions

Even though the focus is likely to be on the child whose parents have divorced, it is crucial to spend one or two sessions with the parent or parents. In rare cases, there is an opportunity to meet and listen to the noncustodial parent, but do not expect this to occur often. Typically, sufficient animosity exists between the divorced parents to prevent cooperation from the absent parent.

In sessions with the parent, learn about how the parent and children are adapting to a single-parent lifestyle. Use the following questions (see also the chapter handout) to facilitate the discussion:

1. How are you doing financially since the divorce? Are you getting appropriate child support? Have you returned to work outside the home since the divorce?
2. How are you experiencing living without a spouse at home?
3. How have the children expressed their fears and anxieties since the divorce?
4. Is your ex-spouse keeping in touch with the children?
5. What are the children like when they return home after spending time with the absent parent? Do they seem to want to visit this parent?
6. How are the children doing in school? Have you talked with their school guidance counselor and teachers about the change in the family?
7. How is discipline going for you? Do you have any special concerns?
8. Have you seen any significant change in how the children are sleeping, eating, or playing?
9. Are the children asking you questions about the divorce, and, if so, how do you answer them?
10. What is the role of God and church in your life now? Are you getting support from your religious community?

While asking for this information from the parent in the first session or two, remember to build an empathic relationship with him or her to facilitate a successful counseling experience with the children. Meet with the parent for a few minutes either before or after the sessions with the children. The parent should be able to provide a progress report on how the counseling is helping and discuss any new concerns that may have surfaced.

Focus the first session with the children on relationship building. Have patience. You cannot hurry a child and still get good results. Be prepared to play games as icebreakers, watch videos relating to how other children have managed the divorce of their parents, and "just talk" about school, friends, family, and anything else the children want to discuss. Do not be surprised or disappointed if children resist the counseling process. This is to be expected. Children are warned all of their lives to avoid talking to strangers, and until a counseling relationship is established, the counselor is a stranger. Go slowly, and play a lot in the beginning sessions.

Following sessions should allow further investigation into the children's thought processes and feelings. Use coloring books (if age appropriate) and "finish this story" exercises to get the children started in the early stages of each session. Focus on reinforcing the children's adjustment and always talk positively about both parents. If the children express anger about their parents, listen but do not agree. However, do not argue the point either. If a child asks, "Is it okay for me to get mad at my dad?" say, "What really matters is what you think or feel. There are no rules about how a young person like you should react. So you can say anything you want here, and I won't get upset or tell your mother."

As the counseling process continues, keep checking with the parent to see if the children are realizing and meeting the goals you established together in the beginning. Terminate the counseling when the appropriate goals have been achieved and no new issues have entered the picture, or when the parent believes enough improvement has been achieved. Remember that coming to counseling sessions is inconvenient for everyone, and especially so for a single parent trying to do everything alone. Appropriate termination will be a welcome accomplishment.

Vignette

Joshua was ten years old and an only child when I met with him for divorce adjustment counseling. Joshua's father has primary custody, and Joshua had been living with his father since his parents' divorce thirteen months earlier. My initial session with his father revealed that the divorce had been very acrimonious, and even though Joshua's mother had previously agreed to the custody arrangements, she now planned to contest the agreement and wanted either sole or equal custody of their son. I never had an opportunity to meet the mother, but the story I heard from both Joshua and his father was that she had become a most difficult person to live with before the divorce and her anger had grown greatly since.

My initial session with Joshua was positive. He was a verbal child who was not at all reluctant to talk and share his feelings with me. Joshua appeared to be genuinely frightened about the possibility that he would have to begin spending more time with his mother. He did not want to see her when his visits were scheduled, and even though his father was good about insisting that he spend those scheduled times with her, Joshua stated, in the strongest terms, that he "hated" the visits. When asked about why he had such strong feelings about the visits, he reported that his mother continually put his father down and tried to bribe or threaten him into taking her side. Clearly, Joshua was and had been closer to his father, and the more his mother tried to persuade him to take her side, the stronger his resistance became. Thus, the custody battle began.

Joshua had been raised in the church. He had made an independent decision to accept Jesus as his personal savior at age seven. He and his father attended a good church in the area, and Joshua was active in AWANA and Sunday school. This is all to the good, of course, but Joshua was also hearing a lot at church about obeying and honoring parents. He had some serious questions about what to do in regard to his mother. Should he argue with her when she said mean things about his father? What should he say when his mother told him she loved him much more than his father did and that he would have a better life and more fun if he lived with her? Joshua was a sharp kid and sensed that his mother was trying to manipulate him, but we needed to talk about how he could handle the situation.

My basic approach to helping Joshua with his mother was to emphasize that he, even as a child, had a right to close his ears to nasty things said about either parent. I suggested that, when his mother went on one of her reported tirades about his father, he say, respectively but firmly, that it made him uncomfortable when she said negative things about his father and that he wanted to go to his room. I strongly emphasized to Joshua not to argue with his mother but instead just not respond. Of course, this would be difficult for any child, but Joshua needed to know that he was not being a bad son by refusing to listen to his mother's negative perceptions about his father. We engaged in role-play to illustrate an appropriate way of handling the situation. Acting as his mother, I would repeat things that Joshua had reported she had said. Then Joshua and I would practice his response—what he would say and how he would say it. The emphasis was on respect for his mother combined with his right not to listen to her negativity.

Here are some examples of the role-playing:

MOM: Joshua, you know every child is supposed to be with his mother. That's the way God intended it to be, and that's all I am trying to do.

JOSHUA: Mom, you know I love you, but I'm just a kid. I can't help what the court decided about where I should go. It isn't my fault.

MOM: I wish your father wouldn't be so hard to get along with. He's always fighting with me. That's the real reason we got divorced in the first place. I hope you understand that the divorce is all your father's fault.

JOSHUA: Can I go to my room now?

MOM: If we go to court to get the custody changed, will you help me? You know how much I love you, Joshua. All I want is the best for you. You know that, don't you?

JOSHUA: Mom, it makes me feel badly when you talk to me like that. I am just a kid, and I don't think it's fair to put me in the middle of the fight you are having with Dad. Can I go to my room now?

These role-plays helped Joshua learn the right words to say when put into an uncomfortable spot by his mother. We rehearsed these and many others on a regular basis in our sessions, and Joshua would suggest new ones after visiting his mother. As he left a session for the week, anticipating a weekend visit with his mother, I would say to him, "Now, Joshua, are you remembering the answers we rehearsed? Remember to treat your mom with respect, even when she says things that make you feel uncomfortable."

My role as counselor with Joshua was one of support, analysis, and problem resolution. Joshua needed support to do and say the right things when he was with his mother. He needed to have an adult such as myself tell him that his feelings were justified and that any other child would feel the same. I knew that children generally do not talk with their friends about family problems, so Joshua had likely never discussed this situation with anyone outside his family, except me. Having no grounds for comparison, Joshua needed input from me, as well as from his father, to confirm that he was behaving correctly.

The specific area of analysis came up when Joshua wanted to know why his parents had gotten the divorce, why they could not get along even now, and why his mother was behaving the way she was. He wanted to know who was at fault in the divorce, and he, as with many children in his situation, feared that maybe he was somehow the cause of it all. We explored each of these concerns together.

Problem solving became our priority either when Joshua was getting ready to visit his mother or when he had just returned from a visit. These situations were equally anxiety producing for Joshua. We worked on strategies he could use to deal with this anxiety, including role-playing, as described earlier; writing letters to his mother and father, which he would probably never send but which would allow him to express his thoughts and feelings about the breakup of his family; and the empty chair technique, wherein Joshua would speak to an empty chair as if he were talking to his mother or father. This allowed him to express his anger and other negative emotions in a safe and caring atmosphere.

Because Joshua was a Christian and a regular at church and Sunday school, I felt it appropriate to take a portion of each session, usually the last ten minutes, to share a Bible verse that I thought might be appropriate in helping Joshua. Some of the verses are included at the end of this chapter, and all focus on varying aspects of my client's concerns. They deal with justified and unjustified anger, respecting parents, dealing with sadness and depression, feeling responsible, and feeling like a failure. We explored what the Bible had to say about the guidance of the Holy Spirit for every believer, even children Joshua's age, and how we all needed to rely on godly guidance in times of trouble. It was important that Joshua be "armed" with biblical input that would prepare him to deal with both his present and his future concerns.

My counseling with Joshua terminated when his father took a job in a neighboring county. He was able to arrange counseling for his son in the immediate area, and though I wished I could have continued with Joshua, the move was the best thing for the family. I felt that I had done what I could to help this boy deal with, aside from God's intervention, an almost impossible problem. Often, Christian counselors have to deal with not knowing how counseling turns out for a client. I had no way of knowing what developed with Joshua and his family after they moved, and it would not be appropriate to make contact to find out. Even though Joshua's father had said he would "keep me posted," it did not really happen. I had the opportunity to share information with Joshua's new counselor in his new location, with written permission from Joshua's father, but that is the best I could do. Ambiguity such as this is one of the more difficult realities of Christian counseling.

Suggestions for Follow-Up

All a counselor can do in these situations is to invite the client to stay in touch after the termination of counseling. At times, counselors can schedule follow-up appointments for clients, but the reality is that clients rarely keep these appointments. If follow-up sessions are possible, use them to fine-tune coping strategies and solutions to better adapt to the always-unexpected changes in the client's life. Moreover, of course, the best follow-up strategy of all is prayer.

Contraindications

A child has to feel safe to benefit from counseling, and the strategies employed with Joshua posed no risks. Counselors should remain alert to signs of mental, emotional, or physical abuse and contact one of the local child protective agencies if any such signs surface.

Resources for Professionals

Coleman, W.L. (1998). *What children need to know when parents get divorced.* Minneapolis, MN: Bethany House.

Collins, G.R. (1995). *Family shock.* Wheaton, IL: Tyndale House Publishers.

Girard, L.W., and Freedman, J. (1991). *At Daddy's on Saturdays.* Morton Grove, IL: Albert Whitman and Company.

Hart, A. (1997). *Helpig children survive divorce.* Dallas, TX: Word, Inc.

Henderson, D.A., Thompson, C.L., and Rudolph, L.B. (2003). *Counseling children with infotrac.* Belmont, CA: Wadsworth.

Magid, K., and McKelvey, C.A. (1989). *High risk: Children without a conscience.* New York: Bantam Books.

Miller, D.R. (1994). *Counseling families after divorce.* Dallas, TX: Word, Inc.

Powell, J. (1999). *Talking about family breakup.* New York: Raintree Steck-Vaughn Publishers.

Resources for Clients

Blackstone-Ford, J., Ford, A., Ford, M., and Ford, S. (1998). *My parents are divorced too: A book for kids by kids.* Washington, DC: Magination.

Cole, J. (1997). *My parents' divorce (How do I feel about).* West Sussex, UK: Copper Beech Publishing.

Hodges, W.F. (1986). *Interventions for children of divorce: custody, access, and psychotherapy,* New York: John Wiley & Sons.

Kimball, G. (1994). *How to survive your parents' divorce: Kids' advice to kids.* Chico, CA: Equality Press.

Krasny-Brown, L., and Brown, M. (1986). *Dinosaurs divorce: A guide for changing families.* New York: Little, Brown and Company.

Lansky, V. (1998). *It's not your fault, Koko bear.* Minnetonka, MN: Book Peddlers.
Rankin, D., and Thomas, S. (1998). *Divorced but still my parents.* Austin, TX: Springboard.
Weitzman, E. (2003). *Let's talk about your parents' divorce.* New York: Rosen/PowerKids.

Related Scripture

Listen to your father, who gave you life, and do not despise your mother when she is old. (Proverbs 23:22 NIV)

I write to you, dear children, because your sins have been forgiven on account of his name. (1 John 2:12 NIV)

A wise son brings joy to his father, but a foolish man despises his mother. (Proverbs 15:20 NIV)

When I was a child, I talked like a child, I thought like a child, I reasoned like a child. When I became a man, I put childish ways behind me. (1 Corinthians 13:11 NIV)

If a man curses his father or mother, his lamp will be snuffed out in pitch darkness. (Proverbs 20:20 NIV)

Though my father and mother forsake me, the Lord will receive me. (Psalm 27:10 NIV)

Questions for Newly Single Parents

1. How are you experiencing living without a spouse at home?

2. Is your ex-spouse keeping in touch with the children?

3. How have the children expressed their fears and anxieties since the divorce?

4. How are you doing financially since the divorce? Are you getting appropriate child support? Have you returned to work outside the home since the divorce?

5. What are the children like when they return home after spending time with the absent parent? Do they seem to want to visit him or her?

6. How are the children doing in school? Have you talked with their school guidance counselor and teachers about the change in the family?

7. How is discipline going for you? Are there any special concerns?

8. Has there been any significant change in how the children are sleeping, eating, or playing?

9. Are the children asking you questions about the divorce, and if so, how do you answer them?

10. What is the role of God and church in your life now? Are you getting support from your religious community?

SECTION III: HOMEWORK, HANDOUTS, AND ACTIVITIES FOR CHILDREN AND ADOLESCENTS

– 27 –

Three Wishes

Philip J. Henry

Guiding Scripture

. . . he will give you the desires of your heart.

Psalm 37:4 (NIV)

Type of Contribution: Exercise, Handout

Objective

Children express the desires of their hearts while learning how to ask God for their requests. Doing so not only helps children with their current situations but also teaches them that God is a source of help and can be called on in future times of trouble.

Rationale for Use

Children are naturally curious about life. Their world is made up of play, both physical and emotional, that highlights their internal states of feelings, needs, hopes, and desires. This exercise seeks to use children's natural playfulness to help them address current distresses and concerns as well as to teach them deeper spiritual truths.

In scripture, we see that we are to respect the personhood of the child and his or her world and to take it seriously. Most of all, we are to help the child connect, in an age-appropriate way, with God, thereby helping that child find out how faithful and loving He is and how great a source of wisdom and comfort He can be. The child can then feel more confident to bring concerns to God and to begin understanding the walk of faith.

At times, children may have difficulty understanding themselves and their feelings. While this is normal for this stage of development, it can be problematic if children's feelings lead to unwise choices or if fears or other unwanted emotions begin to crowd out and intrude upon everyday life. This will inevitably impede healthy functioning in children. The therapist can help by encouraging the child to explore and express the feelings, needs, hopes, and dreams following experiences of these emotions. This is especially important if the possibility of trauma exists and there are areas where healing may need to occur.

The context of wishes is often a place that is tender or injured. The therapist should be very aware and familiar with the signs of abuse or trauma and explore these where this is appropriate. Throughout the process, the therapist should be aware of the child's cognitive, emotional, and spiritual development and identify the child's perception of God and the way He has worked in

The Christian Therapist's Notebook

doi:10.1300/5334_28

his or her life. This will aid in having the session fit with the needs of the child and his or her world.

By having the child imagine God granting him or her three wishes, you can assist the child in expressing his or her hopes, fears, and dreams. This insight can show how the child's thinking about God has developed and can aid your leading the child to a closer, more loving relationship with God.

Instructions

Take the time to talk with the child and connect relationally before you begin. Find out about his or her school friends, family, and life from his or her perspective. Then, introduce the "Three Wishes" exercise by saying, "If you had a wishing well and God gave you three wishes, what would you wish?" On the other hand, if the child is young enough and is willing, you might have him or her color or draw on "The Wishing Well" handout before starting. Then you might proceed by asking the child to imagine that God is offering him or her three wishes. Ask the child to write or draw on the handout what those three wishes might be.

Very often, the child will quickly become engaged in the task. Some children list or draw all three in only a few minutes. Other children, perhaps more inhibited because of newness to counseling or insufficient comfort level, take more time to warm up to the exercise. Do not be discouraged by this; rather, let the child have the time and space to explore, feel, and think at his or her own pace. As the child works, watch how he or she approaches the task: Is the child direct, bold, reluctant, hesitant, confident, or distracted? This observation will give you some idea of how the child faces the tasks in his or her life. If the child does draw, look at the colors chosen, and the movement that the child makes as he or she draws. Observe his or her motor control, facial expression, and ability or inability to concentrate. Note what features in drawing take the most time or have the most detail. All of these observations will help you understand the world of the child and are important while finding and defining the context for helping him or her.

As the child works, explore why he or she wants each of the wishes and how it would affect other people and situations in his or her life. Engage the child in a dialogue about what his or her wishes mean. (*Note:* For some children this will not work because such questions will only disturb the focus on their task. For these children be patient and wait until they finish. Once the work is complete, such children are usually more than willing to explain, in detail, the choices and thoughts about the wishes.) Be curious. Most of the time wishes stem from other issues that surround important matters in the child's life. Be aware of themes for wishes relating to success, failure, sadness, competition, mastery, family, disappointment, weakness, strength, fear, or anxiety, for example. Explore with the child other areas having similar themes. Find out how far each of these themes extends into the child's life and how each influences the child's thoughts, feelings, and behaviors.

If there is time and the child is willing, ask him or her about what would happen if the wishes were granted. Explore how the child's world would change if each wish were granted. What specifically would be different? How would he or she be different? You may also discuss what would occur if the wishes were not granted. Realize that this may be a very real possibility. For example, if a child's parents are going through a divorce, one wish might be for his or her parents to get back together. This may not be something that the child has any control over. Talk with the child about these possibilities when necessary.

If it is appropriate and seems to flow naturally from your conversation, talk with the child about his or her concept of God and prayer. Find out what the child thinks about God. Most of the time, this will be dictated by the beliefs of his or her parents or by his or her religious upbringing. However, some children are free thinkers, even at a young age. Ask the child how he or she sees God. Is He like a waiter, a judge, a bully, or a friend? Help the child to see God as an ally who does not always say yes, but who always loves.

If it is appropriate and the child's parents have given consent, ask the child if he or she would like to pray about the wishes. Talk to the child and teach him or her about prayer, how it is like talking to a friend who wants to help you. Children are often better at simple prayers than adults tend to be, so let the child pray if he or she would like. Have the child tell you what he or she would like to say, and then using the child's name, ask God for the request in as simple terms as possible. Make sure to check with the child after you pray to see what he or she thought and if things are okay with him or her. Allow the child to take the handout home, but make a copy for your file to refer to during coming sessions.

Vignette

As the session began, Jack, a seven-year-old client with red hair and freckles, stared nervously at his swinging feet. Jack's parents had sent him to therapy after his school had contacted them regarding some academic and behavioral problems. The school had reported that Jack had been withdrawing from his peers, would not participate in class, appeared to be distracted, and was, on more than one occasion, becoming weepy in class. At times, he also had lashed out angrily at other students when teased about his crying. Although he did not physically fight others, he had engaged in some loud verbal sparring in the hallway and in the boy's bathroom, which was broken up only through the teacher's intervention.

Six months prior to the session, Jack's mother had been diagnosed with breast cancer. This was the second time she had received this diagnosis, and this time an aggressive cancer had forced her to undergo treatments that had taken a toll on her physically, emotionally, and spiritually. She appeared pale, thin, and weak went I met with her, but she smiled as she talked about her son. While hoping for the best, she knew her prognosis was questionable, and at the time of Jack's first session, she had already begun tests to see if the cancer had spread. Jack's father, a pastor, also attended the first session, and he readily admitted that he struggled with the current situation. He also appeared to be worn and tired. Jack's parents gave some initial information and talked for a few moments before leaving Jack in the office with me.

As the session began, I asked Jack about school. He reported that it was okay and did not elaborate. I asked him to think of his favorite class, and he reported that it was music. Jack enjoyed singing and played the trumpet in the school orchestra. After about ten to fifteen minutes, the subject shifted to sports and his favorite teams and players, to video games, favorite foods, and other mostly neutral subjects.

As Jack began to be more comfortable, his foot swing decreased, and he became more engaged in the conversation. Taking out the Wishing Well handout, I asked him to think of what he would wish for if God would grant him three wishes. He sat there for a moment and stared at the paper. "If you would like," I suggested, "I have some markers, and you could draw your wishes on the front or back of the paper." Jack took the markers and began to draw. The first thing he drew was a sports car. As he worked, I asked him about the car, and Jack reported that, if he had the car, he would drive it fast to get away, if he wanted to. I did not ask what he wanted to get away from, but I did make a note to myself that his withdrawing from peers and others was a theme I might want to address later.

Jack continued to draw what appeared to be a baseball diamond in a stadium. He explained that he would like the ability to hit a homerun every time he was up to bat. He would join the major leagues and make a lot of money. His family, friends, and other people would come to see him score and admire how he could play. With the money, he could help people who needed it.

For his final drawing, Jack drew a dog. He said he had always wanted a dog but his parents had never agreed to this. His parents had promised to consider getting a dog for his birthday, which was now less than two months away.

I then asked Jack which of the three wishes he thought had the best chance of actually happening. He replied that he thought the dog for his birthday was most likely. When I asked him what would change for him if he got this wish, he stared into space and said that the dog would protect him and be with him when his parents were busy. He mentioned that his mother often had to go to treatment or had to lie down and that his father was very busy with work. A dog could play in the yard with him and would protect him. We talked for some time about different kinds of dogs and the pluses and minuses of each kind.

I then asked Jack about the race car. "What would be the best thing to get away from in the car?" I asked. He replied that school seemed to be too long and that he would like to make it shorter by escaping in the car. I asked if there could be anything else he would like to leave, and he mentioned that when he had to stay with his aunt sometimes, he would want to get in the car and go home, but he knew he had to stay until things were better. Throughout this time, Jack appeared to be very somber, on the edge of crying. I let him talk, and he regained control but remained very intense.

As we talked, I asked Jack what he thought about God. Jack said he did not know. He said his father was a pastor and his mother had been involved in the church, but he was unsure about God. He thought that God was okay but was not interested or involved in everything. "He watches what we do" is what Jack said.

I went back to the handout and asked Jack about the second picture. He told me that if he were a great baseball player, he would have lots of money and could buy anything he wanted for himself and his family. He would buy his mom and dad their own race cars so they could drive around together. "It sounds like all of you would like to get in your cars and leave," I said. He wholeheartedly agreed with that.

Our conversation then shifted suddenly to talking about his mother. We talked about how she had found out about the sickness, what she had gone through in treatment, her sickness following chemotherapy, and his fear about what he thought would happen to her. Moreover, we talked again about God. Jack wondered why his mother had gotten sick. We explored why his father, as a minister, could not pray her back to health. He discussed his fears and his desire to have everything be okay.

Since it was getting near the end of the session, I thanked Jack for talking with me. I asked him if he would think about praying to God about his concerns. He agreed to do that, or at least to think about doing that. I asked him if he would mind if I prayed. He said that it would be fine, so I prayed briefly for Jack and his family. I then walked out with him and made an appointment for the next week.

Suggestions for Follow-Up

This exercise can become a great child therapy starting point. The feedback from the child can provide the therapist with insight into areas the child may have had difficulty verbalizing. Make a copy of the handout for the file and let the child take his or her original one home. Using the child's handout can be an excellent way to begin discussions with parents about sensitive issues as seen from the child's perspective. In additional sessions, you will probably address the themes or issues that the child chose to draw or list, so note these somewhere in the treatment plan or file.

If the child has mentioned a wish that uncovers or acknowledges an area of abuse or trauma, the therapist can begin addressing the impact of the specific event. Do explore these without great care and perseverance. When necessary, report any instances of suspected abuse and make appropriate referrals.

This exercise may give the child hope toward happiness and peace through a relationship with God.

Contraindications

This exercise is contraindicated when the therapeutic task is to ensure the safety and well-being of the child or the parents, or when the child has hesitations regarding the religious content.

Resources for Professionals

Dobson, J., and Dobson, S. (2002). *Night light for parents: A devotional.* Sisters, OR: Multnomah Publishers, Inc.

Fortune, M., and Miles, A. (2002). *Violence in families: What every Christian needs to know.* Minneapolis, MN: Augsburg Fortress.

Foxman, P. (2004). *The worried child: Recognizing anxiety in children and helping them heal.* Alameda, CA: Hunter House.

Gilham, J., Jaycox, L., Reivich, K., and Seligman, M.E. (1996). *The optimistic child: Proven program to safeguard children from depression and build lifelong resistance.* New York: Perennial.

Hart, A. (1997). *Helping children survive divorce.* Dallas, TX: Word.

Kearney, T.R. (2001). *Caring for sexually abused children: A handbook for families and churches.* Downers Grove, IL: InterVarsity Press.

Kroeger, C.C., and Nason-Clark, N. (2001). *No place for abuse: Biblical and practical resources to counteract domestic violence.* Downers Grove, IL: InterVarsity Press.

Langberg, D.M. (1999). *On the threshold of hope: Opening the door to hope and healing for survivors of sexual abuse.* Wheaton, IL: Tyndale House.

Rogers, M. (2004). *The hurt that the feel.* Birmingham, AL: New Hope Publishers.

Shelly, J. (1982). *The spiritual needs of children.* Downers Grove, IL: InterVarsity Press.

Resources for Clients

Brooks, R., and Goldstein, S. (2002). *Raising resilient children: Fostering strength, hope, and optimism in your child.* New York: McGraw Hill.

Carroll, J. (2000). *The queen who lost her castle: A search for love and acceptance.* New York: Writers Club Press.

Chapman, G., and Campbell, R. (1998). *The five love languages of children.* Chicago, IL: Moody Publishing.

Dobson, J. (1992). *Hide or seek: How to build self-esteem in your child.* Grand Rapids, MI: Baker/Revell.

Hegstrom, P. (2001). *Broken children, grown-up pain: Understanding the effects of your wounded past.* Kansas City, MO: Beacon Hill.

McDonnell, R. (1997). *God is close to the brokenhearted: Good news for those who are depressed.* Cincinnati, OH: St. Anthony Messenger.

Pinto-Wagner, A.P. (2002). *Worried no more: Help and hope for anxious children.* Lighthouse Point, FL: Lighthouse.

Pudney, W., and Whitehouse, E. (1996). *A volcano in my tummy: Helping children to handle anger: A resource book for parents, caregivers and teachers.* Gabriola, British Columbia, Canada: New Society.
Riley, D.A. (2001). *The depressed child: A parents guide for rescuing kids.* Dallas, TX: Taylor Publishing.
Webb, N.B. (Ed.) (2002). *Helping bereaved children: A handbook for practitioners,* Second edition. New York: Guilford.

Related Scriptures

O Lord my God, I called to you for help and you healed me. (Psalm 30:2 NIV)

Forgive as the Lord forgave you. (Colossians 3:13 NIV)

We live by faith, not by sight. (2 Corinthians 5:7 NIV)

He heals the brokenhearted and binds up their wounds. (Psalm 147:3 NIV)

"For I know the plans I have for you," declares the Lord, "plans to prosper you and not to harm you, plans to give you hope and a future." (Jeremiah 29:11 NIV)

. . . you are in Christ Jesus, who has became for us wisdome from God—that is, our righteousness, holiness and redemption. (1 Corinthians 1:30 NIV)

Blessed are the poor in spirit . . . (Matthew 5:3 NIV)

For the word of God is living and active. (Hebrews 4:12a NIV)

. . . but your grief will turn to joy. (John 16:20 NIV)

The Wishing Well

If God granted you three wishes, what would you wish?

I wish ____.

I wish ____.

I wish ____.

– 28 –

Magical Sunglasses

Lori Marie Figueroa

Guiding Scripture

. . . bound up in the heart of a child . . .

Proverbs 22:15 (NIV)

Type of Contribution: Exercise, Handout

Objective

The objective of this exercise is to help children who may have been abused, physically or sexually, by exploring their feelings in a safe environment, while showing the children that God is a source of hope.

Rationale for Use

Child abuse is a serious public concern, and one of the greatest threats to a child's well-being. According to Tallahassee's Florida Department of Health, in the fiscal year 2002-2003, reports of child abuse or neglect made to the Florida Abuse Hotline totaled 188,257; Florida reported that seventy-nine children had died as a result of abuse or neglect.

Therapists can use imaginative exercises, called "play therapy," to gain insight into a child's progress through the developmental stages of emotional, spiritual, and cognitive growth. A child's age may not necessarily match with the appropriate developmental stages. For example, a ten-year-old can have the physical body of a twelve-year-old, but yet the emotional development of a five-year-old. Explore any such inconsistencies to determine the cause of any maladjustment that is impeding the child from healthy growth.

Access to all forms of media can expose children to quite hostile images even at young ages. Such images send mixed messages to children about what is right and what is wrong, and these conflicting messages can negatively affect a child's spiritual development. It is vital to identify people and/or events that have harmed the child. However, the child must first feel safe in the counseling relationship before being able to share his or her feelings and thoughts, either directly or indirectly.

Young children have basic needs that include feeling loved and safe. Parents play a big part in fulfilling the innate needs of children. Unfortunately, divorce, separation, death, neglect, or abuse often cause these needs to be left unmet. Simple acts of kindness, displayed through non-

The Christian Therapist's Notebook

doi:10.1300/5334_29

verbal communication as well as tone of voice, can influence a child's perception on how these needs are being met.

Through play therapy, therapists can begin to understand the desires of the hearts of children. Christian therapists can show children that God is a source of hope and encourage children to turn to God in times of need by teaching them simple prayers. Such spiritual guidance can have long-lasting impacts on the future development of children.

Instructions

Using the handout at the end of the chapter, explain to the child that God has given him or her a pair of magical sunglasses. Instruct the child to color the glasses and then cut them out; assist the child only if necessary. Ask the child to put on the glasses and to close his or her eyes. Tell the child that when he or she opens his or her eyes that the child's house and life will be the way he or she wants it to be, not necessarily the way it is now. This is similar to the miracle question, as posed by solution-focused therapists (Selekman, 2002).

Ask the child what he or she sees, how he or she feels, who is there, and why the child likes what he or she sees. Therapists should take special note, not only of the items the child describes, but also of any significant people whom the child purposely excludes from the ideal scenario. Areas of concern may include a child's lack of trust, sadness, anger, confusion, guilt, depression, fear of abandonment, stress-related illness (e.g., headaches or stomachaches), low self-esteem, or mixed feelings toward adults in the family. Help the child to explore how his or her life would change if it stayed the way he or she sees it through the glasses.

Now have the child remove the glasses. Ask the child to describe how his or her life really is. Ask open-ended questions that lead the child to explain further any areas of concern. Next, ask the child if God sees his or her life and home as it is now or as it appears through the magical sunglasses. Finally, ask the child to name any problems he or she is willing to share. Discuss ways to help resolve these problems. Brainstorm solutions by encouraging the child to draw pictures of the world he or she saw through the magical sunglasses. End the exercise in the final therapy session by instilling a sense of hope in the child through giving him or her something to look forward to—the dreams the child shared when looking through the magical sunglasses.

Vignette

Miquela, a Caucasian thirty-year-old woman, brought her son, Samuel, age five, to therapy. Samuel had been wetting his bed for the past three months. He had also complained to his mother about having nightmares. He was afraid to be left alone. The last time Miquela had taken Samuel to the usual babysitter, the boy had cried and run after her. The babysitter, a twenty-year-old Caucasian girl with a background as a nanny, had told Miquela not to worry. Miquela explained that Samuel did not even want to go to his cousin's house if Miquela was not present. This was a notable change, since Samuel adored his cousins and was used to visiting them on a weekly basis.

During the first session, the therapist saw Miquela and Samuel together. Samuel was very quiet and clung to his mother. The therapist attempted to build trust and rapport with the child through play therapy. Samuel was resistant at first. However, since his mother was present, Samuel appeared to feel safe enough to participate. Samuel played with a house and displayed a mother, father, and little boy happily living in the house. He purposely closed the door of the playhouse tightly. When asked why he had done that, Samuel explained that the locked door would keep bad people from hurting the little boy doll.

In the next session, the therapist introduced the "Magical Sunglasses" exercise. Miquela, the mother was again present, but she mostly nodded and listened, intervening only to help Samuel cut out the sunglasses. Next, the therapist asked the child to put on the glasses and to close his eyes. Samuel became scared and started crying. Miquela reassured her son and even held his hand.

The therapist told Samuel that when he opened his eyes, looking through the glasses, his house and his life will be the way he wants them to be, not necessarily the way they are now. The therapist asked Samuel to describe what he saw, how he felt, who was with him, and why he liked what he saw in the glasses. Samuel described the house, his parents, and his feelings of love and safety when he was there. He said that, with the magical sunglasses, he did not need a babysitter. The therapist took special note of this comment and made a mental note to explore this issue further later. Samuel described how happy he was when his parents were around and how sad and scared he felt when they were gone.

When Samuel removed the glasses, the therapist asked him to describe how his life really was. Samuel described school and his life at home. The therapist asked open-ended questions about Samuel's babysitter. Samuel explained that he wished he had a brother or sister, but that, if he did, he would not want him or her to go the babysitter. When asked why he felt this way, Samuel started crying. He turned his face away from his mother, started shaking, and seemed scared. Through further exploration, the therapist determined that Samuel's babysitter had sexually abused him.

In a final session, after the abuser had been convicted, the therapist asked Samuel if God saw his life and home as it is now or as it appeared through the magical sunglasses. Samuel was unsure about how to respond. The Christian therapist explained God's love for Samuel. Samuel stated that God probably used the glasses because, if He saw what really happened to Samuel, He would get mad. The therapist acknowledged Samuel's feelings.

Finally, the therapist asked Samuel if he would change anything about his life. He said that he wished he did not have any more nightmares about a monster hurting him. The therapist encouraged Samuel to draw pictures of the happy world he saw through the magical sunglasses before going to bed. The therapist gave Miquela the homework assignment of praying with Samuel every night before putting him to bed.

Suggestions for Follow-Up

In future sessions, the therapist can revisit this exercise by using the magical sunglasses as a tool to help the child communicate whenever he or she seems afraid to speak. In addition, the therapist can follow up on the child's home life by making sure any unsafe situations have improved.

Contraindications

This exercise is contraindicated if the child is afraid to put the sunglasses on or feels uncomfortable participating in the pretend exercise. It may also be contraindicated if the child's parents are reluctant to allow the child to participate in therapy because, as a result, the child may be unwilling to open up and share areas of personal concern.

Resources for Professionals

Burkhardt, S.A., and Rotatori, A.F. (1995). *Treatment and prevention of childhood sexual abuse: A child-generated model.* London, UK: Taylor and Francis Group.

Cattanach, A. (1993). *Play therapy with abused children.* London, UK: Taylor and Francis Group.

Fortune, M., and Miles, A. (2002). Violence in *families: What every christian needs to know.* Minneapolis, MN: Augsburg Fortress.

Hegstrom, P. (2001). *Broken children, grown-up pain: Understanding the effects of your wounded past.* Kansas City, MO: Beacon Hill.

Hughes, D. (1999). *Building the bonds of attachment: Awakening the love of deeply troubled children.* Northvale, NJ: Jason Aronson.

Jernberg, A., and Booth, P. (1999). *Theraplay: Helping parents and children build better relationships through attachment-based play, Second edition.* San Francisco, CA: Jossey-Bass.
Kearney, T.R. (2001). *Caring for sexually abused children: A handbook for families and churches.* Downers Grove, IL: InterVarsity.
Keck, G. and Kupecky, R.M. (2002). *Parenting the hurt child: Helping adoptive families heal and grow.* Colorado Springs, CO: Pinon Press.
Kroeger, C.C., and Nason-Clark, N. (2001). *No place for abuse: Biblical and practical resources to counteract domestic violence.* Downers Grove, IL: InterVarsity.
Langberg, D.M. (1999). *On the threshold of hope: Opening the door to hope and healing for survivors of sexual abuse.* Wheaton, IL: Tyndale House.
Reeves, R. (2004). *The hurt that they feel.* Birmingham, AL: New Hope Publishers.
Selekman, M.D. (2002). *Solution-focused therapy with children: Harnessing family strengths for systemic change.* New York: The Guilford Press.
Shelly, J.A. (1982). *The spiritual needs of children.* Downers Grove, IL: InterVarsity.

Resources for Clients

Brooks, R., and Goldstein, S. (2002). *Raising resilient children: Fostering strength, hope, and optimism in your child.* New York: McGraw Hill.
Carroll, J. (2000). *The queen who lost her castle: A search for love and acceptance.* New York: Writers Club Press.
Dobson, J., and Dobson, S. (2002). *Night light for parents: A devotional.* Sisters, OR: Multnomah.
Gilham, J., Jaycox, L., Reivich, K., and Seligman, M.E. (1996). *The optimistic child: Proven program to safeguard children from depression and build lifelong resistance.* New York: Perennial.
Hess, P., and MacDonald, A. (2003). *The pig in a wig.* Atlanta, GA: Peachtree.
Hostetler, B., and Mcdowell, J. (1998). *The new tolerance: How a cultural movement threatens to destroy you, your faith, and your children.* Wheaton, IL: Tyndale House.
Klass, S.S. (1993). *Rhino.* New York: Scholastic.
Payne, T., and Payne, J. (2004). *Hippo-not-amus.* Colwall. UK: Orchard Books.
Wilson, K. (2004). *Hilda must be dancing.* New York: Simon and Schuster.
Ziglar, Z. (1988). *Raising positive kids in a negative world.* Fullerton, CA: TDM/McGraw Hill.

Relevant Bible Verses

Be imitators of God, therefore, as dearly loved children. (Ephesians 5:1 NIV)

Train a child in the way he should go, and when he is old he will not turn from it. (Proverbs 22:6 NIV)

For you created my inmost being; you knit me together in my mother's womb. (Psalm 139:13 NIV)

. . . Let the little children come to me, and do not hinder them, for the kingdom of God belongs to such as these. (Mark 10:14 NIV)

God is our refuge and strength, an ever-present help in trouble. (Psalm 46:1 NIV)

Even a child is known by his actions, by whether his conduct is pure and right. (Proverbs 20:11 NIV)

And whoever welcomes a little child like this in my name welcomes me. (Matthew 18:5 NIV)

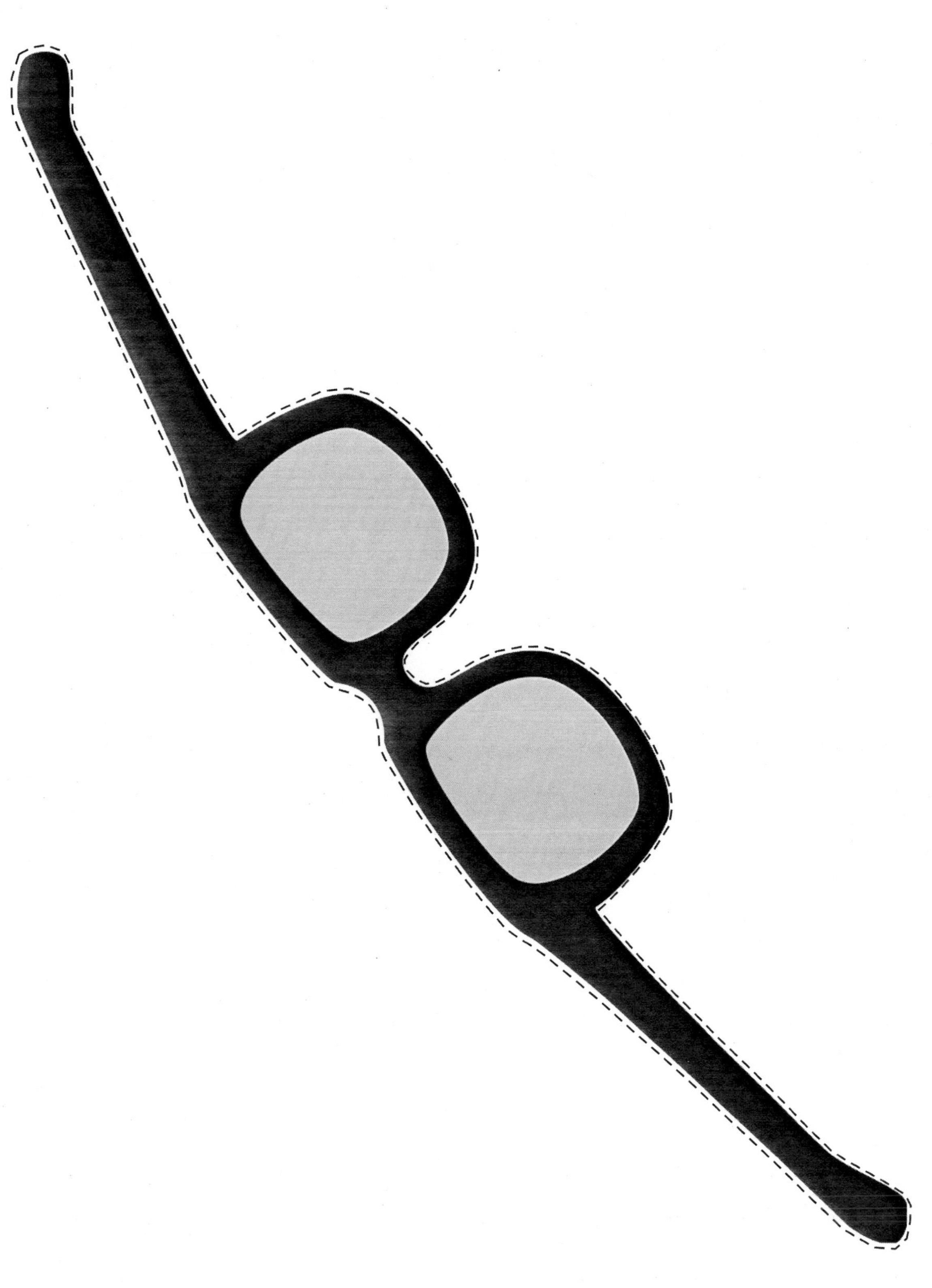

– 29 –

Lions, Tigers, and Bears

Lori Marie Figueroa
David R. Miller

Guiding Scripture

Do not be anxious about anything . . .

Philippians 4:6 (NIV)

Type of Contribution: Exercise, Handout

Objective

Children experience anxiety, as do adults, but with different images and less developed ways of dealing with their fear. Children experience panic attacks because of school pressures and family problems. The death of a close family member, such as a grandparent, can create anxiety pressures that children are unable to deal with and could result in long-term psychological problems or even physical illness. Although children can understand what fear is, expect them to be unaware of how unresolved fear can hurt them and what they can do to feel better. Fear is common in the Bible. Even Jesus experienced a brief period of what we understand to be fear just before his crucifixion. Through a more complete understanding of the love of God, many children can have their anxiety reduced and thereby begin to feel better.

Rationale for Use

Anxiety hurts! Most adults have the mental, psychological, and spiritual maturity to recognize the fear and anxiety they are feeling and to take steps to deal with it. When a child has been traumatized, the needed maturity and experience are absent or incomplete. Just as adults sometimes choose sinful or harmful strategies to deal with their fears and anxieties, children, if left unguided, will just as often adapt in unhealthy ways.

The core of anxiety for children, as it is for adults, lies in not trusting the significant people in one's life for protection and care. Imagine a family driving on a vacation and experiencing a serious accident. Imagine that all survived, but with serious injuries to both parents and only minor injuries to the two brothers, ages six and nine, in the backseat. Also imagine that this is a Christian family and that the boys in the backseat have been raised in the church and have heard of the love and protection of God for as long as they can remember. Now something bad has happened to cause them to question what they thought they knew.

The Christian Therapist's Notebook

doi:10.1300/5334_30

Witnessing their parents and caregivers, their protectors, injured produced in these boys fears and anxieties new to them. The six-year-old apparently regressed to an earlier age as a result of the trauma, losing the toileting skills he had acquired at age three and a half. He woke up crying for his mother almost every night after the accident and refused to talk about the accident to anyone except his older brother. His play became more aggressive and destructive and he refused to attend his Sunday school class anymore. He reported nightmares almost every night. In addition, he gained weight through raiding the refrigerator late at night when everyone else was in bed.

The nine-year-old brother did not regress to such an extent after the accident but did experience a decline in his school grades. He was unable to explain why this was happening but complained that he could not pay attention as easily as he had once done. His parents wondered if events, such as auto accidents, can cause attention deficit disorder. Unlike his younger brother, who would not talk about the accident, the nine-year-old has not stopped talking about it. He has experienced slight mood swings and been described as depressed by his teacher. He has not enjoyed playing as much as he did before, and his play has featured themes of accidents. He also has complained of headaches and stomachaches and of feeling tired a lot.

These two boys serve to illustrate the damage a traumatic event can cause. We could say that these boys have temporarily lost their faith and trust in God as protector and provider, and because of this, they are coping as best they can. Two things will need to happen if they are to recover to a level of functioning near where they were before the accident.

First, they will need to experience the day-by-day care and safety of normal family life. This will reassure them that God is still in charge, and while we do not know why the car accident happened, they can know that God still loves them and wants them to be safe. Second, these boys need to stay in church, as they did before the accident, and remember, through worship and lessons, that God never changes and that His love is forever. God's love will be felt more than learned by children, but these lessons are not futile.

Instructions

Though you will not be doing family therapy in cases of fear and anxiety in an individual child, you will certainly need to get to know the family as a unit to counsel the child successfully. Observe how the family members interact with one another, which parent is more dominant, and which of the children is dominant or submissive. This will allow you to generally get a Spirit-led feeling for the family dynamics. You will see the child individually for two primary reasons: the first is that parents or siblings might be a cause of the child's anxieties, and the other is that the child may not feel free to speak his or her true feelings in front of the parents. So, start with a family session and then move on to individual meetings with the child.

Use the chapter handout with the lion, tiger, and bear picture to engage the child. Ask the child to color in each animal and to give each animal a name. Note the colors used; lighter colors can suggest a friendlier and less frightening perspective than darker, more vivid colors. Ask the child to choose one animal to represent the scary things in his or her life and then talk about what those things are. If the child seems reluctant to talk, be patient and select other activities or games to help make the child feel more comfortable. If you have experienced some traumatic events yourself as a child, share those experiences with the child and talk about how you felt and what helped you to recover.

Talk about God with the child to get a feeling for his or her level of spiritual understanding and maturity. Talk to the child about prayer and pray with the child in a very simple and straightforward way, both at the beginning and end of each session. Be sure to use language and concepts that are age appropriate. This ensures understanding and will allow you to hear and apply the messages at the child's level. Support the child's positive sense of self by communicating your confidence that, with God's help, the child can overcome the terrible events that have happened. Self-esteem is always fragile in younger children, and thus the first emotional aspect to suffer when a traumatic event occurs.

Encourage the child to ask questions of you about anything. Many children learn to avoid questioning adults because they come to understand such questioning is disrespectful. Make sure the child has a name for the common feelings you will be discussing in your sessions. Do not assume that the child knows what "depressed," "anxious," or "traumatic" means. When you use a word such as these, say to the child, "The word *traumatic* is just a grown-up word for something bad that happens to somebody. So if I say 'traumatic,' what will you think it means?" Wait for an answer, clarify if necessary, and then move on.

Use coloring and game playing in your sessions. Children have limited tolerance for adult speech, and a wise Christian counselor will get a child to talk while doing other activities. Games, workbooks, pictures to color, and puzzles assist the child to talk within a nonthreatening environment, helping the child to deal with and correct negative emotions and confusion. Avoid explaining too much to the child about what you are doing and why. The rule with children is to keep the process as simple and as uncomplicated as possible. Most important, always make it fun!

For children with a churchgoing background, use pictures of Old Testament–type warriors or soldiers or heroes of the faith in a "color-me-in" format. As the child is coloring the "superhero," ask the child to guess how the person he or she is coloring was feeling when that event happened. If you are using David and Goliath, for example, ask about how young David might have felt as he first faced his brothers and then faced the giant. Ask your young client if he or she has ever felt that way, and listen carefully to the words he or she chooses to explain his or her feelings. Clarify gently and only as necessary. You do not want to put yourself in the position of being a teacher with the child. Talk about how God protected the figure being colored and how God has always protected those who believe in him. Avoid too much exploration of this issue because, as mentioned, the child may seek an explanation of why the traumatic event happened in the first place.

Explore positive and negative ways of handling problems. Be careful to stay at the child's level of understanding. Feel free to suggest alternate ways of handling problems similar to those experienced by the child. When the child comes up with a good alternative or responds positively to one of your suggestions, give generous and genuine praise to the child as a way of reinforcing good decisions. Remember, you are a significant adult in the child's life during the counseling process, and you should be encouraged to use your adult power to reward the child as a tool in effective counseling.

Reinforce your young client's positive perceptions of parents and God the Father as protective and harmless elements in the child's life. Talk about God being a God of love only, a God who is sad every time a child is hurt and happy when the child gets better. Often after a traumatic event, such as a car accident or house fire, the child is frightened not only of the actual event but also of the implications about the fallibility of his or her parents. Reinforce the idea that accidents can happen, but that God is always in charge and wants people to get better as soon as possible; this, of course, includes feeling better emotionally.

Work at the child's pace and level of understanding. Use words the child can understand and model Christian faith at all times. You are more than a counselor when your client is a child. You are also a role model of loving, caring, protective, wise adult concern, just like the child's parents. You need to remember that parents are the first heroes a child ever knows, so you will want to reinforce the power and wisdom that the child perceives in his or her parents at every opportunity. Downplay parental responsibility for the trauma and emphasize instead that the child has many caring adults, including God, looking out for his or her welfare.

Vignette

Barry was a ten-year-old student at a local Christian school when we met. Barry was a slightly above-average fourth grader who seemed to like school, and the adults in his life described him as a generally happy child. Barry's parents had divorced when he was seven, and though Barry got along well with his stepfather, he was struggling in other areas. Barry was also an only child.

Barry was afflicted with an incurable disease, once known as "elephant man's disease," but more accurately known as neurofibromatosis, a genetic condition that causes disfigurement externally, with an abundance of fibroid tumors internally. Even considering today's better medicines and treatments, it is difficult to control fibroid tumors, causing patients such as Barry to experience a shortened life span. Barry had been in the hospital a lot in his short life, and his prospects for recovery and control of the disease were not very good.

Barry was suffering from the physical ailments of joint pain and facial disfigurement, but he was also suffering from the emotional stress of teasing by his schoolmates. While not afflicted by the uncontrolled physical disfigurement of patients from years ago, Barry nonetheless looked very different, and kids, being kids, teased him continually. He handled this rejection through isolating himself from other children, complaining that he could not do the group activities at school, such as on the playground and in physical education class; he felt safer in the classroom under the protection of the teacher.

Barry was certainly traumatized by the effects of his incurable disease, but he was also being traumatized by the rejection of his biological father. Since the divorce, Barry's father had gradually seen less and less of his son, culminating in Barry not seeing or hearing from his father in almost six months. This "double trauma" was what motivated Barry's mother to seek counseling for him.

Our counseling began with a split session, the first part involving Barry's mother and me. We discussed Barry's medical status, school and family situation, and history with his biological father. During this time, Barry was in the waiting room with his stepfather. Barry's biological father had been a good husband and father until his son's diagnosis of neurofibromatosis, and learning that this disease was genetic, treatable but incurable, and inherited from the father's side of the family. To Barry's father, this apparently meant that he was responsible for his son's illness. His mother felt that this knowledge was more than her husband could bear, and the marriage began to suffer and die, as Barry's father became more and more detached from his son.

The second portion of the first session included Barry's mother and stepfather as well as Barry. The focus was an explanation of what the problem seemed to be (leaving out the issue of the biological father for now) and what we might be able to accomplish in counseling. We talked about the importance of their Christian faith, which was very sound at the time, and about how God loved all children, especially those who are different in some way. I asked Barry to tell me, in front of his parents, about his disease, his treatments, and his feelings about how he was doing. Barry was reasonably well educated and had good verbal skills, so he was able to express himself well.

Each following session began with a private conversation with Barry's mother, who provided updates on Barry's health. Then, for the major portion of each session, I would interact with Barry in my office, playing therapeutic games, drawing and coloring, and sometimes just "messing around," such as playing catch with a tennis ball. It was important that this child see me as a safe and reasonably "fun" person. I wanted Barry to want to return to counseling because I knew this would not be a short-term process.

It is important to note that this ten-year-old was happy with his life. He loved his mother and liked his stepfather; he knew many people, including very involved grandparents, loved him, and he knew he was smart. Nevertheless, he was confused about why others singled him out to have this serious illness and why his "real dad" did not come to see him anymore.

Sessions involved me drawing Barry out of the shell he had created for himself from the incessant teasing at school, and I did this by playing games with him and listening to what he had to say. When he colored and drew pictures, we talked about the colors he chose and the meanings of his drawings. He agreed to let me keep some of the colorings and drawings, and I would tape them to my office walls just before his visits to remind both of us what had happened in previous sessions. It was also helpful for his mother to see his creations in our brief interactions before each session.

I arranged to have a session with Barry's biological father, who still lived in the area. Barry's mother agreed to this but did not tell Barry about it at the time. I did not want Barry thinking about his father too much until I had learned more about the father's side of the story.

I learned what I had expected to learn from Barry's father. This Christian man had been, as he said, unaware of the genetic predisposition to neurofibromatosis and was just about destroyed with guilt. He had stopped going to church and had started using alcohol soon after the original diagnosis, which became one of the presenting problems in the divorce decree. He had no close relationships, except at work, and spent most of his free time alone or with his parents, Barry's paternal grandparents. While this man was not my client, I was very concerned for his welfare and suggested that he try to get some help with his guilt, to which he responded in the negative. Guilt was what was destroying this once good father, and guilt was keeping him from seeing his son. He explained to me the pain he experienced when he saw his son and realized that he was the reason Barry was disfigured and in pain. He just could not bear it, he said, and I realized that renewed contact with Barry was not in the immediate future. I offered to pray with him, but he refused and left in tears. I have never seen a more burdened person, and I saw then that it was best for Barry not to see his father in that state.

I received permission from Barry and his mother to visit his school and to talk with his teacher and guidance counselor. While I would not normally be so proactive, I felt that talking to school personnel was necessary. It was a good meeting. Both the teacher and guidance counselor were unaware of the full extent of the teasing Barry was experiencing. The teacher suggested that the guidance counselor talk with the class when Barry was not there and try to sensitize them to Barry's condition. The feeling was that this would increase empathy for Barry and would reduce the teasing, which it eventually did. In fact, his classmates became so supportive that they would come to his defense on the playground or elsewhere in school if anyone picked on him. I was, of course, very pleased with this result.

I continued seeing Barry for more than a year, and during that time, his condition worsened, improved, and then worsened again. Many appointments were cancelled at the last minute because Barry was admitted into the hospital or was just too sick at home to come in for the session. I was always careful to contact Barry by phone or send a simple card when he was sick, and he seemed to enjoy my attention. Eventually, I lost contact with Barry and his family, and I later heard that they had moved some distance away because of a job change for his stepfather. I do not know what became of this child, which, in itself, is one of the hardest things to get used to about counseling. I felt I had helped Barry through a tough time in his life, and I prayed that he had someone else in his new town and new school who would continue helping him.

The case of Barry reminded me of what I had learned in graduate school: We counselors are not healers, but the hands of the healer Himself; God uses us to help others but we are not the only ones to help. I was impressed again that God will provide the human helpers His people need, and it continues to be a great privilege and honor to be counted among the cadre of Christian counselors used by God.

Suggestions for Follow-Up

Using animal imagery can be helpful in getting a reluctant child to open up in counseling. Using games and imaginary stories, puzzles, and videotapes can help a child become aware that names might exist for his or her feelings. When the feelings have names, they are usually easier to manage.

Follow-up with children is truly follow-up with parents. You will want to check on the child's progress, but you should do so *only* through the parents. Counselors do not have the freedom to contact children without parental permission and knowledge, and we Christian counselors have to be very careful about approaching clients or former clients in church to ask how they are doing. One approach with child clients and their parents is to agree only to say hello in church or in any public setting to avoid violating confidentiality, an approach that is generally acceptable to both clients and parents.

Contraindications

Using animal and imaginary imagery with children is contraindicated if the child is unable to feel at ease in the experience or if the sessions produce bad dreams or nightmares. A child with physical illness issues such as Barry experienced must be feeling physically well enough to pretend, play games, and imagine. If need be, counselors should wait until the child feels better to get back to work.

Resources for Professionals

Borgman, D. (2003). *Hear my story: Understanding the cries of troubled youth.* Peabody, MA: Hendrickson Publishers, Inc.

Collins, G.R. (1995). *Family shock: Keeping families strong.* Wheaton, IL: Tyndale House Publishers, Inc.

Crabb, L. (1977). *Effective biblical counseling.* Grand Rapids, MI: Zondervan Publishing House.

Wright, H. (2003). *The new guide to crisis and trauma counseling.* Ventura, CA: Regal Books.

Resource for Clients

Rockwood, E. (1999). *When prayers are not answered.* Peabody, MA: Hendrickson Publishers, Inc.

Related Scriptures

> Though my father and mother forsake me, the Lord will receive me. (Psalm 27:10 NIV)
>
> As a father has compassion on his children, so the Lord has compassion on those who fear him. (Psalm 103:13 NIV)
>
> How great is the love the Father has lavished on us, that we should be called children of God! (1 John 3:1 NIV)

– 30 –

Self-Esteem

David R. Miller
Philip J. Henry

Guiding Scripture

I praise you because I am fearfully and wonderfully made.

Psalm 139:14a (NIV)

Type of Contribution: Exercise, Handouts

Objective

Children enter this world with a mixed bag of self-esteem. From one perspective, the child is king of the universe, with all things revolving around him or her and all things created for his or her own sole enjoyment. Children are egocentric to a fault. A child may say things like, "Why is the moon following us?" and "I'm so glad God made it sunny for my birthday party." At the same time, though, the child feels incredibly frustrated because his or her short stature and limited knowledge makes him or her feel inferior to just about everyone else. Add to this conflicted mix the varying role and influence of parents and their individual personalities and upbringing, the role of siblings and other family members, and the general environment, and we can see that self-esteem, like children, will come in all shapes and sizes.

This mix of influences produces many children with good feelings about themselves, and for whom almost no amount of sad or unfortunate experiences will make them feel that they are less than they believe themselves to be. Then there are those children we see in the counseling office, whose parents believe they are struggling with low self-concepts and inadequate self-esteem and who would like our help in raising the children's self-esteem to an age-appropriate level. Parents and counselors know that elevating the self-esteem level of a child or teen is not easy. Self-esteem is not created in a vacuum, and it will not change overnight in a counselor's office. Self-esteem is an important issue and worthy of our time and attention.

Rationale for Use

Young people with lowered levels of self-esteem are more at risk for any problem we can imagine, when compared to age-mates with higher levels of self-esteem. Children exhibiting lower self-esteem experience higher levels of incidents involving drug abuse, criminality, unwed pregnancy, early death by homicide or accident, mental instability, academic underachievement, sexual confusion, suicide, and self-mutilation.

The Christian Therapist's Notebook

doi:10.1300/5334_31

While it is true that children's level of self-esteem does not create itself, it is also true that we are unable to explain personality variables in some children that lead to lower levels of self-esteem, despite the best family and school experiences possible. Mainly, lower self-esteem is much more prevalent in financially stressed families and in families having an addicted or alcoholic parent, a chronically mentally ill parent, or a parent who is physically disabled.

Early intervention is the key to resolving self-esteem issues. A child who has lived with lower self-esteem for five years of his or her eight years of life will recover much more easily than a teenager who has experienced lower self-esteem for twelve of his or her fifteen years. Anyone can be helped, but, if possible, early intervention is the answer. Of course, you as counselor have no control over the children brought to you by parents; you can work with only those who are presented to you. Dealing with children will cause you to reexamine your own childhood experiences to make sure you have dealt with your own issues, if any; this is necessary to keep your experiences from contaminating the counseling process.

Instructions

Because your client is a person under the legal age of majority (differs from state to state), you will need to meet with the parents for the intake session and perhaps another session to obtain the necessary information about your young client. During your intake session, focus on early childhood experiences of all types. This will include traumatic experiences, such as the death of a family member, automobile accident, hospitalization of the child for more than a day or two, or any prolonged time when a parent was gone from the home for any reason. Also be aware of any major changes in the child's family status, including relationships with stepsiblings and a stepparent, religious experience, and academic history. The goal is to gain a general sense of what it must have been like for this child growing up in a home with these experiences and with these people for parents.

Using the handout "Self-Esteem Questions for Parents" at the end of this chapter, ask the parents the following questions:

1. Tell me, what makes your child different from the other children? What makes him or her special?
2. What are your hopes for your child? What do you want for him or her?
3. What is the worst thing that has happened to your family since the birth of your son or daughter? What is the best thing?
4. Compared to the other children you know, where would you place your child's academic abilities?
5. Has your child made a spiritual commitment to Christ? If so, what can you tell me about it?
6. Does your child feel popular and accepted by his or her peers?
7. Would you describe your child as primarily a leader or a follower?
8. Other than self-esteem, what concerns or worries you most about your child?
9. Has your child ever lived away from either or both of you for more than a week or two? If so, what were the circumstances?
10. When your child improves his or her self-esteem, how will you know it? What will be some signs that self-esteem is improving?

The answers to these questions, plus the normal intake information you are receiving, should enable you to begin understanding the major issues in the life of the family and the child that could lead to his or her reduced levels of self-esteem. Remember, self-esteem for anyone comes from congruence between personal expectations and personal feelings that those expectations are or are not being met. Low self-esteem is not an inborn attribute; rather, it is acquired through years of being raised within a family system, with all the variables and influences to which each of us is vulnerable.

Self-esteem is built on felt congruence between what the person feels his or her ability level to be and what he or she believes his or her performance levels are. In other words, the person asks, "Am I doing what I believe I should be doing?" Five areas combine to construct self-esteem for all relatively normal human beings, regardless of age. You, as the child's counselor, can apply these five areas as a means for analysis:

1. Spiritual self-esteem based on congruity between belief and behavior
2. Academic self-esteem based on agreement between school achievement and perceived level of ability
3. Social self-esteem, based on perceptions of what family and friends think about the person (e.g., liked or disliked, admired or disdained)
4. Emotional self-esteem based on personality and changing emotional states, or what the individual likes or dislikes about himself or herself
5. Physical self-esteem based on self-perceptions about personal appearance and physical abilities

You may find it helpful to use the "Five Areas of Self-Esteem" handout at the end of the chapter as a guide. You will note there are appropriate Bible verses to use with the handout.

Once you have an understanding of family background and the underlying foundational building blocks of self-esteem, you can now begin the counseling process with the child or adolescent, starting with parent-described self-esteem issues. You will want to listen for descriptions of feelings and experiences that will provide you with insights into how this young person feels about himself or herself. At the same time that you are listening for insights, you are also providing the child or teen with the experience of a listening adult, one who does not interrupt, criticize, correct, or command. You are genuinely interested in this young person, and you want to hear what he or she has to say.

Just as parents model God to their young children, you are setting an example of godly love and concern. You are communicating the child's importance simply by attentive listening and affirming responses that should lead the young client to trust you and want to confide in you. Emphasize the uniqueness of every individual, and explore perceptions about gifts and talents, clarifying if necessary that God has given every believer at least one gift or talent, and that the great majority of Christians have more than just one or two gifts.

You will need to invest in a supply of appropriate tools to use in exploring self-esteem. In addition to the checklist at the end of the chapter, you will need some magazines, scissors, paste or clear tape, markers, crayons, and a few sheets of large poster board in a neutral color. You will instruct your young client to use these materials to build a self-esteem collage of things he or she is interested in and at which he or she excels. Emphasize to the client that being good at something is learned, and that sometimes it takes a lot of practice and hard work to become really good at something. Such an emphasis is important because young people tend to be impatient with themselves. If children hold unrealistic expectations of themselves, a sense of failure and incompetence can set in quickly. Preach patience to your young client!

As we get ready to look at the vignette of a self-esteem-challenged young person, as emphasized before, please remember that the child or teen has had a lifetime, however brief at this point, to develop his or her sense of self-esteem. It is important that you, as counselor, hold realistic expectations for how quickly and how completely you can help this young person develop a level of self-esteem that is more appropriate to his or her age and circumstances. Be patient and gentle with yourself, just as you are asking your client to do.

Vignette

Jason's father was in jail. This single fact seemed to have shaped this eleven-year-old from the head down; he avoided eye contact, spoke in a muffled voice, and sat with hunched shoulders. Jason was a student in a medium-sized Christian school in rural northeastern Florida. Jason's family was now a single-parent family since his father's conviction for a drug offense two years earlier. The arrest and conviction of his father was a shock to everyone who knew the family, and due to the rural nature of the area in which they lived, this included just about everyone. Jason's parents were Christians, as were he and his younger sister, and had been active members of the largest church in the county.

Jason and his sister attended the Christian school that was a ministry of his church, and even though the family income had dried up since his father's incarceration, an anonymous person in the church had been paying their tuition since the arrest. The part-time guidance counselor at the school brought Jason to my attention after receiving reports from some of Jason's teachers about the downward slide of his academics, as well as his changing social world. This boy's grades had suffered greatly when his father was first arrested but had rebounded after the father was convicted and went away to prison. Now his grades were clearly on the way back down again. An additional concern was that Jason had become more isolated, both at school and in the neighborhood. He sat alone on the playground during recess and by himself in the lunchroom, eating quietly and looking sad. The principal of the Christian school called Jason's mother and suggested that counseling might be in order, given the negative changes everyone was seeing. She agreed and called me for our first appointment, which would be with his mother only.

Mrs. Bennett, Jason's mother, was a carefully dressed woman in her late thirties who exhibited some of the same facial characteristics and body language I would see in her son. I would characterize her as embarrassed, possibly feeling guilty or responsible for what had become of her family, yet determined to help her son if she could. Her eyes expressed sadness more than anything else, and tears came to the surface when we discussed her children. She told me how concerned she had become about Jason spending so much time in his room alone, playing videogames or watching television. She had taken her son to the pediatrician because she was worried about depression or bipolar disorder, but the doctor had wisely suggested that his emotional downturn was situational, caused by his father's imprisonment, and was not something that medicine would help at this time. The pediatrician suggested counseling, which coincided with the recommendation of school personnel.

The intake session continued with a detailed developmental history of Jason, which was unremarkable, and concluded with Mrs. Bennett's impressions of how Jason had understood and internalized the effect of his father's actions in bringing about the changes in their family. Jason had been a normal boy before the departure of his father, and we had every reason to believe that we could build on his strengths and get him back to more normal levels of self-esteem and social behavior. I recommended that, if she could afford it, a visit to a Christian bookstore to examine some titles dealing with self-esteem in children as well as children dealing with trauma. She agreed, and we made the first appointment for Jason to come in the next week.

The first session began with me, Jason, and his mother meeting together to discuss why we were all there that day. I like to have the parent present for this session to go over the basic rules of counseling with young people. I let Jason know that my only intent was to help him feel better about things, and I shared with him that I would not talk to his mother about anything we talked about unless it involved danger to himself or someone else. I mentioned that Jason could talk to his mother or anyone else about what we did in the office, but I would not. I have found with experience that an opening such as this helps the young person feel safe within the structure of the counseling office. It also helps him or her understand that, while the parent may have scheduled the counseling, my client is the child or teenager and I will honor that relationship.

Once we had covered the ground rules, Mrs. Bennett left the office, and for the rest of the session, Jason and I played checkers. I asked him gentle, open-ended questions, such as "What's your school like?" and "What do you like to do for fun when you're home?" Mostly, however, we just played checkers, with Jason winning a little more than half of the games. During our games, I asked a few questions, to which Jason simply answered "yes" or "no," for the most part. This is a normal first session with older children and teens, as young clients need to feel comfortable in the office and with the counselor before opening up, and that can be accomplished only by starting slowly. I had clearly explained this process to Mrs. Bennett because I did not want her to be upset when Jason came home and said we had just played games during the session and I did not "make" him talk about anything at all. In preparation for the second session, I asked Jason to think about different questions that he might like to ask me, given that I worked with children his age so often. He did not have to ask me anything, but I wanted to invite him to do so. I ended our first session without assigning homework because I wanted Jason to leave feeling as if it had been an easy and good session, nothing complicated or uncomfortable.

I began my second session with Jason by allowing him to choose a game to play from the selection in the office; he chose checkers again. We played only two games this time; then I told him it was time to do a little work. I asked him to tell me about his father leaving the home, and I followed with asking him how that made him feel. This was difficult for Jason, and I had to be patient while he thought about what he wanted to say. I then shared with him the perceptions of those who knew him: they believed he was feeling low about himself. I then asked if this was true. He agreed that he felt different after his father went to jail, and it just had not been the same since. We talked about what it would take to get him back to feeling better about himself, considering that we could not change what had happened with his father. He said, "I guess I'll just have to get used to it."

I decided we needed to explore these issues in a concrete manner, so he and I developed a "self-esteem improvement plan" to explore the five areas of self-esteem mentioned earlier, one at a time. When we had made enough progress on one area, we would move on to the next one. Jason seemed excited about the plan and liked the idea of us working together, rather than us just talking and me telling him what he should do. We started with his spiritual self-esteem, which we based on the congruity, or agreement, between what Jason felt should be his level of spirituality and the level it actually was, at least as he saw it. As homework, I asked Jason to look up and carefully read specific Bible verses so that we could discuss them during our next session. We combined an analysis of the verses with continued counseling to help him internalize the lessons God had for him. The substance of our "self-esteem improvement plan" follows:

Spiritual Self-Esteem: Consistency Between Belief and Behavior

> I have fought the good fight, I have finished the race, I have kept the faith. Now there is in store for me the crown of righteousness, which the Lord, the righteous Judge, will award to me on that day—and not only to me, but also to all who have longed for his appearing. (2 Timothy 4:7-8 NIV)

Discussion points:

1. Does Jason believe he was trying to be a good Christian?
2. Was Jason looking forward to seeing Jesus?

> For the word of God is living and active. Sharper than any double-edged sword, it penetrates even to dividing soul and spirit, joints and marrow; it judges the thoughts and attitudes of the heart. (Hebrews 4:12 NIV)

Discussion points:

1. Was Jason reading his Bible?
2. How did he feel about the importance of the Bible?

> Then he adds: Their sins and lawless acts I will remember no more. (Hebrews 10:17 NIV)

Discussion points:

1. Does Jason understand God's forgiveness?
2. Does Jason feel forgiven when he confesses his wrong behavior to God?

> And that is what some of you were. But you were washed, you were sanctified, you were justified in the name of the Lord Jesus Christ and by the Spirit of our God. (1 Corinthians 6:11 NIV)

Discussion points:

1. Does Jason understand sanctification and justification?
2. Does Jason really believe he is being washed clean by Jesus?

Academic Self-Esteem: Achievement and Self-Awareness

> Brothers, I do not consider myself yet to have taken hold of it. But one thing I do: Forgetting what is behind and straining toward what is ahead, I press on toward the goal to win the prize for which God has called me heavenward in Christ Jesus. (Philippians 3:13-14 NIV)

Discussion points:

1. Is Jason trying his best to succeed in school?
2. Does he feel his efforts are being rewarded?

> For God did not give us a spirit of timidity, but a spirit of power, of love and of self-discipline. (2 Timothy 1:7 NIV)

Discussion points:

1. Is Jason willing to take on new academic challenges?
2. Does he exercise self-discipline in the area of schoolwork?

> Do nothing out of selfish ambition or vain conceit, but in humility consider others better than yourselves. (Philippians 2:3 NIV)

Discussion points:

1. If Jason is being successful in school, is he humble or arrogant?
2. Is he helpful to others at school?

Social Self-Esteem: Awareness of How Others (Friends and Family) See Him

> A man of many companions may come to ruin, but there is a friend who sticks closer than a brother. (Proverbs 18:24 NIV)

Discussion points:

1. Does Jason feel his friends are those of whom God approves?
2. Does Jason feel Jesus to be a best friend?

> I am a friend to all who fear you, to all who follow your precepts. (Psalm 119:63 NIV)

Discussion points:

1. Does Jason feel the protective friendship of God?
2. If so, how does this help him in his life?

> Therefore, as we have opportunity, let us do good to all people, especially to those who belong to the family of believers. (Galatians 6:10 NIV)

Discussion points:

1. Does Jason believe he is being helpful in his family?
2. Is Jason involved in helping those outside his family?

Emotional Self-Esteem: Balance Between Internal and External Emotional Expression

> That man should not think he will receive anything from the Lord; he is a double-minded man, unstable in all his ways. (James 1:7-8 NIV)

Discussion points:

1. Is Jason expressing age and situation-appropriate emotions?
2. Does he understand the helpful and hurtful aspects of emotional expression?

> Set your minds on things above, not on earthly things. (Colossians 3:2 NIV)

Discussion point:

1. Considering Jason's age and situation, how much does he focus on earthly versus heavenly things?

> Those who belong to Christ Jesus have crucified the sinful nature with its passions and desires. (Galatians 5:24 NIV)

Discussion points:

1. Is Jason feeling guilty about any present behavior?
2. Does he understand the nature of the battle with sin?

Physical Self-Esteem: Self-Perceptions of Ability and Appearance

> For we are God's workmanship, created in Christ Jesus to do good works, which God prepared in advance for us to do. (Ephesians 2:10 NIV)

Discussion points:

1. How does Jason feel about his appearance and ability?
2. How does he feel his family and age-mates perceive him?

> Do you not know that your body is a temple of the Holy Spirit, who is in you, whom you have received from God? You are not your own; you were bought at a price. Therefore honor God with your body. (1 Corinthians 6:19-20 NIV)

Discussion points:

1. Does Jason understand the concept of the indwelling Holy Spirit?
2. Does he feel he is "managing" his body well?

> I am not saying this because I am in need, for I have learned to be content whatever the circumstances. (Philippians 4:11 NIV)

Discussion points:

1. Is Jason content with his ability and appearance?
2. Does he understand the idea that God created him as he is?

Counselors need to be vigilant in remaining aware of the age and social situation of all clients, but especially young people such as Jason. As you work through the self-esteem evaluation process, be mindful of what is age appropriate and what may fall within the boundaries of different but still within the normal range. Refer to human and child development textbooks for specifics on age-appropriate attitudes, thoughts, and behaviors.

As Jason and I worked through the self-esteem exploration, it became clear to me that, in spite of the difficulty with his father, he was about as normal as could be expected. The counseling process continued for some time and focused on many issues that surfaced in Jason's life, which created challenges for him. Eventually, Jason's mother and I agreed that counseling could terminate, but her son could return at any time, as needed.

Suggestions for Follow-Up

I suggested to Jason and his mother that he should remain active in church and youth activities and try to find someone in the church to whom he could be accountable until his father returned to the family. This person could be a youth pastor or other mature male in the church. Jason's mom accepted this suggestion with a sense of relief. I invited Mrs. Bennett to stay in touch with me as she felt the need, and she agreed.

Contraindications

Counselors should be alert for any evidence of self-destructive thinking, habitual or compulsive reactions (such as germ phobia or nail biting), eating disorders, and any other "beyond the boundary" type of behavior. When in doubt, get the opinion of another professional.

Resources for Professionals

Adams, J. (1986). *The biblical view of self-esteem, self-love and self image.* Eugene, OR: Harvest House Publishers.

Bradshaw, J. (1988). *The family: A revolutionary way of self-discovery.* Deerfield Beach, FL: Health Communications, Inc.

Resources for Clients

Meier, P., Ratcliff, D., and Rowe, F. (1993). *Child rearing and personality development.* Grand Rapids, MI: Baker Books.
Metclaf, L. (1997). *Parenting toward solutions.* Englewood Cliffs, NJ: Prentice Hall.
Payne, A. (2002). *You may lose your balance, but you can fall into grace.* Birmingham, AL: New Hope Publishers.

Related Scripture

I praise you because I am fearfully and wonderfully made. (Psalm 139:14a NIV)

Finally, brothers, whatever is true, whatever is noble, whatever is right, whatever is pure, whatever is lovely, whatever is admirable—if anything is excellent or praiseworthy—think about such things. (Philippians 4:8 NIV)

Self-Esteem Questions for Parents

1. Tell me, what makes your child different from other children; what makes him or her special?

2. What are your hopes for your child? What do you want for him or her?

3. What is the worst thing that has happened to your family since the birth of your son or daughter? What is the best thing?

4. Compared to the other children you know, where would you place your child's academic abilities?

5. Has your child made a spiritual commitment to Christ? If so, what can you tell me about it?

6. Does your child feel popular and accepted by his or her peers?

7. Would you describe your child as primarily a leader or a follower?

8. Other than self-esteem, what concerns or worries you most about your child?

9. Has your child ever lived away from either or both of you for more than a week or two? If so, what were the circumstances?

10. When your child improves his or her self-esteem, how will you know it? What will be some signs that self-esteem is improving?

Five Areas of Self-Esteem

SPIRITUAL SELF-ESTEEM: CONSISTENCY BETWEEN BELIEF AND BEHAVIOR

2 Timothy 4:7-8 (NIV) — *I have fought the good fight, I have kept the faith. Now there is in store for me the crown of righteousness, which the Lord, the righteous Judge, will award to me on that day—and not only to me, but also to all who have longed for his appearing.*

Discussion points:

1. Do you believe you are trying to be a good Christian?
2. Do you look forward to seeing Jesus?

Hebrews 4:12 (NIV) — *For the word of God is living and active. Sharper than any double-edged sword, it penetrates even to dividing the soul and spirit, joints and marrow; it judges the thoughts and attitudes of the heart.*

Discussion points:

1. Are you reading your Bible?
2. How did you feel about the importance of the Bible?

Hebrews 10:17 (NIV) — *Then he adds: His or her sins and lawless acts I will remember no more.*

Discussion points:

1. Do you understand God's forgiveness?
2. Do you feel forgiven when you confess your wrong behavior to God?

1 Corinthians 6:11 (NIV) — *And that is what some of you were. But you were washed, you were sanctified, you were justified in the name of the Lord Jesus Christ and by the Spirit of our God.*

Discussion points:

1. Do you understand sanctification and justification?
2. Do you really believe you are being washed clean by Jesus?

ACADEMIC SELF-ESTEEM: ACHIEVEMENT AND SELF-AWARENESS

Philippians 3:13-14 (NIV) — *Brothers, I do not consider myself yet to have taken hold of it. But one thing I do: Forgetting what is behind and straining toward what is ahead, I press on toward the goal to win the prize for which God has called me heavenward in Christ Jesus.*

Discussion points:

1. Are you trying your best to succeed in school?
2. Do you feel your efforts are being rewarded?

2 Timothy 1:7 (NIV) *For God did not give us a spirit of timidity, but a spirit of power, of love and of self-discipline.*

Discussion points:

1. Are you willing to take on new academic challenges?
2. Do you exercise self-discipline in the area of schoolwork?

Philippians 2:3 (NIV) *Do nothing out of selfish ambition or vain conceit, but in humility consider others better than yourselves.*

Discussion points:

1. If you are being successful in school, are you humble or arrogant?
2. Are you helpful to others at school?

SOCIAL SELF-ESTEEM: AWARENESS OF HOW OTHERS (FRIENDS AND FAMILY) SEE HIM

Proverbs 18:24 (NIV) *A man of many companions may come to ruin, but there is a friend who sticks closer than a brother.*

Discussion points:

1. Do you feel your friends are those of whom God approves?
2. Do you feel Jesus to be a best friend?

Psalm 119:63 (NIV) *I am a friend to all who fear you, to all who follow your precepts.*

Discussion points:

1. Do you feel the protective friendship of God?
2. Is so, how does this help you in your life?

Galatians 6:10 (NIV) *Therefore, as we have opportunity, let us do good to all people, especially to those who belong to the family of believers.*

Discussion points:

1. Do you believe you are being helpful in your family?
2. Are you involved in helping those outside your family?

EMOTIONAL SELF-ESTEEM: BALANCE BETWEEN INTERNAL AND EXTERNAL EMOTIONAL EXPRESSION

James 1:7-8 (NIV) *That man should not think he will receive anything from the Lord; he is a double-minded man, unstable in all his ways.*

Discussion points:

1. Are you expressing age- and situation-appropriate emotions?
2. Do you understand the helpful and hurtful aspects of emotional expression?

Colossians 3:2 (NIV)	*Set your minds on things above, not on earthly things.*
Discussion point:	1. Considering your age and situation, how much do you focus on earthly versus heavenly things?
Galatians 5:24 (NIV)	*Those who belong to Christ Jesus have crucified the sinful nature with its passions and desires.*
Discussion points:	1. Are you feeling guilty about any present behavior? 2. Do you understand the nature of the battle with sin?

PHYSICAL SELF-ESTEEM: SELF-PERCEPTIONS OF ABILITY AND APPEARANCE

Ephesians 2:10 (NIV)	*For we are God's workmanship, created in Christ Jesus to do good works, which God prepared in advance for us to do.*
Discussion points:	1. How do you feel about your appearance and ability? 2. How do you feel your family and age-mates perceive you?
1 Corinthians 6:19-20 (NIV)	*Do you not know that your body is a temple of the Holy Spirit, who is in you, whom you have received from God? You are not your own; you were bought at a price. Therefore honor God with your body.*
Discussion points:	1. Do you understand the concept of the indwelling Holy Spirit? 2. Do you feel you are "managing" your body well?
Philippians 4:11 (NIV)	*I am not saying this because I am in need, for I have learned to be content whatever the circumstances.*
Discussion points:	1. Are you content with your ability and appearance? 2. Do you understand the idea that God created you as you are?

– 31 –

It's Just Like Me

Philip J. Henry

Guiding Scripture

As a man thinketh in his heart, so is he.

Proverbs 23:7 (KJV)

Type of Contribution: Exercise, Handout

Objective

The goal of this exercise is to facilitate the therapeutic connection with the adolescent by encouraging the client to begin talking about himself or herself. This will aid the client in examining the conclusions regarding his or her self-concept. The ability to name, communicate, and adjust these conclusions is a key factor in reaching a successful outcome in counseling.

Rationale for Use

For the adolescent, the world is full of action and discovery. On the outside, he or she engages in a variety of new activities, has the opportunity to meet and connect with an ever-widening group of people, and is able to try out new and unique behaviors. Inside as well, the teen is a buzzing hive of activity.

Foremost in these endeavors is the development of a God-given identity. The developing mind considers self in relationship to others, the future, and hundreds of other facts and scenarios all at the same time. The laboratory of the heart examines the endeavors in the outside world as well as the self's inward workings. As a result, an identity begins to emerge.

Scripture teaches that it is the inside activity that guides the direction of self-concept. A person truly is the way he or she thinks. True self-concept comes to the surface by who the person is when no one is watching. While anyone can put on a mask and fool people into thinking that he or she is quite different from what goes on inside, eventually a person's life will begin to become on the outside the way that he or she is on the inside.

Teens usually come to counseling with some problems related to thoughts about themselves. This exercise allows adolescents to express how they think about themselves and seeks to accomplish the following:

1. Explore and understand the current internal world of the client.
2. Identify thoughts about self that might be a barrier or a help in the client's life.

The Christian Therapist's Notebook

doi:10.1300/5334_32

3. Help discover the process the teen uses to make decisions, particularly those related to self and God.
4. Identify the negative ideas of self and others that have developed.
5. Challenge the teen to think in a more positive and optimistic manner regarding himself or herself.
6. Identify the teen's thoughts about how God views him or her and what He desires for the teen's life.
7. Search for areas for internal growth and strength.

Instructions

Taking out the "It's Just Like Me" handout at the end of this exercise, ask the client if he or she is willing to fill out a sheet that would help you get to know him or her a little. Assign this as homework or take time to let the client complete it during the session. This can be a difficult task for a teenager, so allow enough time for him or her to do this. If the client hesitates, say you are sure he or she can come up with some answers without thinking too hard about them. If you sense further resistance, tell the client that he or she can lie on one or two, which often breaks the ice with most teens.

When the client is finished, begin with the first item on the list. Once finished covering the entire list, ask for an example of one description the client feels is true—what he or she truly thinks is important. You might want to clarify confidentiality issues if you sense hesitance to continue on the part of the client. Take your time with the client, and let him or her give you a couple of examples for each completed sentence. Often, you will witness the client's opinions developing as he or she is sharing these thoughts. This type of interaction often triggers the brain. allowing the client to be open to "Aha!" discoveries, often in midsentence. Take time to challenge the client if what he or she says does not match his or her actions, body language, or nonverbal cues. The careful and correct course of action will give you greater credibility with the adolescent client, as he or she comes to know you as someone who has insight and who may have knowledge that might be helpful to him or her. Allow the client to talk about life and self as he or she wishes.

The goal is not completion of the assignment but the examination of the client's view of self and his or her development in understanding both self and the implications of his or her thinking. Issues of family, drugs, sex, school, failure, success, choices, secrets, and trauma can emerge during this exercise because these significant issues naturally relate to the client's view of self.

Ask the client what he or she believes God thinks of him or her. If God were filling out the handout, what would He write? If the thoughts the client attributes to God are negative, examine the origins of these ideas. If appropriate, lead the adolescent client to examine the "Steps to Peace with God" handout, provided in Chapter 40.

Vignette

Pedro walked into the counseling office looking like a lost puppy. He had sad droopy eyes, a great deal of acne covering his face, a thin, somewhat underdeveloped body, even for a thirteen-year-old, and an expression that appeared to be apologizing for just existing. When I introduced myself, he looked at the floor intently and mumbled so quietly that I was not sure what he had said. He seemed to be very nervous.

Pedro was the youngest of three children, having two older sisters. His parents were both teachers. His mother worked in a local Christian elementary school, while his father taught in a public high school and was the high school football coach. Pedro was struggling in school and in life. He had been attending the Christian school where his mother taught, but because he had continued to fall behind the other students, he transferred to a public school that offered special education classes that his parents felt would best fit Pedro's learning style and level.

That Pedro had recently been involved in an altercation with another boy at school triggered the referral to counseling. It apparently was quite the lunchroom scene: flying trays, tossed drinks, and hurled food—all worsened by Pedro's not stopping his behavior when a teacher's assistant, a teacher, and a vice principal tried to intervene. Pedro was suspended for ten days as a result of the incident.

I began the session by asking Pedro to tell me why he thought he was coming for counseling. His reply was brief: "Because my mother made me." Later I discovered that his mother had bribed him with a new Xbox game. I mentioned that I had heard he had switched to a new school. When I asked him about his new school, he said that he liked it better than Piedmont Academy, the Christian school where his mother still worked. I thought, "Wow, a big fight and all this hassle, and he still likes it better than his old school! Piedmont must have not been good." I asked what he liked about the new school, and he said that the classes were smaller, the schoolwork was easier, and teachers usually left him alone.

This less than lively interaction continued for another ten minutes, with me asking questions and him answering them grudgingly. At that moment, I thought to myself that this might become the longest hour in the history of the world. I could not believe when I looked at the clock that only ten minutes had passed. Then we reached a new low. When I asked Pedro to give me three words he would use to describe himself, he said, "dumb, stupid, and ugly." I realized then that this was not going to be an easy process. However, this did give me some insight as to where his anger could be originating.

Taking the "It's Just Like Me" handout, I explained to Pedro that I needed him to help me understand a little bit of what it is like to be in his shoes. Pedro just stared at me. "Why?" he asked. I replied, "If you could help me understand a little bit of what it is like to be you, I think that you and I can work together to make things better. This sheet is all about you, and you are the expert on you."

Pedro agreed to "help me" with the caveat that I would write down what he told me. For the first line Pedro offered "late," explaining that he was late to everything. I mentioned that he had not been late to the session, but Pedro explained that his mother had made sure he was on time by picking him up from school and taking him directly to the office. At this point, we talked about his mother and her many demands. For a teen who is just barely making it in school, Pedro's mother was a little too demanding of him.

Next, Pedro told me to write down "artistic," believing himself to be an artist of sorts. He showed me his notebook with some comics he had drawn. They were good, and I told him so. Next, he chose "musician." I discovered that Pedro was hoping to learn the drums and loved to listen to music. He watched MTV whenever possible and could name about twenty groups that were his favorites. I was not familiar with some of the bands he mentioned, so I asked Pedro if he would mind bringing a selection of his favorite music to the next session. For the first time, he smiled.

Throughout the rest of the session, this exercise helped me to learn more about Pedro. I learned that he hated sports when he told me to write down "unathletic" on one of the lines. He saw himself as a failure because he was never going to play football, something his father desired. I learned that several of his friends had started to use drugs, although, so far, he was not; he had tried drinking, however, several months ago. I learned that he felt out of place going to church, and that he was questioning his belief in God. We talked for a while about his changing beliefs. He was not negative; he was just unsure and questioning, so I told him that I thought God allows us to question. I learned he was a skater, that he wanted a tattoo of an eagle, that he felt as though he "messed up" all of the time, that he enjoyed most fast foods, but loved cheese fries.

In the following weeks, I asked Pedro to bring in some magazines, and he made a very elaborate collage titled "Pedro." As he worked, we talked about how things were going. He had returned to school, following his ten-day suspension for the lunchroom fight, which I learned had been instigated by a racial slur. As he worked, we talked, and I told him that God had given him some good abilities and talents.

I talked with Pedro's parents about the racial remarks that some of the other boys had made, and his parents met with the school administration. Pedro transferred to a different lunchtime, and the administration disciplined the other boys for their part in the conflict.

I used the exercise and the collage in one more way. I met with Pedro's parents without him and had his parents comment on Pedro's exercise and collage. We talked about his progress and about the importance of developing what God had given Pedro, even if it meant putting their desires aside. Pedro's mother and his father came to understand the importance of this, which in turn allowed them to encourage development of the gifts God had given their son.

Pedro began drum lessons and was able to transfer into a regular art class. Pedro ended the year with a B average and no other incidents at the school.

Suggestions for Follow-Up

Often, those with low self-esteem find it difficult to see any positives about themselves. Adolescents, ostracized by others, may be experiencing an ugly-duckling phase, feeling like a scapegoat, or struggling to find good in themselves. This exercise is a good beginning, allowing an ongoing exploration of adolescents' pain and encouraging the development of the skills needed to communicate and manage life.

Work with the client to find areas of strength and interest, and help him or her focus more time and attention on what he or she does well. Support the client in finding God's will in addition to His plan for the client's life and his or her unique design and purpose.

Note: This may be a good time to pray with and for the client, providing he or she identifies and is willing to try to connect with God as a source of help. Be sure the client realizes God is not a butler who gets things for him or her or a candy machine that takes in prayers like money and dispenses goodies. Emphasize the long-term plans that God may have for him or her because this is something the young client might not see.

Contraindications

You cannot make people talk about themselves if they do not want to or if they are not ready. Do not use this exercise if the client is not open to speaking about personal matters. This will only widen the distance you will have to bridge in order to connect effectively.

Alternative Exercise

If the client resists an exercise this intimate, have the client draw himself or herself doing things that he or she likes or make a collage that is all about him or her. As the client works, talk with him or her and then discuss the items that he or she has chosen for the collage.

Resources for Professionals and Parents

Brandt, H., and Skinner, K.L. (2002). *I want to enjoy my children: Biblical principles for parenting.* Sisters, OR: Multnomah.

Dobson, J. (1982). *Dare to discipline.* New York: Bantam.

Dobson, J. (1992). *Hide or seek: How to build self-esteem in your child.* Grand Rapids, MI: Baker/Revell.
Dobson, J., and Dobson, S. (2002). *Night light for parents: A devotional.* Sisters, OR: Multnomah.
Hart, A. (1997). *Helping children survive divorce.* Nashville, TN: W. Publishing Group.
Hemfelt, R. (1990). *Kids who carry our pain.* Nashville, TN: Thomas Nelson Publishers.
Hostetler, B., and McDowell, J. (1998). *The new tolerance: How a cultural movement threatens to destroy you, your faith, and your children.* Wheaton, IL: Tyndale House.
Huggins, K.(1989). *Parenting adolescents.* Colorado Springs, CO: NavPress Publishing Group.
Scott, B. (1997). *Relief for hurting parents.* Lake Jackson, TX: Allon Publishing.
Ziglar, Z. (1988). *Raising positive kids in a negative world.* Fullerton, CA: TDM/McGraw Hill.

Resources for Clients

Helmer, D.S. (2003). *Let's talk about feeling sad.* New York: Rosen/Powerkids.
Hennigan, B., and Sutton, M.A. (2001). *Conquering depression: A 30-day plan to finding happiness.* Nashville, TN: Broadman and Holman.
Horner, S. (2004). *What is God's design for my body.* Chicago, IL: Moody Press.
Huggett, J. (1985). *Sex and friendship.* Downers Grove, IL: InterVarsity Press.
McDonnell, R. (1997). *God is close to the brokenhearted: Good news for those who are depressed.* Cincinnati, OH: St. Anthony Messenger.
McGee, R. (2003). *Search for significance.* Nashville, TN: W. Publishing Group.

Related Scriptures

> Make a careful exploration of who you are and the work you have been given, and then sink yourself into that. Don't be impressed with yourself. Don't compare yourself with others. Each one of you must take responsibility for doing the creative best you can with your own life. (Galatians 6:4-5 MSG)

> Each one should test his own actions. Then he can take pride in himself, without comparing himself with somebody else, for each one should carry his own load. (Galatians 6:4-5 NIV)

> Investigate my life, O God, find out everything about me; cross-examine and test me, get a clear picture of what I'm about; see for yourself whether I've done anything wrong—then guide me on the road to eternal life. (Psalm 139:23-24 MSG)

> The crucible is for silver and the furnace for gold, but the LORD tests the heart. (Proverbs 17:3 NIV)

> Do not let anyone look down on you because you are young, but set an example for the believers in speech, in life, in love, in faith, and in purity. . . . Do not neglect your gift. (Timothy 4:12, 14a NIV)

> I write to you, young men, because you are strong, and the word of God lives in you, and you have overcome the evil one. (1 John 2:14b NIV)

> Above all else, guard your heart, for it is the wellspring of life. (Proverbs 4:23 NIV)

It's Just Like Me

1. It's just like me to ____________________.

2. It's just like me to ____________________.

3. It's just like me to ____________________.

4. It's just like me to ____________________.

5. It's just like me to ____________________.

6. It's just like me to ____________________.

7. It's just like me to ____________________.

8. It's just like me to ____________________.

9. It's just like me to ____________________.

– 32 –

If I Had Faith . . .

Philip J. Henry

Guiding Scripture

And without faith it is impossible to please God.

Hebrews 11:6a (NIV)

Type of Contribution: Exercise, Handout

Objective

The goal of this exercise is to move the client from a life of doubt to a faith-filled life, by helping him or her to consider how greater faith might affect the various aspects of his or her life and how he or she might take steps to develop this type of faith. Since there is never a time in the Christian life where faith is not a priority, the answer to much of what a client faces in his or her life is a *faith-full* response.

Rationale for Use

For the Christian, faith is the rubber of belief meeting the road of reality. The Bible says that if one has the faith of a mustard seed, he or she can see tremendous changes in life and in the world. Believing faith pleases God and is powerful in prompting changes in actions and attitudes, as well as in facilitating emotional and spiritual growth.

By having the client think about how his or her life would be different with faith, this exercise helps the client examine the areas that are faith-filled and those which have room to grow (i.e., areas of unbelief). Clients also can highlight the behavior, attitudes, actions, or emotions that might coexist with a life of faith and how his or her life might be different with faith. Scripture can be key in this process, helping to plant the seeds of faith.

This exercise can help the client face life *faith-fully* by helping him or her to do the following:

1. Understand a biblical view of faith.
2. Conceptualize what a walk of faith might look like, a necessary step to having the client apply faith to life.
3. Explore areas where biblical faith is sound and those areas where it needs to grow.

The Christian Therapist's Notebook

doi:10.1300/5334_33

4. Move from a pessimistic, negative worldview to one of optimism and faith, a vital part of establishing a vibrant life of faith.
5. Identify initial steps necessary for faith to grow.
6. Find faith in Christ.

Instructions

Begin the session by discussing with the client what he or she thinks about faith. Make sure the client understands that having faith does not mean he or she never sins or makes a mistake. A life of faith means a trusting relationship with God is present, one that allows the individual to face his or her life with confidence, even in the face of obstacles and adversity.

Read Hebrews 11:6 and talk with the client about how God can work in only the areas of our lives where faith is alive and well. Explain the concept of biblical faith and its life-changing effects. Give other biblical examples of faith that please God (Noah, Abraham, David, Gideon, Jesus, etc.). Examine at least one of these individuals in detail. Make sure the client realizes that you are not suggesting that he or she must live a life of perfection. However, as in the lives of the biblical characters, which were full of faults and mistakes, faith can grow in the frailest of human environments. Have the client read several of these Bible stories, looking for how the individuals responded in faith, for homework.

Once you feel the client has a basic grasp of what faith is, introduce the "If I Had Faith" exercise. Ask the client how his or her life would be different if this kind of faith were a part of it. Have the client imagine how the areas of his or her life, as outlined in the chapter handout, would change if faith were present. Ask the client to talk about how he or she might change if he or she were to move in the direction of faith. Allow the client to dream, imagine, break the chain of doubt, and let his or her imagination soar. This is not the time for realistic thinking. That will come later.

As a final step, you might ask the client how faith would change his or her relationship with God. If he or she has not made a commitment to Christ, this would be a good time to introduce him or her to this idea (see the handout "Steps to Peace with God" in Chapter 40).

Vignette

Don, a middle-aged executive, had initially attended therapy for a plethora of symptoms, ranging from sleeplessness to worry and depression. Don was a no-nonsense business type, not the sort of client who would come to counseling unless things were seriously wrong. Therefore, the counselor paid intense attention to what Don said, while asking a few key questions. Many of the problems the counselor discovered related to difficulties Don had encountered when his business hit an unforeseen slump.

Don owned a plumbing supply business. For many years, he made a good living. As his business grew, he employed members of his family and his church. Don had been attending First Presbyterian Church for over twenty years and was active on several committees.

After an initial session, the therapist concluded that, not only was Don having a financial crisis, he was also having a crisis of faith. Many of the things Don held onto for years without questioning now felt challenged. Like muscles that had atrophied from lack of use, Don's faith, after years of stagnation, seemed to protest from overexertion.

At the start of the second session, the therapist reviewed Hebrews 11:6 (NIV): "And without faith it is impossible to please God." This was a verse familiar to Don from his years of church attendance, but as he discussed this verse with his counselor, he readily admitted that his faith had seen better days. "I know that I should have more faith, but I am stuck," he reported. The counselor investigated where Don thought he was stuck and how he thought he could get unstuck. Next, the counselor asked Don to think of biblical characters who had lived lives of faith, and they discussed some of these together. Most prominent of these characters was Joseph. His persistent faith, even after tremendous testing, was something that Don said he wished he possessed. On one level, he said he knew that things would be okay, but on another he was not sure. One minute, his faith seemed to be strong, and the next, it caved in.

Then, the counselor took out the "If I Had Faith" handout and asked Don to think about how his life would be different if he had faith. At first, Don complained that he did not have faith, so completing the handout was useless. Nevertheless, after a brief time, he agreed to try to think about how faith would change his life.

The first thing Don said would be different would be his fears. "If I had faith, I suppose I would not worry so much, especially about how bad business has been lately," he said, laughing. "I guess I would also sleep better at night. At night, I lie in bed and think of all the people I might have to lay off and all of the bad things that might happen."

As they spoke, Don continued to talk about various parts of his life and the possible changes in his life if he really believed and had faith. "I guess my attitude would also be better," he replied. "I have been stressed, negative, and a bear to be around. I used to be so grateful for what I had, but lately, I keep focusing on what I might lose. In addition, I suppose that I would pray more if I had faith. I know that I should pray, but I guess I have not prayed because I have given up." Don talked about how he also had recently withdrawn from his wife, family, and friends and had even stopped showing up at the office some days. He also avoided church and the people in church who were close to him.

Don continued to work through the handout, focusing on faith and the things that would be different with a strong, growing faith. As the session continued, it became clear to Don that he would have to live his life in a very different way if he was to live a life of faith.

Don thought of when he had started the business and remembered the difficulties in the past when he had encountered rough times. Along with the counselor's help, he began to remind himself of God's faithfulness. "I started the business with nothing," he commented. "I think I would have killed to have half of what God has given me now."

As the session ended, Don's counselor assigned the task of memorizing Hebrews 11:6 and reading the story of Joseph and Gideon, asking Don to notice how faith changed what seemed to be impossible situations. The session ended with the counselor asking Don to pray. Don, with some emotion, asked God to help him as he struggled to regain a life of faith.

Suggestions for Follow-Up

This exercise attempts to trigger and plant possibilities in the mind and heart of the client, to help him or her consider how his or her life would be different if he or she had faith in God. This is the perfect place to use Scripture to help the client fully understand the faith concept. It might help to have the client memorize key scriptures or Biblical phrases that would remind him or her to view the world through the eyes of faith.

Contraindications

This exercise is contraindicated when denial is an issue or the client is avoiding doing or dealing with something in favor of a hypothetical, spiritual, or theoretical discussion. This exercise is for those who are willing and need guidance, and not for those who are resistant and need confrontation or motivation.

Resources for Professionals

Bauman, L. (1997). *Ten most troublesome teenage problems and how to solve them.* New York: Birch Lane Press.
Brandt, H. (1997). *The heart of the problem.* Nashville, TN Broadman and Holman Publishers.
Dacey, J., and Kenny, M. (2000). *Adolescent development.* Dubuque, IA: WBC Brown and Benchmark.
Gallup, G., and Jones, T. (2000). *The next American spirituality: Finding God in the twenty-first century.* Colorado Springs, CO: Chariot Victor Publishing.
Minirth, F., and Meyer, P. (1994). *Happiness is a choice.* Grand Rapids, MI: Baker Books.
Walker, S. (2001). *Driven no more: Finding contentment by letting go.* Minneapolis, MN: Augsburg Fortress Publishers.
Wright, H. (2001). *Recovering from the losses of life.* Old Tappan, NJ: Fleming H. Revell Co.

Resources for Clients

Eldridge, J. (2000). *Wild at heart: Discovering the secret to men's souls.* Nashville, TN: Thomas Nelson, Inc.
Gunderson, G. (2003). *Biblical antidotes to life's toxins.* Peabody, MA: Henderson Publishers.
Langberg, D. (1999). *On the threshold of hope: Opening the door to healing for the survivors of sexual abuse.* Wheaton, IL: Tyndale House Publishers.
Maxwell, J. (1992). *The winning attitude: Your key to personal success.* Nashville, TN: Thomas Nelson Publishers.
Maxwell, J. (2000). *Failing forward: How to make the most of your mistakes.* Nashville, TN: Thomas Nelson Publishers.
Robinson, J. (1996). *Knowing God as father.* Ft. Worth, TX: Life Outreach International.
Schuller, R. (1985). *The be happy attitude.* Waco, TX: Word Books.
Schuller, R. (1993). *Life's not fair, but God is good.* Nashville, TN: Bantam Books.

Related Scriptures

Now faith is being sure of what we hope for and certain of what we do not see. (Hebrews 11:1 NIV)

And without faith it is impossible to please God, because anyone who comes to him must believe that he exists and that he rewards those who earnestly seek him. (Hebrews 11:6 NIV)

Trust in the Lord with all your heart and lean not on your own understanding; in all your ways acknowledge him, and he will make your paths straight. (Proverbs 3:5-6 NIV)

For everyone born of God overcomes the world. This is the victory that has overcome the world, even our faith. (1 John 5:4 NIV)

Therefore, since we are surrounded by such a great cloud of witnesses, let us throw off everything that hinders and the sin that so easily entangles, and let us run with perseverance the race marked out for us. Let us fix our eyes on Jesus, the author and perfecter of our faith, who for the joy set before him endured the cross, scorning its shame, and sat down at the right hand of the throne of God. Consider him who endured such opposition from sinful men, so that you will not grow weary and lose heart. (Hebrews 12:1-3 NIV)

If I Had Faith . . .

Attitude

Actions

Beliefs

Family

Fears

Prayer

Social life

Future

– 33 –

The Prodigal Child

David R. Miller

Guiding Scripture

. . . he who rebels against the authority is rebelling against what God has instituted . . .

Romans 13:2 (NIV)

Type of Contribution: Exercise, Handout/Homework

Objective

Stress is rarely more prevalent than when a parent and child are at odds with each other, and perhaps with God as well. Counseling a rebellious child and one or two upset parents requires maturity and discernment on the part of the Christian counselor. Subjects for the counseling process with the child or adolescent include the importance of submission and prayer while still in the parent-child sphere of life, God's perspective on humility and obedience, the role of faith in the process, the consequences of continued rebellion and sin, and the rebirth of family harmony. Note that parents are likely to contribute to the stress in the parent-child relationship and may require help refocusing on their parental role as outlined in the Bible.

Rationale for Use

As the Christian family continues to experience ever greater stress and pressure from the secular world in which we all live, counselors may intervene and help resolve these significant family crises. Counselors will face a three-part challenge.

First, consider the wants and needs of the parents; if you are dealing with a two-parent family, ever less frequent these days, you will need to consider the individual personalities of each parent, how these divergent personalities come together in parenting, and the points at which they diverge. Is one parent more in charge of the "target" child? What is the child's relationship with the same-sex parent? What is his or her relationship with the opposite-sex parent? Are the parents fighting for power as they strive to resolve this rebellious situation in their family? How close to God do these parents seem to be? Is one closer than the other is? You also face the challenge of having the child see you as a "parent advocate" because, in all cases of rebellion in the family, the marriage too is under stress.

Second, consider the needs and desires of the child or adolescent. Counselors will not be successful in situations requiring family counseling unless serious time and attention focuses on the inner thoughts and feelings of the dependent young person, the target child causing family tur-

The Christian Therapist's Notebook

doi:10.1300/5334_34

moil. We can assume that God wants this young person to be in conformity to His plan for family life, which, of course, includes an appropriate superior-subordinate position, as related to the parents and the child or adolescent. We know the young person will be happier and more stress free when he or she gets back into an acceptable relationship with his or her parents.

Third, we must be cognizant of what God wants for this family. The family is the seedbed for all good things that happen during childhood. God provides the family to bring glory to Him and peace and happiness to His creation. The more a family conforms to godly principles, the better off everyone will be. A Christian family in a state of upset is a poor testimony in the community and within the body of believers connected to the family. We do not expect families to be perfect, but we do expect Christian families to deal appropriately with problems as they arise and to follow biblical principles in seeking solutions. God smiles on the Christian family in which all members are in submission to Him, considerate of one another, and remain mindful of the leadership of God in family matters.

Instructions

As you schedule your counseling sessions, you will want to meet with the child or adolescent first, then with his or her parents, and then with everyone together for at least one session. You need to speak privately with the family members involved because a child or teen at odds with parents is unlikely to be open and honest with you in front of his or her parents. Parents, too, may have a hard time saying what they really want to say while their son or daughter is there listening. We are not suggesting secrecy but, rather, giving all parties to the dispute an opportunity to state their cases without fear of correction or judgment.

Media resources, such as the video *The Prodigal Son,* can be useful to the counseling process. You can either view videos during the session, with discussion following, or assign the activity as homework for the parents and child to do together, so that they can discuss it during their next session together with you.

The power of prayer is all-important in resolving family crises. Act as an appropriate example of a person who believes in answered prayer through opening each counseling session with prayer, asking for prayer requests from the family members, and being spiritually optimistic that God will answer the prayer requests involving this family. It may prove beneficial to share a brief testimony of how prayer has worked in the lives of other, unidentified families.

When working with the rebellious child, listen for his or her story. Let the child tell you what he or she thinks is the real issue for which the rebellion is only a symptom. Listen to the child or adolescent communicate how unfair and unreasonable his or her parents are—how the parents do not like his or her friends, how they do not understand what is going on at school—and how he or she hates, absolutely hates, the youth group at church. Listen uncritically and nonjudgmentally. Remember, the young person is probably testing you with his or her negative statements, believing that you, as another adult, will probably just take the side of the other adults, his or her parents. When you resist the temptation to be corrective and parental with this young person, you gain much needed credibility.

When focusing on the parents, the same recommendations apply as when counseling the young person. Listen, listen, listen! Each parent should have a story to tell about what the rebellion has done to him or her and how he or she is feeling. You will probably get tears from the mom and anger from the dad, but work hard to avoid interrupting these emotions. Remember that these Christian parents undoubtedly feel as though they have failed both their child and God. You will very likely hear that they have consulted with church leaders and tried to apply their suggestions with little or no success. You will hear that their marriage is suffering, that their sex life is on hold, and that they cannot even go out to dinner without thinking and talking about this rebellious child or teenager. Accept their thoughts and feelings uncritically. There may be a time later when you can work in a more corrective and therapeutic mode. When meeting with the parents, use the "Balance Sheet" handout at the end of this exercise. Ask the parents to complete the handout together, listing their child's assets and liabilities. Help them to first focus on the assets, the positives, and express thankfulness for the good qualities. Then, help them move to listing the areas needing improvement. Let them work through discussing each list and coming to consensus on the items. This will give you a good glimpse into their communication and perhaps conflict over the child.

Use homework assignments as much as the family will accept. Most family members are likely to be very busy, so avoid requiring more than an hour a week of family activities, counseling homework, and writing assignments. In the beginning, assign homework individually to each parent and to the target child or adolescent. With the child or teenager, you may need to agree to keep completed homework confidential, at least for a while, until trust is reestablished at home. This may take some time.

You may find it useful to ask each of the family members to keep a private journal during the week to bring in and share, in confidence, in the counseling session. Do not present this assignment as homework but, rather, as an aid to counseling, a way to help you, the counselor, learn as much as possible about the family in the shortest time. Remember, most parents will be thinking that the family will get the help they need in six or fewer sessions, or they will think counseling is not going to work. Be careful to remain optimistic and to interpret counseling in the most positive light possible. As long as parents believe the family is making progress, they will probably return for another counseling session.

Use biblical resources carefully. We do not want to add to the guilt already felt by all involved members of the family. You can provide one or two Bible verses for the young person and his or her parents to look up, read, and be prepared to share thoughts on when they return to counseling. Typically, Christian parents will not feel like they are receiving Christian counseling unless the Bible is a resource utilized on a regular and significant basis. While we do not want to turn the counseling session into Bible study, we will want to rely on foundational Bible passages for information and Spirit-led guidance.

Vignette

Jason was seventeen years old when I met him and his parents, John and Amanda, through the counseling outreach center of our church. Jason attended public school but was heavily involved in youth activities at our church and considered a leader by our youth pastor and his assistants. John, Jason's father, was being considered for the office of deacon at the time of our first session, and he felt added pressure to get the family situation resolved. John valued the deacon office very highly and did not want to do anything that, in his mind, might disqualify him from that office.

John and Amanda both worked full-time, and Jason had an after-school job at a fast-food restaurant. Jason was an only child. This family had been active in our church longer than I had been there, and Jason happily and proudly stated that he "grew up in the church."

The problem was Julie, a girl whom Jason had been dating since the two met in one of their classes at school. Julie was a professing Christian girl with an impeccable reputation who was well thought of by everyone, with the exception of Jason's mother, Amanda. Amanda was convinced that Julie was not the girl for her son and had persuaded her husband, John, to support her feelings on this. Jason, as you would imagine, was very upset and refusing to break off the relationship with Julie, unless his mother could tell him why he should do as she said. Jason felt that, as a senior in high school and because he had never been in major trouble, he should have the freedom to choose his own friends, including girlfriends.

This was becoming a major crisis for this family—neither side would budge! Jason's parents were beginning to worry that they were risking a chasm in their relationship with their son, which troubled them greatly. Jason, as frustrated as he could be, did not understand why his parents (mainly his mother) did not like Julie. It was clear to me that Julie was becoming a symbol of blossoming independence for Jason and loss of parental control for his mother, and I could imagine Jason committing to Julie even if only to prove to his parents that he could make his own good decisions.

Therapy began with a family session in which each person was allowed to state his or her concerns and possible solutions to improve the situation. I modeled active listening for them, encouraging them to talk, requesting clarifications, asking open-ended questions, making good eye contact, offering verbal responses, and maintaining complete neutrality within the session. I ended the session with the suggestion that we place certain issues on hold until the next session. Jason agreed to refrain from seeing Julie until then, and his parents agreed to avoid raising the issue of Julie with their son. This, I thought, would give all members of the family a reminder of how good things used to be and might serve as a motivator for compromise.

I split the second session between Jason and his parents. I saw Jason first because I wanted him to feel an equal partner in resolving this issue. I promised him complete (within legal limits for a minor) confidentiality by assuring him that I would not share any of our conversation with his parents unless he wanted me to do so. We focused on alternate strategies for bringing his parents around to his position. Jason suggested that it might be a good idea if he and Julie "cooled it" for a while, meeting only at church, with his parents' knowledge. To encourage Jason, I reminded him of his coming emancipation at age eighteen but tempered that with a discussion of the biblical command, not a request, that he honor his parents. Jason left the session encouraged.

During the parents' portion of the second session, I listened to their concerns; Amanda did most of the talking. I was reminded again that these two appeared to be very solid, caring, concerned Christians who were trying to do their best for their son. I asked them first to work through the "Balance Sheet" handout, discussing and listing together their son's assets (what qualities of his that they were thankful for) and liabilities (areas in their son's life needing improvement). They did a good job of recognizing their son's strengths. They differed somewhat in their assessments of the areas they felt needed improvement in Jason's life. Amanda was harder on Jason and seemed to expect more of him. I gained valuable insight into their communication with each other and how the subject of their son could at times put them at odds. I spent a few minutes discussing this with John and Amanda. I encouraged them, especially Amanda, not to lose sight of the many fine qualities that Jason possessed. We then discussed the possibility of their refusal to bend a little with Julie as potentially pushing Jason into an open act of rebellion; we reviewed the biblical command to avoid putting obstacles before children. Perhaps they were risking losing their son altogether by refusing to compromise on the Julie issue. We prayed for guidance; I asked each of the parents to lead in prayer for wisdom, and then I closed with prayer.

I saw Jason alone for the third session. We discussed the home situation and the feelings he had now that he and Julie were a little more "platonic" in their relationship, as they waited for the situation to be resolved. Jason stated his surprise that both he and Julie felt better with their relationship on hold for the moment. They were willing to let this situation continue as it was for a while, which I thought was a sign of maturity for these teenagers. Jason also commented on how good it felt at home without the turmoil they had been experiencing. The remainder of the session focused on encouragement for Jason that the situation would be resolved soon.

The fourth session was with John and Amanda, who agreed that things were much better at home, even while they recognized that something still must be done. I encouraged them to continue to pray and to rely on the guidance of the Holy Spirit, as they waited for God to lead them toward a solution. I mentioned the emancipation issue for Jason as a means of encouraging compromise. It was during this session that John seemed to come out of himself and assume or regain leadership of the family. He stated a willingness to compromise and let Jason and Julie date, as long as some of those dates included activities at home and maybe, once in a while, involved some family games and so on, which Amanda, to my slight surprise, agreed. We ended the session with their promise to talk to Jason about their decision, which would include an invitation for Julie to come for dinner and spend the evening after dinner with Jason.

The fifth and final session was with all three of the family members. We reviewed the reasons for their initial visit and the progress they have made in resolving this family crisis. I focused on encouraging them in their progress, but I tempered that encouragement with a warning not to expect things to be perfect in a family with an only child who was growing to independence, and who would soon strike out on his own, as God led him. Jason talked about his plans for college, which seemed to please his parents. I noticed that Julie seemed to be less and less the focus of the family conversation.

Suggestions for Follow-Up

We ended our last session with my request that they make an appointment to come back in four weeks for a progress report. It is my experience that these appointments are usually not kept if things are going well, which is what happened with this family. I had the advantage of seeing them in church, and I was able to determine that Jason and Julie were still dating occasionally, and the family appeared to be in good shape.

Counselors should frame the discussion of follow-up sessions by reviewing the case notes and analyzing the sessions. Were issues avoided that should have been explored? Was neutrality maintained? Did all family members seem satisfied with alternatives and the way the crisis was resolved? Was God honored by everything that happened in the sessions?

The number of sessions will vary, as will the issues, of course. Remember, you are the conduit for God's grace and wisdom to your hurting clients. God has called you to a very special ministry.

Contraindications

Anytime an adolescent is involved in family issues, evaluate him or her for signs of depression and suicidal ideation. A referral to a psychiatrist would be appropriate if such signs became apparent. It is also necessary that all involved family members be a part of the therapy process. Evaluate for and eliminate issues of abuse and neglect before counseling proceeds.

Resources for Professionals

Collins, G. (1993). *The biblical basis of Christian counseling for people helpers.* Colorado Springs, CO: NavPress.

Dykstra, R. (1997). *Counseling troubled youth.* Louisville, KY: Westminster John Knox Press.

Resources for Clients

Chapman, G. (2000). *The five love languages of teenagers.* Chicago, IL: Northfield Publishing.

Crabb, L. (1988). *Inside out.* Colorado Springs, CO: NavPress.

Pratt, M. (2004). *When my faith feels shallow: Pursuing the depths of God.* Birmingham, AL: New Hope Publishers.

Related Scriptures

All your sons will be taught by the Lord, and great will be your children's peace. (Isaiah 54:13 NIV)

How can a young man keep his way pure? By living according to your word. (Psalm 119:9 NIV)

Fathers, do not exasperate your children; instead, bring them up in the training and instruction of the Lord. (Ephesians 6:4 NIV)

Balance Sheet

My Child's Assets and Liabilities as of (date) ________

Assets (What I'm thankful for)	**Liabilities** (Areas needing improvement)
____________________	____________________
____________________	____________________
____________________	____________________
____________________	____________________
____________________	____________________
____________________	____________________
____________________	____________________
____________________	____________________

– 34 –

Just for Today

Philip J. Henry
David R. Miller

Guiding Scripture

But seek first his kingdom and his righteousness and all these things will be given to you as well. Therefore do not worry about tomorrow, for tomorrow will worry about itself. Each day has enough trouble of its own.

Matthew 6:33-34 (NIV)

Type of Contribution: Exercise, Handout

Objective

This exercise will help ground the client in the present, by focusing on the "now" priorities that God has for his or her life. To do this, the client must let go of all that is in the past and withdraw from plans and possibilities of the future. The "now" of God is the best way to live in this present reality.

Rationale for Use

Clients often come to therapy with sets of complex problems that are interwoven. Their past, present, and future feel tied up together by knots of worry and anxiety, which can lead to questions such as these:

What will I do about . . . ?
How will I . . . ?
When and where will I . . . ?
What if I had only not . . . ?
What will I do if . . . ?

And round and round it goes . . .

The force of the past and the future can squeeze the client into an unhealthy present that can very literally drive him or her crazy. The Bible speaks directly to this disregard of the present, labeling it as harmful and, at the same time, silly. Disregard of the present is harmful because it disconnects a person from God, and from others, and injures the body and spirit; it is silly or foolish because little or nothing is gained in trying to live beyond today. The client's stress and

The Christian Therapist's Notebook

doi:10.1300/5334_35

worry may build up and up until his or her days seem filled with anxiety and the nights devoid of rest and sleep. This way of living will never lead to peace.

There is a better way to live. The secret, according to Jesus, is to live in the present, putting God's priorities first. Once realization sets in on what is truly important, one may prioritize life accordingly.

This can help a person realize that things are only as important as he or she deems. A person can choose to let go of worry and release the present day into God's hands. When both cognitive choice and mental focus are on God and His priorities, life will find a restful peace.

This exercise seeks to help the client understand how his or her anxiety may rise as he or she focuses on the past and future, while learning how peace can come from staying in the present moment. To do this, the client must identify the biblical priorities in his or her life as well as the barriers that prevent him or her from considering God's priorities. Then the client can feel free to explore ways of staying in the God-controlled moment and discover how to release past and future cares.

Instructions

Many people do not tie their current anxiety, depression, or hopelessness with their life focus. Life just happens and the moods and internal struggles they face seem to come and go mysteriously. Before beginning this exercise, counselors should teach clients about how staying in the present can be beneficial to them.

Take a Bible and read Matthew 6:25-34 (NIV) with the client. Take time to let him or her hear Jesus' words: "Therefore I tell you do not worry about your life. . . . But seek first His kingdom. . . . do not worry about tomorrow. . . . Each day has enough trouble of its own." Talk with the client about how worrying or being preoccupied with events in the past or future possibilities is not helpful.

Often at this point, some clients who have major issues will argue for special exemptions so they can have a license to worry. The typical argument goes something like this: "No one has had my past" or perhaps "The things that I am facing in the future are unique." Therefore, clients reason they should be allowed to worry. Do not fight this, for some of it may be true. Some people have faced tremendous hurts in the past or enormously crushing experiences loom in their future. Rather than disagree with clients and their logic, return to the truth of scripture to see if they can have some success in understanding that they can live only for today, even if everything they face or fear is true.

Ask the client if he or she would be willing to look at the focus of his or her life. If the client consents, take out the "Just for Today" handout and start by asking the client to consider thinking about issues from the past that are concerning him or her. Ask the client to identify five things that he or she thinks about his or her past that cause him or her to have stress or anxiety. If the client has been in therapy before or with you for some time, this should be an easy task.

Talk briefly about each of the problem areas from the past. Do not minimize the problems in the past, but also do not allow them to dominate the discussion. The focus here is not to hear a retelling of past traumas but to understand how the past influences the present. Have the client rank these troubling past events in order of importance. Then list them on the handout from 1 to 5. Ask the client for some details about what he or she is thinking about when he or she begins to feel anxious or troubled. Help the client to see how these past events have control over him or her and how these events rob him or her of present peace and tranquility.

For some clients, this will be very unsatisfying. Some people have a big investment in keeping ties to the past, for a number of reasons. In spite of this, see if you can move the client to a present focus, looking back on the events and realizing their present implications rather than living in them. Listen for words or phrases that convey a sense of fatalism, such as the following:

It hasn't been the same since . . .
If only I had . . .
If only I had not . . .
My life changed after . . .

See if the client can identify how looking backward has influenced his or her present life. Gently highlight how different this is from focusing on God and His priorities. If the wounds are too fresh at this point, consider returning to this exercise later. Otherwise, plant the seed of change now, but do not spend a lot of time trying to have the client integrate something that he or she is not ready to receive.

Next, ask the client questions about the future and what he or she fears might happen. Have him or her think of five things that cause his or her anxiety or stress concerning the future. Again, as with the past, take some time and really listen to the client. These questions may be more difficult for some clients because, although future worries may be very powerful, they are often hard to articulate. This actually is part of the difficulty with many clients. The future preys on the present, yet clients lack the awareness or the ability to verbalize or conceptualize this fact. Help the client to see what part each of the future worries plays in his or her life. Once he or she has a list of the five issues, have him or her rank these and in the "future" section of the handout.

Review the scripture verse printed on the handout with the client. Show the client that anxious living places the fears and anxieties of the past and present first in his or her life, while the way of peace is found by placing God first and living each day in the present. Discuss the importance of seeking God and His righteousness first. Say, "If you were going to make God a priority in your life, what would be first?" Have the client list five things that would happen when God becomes the focus and His priorities become first in his or her life. List the five changes at the bottom of the handout, to identify the way of peace. See if there is one of these where the client can begin. If the client is willing, pray, centering your prayer on this revolutionary change in focus that he or she is attempting.

Although this seems like a simple exercise, it is not. It is a clash of philosophies. To move from a past- or future-focused life to one in which the client seeks to live in the present with God's priorities will take time and perseverance.

Vignette

Sally, a twenty-nine-year-old computer programmer, came into her session with a wadded tissue that she continued to alternately wring and use to dab the corners of her eyes. It looked as if she was not having a good day.

She had been in therapy with Dr. Dona Jones for three months and, during that time, had made good but inconsistent progress. Originally, she had come to therapy after her best friend's wedding. This happy time for her friend triggered unhappiness and fears for her that she was getting older, fatter, and less attractive, and that she would never get married, something that she felt she desperately wanted and needed. This led to more anxiety and sleeplessness, and, finally, when she began having some problems at work, another friend suggested she attend therapy.

After listening to Sally share some of the trials of her day, Dr. Jones asked if she would mind if they read a few Bible verses together that might help her refocus. Sally, a regular member of a nondenominational church, had already shared much about her faith, so this was a very natural thing to do. Dr. Jones handed Sally a copy of Matthew 6:25-34 and asked Sally to read the first verse. They then read a few more verses and talked about the meaning of each. Through the next ten minutes, Sally and Dr. Jones talked about the passage and about worry. At the conclusion, Sally agreed that she wished she was not so bothered about her past or worried about the future.

Some changes were coming in her workplace, which was making her upset today. She stated that she wanted to put God first in everything, but she was not sure how to make the change.

Dr. Jones asked Sally if she might consider working on an exercise that might help her take a step in the right direction. Sally agreed, and Dr. Jones took out a copy of the Just for Today handout and began to explain it to Sally. "That looks like me," Sally volunteered, as she looked at the picture. "The past and future seem so big to me, and I feel so small." With that, Sally let out a little sob and wiped her eyes with her wadded tissue.

"Well," said Dr. Jones, "let's take a look at these big issues and see if we can put them in a better perspective. Can you think of five things in the past that take your focus off the present and turn your focus away from God?" Sally first indicated that she often thought of an old boyfriend. "Ever since I broke up with Mark, my life has not been the same. I should have never done that. It was a big mistake." Mark had been an old boyfriend who, in Sally's memory, had gotten better with age. The longer she was away from him, the better she remembered him to be. He had been unfaithful to her, and while he attended church with her on some occasions, he had a serious drinking problem. In the end, she had refused to see him anymore and broke off the relationship. As time progressed, when no one new appeared on the horizon, Sally began to pine for him. This first issue took a while to talk about, and Dr. Jones tried very hard not to let this become a repetition of past sessions in which Sally had complained about losing Mark but then did nothing to change herself. The next four past issues Sally listed were bad choices of career, problems with her parents, choices concerning her move away to a new city, and choices of cars. Currently, Sally had a clunker that she caused her to worry constantly about it breaking down.

After talking about how all of these issues twisted her up with worry, Dr. Jones turned to asking her about the future. Sally's first issue was the fear that she would never find someone to love her and to share her life. She talked about several of her friends who had married in the past two years and reported that, on occasion, especially when she was not busy, she spent a great deal of time worrying about not having this kind of a future. Next, she mentioned her fear regarding her job. She had moved to the city to work with her present employer, but restructuring had meant that many people in her division had been laid off or transferred to other cities. Sally also mentioned her parents' health, her lack of financial resources for retirement, and, finally, after not being able to come up with anything else, her concerns about her health in the future. As they talked, Dr. Jones tried to highlight those things which loomed as potential problems and those things which were merely fears. She tried to help Sally think about how her focus on the future prevented her from really living in the present.

With about fifteen minutes left in the session, they turned to talk about God's priorities and the ways Sally could live more comfortably in the present. The first priority that Sally chose was church attendance. Sally admitted that she recently had not been faithful in her church attendance. When she had dated Mark, she had found that he would often try to look for an excuse not to go, and she had found it easy to go along with his perspective. As a result, she had gotten out of the habit of going to church regularly. Along with this, she reported that her relationship with God had grown "stale." She had not read her Bible in months and did not pray in any consistent manner. Dr. Jones and Sally talked about some ways she could work on her devotional time and strengthen herself spiritually. In this discussion, Sally talked about going to a singles Bible study at her church that a friend attended. Sally said that she knew it would be good for her, but so far she was not motivated to go.

The session ended with Dr. Jones asking Sally to take a copy of the handout home and encouraging her to come up with more of God's priorities for her in the present. Dr. Jones led Sally in a prayer, asking God to help her make the present more meaningful, and the session ended on the hour.

Suggestions for Follow-Up

This exercise gives the client a clear view of the areas that are priorities in his or her personal life. Make a copy of the handout, and in following sessions, work to see if the client is willing to make a commitment to move in the direction that places God's priorities first in his or her life. If the client continues to be anxious, go back over the handout and begin to identify, in a systematic way, how he or she can move on to a more peaceful way of life.

Some of this is a choice. Challenge the client to realize that he or she could not live his or her life with his or her own priorities first and still find peace. Have the client memorize Matthew 6:33-34 or write this Guiding Scripture on a card as a reminder of how the client can find peace.

Contraindications

This exercise is contraindicated if the client shows psychopathology that prohibits him or her from thinking in an organized way, or if his or her anxiety is so great that it demands an immediate intervention, either medical or therapeutic.

Resources for Professionals

Adams, J E. (1986). *The Christian counselor's manual.* Grand Rapids, MI: Zondervan Bible Publishers.

Anderson, N. (1999). *Freedom from fear: Overcoming worry and anxiety.* Eugene, OR: Harvest House Publishers.

Bauman, L. (1997). *Ten most troublesome teenage problems and how to solve them.* New York: Birch Lane Press.

Foster, R. (1998). *Celebration of discipline: The path to spiritual growth.* New York: HarperCollins.

Garrod, A., Kilkenny, R., Powers, S., and Smulyan, L. (2002). *Love me for who I am.* Richmond, VA: Pearson Education.

Twoey, E. (2002). *Proteen: A positive approach to understanding adolescents.* Cleveland, TN: Pathway Press.

Resources for Clients

Blackaby, H. (1998). *Experiencing God.* Nashville, TN: Broadman and Holman.

Dillow, L. (1998). *Calm my anxious heart.* Colorado Springs, CO: NavPress Publishing Group.

Gregg-Schroeder, S. (1997). *In the shadow of God's wings: Grace in the midst of depression.* Nashville, TN: Upper Room Books.

Jeffress, R. (1996). *Guilt-free living.* Wheaton, IL: Tyndale House Publishers.

Lewis, C.S. (2001). *The problem of pain.* San Francisco, CA: Harper San Francisco.

Meyer, J. (2002). *Be anxious for nothing.* Iberia, MO: Dake Publishing.

Robinson, J. (1996). *Knowing God as father.* Ft. Worth, TX: Life Outreach International.

Schuller, R. (1985). *The be happy attitude.* Waco, TX: Word Books.

Stanley, C. (2003). *Finding peace: God's promise of a life free from regret, anxiety and fear.* Nashville, TN: Thomas Nelson Publishers.

Swenson, R. (1999). *The overload syndrome: Learning to live within your limits.* Colorado Springs, CO: NavPress Publishing Group.

Swindoll, C. (2003). *Strengthening your grip.* Nashville, TN: W. Publishing Group.
Vredevelt, P. (2001). *Letting go of anxiety and worry.* Sister, OR: Multnomah Publishers, Inc.
Walker, S. (2001). *Driven no more: Finding contentment by letting go.* Minneapolis, MN: Augsburg Fortress Publishers.
Wright, H. (2001). *Recovering from the losses of life.* Old Tappan, NJ: Fleming H. Revell Co.

Related Scriptures

Give your entire attention to what God is doing right now, and don't get worked up about what may or may not happen tomorrow. God will help you deal with whatever hard things come up when the time comes. (Matthew 6:34 MSG)

Cast your cares of the LORD and he will sustain you; he will never let the righteous fall. (Psalm 55:22 NIV)

Therefore I tell you, do not worry about your life, what you will eat or drink; or about your body, what you will wear. Is not life more important than food, and the body more important than clothes? Look at the birds of the air; they do not sow or reap or store away in barns, and yet your heavenly Father feeds them. Are you not much more valuable than they? Who of you by worrying can add a single hour to his life?

And why do you worry about your clothes? See how the lilies of the field grow. They do not labor or spin. Yet I tell you not even Solomon in all his splendor was dressed like one of these. If that is how God clothes the grass of the field, which today is here and tomorrow is thrown into the fire, will he not much more clothe you, O you of little faith?

So don't worry, saying, "What shall we eat?" or "What shall we drink?" or "What shall we wear?" For the pagans run after all of these things, and your Father knows that you need them. But seek first His kingdom and His righteousness, and all these things will be given to you as well. Therefore do not worry about tomorrow, for tomorrow will worry about itself. Each day has enough trouble of its own. (Matthew 6:25-34 NIV)

Do not be anxious about anything, but in everything, by prayer and petition, with thanksgiving, present your requests to God. And the peace of God, which transcends all understanding, will guard your hearts and your minds in Christ Jesus. (Philippians 4:6-7 NIV)

Just for Today

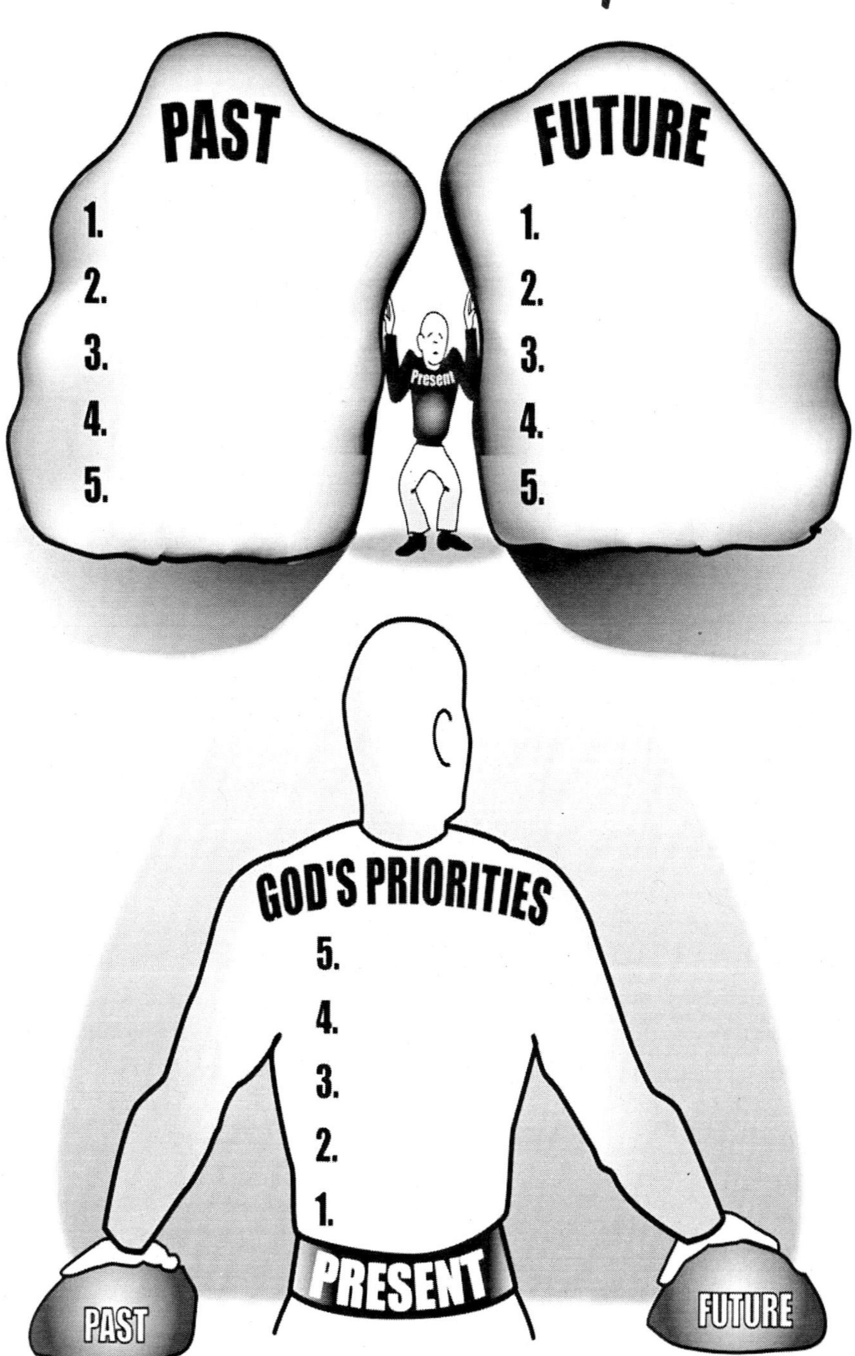

But seek first his kingdom and his righteousness and all these things will be given to you as well. Therefore do not worry about tomorrow, for tomorrow will worry about itself. Each day has enough trouble of its own.

Matthew 6:33-34 (NIV)

– 35 –

All About Suicide

David R. Miller
Philip J. Henry

Guiding Scripture

How long O Lord? Will you forget me forever? How long will you hide your face from me? How long must I wrestle with my thoughts and every day have sorrow in my heart? How long will my enemy triumph over me? Look on me and answer, O Lord my God. Give light to my eyes or I will sleep in death; my enemy will say, "I have overcome him," and my foe will rejoice when I fall. But I trust in your unfailing love and my heart rejoices in your salvation. I will sing to the Lord, for He has been good to me.

Psalm 13 (NIV)

Type of Contribution: Exercise, Handout

Objective

One of the most anxiety-producing experiences for any therapist is realizing that a client is or may be self-destructive. A client may exhibit overt signs, including suicidal thinking and comments, note or letter writing with a self-destructive theme, giving away important possessions, breaking off important relationships, and active suicidal planning. Covert signs of suicidal intention include risky, dangerous, or "thrill-seeking" behavior; careless sexual activities; and addictions. At these times, a client will have diminished capacity to think clearly and problem-solve along with great ambivalence about life and death. Spiritually, the person may feel under assault, threatened, attacked, and, most of all, distant from God. This exercise will provide the counselor with diagnostic tools and therapeutic remedies to help the suicidal client.

Rationale for Use

People considering suicide usually do not want to die; they just do not want to continue living as they have lived. Ambivalence is the prime mental state of a suicidal person, and this ambivalence gives hope to the helper. Christian counselors can build understanding by considering the cases of suicide or suicidal thinking in the Bible. For example, Samson took his own life, as recorded in Judges 16:29-30. The story of Saul killing himself is told in 1 Samuel 31:4-5. Ahithopel, David's rejected counselor, committed suicide, as revealed in 2 Samuel 17:23. Zimri the traitor took his life, as seen in 1 Kings 16:18. Of course, adding to the list, Judas, the betrayer of Jesus, hanged himself, as told in Matthew's gospel (27:5).

The Christian Therapist's Notebook

doi:10.1300/5334_36

Some people recorded in scripture only wished to die but did not complete the act, such as Job, as indicated in Job 6:8-11, 10:1, and 14:13. Jonah asked God to kill him, as recorded in Jonah 4:8. The apostle Paul wanted to die, as noted in 2 Corinthians 5:8. Today it is difficult to imagine the forces operating behind Bible characters who considered or committed suicide; life was so different then. However, two things remain constant: the love of God and the sin of human beings. It is the love of God that sustains His children, and this hope ultimately comes through trusting in the salvation offered through Jesus, regardless of the depth of the negative state of mind brought on by individual or corporate sin.

Instructions

Suicide is a self-decreed, self-intended wish for and attainment of death. A suicide attempt is a self-destructive action with death as the ambivalently expected result. However, what is it when a person makes a suicide gesture, such as overdosing on a nonfatal drug, and then calls for help? The term that applies to this behavior is *parasuicide,* which describes self-destructive behavior for which the intent is something other than death.

A counselor needs to be able to diagnose the state of mind and self-destructive intent of the person correctly. Clearly, a person who took too many aspirins and then called 911 is in a different category of risk than the person who took a potentially fatal dose of a substance and was rescued against his or her will.

Consider the possible causes of suicide, which come from crises of many sorts, including marital or relationship problems, separation or divorce, death of a loved one, failure and self-devaluation brought on by the loss of a job or demotion, a general loss of meaning or hope in life, and a broad range of inner conflicts. Christian clients will experience a similar range of concerns, but the issues are likely to center on felt spiritual failure, such as failing to respond to the leading of the Holy Spirit at a previous point in their lives, sinful moral failure, or an inability to accept God's grace, love, and forgiveness.

People who are suicidal are depressed. Though people may feel "down in the dumps" at times, most react to negative feelings by engaging in more acceptable behaviors, such as sleep or entertainment, talking to a trusted friend, praying for God's help, getting some physical exercise, eating, or just waiting for the feeling to pass. When we experience sadness or depression, especially for no apparent reason, we know those feelings will eventually pass and we will feel better. However, for some people, this may not always be true. The following is a list of several types of depression:

1. *Reactive depression* is depression caused by a specific happening or event that occurs outside the person's body. Examples could be a hurricane sweeping through and destroying a person's home, or a severe financial loss as a result of an automobile accident. Perhaps a parent is dealing with a teenager or adult child who is living far from the Lord and the parent feels responsible. Many possibilities exist.
2. *Endogenous depression* is caused by a change in body chemistry. Hormonal changes of menopause, adolescence, pregnancy, and aging are some factors at work in this type of depression. Endogenous depression creates a change in brain chemistry that can throw a person's normal emotional balance into chaos. Medical intervention is often used with depression of this type.
3. *Neurotic depression* reflects a deeply seated personality malfunction that has probably been in place during all or most of the person's life. This type of depression is extremely difficult to treat medically or therapeutically. Depression of this type reflects the failure experienced by a person who has tried to adapt to life's challenges and has consistently failed.

Counselors must be diagnosticians with the ability to determine the risk, intentions, and means of a client experiencing suicidal thinking. Counselors must ask questions and attempt to get as complete a history as possible to know the level of danger. Look and listen for signs of erratic sleep patterns (e.g., too much or too little sleep), general feelings of boredom, and loss of appetite for food, fun, sex, or activity. Many depressed people experience problems with personal hygiene, such as a sloppy and careless appearance or wearing the same clothing for several days. Depressed clients may experience weeping attacks for no apparent reason, they may break off interactions with friends and family, and they may feel ill and unhealthy without an apparent physical cause.

In obtaining a history of the depressed person, be on the alert for prior suicide attempts or gestures, comments orally or in writing indicating a self-destructive intent or preoccupation with death, as well as the types of movies and reading material chosen. Also, look for risky or self-abusive behavior, such as self-mutilation; any clear signs of mental illness, including hallucinations or delusions; an overwhelming sense of guilt or shame; and obsessive self-doubt and intense fears without apparent cause. The only way to receive the needed information is to listen to the client and to ask careful, nonaccusatory, open-ended questions of the client and, in some cases, the client's friends and family.

Consider these several strategies for helping a client engaging in suicidal thinking and showing some or many of the warning signs previously mentioned:

1. Listen for the feelings behind the words your client is using to describe his or her situation. How does your client see his or her world? Intensity of emotion is one way to determine risk level. Be alert to less obvious indicators of emotion, such as words chosen, facial expression while talking, such body language as wringing hands or fidgeting, and general appearance. Listen for emotions attached to comments or questions about God. Are the comments about God negative or positive? Why?
2. Begin cooperatively developing a no-harm contract with the client. Use the No-Harm Contract provided as a handout at the end of this exercise. Professionals know that suicidal people are far less likely to commit a self-destructive act if they have agreed to and signed a no-harm contract. This is a major tool in helping suicidal clients and should not be overlooked. Once your client understands the nature of a no-harm contract, attempt to get him or her to sign it. An example of such a contract is included as a handout at the end of this chapter.
3. Assess the client's support system. Is his or her family close by or at a distance? What would the client do, under normal circumstances, if he or she needed help from family? If the client is away from family, are there friends to call? Is your client involved in a church, and if so, could the pastor or others be helpful?
4. Learn as much as possible about the client's spiritual condition. How does your client see God in the process of dealing with his or her depression? What does your client believe about guilt, sin, and God's forgiveness? Has your client had experiences in which he or she was condemned by a religious authority figure for misbehavior of some type? It is not uncommon for a person to have had a negative experience with religion as a child and still be suffering from it as an adult.
5. Can your client verbalize recovery? Can he or she tell you what life would be like without depression? If so, how detailed is the description? Is God an element in life after recovery, and if so, how does your client express his or her thinking?
6. Be affirmative and supportive in your counseling. The client must see you as a caring helper who also knows what you are doing. The more you express humility in your ability to help, the more hopeless your client will feel. Be assertive about your ability to help, and

express a willingness to "go to bat" for your client, if necessary. Passivity is not an effective counseling strategy when helping a depressed and potentially suicidal person.

7. Make a firm appointment for the next session; as with a no-harm contract, people usually will not break an agreed-to appointment. If you can get your client to promise to come back for the next session, which should never be more than one week away, you can be reasonably sure that he or she will be safe until then. As a part of the safety arrangements, work out a way you can be reached in an emotional emergency, and make it clear that you will be available, if possible. Working with a depressed and possibly suicidal person takes more commitment from the counselor than do standard counseling situations.

A Gentle Reminder of What to Say or Not Say to a Client

When your client says, "Sometimes I think I'd be better off dead, but I'd never really kill myself" . . .

Don't say	Instead say
"You'll feel better soon." "Why are you feeling so hopeless?"	"What's bothering you, John?"

When your client says, "I think about death a lot" . . .

Don't say	Instead say
"Don't talk that way." "You have so much to live for." "You know God wants the best for you."	"How long have you felt this way?" "Can you tell me a little more about how you have been feeling?"

When your client says, "I feel so embarrassed about being depressed. People at home will be watching me all the time now" . . .

Don't say	Instead say
"Well, people are people, after all." "You'll just have to deal with it."	"Let's talk about your sense of embarrassment." "Do you think God wants you to get better?"

When your client says, "When my husband left me, I knew right away that I would not be able to live without him" . . .

Don't say	Instead say
"No wonder you're so unhappy." "I would be miserable if that happened to me too."	"That must have been quite a shock." "I think anyone would be temporarily destroyed by a loved one leaving."

When your client says, "I can't go on feeling this badly. My pain is too much for me to bear" . . .

Don't say	Instead say
"No need to worry." "We have lots of ways to help with depression."	"I can see you are in real pain right now." "I want you to know that I am committed to you getting better, and I believe we can do it, with God's help."

Vignette

Allyn was almost twenty-one years old when we met. Allyn was a committed Christian and member of a solid evangelical church in a city about forty minutes away from my office. He lived with his parents and maternal grandmother in the family home, the only home he had ever known. This young man seemed to be normal, if a little immature in some ways. As we talked, I learned about his commitment to God and his church, that he was very much a "homebody," that he had dated only occasionally, and that he had never had a serious romantic relationship, much less come close to getting married. In fact, one of the few smiles I saw on Allyn's face was when I asked the question about getting married, which he apparently saw as either funny or ridiculous.

Allyn was depressed because he was in trouble, serious trouble, and trouble from which neither I nor anyone else could save him. This Christian and solid church member had been arrested for sexually abusing two boys, ages five and eight, for whom he occasionally babysat while their divorced mother had to be out of town on business. The abuse involved inappropriate touching and was made public only after Allyn had refused to agree with something the older boy had asked him to do sexually. The older boy then became angry and told his mother what had been going on. She had Allyn charged, and he was arrested, booked, and then jailed for a short time in his hometown police building. His parents placed bond, and he was allowed to return home, with the understanding that he could have no contact with the two boys or anyone else under the age of eighteen. His family was, to say the least, shocked and dismayed at their son's behavior. Allyn readily admitted the behavior and attempted to explain himself by saying that, while he knew what "they" had done was wrong, he did not know it was illegal and claimed surprise at his arrest.

Fast-forward to the time of our first counseling appointment, and we find Allyn now fully aware of the serious penalties for child sexual abuse and with the understanding that he could spend more than a decade in prison for the offense. He told me that his lawyer was certain that Allyn would get some prison time and that the best he could hope for would be a year or two in a minimum-security facility. This was the first time Allyn had been in any kind of trouble, and that would work in his favor.

Allyn was distraught. His family was upset with him. The few friends he once had, now would have nothing to do with him. He had been fired from his job once the story made the newspaper, and he had stopped going to church out of extreme embarrassment and guilt. With tears in his eyes, he told me that no one had contacted him from his church to offer support or prayer. He was not sleeping, he was gaining weight, his personal hygiene was slipping, he was depressed and anxious "all the time," and he had seriously considered killing himself to save everyone else the trauma of a trial.

His attorney referred Allyn to me because of my experience in dealing with sexual offenders and, more important, because he was afraid that Allyn might actually take his life. My challenge, according to his lawyer, was to keep him alive through preparation for the trial and the trail itself, at which I would be called to testify as a witness in Allyn's defense. His lawyer felt that Allyn's sentence would be, in his words, "manageable" and that his client could come out of this process an older and wiser person who could go on to have a mostly normal life.

My first session with this young man involved completing normal intake forms and getting information on all the mundane but important parts of his life, job, church, school, friends, and family. I asked questions about his physical and mental health history, important memories from childhood and adolescence, family and work relationships, and sexual issues. I learned that Allyn was still a virgin, that he held very conservative attitudes about television and movies, and, on those few occasions he had dated, that he was a complete gentleman.

During the intake session, which lasted one and a half hours instead of the normal fifty minutes, I tried to draw my client into a discussion of his feelings about what he had done that had resulted in his arrest. His guilt, however, was so powerful that he was reduced to sobbing tears when he tried to talk about it. I decided to take a more indirect path and turned the discussion to his family and church experiences; this was both more productive and helpful in building a counseling relationship. I knew that I could not expect this "stranger" to reveal his innermost thoughts unless and until he trusted me. I had to empathize with both his situation and the depression he was suffering. I asked him to share some of his best memories with me as a way of bringing the emotional level up to a point where Allyn could verbalize his feelings.

At the end of the first session, I took some time to explain a "no-harm" contract to Allyn, and then asked him if he was agreeable to signing it. He took some time to think about it, which caused me even more concern about him, but then agreed to sign it. Because of his hesitation, I emphasized again that I was going to trust him, just as I was asking him to trust me. I gave him the necessary emergency phone numbers and suggested he start reading through the Book of Psalms in preparation for our next session. I prayed and asked God to protect this struggling young Christian, emphasizing God's all-knowing control and wisdom.

Because of the legal issues involved in his arrest, I requested and received permission from Allyn to talk to his parents and his lawyer, if I thought I needed to. I called his parents and, without sharing anything Allyn and I had talked about, told them of my concerns about depression. I then asked if they had any firearms in the home, as the family lived in a primarily rural area. It turned out that Allyn's father had one handgun and several shotguns and rifles. I explained my concerns and suggested to them that they take the weapons away or securely lock them until the situation was resolved, to which they agreed. While this kind of proactive intervention is not common in most counseling, it may be appropriate for suicidal clients.

Our second session involved exploring Allyn's awareness of his depression, its causes, and some possible cures. He had equally strong reasons to remain alive as he did for ending his life. He trusted God (he said), and he really believed that when everything was finished, he would be okay. The process worried him. He was interested in protecting everyone from the details of what he had done. He wished to spare the boys from a courtroom experience that might be difficult, and he wanted to spare his parents and grandmother the trauma of listening to the terrible things he had done. Allyn had confessed, but there would still be a public hearing to determine his sentence. Again, we talked about the providence and protection of God, and I challenged this young man to say aloud what he was thinking, a difficult thing to ask of anyone in this position.

Our third session followed up on my instructions that Allyn spend some time reading those stories in the Bible having to do with depression, suicide, or suicidal thinking. He had done some reading in Psalms, as I had suggested, and he was beginning to develop an awareness of life outside his problems. He was learning that even very serious problems pass away and that he could trust God in whatever arena he found himself, even prison.

The following sessions were supportive; Allyn seemed to respond to my concern for his welfare in a positive way. We explored all areas of his prearrest life, and we continued to learn more about the forces that led up to his sinful and illegal behavior. I was doing what I needed to do. I was helping to keep this young man alive, and at the same time, we were engaging in counseling aimed at revealing his problems and correcting the wrong thinking that had gotten him into trouble. Allyn was later convicted of his crime and sentenced to two years in a minimum-security prison in our state, with eight years of probation to follow his release. I lost contact with my client after the conviction; he did not write me from prison, nor did I contact him. He was going to get on with the rest of his life, and I hope and pray that he did.

Suggestions for Follow-Up

In order for a no-harm contract to work, a counselor must prepare to be "on call" during the crisis period. Most suicidal people experience real risk for only a few days or weeks and then need less support. The counselor must be a strong but warm advocate for the client's well-being and be prepared to become actively involved in protecting the client, if the need arises.

Contraindications

Counseling a self-destructive person requires having options available at any moment. The counselor should understand the legal ways a person can be hospitalized against his or her will, and these vary from state to state. If the client is in clear and present danger at a given moment, the safety of the client always takes precedence over any counseling needs or issues.

I have never worked with a suicidal client alone. I always had people in reserve I could call on, such as family members, a pastor, and the police. Counsel suicidal people in a location where other professionals are available in case of a crisis.

Resources for Professionals

Curran, D.K. (1987). *Adolescent suicidal behavior.* Washington, DC: Hemisphere Publishing Corporation.

Kirwan, W.T. (1984). *Biblical concepts for Christian counseling.* Grand Rapids, MI: Baker Book House.

Shneidman, E. (1985). *Definitions of suicide.* New York: John Wiley and Sons.

Resources for Clients

Warren, R. (2002). *The purpose driven life: What on earth am I here for?* Grand Rapids, MI: Zondervan.

Wright, N. (1998). *Winning over your emotions.* Eugene, OR: Harvest House Publishers.

Related Scriptures

> For in my inner being I delight in God's law; but I see another law at work in the members of my body, waging war against the law of my mind and making me a prisoner of the law of sin at work within my members. What a wretched man I am! Who will rescue me from this body of death? Thanks be to God—through Jesus Christ our Lord. (Romans 7:21-25 NIV)

> Jesus answered, "I am the way and the truth and the life. No one comes to the Father except through me." (John 14:6 NIV)

> So do not throw away your confidence; it will be richly rewarded. You need to persevere so that when you have done the will of God, you will receive what He has promised. For in just a very little while, He who is coming will come and will not delay. (Hebrews 10:35-37 NIV)

No Harm Contract

I, ________________________________, agree not to kill myself, harm myself, or attempt to kill myself for the time period beginning now ________________ until ________________.

I agree to come to my next appointment on ____________ at ___________ with ________________________________.

I agree to get rid of things that I have thought about using to kill myself.

I agree to call the crisis numbers on the crisis card given to me today by ______________________ should I have the urge to kill or harm myself.

I realize that this contract is part of my therapy contract with my counselor at ____________________________.

____
Signature of Client

____
Signature of Counselor

____
Date and Time

– 36 –

Self-Injury

Emery D. Twoey
Philip J. Henry

Guiding Scripture

Scorn has broken my heart and has left me helpless; I looked for sympathy, but there was none, for comforters, but I found none. . . . I am in pain and distress; may your salvation, O God, protect me.

Psalm 69:20, 29 (NIV)

Type of Contribution: Exercise, Handout

Objective

Self-injury, paradoxically, is often an attempt to escape pain, to comfort oneself, and, sometimes, to reach out for help. The person engaging in self-injury/mutilation is causing pain to the physical body to counteract the pain brought on by external persons or circumstances perceived to be difficult to control or impossible to manage.

Physical self-wounding may be obvious and clearly indicate the pain of the client, or the injuries may be concealed, a closely held secret, unknown even to close friends and family members. A variety of factors may prompt self-injury, but one thing is sure: the Christ of the cross knows each pain. The forces pushing the person to self-injure and/or self-mutilate are reflected in the Psalm of the Guiding Scripture and can be soothed and healed by the God who loves.

Rationale for Use

Human beings tend to place the safety of self at the top of the importance hierarchy. Most of us are able to understand self-destructive acts, such as suicide and self-injury, on only an intellectual level. Hurting self is an act so foreign to most, including counselors, that many have a difficult time trying to help when called upon to do so. People tend to react by sympathizing with the pain being experienced and working to resolve that immediate pain, often to the detriment of dealing with the more deeply seated reasons for the self-injurious behavior.

Self-injury is an attempt at self-treatment for some real or imagined pain caused by internal guilt and self-loathing or external persons or circumstances. The one who self-injures is attempting self-medication, of a sort. He or she is feeling pain, physical or psychological or both, and believes that this pain is beyond treatment, beyond understanding by others. Clients who self-injure or self-mutilate themselves are panic-stricken with a sense of helplessness, just as the

The Christian Therapist's Notebook

doi:10.1300/5334_37

suicidal person feels driven to the wall with no avenue of escape. Helplessness and hopelessness are common threads that bind all self-injury clients together and help the counselor understand and effectively treat these people.

Counselors will want to help the self-injury client understand that the pain he or she is experiencing is not unique to him or her and that others have found peace and healing in the God of love. Do not minimize the sense of helplessness and hopelessness. Do not try to talk the client out of his or her pain, and do not try to convince the client that he or she is wrong in what he or she is doing. Instead, attempt to show the client another way to deal with the very real pain. Helping the client turn his or her eyes away from self and more toward God will be a slow and perhaps tedious process, but there is no other option. No medicine can turn the client's pain away permanently. No alcohol or drug will anesthetize for the long run. Only God can answer the need.

Instructions

You will need to do a very thorough personal history intake with your client who is self-injuring. Be patient in the beginning and remind yourself that time will be saved, rather than wasted, by getting a complete psychological and personal history. Be careful to ask direct questions about when the self-injuring began, and be prepared to adjust your timeline as the client comes to trust you more and eventually tells you the "real story" behind the behavior.

You may need to involve parents. Self-injury is very common among adolescents and young adults, and in some cases, you may need parental consent and information to proceed with counseling. This can be a challenge because parents may be involved at some level in the motivation for the self-injurious behavior.

Ask your client to tell you where the pain lives inside his or her body. Ask what color the pain is, what it smells like, and what it looks like. Personalize his or her pain by asking your client to give the pain a name. All of this helps to "materialize" the pain the client is experiencing and serves to raise your credibility as a counselor who believes in the pain this client is experiencing.

You believe your client! You are not ridiculing the fear and self-loathing your client feels. You are not repeating what he or she has so often heard, that this is a phase he or she will soon pass through. You believe! You are not telling your client that the most important thing is that he or she stops the self-hurting. You are not recommending a search of his or her room for instruments used to inflict the pain. You are different! You are listening without criticizing or correcting. You are listening without being parental or excessively clinical because you believe the pain is real and want to help your client deal with it, with God's help.

Ask your client to tell you about some "typical" self-injury experiences. Listen for what was happening just before and just after the self-injury occurred. Use the "Grid of Pain" handout to help your client grade the level of pain experienced then and now. Use the handout also as a homework assignment; ask your client to find magazine clippings and "cut and paste" triggering images onto the grid. Encourage your client to find other images that might trigger his or her self-injury or that "other people" might find to be triggers. Be careful to explain that triggers are simply things that cause the client to hurt or that recall a previous hurt which then needs to be dealt with by self-inflicted pain. Ask your client to talk about how the pain helps him or her. Is the pain a friend or an enemy? Would he or she like to be pain free, or does he or she feel that pain is a necessary companion in order to deal with life's challenges, both past and present?

Ask your client to show you how he or she hurts himself or herself. The typical client response is one of embarrassment and unwillingness, but do gently persist with your questioning. Ask to see the marks self-injury has left on the client's body, but be careful to stay within the bounds of an appropriate counselor-client relationship. You do not need to see marks or scars on personal body areas, as this would violate both counselor and Christian ethics. Most self-injury and mutilation will be to the arms and legs, and primarily where the marks can be hidden by clothing. Unlike people with tattoos, clients with self-inflicted marks or scars are more likely to want to keep them hidden and away from questions or criticism by family or friends.

Explore both preinjury and postinjury feelings. Ask your client to describe the last event of self-injury. You are more interested in feelings than behaviors at this point in counseling. How was your client *feeling* during the hour or two just preceding the injury? How did your client *feel* immediately after, and how long was it before the relief of self-inflicted pain faded and the old guilt, shame, and self-loathing returned? What was the client thinking while he or she prepared the self-injury? Look for any rituals that may have developed around the self-injury event and explore their meanings with the client. Christian clients may actually pray before the self-injury. If this is the case with your client, explore the purpose of his or her prayer. Is he or she asking for forgiveness for what is about to happen, or is he or she asking God to take away the need for pain? Ask your client to use the Grid of Pain handout at the end of this chapter; direct the client to find pictures from magazines that represent things that have caused him or her pain, or simply to write down the words or names of things that have been pain sources for him or her; then discuss each of these items with your client.

Suggest, as a part of counseling, that there might be "half-steps" the client could use to meet his or her need for self-inflicted pain without the danger and scarring of behavior such as cutting the skin. For example, suggest the client immerse a hand in ice water as an alternative to self-injury. This kind of strategy is employed only as a temporary tactic while getting the client to the point in counseling where pain is no longer needed or sought.

Finally, focus repeatedly on the pain and suffering experienced by Jesus, how he was bruised for our iniquity and whipped for our transgressions. Gently talk about how Jesus lived, died, and was resurrected so that we human beings would not have to suffer the pain He bore on the cross. Suggest that when the client self-injures, he or she is rejecting the purpose of the cross and that, by his or her behavior, he or she is making a strong statement that the suffering and death of Jesus, while sufficient for the forgiveness of all other human beings, is not adequate for the client. Is this what the client believes? Be gentle on this point. Avoid preaching or teaching. You are simply opening up an alternate way of thinking for your client. You are not suggesting he or she has been wrong or sinful because you want to be careful to avoid adding to existing shame and guilt in the client.

Vignette

I first met Sharon when she was fifteen years old and a student in the Christian school where our two youngest children were enrolled. The school was large, about 1,200 students in kindergarten through grade twelve. Even though our two youngest children were students in the same school, they were in different grades and did not know Sharon.

The school guidance counselor called me after another student had reported seeing Sharon in the girls' room making deep scratches in her wrist to the point of drawing blood. Sharon refused to talk with the girl about what was going on, and in Christian concern, the girl talked to the guidance counselor about what she should do. The guidance counselor called Sharon into the office and, after reminding her that she was not in trouble, asked if she wanted to talk about what was making her feel badly. Denial was Sharon's first response, but the counselor persisted, and eventually Sharon revealed a number of deep scars on her upper arms and legs, marks that were in several stages of healing, indicating a continuous pattern of self-injury. Sharon was extremely embarrassed about her behavior and was unable to explain why she did it, except to say that somehow it made her feel better.

Sharon's guidance counselor felt as if some outside help would be appropriate, and so she called me. Self-injury is a relatively rare occurrence, and it is not surprising that anyone would feel unprepared to deal with it. Because we worked for the same Christian school "system," it was relatively easy for me to introduce myself to Sharon and her parents, who were put at ease when I mentioned that I, too, had children in the school.

Our first meeting involved Sharon, her mother, the guidance counselor, and me. After the guidance counselor shared her first contacts with Sharon following the incident in the girls' room, I explained that my role would be to provide counseling services for Sharon, the goal of which was cessation of all self-injurious behavior. I shared that, while my only goal was to help end the self-destructive behavior, I would need to ask for the full cooperation of both Sharon and her mother in providing background information that might help me understand and help. I explained confidentiality and emphasized that what we talked about in the counseling office stayed there unless, because Sharon was a minor, I needed to talk to her mother about any potential danger or special concerns I might have. This was agreeable, and we scheduled our first session for the following week.

The second session began with Sharon's mother and me alone. This was an information-gathering session during which I asked about Sharon's early years, any traumatic events she may have experienced, how Sharon had handled the divorce of her parents, her general health, and anything else the mother might think pivotal. The only significant issue Sharon's mother mentioned was how hard it was for Sharon to be without her father, who had moved to another state following the divorce and now saw the children only three or four times a year. While Sharon's mother was still unmarried, her father had recently married a woman with two young children. Sharon was the oldest of three girls and had taken on some motherly responsibilities after the divorce, which was a great help to her mother.

The second portion of the second session was my listening to Sharon talk about her family and general experiences. It was important that she learn that I would listen to her without interrupting, correcting, or criticizing, and that I would pay close attention, even though she was "just a teenager." This rapport building is absolutely essential when beginning a counseling relationship with anyone of any age, but it is especially so with adolescents. I recognized that what I was hearing was relatively unimportant, but that my young client was putting me through a test, to see if I would just be another authority figure, like her parents and teachers, or if I had real interest in her. Such testing of counselors is common among adolescents.

The second session ended with asking Sharon to keep a journal of all her activities, including any self-injury episode. While I would not ask to read the journal, I would expect Sharon to read portions of it to me, if requested. I also explained that I would ask to see her arms and ask her mother to keep an eye on the rest of her to keep track of her self-injurious behavior. Such accountability was an important element in helping Sharon to understand that we all were serious about helping her end this dangerous behavior.

Our third session involved a quick five-minute update from Sharon's mother, and the rest of the session was just Sharon and me. Again, I focused on listening, but I was beginning to hear more about fears and feelings, which indicated that Sharon was starting to trust me. It is so important for a counselor to be patient in developing trust and rapport with an adolescent client. There simply is no substitute for relationship building.

Sharon revealed that the self-hurting behavior had begun a few months after the divorce of her parents and had worsened when her father had moved away. Sharon clearly blamed herself for the problems her parents had experienced. She felt that, as the oldest child, if she had done better in school and been more of a help to her mother at home, her parents would not have fought so much and the divorce could have been prevented. Though irrational and untrue, such beliefs are common to children of divorced parents, and even more so among the oldest children.

I asked Sharon if any self-hurting had occurred, and she said, "Just a little," which meant some wrist scratching similar to what had happened at school. She had engaged in this behavior while in her room and in bed, saying it helped her to sleep. She shared that her sadness was most awful at night because that was when she missed her father the most. She said that the pain she felt in her arm helped to keep her mind off the pain she was feeling inside. We talked more about her thoughts and feelings and ended the third session.

Following our third session, Sharon had a bad week. She learned that her father and his new wife were going to have a baby, and this totally depressed her. She had taken a single-edge razor blade from a hiding place in her bedroom and inflicted serious cuts on her upper arms, not enough to require stitches but enough to bleed significantly and upset her mother, who found blood on her sheets. I took this very seriously, of course, but not in a parental or authoritative way, but instead as a doctor might approach it. We talked about the danger of infection and scarring and that she might find herself hospitalized if the behavior occurred too frequently. I explained, during this fourth session, that she was using an unacceptable method to escape the pain of feeling abandoned by her father, and we needed to find another way she could express her feelings without hurting herself.

As the fourth session ended, I asked Sharon to compose a letter to her father, one that she might never send, but that would allow her to express her hurt and anger at what she perceived to be his rejection of her. I suggested she also write a letter to God, asking Him to help her learn how to accept God's forgiveness for not trusting Him and for not taking seriously the work that Jesus had done on the cross. I was careful to avoid an accusatory tone, but I needed this Christian young person to begin thinking about what she really believed about God and Jesus.

Our next session proved to be a real breakthrough for Sharon. She told me that she had been seriously thinking about our talk of the previous week, about the role of God in her life, and she realized she was failing to believe that God was in charge of her life. Sharon said that she had finally realized that her parents' problems belonged to them alone. When I asked about how she had come to this realization, she said that she and her mother had finally had a long talk about the separation and divorce and that, while she missed her dad, she loved and trusted her mother and believed what she was told about the reason for the divorce. "It really wasn't my fault!" Sharon exclaimed. "I don't know why it was so difficult for me to understand that all along. It makes so much sense now."

While I have some professional reservation about sudden turnabouts like this, I could do nothing else but accept what she was telling me as true. I asked about incidents of self-injury and was told that none had occurred since she last saw me. Sharon talked at length about the relief she felt at finally understanding the proper place of responsibility in her family situation. It just seemed that she had grown up quite a lot in one week, and while I tend to be cautious when this happens, I had no reason to doubt her. I talked with her mother alone at the end of the session, and she verified the conversation and promised to keep checking Sharon for fresh injuries.

Our final session ended the week after Sharon went to the altar during church. She asked God to help her with accepting His love and protection and rededicated her life to Him. She enthusiastically told me about feeling closer to God and her parents than ever before, and she finally had found joy in realizing that God the Father never fails and is always there for her. I invited her mother into the office, and we prayed together for Sharon's continued improvement. The session concluded with Sharon promising to meet with me for a follow-up session once a month until school was out, in about four months.

The case of Sharon reinforces the importance of patience and advocacy when counseling teenagers. Counselors need to be gently proactive and willing to demonstrate commitment to and belief in the importance of the adolescent's issues. As is typical with Christian young people, Sharon got in trouble because she confused her earthly father with her heavenly Father, and when one abandoned her, she felt abandoned by both. Once we reframed her thinking about this, we began to see improvement. I cannot emphasize enough the importance of careful listening and empathic understanding in cases such as Sharon's. Thank God we were successful.

Suggestions for Follow-Up

Follow-up in cases of self-injury involves parents or other caregivers, in the case of children or adolescents, and friends and spouses, with adults. In some cases, antianxiety medication might be considered as an adjunct to therapy, and a referral to a psychiatrist is warranted in some cases as well. Encourage your client to stay in touch with you because you care about him or her, and make sure you return phone calls promptly.

Contraindications

In cases of life-threatening self-injury, hospitalization is always a prime referral. If the client feels that he or she cannot voluntarily stop or limit the self-injurious behavior, have parents or spouses come to the office to discuss hospitalization as a firm and desirable option. Professionals have the duty and responsibility, in severe cases, to insist that the client be in a safe environment until his or her condition is under control. If a client is engaging in serious self-injury, a counselor should consider putting therapy on hold until the behavior can be controlled well enough to allow the client to engage in therapy.

Resources for Professionals

Borgman, D. (2003). *Hear my story: Understanding the cries of troubled youth.* Peabody, MA: Hendrickson Publishers, Inc.

Lester, A. (1995). *Hope in pastoral counseling.* Louisville, KY: Westminster John Knox Press.

Resources for Clients

Bradshaw, J. (1988). *Healing the shame that binds you.* Deerfield Beach, FL: Health Communications, Inc.

Carlson, D. (2000). *Overcoming hurts and anger.* Eugene, OR: Harvest House Publishers.

Stewart, D. (2004). *Refuge: A pathway out of domestic violence and abuse.* Birmingham, AL: New Hope Publishers.

Related Scripture

> Do you not know that your body is a temple of the Holy Spirit, who is in you, whom you have received from God? You are not your own; you were bought at a price. Therefore, honor God with your body. (1 Corinthians 6:19-20 NIV)

> Don't let anyone look down on you because you are young, but set an example for the believers in speech, in life, in love, in faith, and in purity. (1 Timothy 4:12 NIV)

> Do not repay evil with evil or insult with insult, but with blessing, because to this you were called, so that you may inherit a blessing. (1 Peter 3:9 NIV)

Grid of Pain

Use the pain grid to grade the level of pain experienced then and now. Find magazine clippings and "cut and paste" triggering images onto the grid including images that might trigger self-injury or that "other people" might find to be triggers.

– 37 –

When I'm Mad

Emery D. Twoey
Philip J. Henry

Guiding Scripture

Go ahead and get angry. You do well to be angry—
but don't use your anger as a fuel for revenge.

Ephesians 4:26 MSG

Type of Conbribution: Exercise, Handout

Objective

Assisting teenagers in understanding how anger disrupts their emotional and social growth involves being able to explore the things that make them angry and introducing them to safe ways to express anger. Doing this requires being able to identify the underlying feelings that accompany anger and the areas where healing might need to occur as well as encouraging adolescents to dialogue with God, even when they feel angry.

Rationale for Use

Anger is a feeling of displeasure, resulting from injury, mistreatment, or opposition, and it usually shows itself in a desire to fight back at the supposed cause of this feeling. Anger is a very common experience and emotion. It is a natural part of the teenage years and may be accompanied by temper outbursts and, sometimes, aggressive behavior. Les Parrott (2000) states that anger is so common during adolescence that many people believe its absence is a maladaptive sign. People expect adolescents to be angry and even slam doors shut now and then. However, for some, anger becomes a chronic pattern of destructive behavior. At times, these emotional outbursts are signs that a young person's anger has reached unhealthy proportions. Teenagers often do not know how to express anger appropriately, and as a result, anger builds, and they explode (McDowell and Hostetler, 1996).

When teens react aggressively, resolution of angry feelings and proper responses to upsetting situations are the goals. Angry outbursts occur when adolescents become emotionally hurt and frustrated. Frustration arises from the feeling that desires, goals, and/or wants are being blocked or needs are not being met. Hurt develops from adolescents thinking someone has wronged them in some way. Often, the only way adolescents know how to respond to these perceived roadblocks is with extreme and aggressive behavior.

The Christian Therapist's Notebook

doi:10.1300/5334_38

Adolescence is a dramatic stage of life for the teenager, who views everything in absolute terms, with little awareness of shades of gray. Therefore, all reactions are intense ones, and for those who have few natural inhibitors, anger is all too often the first response. Many times, what adolescents are trying to say through their anger is that they feel inadequate to the task facing them and need assistance but do not know how to ask for it. Aggression is a natural way to get the attention they need but do not know how to request. Adolescents who react in aggressive, angry ways are usually trying to regain control over their lives because they are incapable of finding workable solutions to their problems. Their inability to communicate causes them to try aggression or intimidation.

To resolve such needs, God's provision for handling anger is critical. Too many teens experience the frustration and anger process. God's word says, "A fool gives vent to his anger but a wise man keeps himself under control" (Proverbs 29:11 NIV) and "Everyone should be slow to become angry, for man's anger does not bring about the righteous life that God desires" (James 1:19b-20 NIV).

Instructions

The first step in working with teens having anger management difficulties is to listen and pay attention to what they are saying about how they are feeling. Many times, you will get an avoidance type of response, such as, "I don't know what is wrong" or "Nothing is wrong." At this point, you may also want to examine body language. This will often give you much-needed information, as teens will appear tense, be closemouthed, or sit in a defensive pose, perhaps even with their backs turned to you. Help the young client to see what his or her body language is saying and to realize how this avoidance behavior is counterproductive. Ask the client to consider how avoidance is part of being angry (McDowell and Hostetler, 1996).

It may be helpful to use the process Neil Warren (1990) suggests in his book *Make Anger Your Ally:* Ask the teen to spell out, in writing, the kind of person he or she wants to be. For example, "I want to be a person people like to be around," "I want to be the kind of person who gets along with others," or "I want to be someone who doesn't have to be arguing with others or in conflict with others." After the teen writes a statement of what kind of person he or she wants to be, he or she should be prepared to repeat it silently throughout the day, especially when beginning to feel angry about something.

Next, discuss with the teen ways to recognize the explosive buildup. Review past expressions of anger, and pick apart the situations that facilitated the feelings of anger. Then, you and the adolescent can begin to identify the situations that cause him or her to become angry. As you identify the situations that cause the anger to intensify, begin to discuss ideas for avoiding the actual aggressive interchange with others. Practice choosing alternative ways of responding. This may be difficult because the teenager probably has reinforcement for acting aggressively, and he or she needs to rethink this pattern of behavior.

Once you have succeeded in getting the teen to talk freely about his or her anger, take out the handout "When I'm Mad" at the end of this exercise. Revisit some of the situations the teen has identified when he or she was angry and write them in the first column of the handout. Talk through each incident, having the teen write in what happened, what he or she wanted, and what the accompanying feeling was. Be prepared for this to take some time. The teen likely will not be able to immediately identify what he or she wanted or what the accompanying feelings were. Discuss these things with the teen, giving the teen plenty of time to think about it. Allow silence and space. Help the teen see that often when we are angry it is because we did not get what we wanted or expected or hoped for in some way. It is of highest importance to help the teen see that there is always another emotion underlying anger. Don't go on until you have helped the teen identify the accompanying feelings.

In the next session, encourage the adolescent to think things through before reacting angrily. Train the teen to think about what he or she wants out of the situation, and to realize that getting angry will probably not achieve the desired results. However, realize that being able to respond in this manner does not mean the anger issues have been resolved.

The next step is to develop a way to channel the anger constructively. Here you will focus your attention on the "why" of anger: "Why am I angry?" Is it frustration or a blockage of a desire? Is it a hurt feeling or threat in some way? Twoey (2002), in his book *ProTeen: A Positive Guide to Understanding Adolescents,* instructs the counselor to try to get to the cause of the problem by exploring the personal issues that surface. To do this, review the behavior and social skills breakdown that occurs during an angry episode, and discuss how the adolescent handled the situation. Twoey reveals that it is very important to understand what the emotions are trying to say while feeling angry. After the attempt to pinpoint the primary feeling, assist the teen in resolving the anger and in understanding what is producing the negative behavior.

In his book *Helping the Struggling Adolescent,* Parrott (2000) recommends Raymond Novaco's anger control technique, which consists of triggers and self-evaluation. Anger usually revolves around certain triggers or events interpreted by the individual in negative ways. Understanding how to interpret situations can lead to reducing the negative and passionate responses to people or situations. This then needs to lead toward self-evaluation. Self-evaluation is the process used to assess how well the teen did in reducing the negative effects of the anger response mode. What kind of self-talk is happening that will change poor responses to healthy ones? Statements such as, "Relax," "I don't have to get upset," and "Chill out" can be helpful mantras for stopping an angry response.

Consider praying with the teenager about overcoming the passion that accompanies an explosive event and enlisting the Holy Spirit's aid in dealing effectively with hurt and frustration. In addition to this, assist the teenager in praying about the situations or individuals that trigger the angry responses.

Vignette

It was a beautiful Saturday morning in the Maddachu household and time to get out of bed and down to breakfast. Ivan could hear his mother yelling at him from downstairs to get up and eat so he could help his father build a utility shed in the backyard. As he made his way to the kitchen, he heard his father tell his mother that Ivan can kiss the car goodbye for the rest of the weekend. "I'm sick and tired of always waiting around for that boy to get in gear when there's work to be done, so he can just forget about using the car!"

When Ivan got to the kitchen, his mother scolded him again for sleeping the day away. "Your father is very upset at you and so am I. You never take responsibility to help around here. Now eat your breakfast and get outside and help your father," she said. Ivan mumbled something to himself under his breath, swallowed his orange juice, and went out the door.

In the backyard, his father was busy organizing the plywood and measuring it to cut into various pieces. He told Ivan to continue nailing the framework together while he cut some more two-by-fours. Ivan, already irritated at his parents, began hitting the wooden frame of the utility shed with many aggressive blows. At one point, as he was hammering, he hit his thumb. This brought on a litany of colorful words in an effort to subdue the pain. After he managed to calm down, his father tried to remind him how unacceptable his behavior had been, and that he had better get it under control. "Acting like a jerk is not going to get this shed built," he chided. Ivan again mumbled a few more choice words under his breath and began to hammer the framework together. At one point, Ivan hit his thumb again, but this time, he began hitting the garden trailer with his hammer, while cursing his bad luck and putting several dents into the fenders of the trailer.

When Ivan was finished throwing his temper tantrum, his father told him to go to his room until he could calm down. All the way to his room, Ivan blamed everyone and everything, including the hammer, for his bad attitude.

The following week, Ivan's father made an appointment for Ivan to see me. When Ivan arrived, it was clear that he did not want to be there and he appeared angry. I considered this fortuitous since Ivan's father had mentioned to me that he wanted Ivan to see me because he "had a problem with anger." I made some small talk with Ivan to try and help him get comfortable, asking about his basketball sneakers, school, hobbies, etc. I then asked Ivan to thing about how he felt when he walked into my office. He was able to admit that he was angry. I asked him why he was angry. Not surprisingly, his response was "I don't know." I patiently kept probing and asking him questions until he blurted out "because my Dad is a jerk." I asked more questions about why he felt that way and when he felt that way. I asked him about other people that made him angry. I asked him about situations that made him angry. I let him freely talk about all the things and people that made him angry. I asked him if he felt he was angry often and he admitted that he was.

I took out the "When I'm Mad" handout and asked Ivan if we could complete it together. He agreed, somewhat unenthusiastically. We listed a number of the examples Ivan and I had talked about of people or situations that made him angry. I then asked Ivan to look at each entry and write in exactly what had happened. We then spent some time talking about what Ivan had wanted in each situation and in what way he did not get what he wanted. We then examined how Ivan felt during each situation and when he did not get what he wanted. Ivan's first and second response to my question about how he felt was "I don't know." He then replied that he felt angry. I had to help him look beyond the anger and see how else he felt. Was he disappointed, embarrassed, shameful, afraid, or in pain? Did he feel inadequate or that he was being put down? It seemed that many of Ivan's angry incidents involved his father. Ivan was finally able to put into words that his father made him feel like a failure, that he was never good enough or could never meet his dad's expectations. These feelings were always expressed, however, as anger.

We talked about ways to handle these feelings besides exploding, and brainstormed ways for Ivan to tell his father how he made him feel. Since we were almost out of time, I introduced several alternative ways to channel and handle anger appropriately and told Ivan we would explore these next time. As homework, I gave Ivan another copy of the "When I'm Mad" handout, asked him to complete the four steps each time he became angry in the coming week, and asked him to bring it with him to the next session to begin our discussion.

Suggestions for Follow-Up

As anger and discussion of anger-related situations arise in subsequent sessions, revisit this exercise and have the client complete the handout again with you. Anger is an unfolding process, so it will likely take several reviews of the material before any significant change takes place. In addition, as the client goes back and identifies the feelings behind the anger in situation after situation, he or she will begin to understand and learn to control the underlying emotions.

Contraindications

Do not attempt this exercise unless the client-counselor rapport can tolerate a little friction. Ensure that the adolescent understands that the therapy process does not seek to alienate his or her parents or to give them the indication that harmful acts are normal.

Resources for Professionals

Bauman, L., and Riche, R. (1997). *The ten most troublesome teen-age problems and how to solve them.* New York: Citadel Press.
Hutchcraft, R. (1997). *Ten time bombs.* Grand Rapids, MI: Zondervan Publishing House.
McDowell, J. (1996). *Handbook on counseling youth.* Nashville, TN: W. Publishing Group.
Parrott, L. (2000). *Helping the struggling adolescent.* Grand Rapids, MI: Zondervan Publishing House.
Trollinger, S. (2001). *Unglued and tattooed.* Washington, DC: Life Line Press.
Twoey, E. (2002). *ProTeen: A Positive Guide to Understanding Adolescents.* Cleveland, TN: Pathway Press.
Warren, N.C. (1985). *Make anger your ally.* New York: Doubleday and Co., Inc.

Resources for Clients

Covey, S. (1998). *The 7 habits of highly effective teens.* New York: Simon & Schuster, Inc.
DeAnda, D. (2002). *Stress management for adolescents.* Ottawa, Ontario: Research Press.
Moles, K. (2003). *Strategies for anger management.* Hawthorn, NY: Wellness Reproductions & Publishing.
Shapiro, L.E. (2004). *The emotional literacy series.* Fairfax, VA: CTC Publishing.
Stewart, J. (2002). *The anger workout book for teens.* Austin, TX: Jalmar Press.

Related Scriptures

A gentle answer turns away wrath, but a harsh word stirs up anger. (Proverbs 15:1 NIV)

A fool gives full vent to his anger, but a wise man keeps himself under control. (Proverbs 29:11 NIV)

But I tell you that anyone who is angry with his brother will be subject to judgment. Again, anyone who says to his brother, "Raca" is answerable to the Sanhedrin. But anyone who says, "You fool!" will be in danger of the fire of hell. (Matthew 5:22 NIV)

My dear brothers, take note of this: Everyone should be quick to listen, slow to speak and slow to become angry, for man's anger does not bring about the righteous life that God desires. (James 1:19-20 NIV)

When I'm Mad

SITUATION OR PERSON THAT MADE YOU MAD	WHAT HAPPENED	WHAT YOU WANTED	ACCOMPANYING FEELING

Friends

David R. Miller
Philip J. Henry

Guiding Scripture

He who walks with the wise grows wise, but a companion of fools suffers harm.

Proverbs 13:20 (NIV)

Type of Contribution: Exercise, Handout

Objective

For the adolescent, relationships with peers are of the utmost importance. Making friends, being with friends, and keeping friendships define who they are and what they do and will be. During this period of development, parents, teachers, ministers, and all others take a backseat to friends. These significant friendships, or sometimes the lack of them, can make or break adolescents.

Therefore, this exercise aims to assist adolescents to explore friendships and identify individuals who might help them in promoting positive change. Conversely, it also aims to assist adolescents to examine relationships that might have a negative effect and to discover their pattern of choosing friends. In addition to this, another goal is to ensure that teenagers consider how positive friendships might influence their thoughts, attitudes, and actions. A final goal is to help adolescents to consider God as a source of friendship and to invite Him into their lives to give wisdom in choosing and making friends.

Rationale for Use

Scripture agrees with the assessment that friends are important. In fact, many passages point to the influence of friends and the importance of choosing them carefully because of their great influence. The old saying "birds of a feather flock together" is appropriate here. Look at the friendships of a teen and you will see the direction he or she is heading and his or her developing destiny. A teen's life will shape and be shaped by those with whom he or she spends his or her time. Spend time with someone, and, before long, your attitudes, values, and even thoughts about God will be the same as that person's.

Adolescents have many obstacles to overcome in order to learn, grow, and become productive. One area of particular difficulty for an adolescent is his or her relationships and his or her desire to fit in. Most adolescents' problems result from the mishandling of normal and predict-

The Christian Therapist's Notebook

doi:10.1300/5334_39

able daily situations. Along with this is the fact that friends are very important in the lives of teenagers. With friends, adolescents can practice and experiment with social behavior, and they can fine-tune behaviors so they will be more acceptable socially. Friends provide adolescents with a means of support in an atmosphere where they can feel secure. Teenagers need affirming relationships that will provide genuineness and encouragement, and friends can foster these affirming relationships.

Instructions

As you begin your sessions with the youngster, try to get him or her to identify the characteristics of the friends he or she has. Let the teen guide the discussion, but help him or her to understand that you are looking for character traits such as honesty, genuineness, politeness, aggressiveness, and so on. Ask the teen to be as honest as possible when sizing up the people with whom he or she spends time.

Then, talk with the teen about the importance of friendships, and see if he or she is open to exploring the influence of these friendships on his or her own behaviors. Explore the type of people he or she befriends and the amount of time he or she is with these friends. While exploring the type of friends your young client has, attempt to get him or her to ponder if his or her friends are healthy for him or her. Do they influence him or her for the good, or do they lead him or her into trouble?

At this point, take out the "Anchor-Lifeline-Noose" handout at the end of this exercise. Read the descriptions at the top of the handout, talking with the client about how friends can be anchors, lifelines, or nooses. Ask the client to think about each of his or her friends and which category each fits into. Have the client write the name of his or her friends in the appropriate column. Notice whether any patterns emerge and discuss how the client chooses who to spend the most time with. Talk about the friends that act as a "noose" in the client's life, and whether the client might consider spending less time with those friends. Discuss the benefits of focusing more time and attention on friends that are "lifelines."

Once you have fully discussed the handout, look at good decision-making skills. How does the teen make the decision to hang out with his or her current friends? Does he or she make a decision primarily because he or she has known these friends for a long time or because they like the same things? Remember, troubled kids will look to associate with other troubled kids. Follow up on this destructive tendency.

Now share how the teen might make positive decisions regarding friends. Counselors can expose teens to better decision making by engaging them in conversation and discussion. The foundation is care, and it centers on listening to each other. You can share experiences and answers to prayer. Your experiences will become the foundation for the teens' decision-making processes. Teens have numerous choices today, but few people help them make good decisions. Role-play "what if" situations with your young client, such as, "What if this happened to you?" or "What would you do in this situation?" This is a terrific way to get inside the teen's mind. As the youth moves into the teenage years, his or her friends become increasingly important mirrors that reflect what is going on in his or her life. This young client's attitudes and values are being shaped by these interactions, and the counselor needs to be mindful of these shaping forces. When confronted with the important challenges of choosing friends, the client should ask himself or herself some questions, such as, "Am I looking at all my options and alternatives?" and "Am I doing the responsible thing here?"

Keep in mind Paul's advice to Titus about life decisions: "For the grace of God that brings salvation has appeared to all men. It teaches us to say 'no' to ungodliness and worldly passions, and to live self-controlled, upright and godly lives in this present age" (Titus 2:11-12 NIV).

The next area to address is how God fits into the equation. What does the teen think God desires in his or her choosing of companions? What kind of friend does the teen think God is? Is He even considered as a friend or just a higher power? Is he a personal God who wants to have a relationship with the teen? Help the teen see how a friendship with God can grow and how He can lead in the process of finding good friends. If the teen has not started a friendship with God, use the "Steps to Peace with God" handout (see Chapter 40) to help him or her begin.

Vignette

Thank God, it's Friday, and school is out for the weekend. Calvin is counting down the minutes until he can get with his friends and skate. The plan is to meet at his house at six o'clock and skate to the plaza parking lot to "ollie" and "half pipe" to their heart's content.

Six o'clock rolled around, and the gang showed up at Calvin's, and then they proceeded down the street to the plaza. Unfortunately, a funny thing happened on the way. One of the boys suggested they check out the abandoned building halfway to the plaza. With no objections, they all squeezed their way through the locked fence and past the no trespassing signs to the back of the building. They could see in the windows, and what they saw was a warehouse with a large open floor, perfect for skateboarding. The problem was that the doors were locked. One of Calvin's friends suggested they return to Calvin's house to get a hammer and pry bar. When they returned to the house, Calvin's mother wondered why they were back so soon but did not give it another thought. The boys took the tools and returned to the warehouse. They broke the lock off the door and went in. Unknown to the boys, a neighbor saw them entering the property the second time and called the police. They had been skating for only several minutes when the police arrived. When the boys saw a police cruiser outside the property, they split.

Everyone got away except Calvin and one other boy. As the police had Calvin spread out over the hood of the police car, his mother just happened to be driving by on her way to the store. Panic-stricken, she pulled over and asked the officer what was going on. He told her Calvin was being arrested for trespassing, and she would have to come down to the station to pick him up. Calvin ended up having to perform hours of community service and pay for the damage to the building, all because he listened to the folly of his foolish friends who abandoned him when the heat showed up. He was also ordered to attend four hours of therapy.

When I met Calvin in my office, he struck me as a personable young man, well-mannered and friendly. We talked for awhile about why he was there, his friends, and skateboarding. His friendships seemed to revolve around skateboarding and it seemed to be important to him to be part of the group. He did not strike me as either a strong leader or a strong follower. I asked him to describe his friends to me, which he did. I asked him about their strengths and weaknesses, who he liked best and why. I asked him which friends his mother liked best. We talked about how he felt about getting caught in the abandoned building and getting into trouble while most of his friends got away.

Taking out the "Anchor-Lifeline-Noose" handout, I asked Calvin to read the descriptions of each type of friend at the bottom of the page. After he did, I asked him to think about his friends and which category each of them might fit into. One by one, we talked about his friends and why they fit best into the category Calvin had chosen. After Calvin finished filling in the page, I asked him what he noticed. He responded accurately that most of the names appeared in the "noose" column (friends who may get you into trouble at times). I asked him whether he thought that was a good thing. He appeared thoughtful, and acknowledged that it was not a good thing. We then talked about some ways that Calvin could change that. I asked him if he knew some teens that would fit into the "lifeline" category. He responded that he did, but that he was not as close to those teens. We brainstormed some ways to build friendships with those teens. We also talked about not spending as much time with some of his friends that tended to get him into trouble.

We reviewed the benefits of friendship with people that build you up and help you do the right thing. Toward the end of the session, I asked Calvin how his friends would characterize him if they were asked to complete the handout. With this foundation laid, we were able to spend the remaining three sessions developing strong decision-making skills, discussing not only how to choose good friends but also how to make wise decisions within those friendships.

Suggestions for Follow-Up

Continue to help the teen think about the results of his or her friendships. Continue to emphasize the importance of changing his or her friendships from the negative ones that were bad influences. Encourage the teen to bring a friend to a session because you will gain a different perspective on the teen's behavior.

Contraindications

If the client is resistant to discussing his or her friends, do not attempt to force this. Nothing shuts a teen down faster than criticism of those closest to him or her.

Resources for Professionals

Dowd, T., and Tierney, J. (1997). *Teaching social skills to youth.* Boys Town, NE: Boys Town Press.

McDowell, J. (1996). *Handbook on counseling youth.* Nashville, TN: W. Publishing Group.

Parrott, L. (2000). *Helping the struggling adolescent.* Grand Rapids, MI: Zondervan.

Schrumpf, F., Freiburg, S., and Skadden, D. (1993). *Life lessons for young adolescents.* Ottawa, Ontario: Research Press.

Trollinger, S. (2001). *Unglued and tattooed.* Washington, DC: Lifeline Press.

Twoey, E. (2002). *ProTeen: A positive guide to understanding adolescents.* Cleveland, IN: Pathway Press.

Resources for Clients

Beisswenger, I., and Eldred, M. (2004). *The way we see things: Middle schoolers look at themselves and issues they face everyday.* St. Louis, MO: Rope Ferry Press.

Brown, L.K., and Brown, M. (2001). *How to be a friend: A guide to making friends and keeping them.* New York: Random House, Inc.

Griffing, E.A. (1987). *Making friends and making them count.* Westmont, IL: InterVarsity Press.

Matthews, A. (1991). *Making friends: A guide to getting along with people.* Chicago, IL: Price Stern Sloan Publisher.

McGraw, J. (2000). *Life strategies for teens.* New York: Simon & Schuster, Inc.

Related Scriptures

> He who walks with the wise grows wise, but a companion of fools suffers harm. (Proverbs 13:20 NIV)

> A friend loves at all times, and a brother is born for adversity. (Proverbs 17:17 NIV)

A man of many companions may come to ruin, but there is a friend who sticks closer than a brother. (Proverbs 18:24 NIV)

Do not envy wicked men, do not desire their company. (Proverbs 24:1 NIV)

He who keeps the law is a discerning son, but a companion of gluttons disgraces his father. (Proverbs 28:7 NIV)

You are my friends if you do what I command. (John 15:14 NIV)

Do not be misled: Bad company corrupts good character. (I Corinthians 15:33 NIV)

My Friends

Anchor	Lifeline	Noose
Anchor—Someone who provides stability but who may hold you back from doing things you would like to or should do.	Lifeline—Someone who is there when you need them. A source of support in trouble. Someone who pulls you to positive things.	Noose—Someone who may be good to hang out with but who may get you into trouble at times.

– 39 –

Bad, Bad, Bad

Philip J. Henry

Guiding Scripture

How long must I wrestle with my thoughts and everyday have sorrow in my heart. . . .
Look on me and answer, O Lord my God.

Psalm 13:2a (NIV)

Type of Contribution: Exercise, Handouts/Homework

Objective

This exercise lets the adolescent client give voice to his or her complaints and helps him or her examine what might be the components of his or her depression. Clients can highlight the bad he or she sees in his or her present world, future, and self. Then, the young client can see whether he or she can make logical sense of his or her life by drawing on God for hope and strength.

Rationale for Use

Living a life of faith at any age does not mean that things will be easy. All life contains hurt and sorrow. Through the Psalms of David, it is clear that he had his times of depression. His life was, by any account, a successful one; however, it also contained a mixture of pain and trouble. When these negative experiences occurred, David was not shy in telling God or anyone who would listen how he felt. In the Psalm of the Guiding Scripture, David clearly communicates his negative emotion to God and to all who read his words. In doing so, he sifts through his emotions and thinking and seeks to find a source of connection with God that will aid him in facing the day.

Adolescence, in particular, is a time when the insanity and the pain of life are very real. Changes in hormones and body abound. Inadequacy, rejection, loneliness, and confusion are common. Doubts about self, fear of the future, and questions about what this life all means also rise to the surface. Through the help of this exercise, clients should be able to express as honestly and completely as possible the negative aspects of their lives and to explore what these negatives mean to them regarding their view of self, others, life in general, and God.

With the help of a good therapist, the client then can begin to identify the component in his or her thinking that might lead to depression and to understand what a true walk of faith might look like. This will aid the client in moving from a pessimistic, negative worldview to one of optimism and faith, by identifying initial steps that would help the client grow in the face of his or

The Christian Therapist's Notebook

doi:10.1300/5334_40

her current trouble and suffering. Finally, the goal of the therapy process is to lead the client to an initial or greater commitment to Christ, who can be a positive support in the midst of a negative and pessimistic world.

Instructions

Adolescents who are depressed often do not present themselves that way. More often, they appear to be angry, defiant, sullen, resistant, or withdrawn. As a result, joining with them to develop a working relationship can indeed by tricky.

Most important is to take the necessary time to listen to the client to facilitate the building of the therapeutic relationship. This may take a week or two of listening to and connecting with the client. Introduce the handout and explain to the client how to proceed; ask him or her to identify the things that are bad in his or her life. School, home, friends, and relationships are great places to start. Allow the client the emotional space necessary for him or her to talk about these bad things in his or her life. Make sure to listen attentively. When the client stops talking, ask him or her to elaborate on any general statements. Listen "between the lines" for indications of the presence of hurt, frustration, hopelessness, and helplessness.

Help the client to see that God, as shown in the Bible, agrees with much of his or her perspective on the world: it is a fallen world, and there is going to be trouble. Give biblical examples of those who voiced their complaints about the world to God, such as Moses, David, Job, and Jeremiah.

Ask the client to imagine how the areas of his or her life identified as "bad" have influenced his or her view of self, of the world, and of his or her future. Let the client sort through the bad parts of his or her life, identifying how each individual part has affected these three areas. Take time to let the client reflect on his or her thinking. Adolescents often are still developing this skill, and some may have more difficulty with reflection than others.

Ask the client to talk about how he or she wishes the world could be different and where he or she sees God fitting into the process. In the spaces between the negatives, see if the young client can identify a message he or she can meditate on that will put the bad into perspective. This may be a biblical passage or one that he or she comes up with that can help him or her to put the negative in perspective or to remember that God cares and can help. During the week, as homework, have the client keep track of when his or her thinking becomes more negative, including the circumstances and thoughts that accompany this change.

Vignette

Derrick came to the session fifteen minutes late, dressed from head to toe in black. He wore black pants and shirt, a black leather jacket, and black army boots. He sat looking down at the floor, with his arms folded and a blank look on his face. As the session began, the therapist asked Derrick the normal intake questions about his being there and the problems he was having. To all the questions, Derrick answered with as few words as possible. At times, the therapist had to repeat the question two or three times before Derrick even responded. What the therapist gained from the interaction was that Derrick's parents, who were concerned about his behavior and choice of friends, had sent Derrick to therapy, and that Derrick was less than thrilled to be there.

As the session continued, it became obvious to the therapist that Derrick struggled to interact with many of the adults in his life. He saw teachers as ogres or monsters, his parents as his jailers, and other adults as part of a conspiracy to make him miserable. Derrick struggled not only with adults but also with his peers, viewing them as suspect too. According to him, they were part of a group who had caved in to social pressure to be popular or successful in school and acted "fake" most of the time. The best way to face the real world, according to Derrick, was with an honest pessimism about the world and those who live in it.

Although Derrick initially presented this hard-shell attitude, as the therapist continued to talk with him, his defenses seemed to soften. Derrick talked about how "messed" up his family was after his parents' divorce, how he hated his father and his new "perfect family," and how much a struggle school continued to be for him. During this discussion, the therapist used all of the necessary attending and listening skills and was actively empathetic. The session ended on a positive note; while Derrick was not chatty, he progressed from being very uncooperative to mildly resistant.

The next session, Derrick was back to his highly resistant mode. He again was dressed all in black, but this time he sported a pair of orange sneakers with black laces. After an initial conversation, the therapist asked about whether Derrick thought he was depressed. Derrick admitted immediately that at times he did feel down, especially when he had a blowup with his father or when he encountered problems at school. The therapist suggested that they write down some of the things that were "bad" in his life, explaining that these things could be connected with how badly he felt.

When Derrick agreed, the therapist took the first "Bad, Bad, Bad" handout, placed it on a clipboard, and gave it and a pen to Derrick. The therapist then asked Derrick to write anywhere on the exercise the things that were bad in his life. The first thing that Derrick wrote was "family," filling the big "A" space in the middle of the paper. Next, he wrote "Mrs. Wright," his math teacher. Derrick had failed algebra once and was not doing well in the class now. With the therapist's help, Derrick managed to fill most of the paper: "moving"; "Doreen," his stepsister; "getting a job and finding a career"; "Lisa," his father's new wife; "walking to school"; "Mr. Ranger," the principal at his school; and "Michael," a peer who was one of his enemies at school.

As he filled the paper, Derrick's mood seemed to lighten a little. He even smiled and chuckled as he put names, events, or problems on the paper, suggesting what he would like to do to solve some of these problems. Taking time, the therapist let Derrick talk about each item as long as he wanted, and although Derrick's language was not the best when speaking of the things he really hated, the therapist stayed connected with him and made him feel that what he had to say was important. The therapist casually mentioned that the Bible had much to say about the bad in the world and read a verse from the Psalms in which David complained about the things around him.

As the session ended, the therapist asked Derrick to take the second "Bad, Bad, Bad" handout home with him, to think about whether the things that he had written about made him feel differently about himself and his current life or whether they affected how he thought his life would be. The therapist wrote some of the items from the first handout in each of the three categories on the second handout: What is bad about today? What is bad about me? What is bad about the future.

The next session, Derrick said that he had not remembered to bring in the handouts; in fact, he said that he had lost them. He was much more interested in talking about a recent fight with his father. Although the therapist tried to redirect him, Derrick would not be derailed from the topic, so the session concluded with talking about his relationship with his father. The therapist gave Derrick another copy of the second handout along with a copy of the first handout that he had completed the previous week.

Again, the following week Derrick showed up without both of the handouts. This time, his therapist asked if he would be willing to fill out the second one in the session, and Derrick agreed. The therapist then explained that his depression could be related to how he thought about the "bad" in his life and how that "bad" colored his view of today, his future, and himself.

Derrick wrote some of the "bad" items from the first handout in each of the three categories of the second handout. As he worked, the therapist highlighted how his thinking about these items could dictate whether he was having a good or bad day. The therapist emphasized the control Derrick had over what he thought about and the way he thought about it. To solidify this point, the therapist allowed Derrick to choose what category an item went in or whether the item did not fit any of the categories. The session ended with an agreement that Derrick would try to notice when and how he thought about the "bad" in his life.

In the next session, the therapist pulled out a copy of the completed second handout from the previous week and asked Derrick how his week had gone. Derrick reported that he had noticed that his bad moods came in relationship to school, especially math class, and on weekends before he went to his father's house. He also reported that math class had the had greatest effect on what he thought of himself. When he thought about how poorly he did in math, he told himself that he was dumb or stupid and that he would never graduate from high school.

Together with the therapist, Derrick came up with an alternate way to think about the math class. He acknowledged that math was not his best subject, but, with help, he could finish the class and get on with his life.

As the session closed, Derrick seemed somewhat hopeful, for the first time in months. The therapist then disclosed some personal struggles from the past that had a similar theme and discussed how faith in God had helped to overcome these troubles. The therapist asked Derrick to pray with him, asking God to help Derrick succeed in addressing his negative issues. Derrick agreed, somewhat hesitantly, and the therapist prayed:

> God I thank you for Derrick and the gifts you have given him.
> I know that he is struggling now with math and with other things.
> Would You show him how he can deal with this class successfully?
> Please help Derrick face the other hard things in his life.
> I ask this in Jesus' name. Amen.

The next week, Derrick reported that he was moving in with his father. His mother had taken a job in another nearby city and would be moving there soon. Derrick would need to end counseling in the near future.

Together, in the final weeks of the counseling sessions, Derrick and his therapist worked on other negative issues and his responses to them. Derrick began to dispute these negatives, and his mood continued to lift. In his last session, he mentioned that he would like to come back to see the therapist for a follow-up session if he came back to visit friends. The therapist reminded Derrick of what he had learned and encouraged him to continue learning about God and thinking in a more positive way.

Suggestions for Follow-Up

The first handout is a good way for a therapist to connect with a depressed client. Defining the bad things in life on paper lets the therapist see what the adolescent is up against in the world and what the therapist must battle for therapy to be successful. Often, simply listening and being sympathetic can be therapeutic to a young client.

Using the second handout along with the first as a homework assignment allows the client to evaluate the thoughts associated with the negatives, not just the negative experiences themselves. Once the client has shared his or her perspectives about self, the world, and the future, the therapist can use these perceptions to identify their associated thoughts and attitudes.

Spiritual issues are often very near the surface during such a process because the client often wonders why God would permit his or her life to be as it is. At this point, the Christian counselor may share the biblical insight that this is a fallen world and that God's will is not always done.

This, however, does not mean that He is uncaring. On the contrary, there is hope and strength for those who look to God.

Examples of how other men and women of faith wrestled with the "bad" in their world can help the client develop a mature view of the world and learn how to face the bad of his or her life with hope and faith.

Contraindications

This exercise is contraindicated when depression is so entrenched or severe that the client is unable to engage actively in the therapeutic process. If the client is too depressed, the retelling of the bad will serve only to strengthen his or her negative perceptions.

Always address suicidal or homicidal ideation immediately with a therapeutic intervention that meets the level of severity. Consider the pursuit of medication, hospitalization, commitment, increased psychotherapy, or other intervention in cases of more severe depression.

Resources for Professionals and Parents

Bauman, L. (1997). *Ten most troublesome teenage problems and how to solve them.* New York: Birch Lane Press.

Coe, K., Faber, A., and Mazlish, E. (1999). *How to talk so kids will listen and listen so kids will talk.* New York: Avon Books, Inc.

Fassler, D.G., Dumas, L. (1998). *Help me, I'm sad: Recognizing, treating and preventing childhood and adolescent depression.* New York: Penguin.

Glasser, W. (2002). *Unhappy teenagers: A way for parents and teachers to reach them.* New York: HarperCollins Publishers, Inc.

Hemfelt, R. (1990). *Kids who carry our pain.* Nashville, TN: Thomas Nelson Publishers, Inc.

Huggins, K. (1989). *Parenting adolescents.* Colorado Springs, CO: NavPress Publishing Group.

Huggins, K. (2003). *Friendship counseling: Jesus' model for speaking life-words to hurting people.* Colorado Springs, CO: NavPress Publishing Group.

McDowell, J. (1996). *Handbook on counseling youth.* Nashville, TN: W. Publishing Group.

McGee, R. (2003). *Search for significance.* Nashville, TN: W. Publishing Group.

Parrott, L. (1993). *Helping the struggling adolescent.* Buffalo, NY: Zondervan Bible Publishers.

Scott, B. (1997). *Relief for hurting parents.* Lake Jackson, TX: Allon Publishing.

Resources for Clients

Anderson, N. (2000). *The bondage breaker.* Eugene, OR: Harvest House.

Carter, L., and Minirth, M. (1995). *The freedom from depression workbook.* Nashville, TN: Thomas Nelson Publishers, Inc.

Eareckson, T.J. (1997). *When God weeps.* Grand Rapids, MI: Zondervan Bible Publishers.

Gregg-Schroeder, S. (1997). *In the shadow of God's wings: Grace in the midst of depression.* Nashville, TN: Upper Room Books.

Hart, A. (2001). *Unmasking male depression.* Dallas, TX: Word Publishing.

Helmer, D.S. (2003). *Let's talk about feeling sad.* New York: Rosen/Powerkids.

Hennigan, B., and Sutton, M.A. (2001). *Conquering depression: A 30-day plan to finding happiness.* Nashville, TN: Broadman and Holman.

LaHaye, T. (1996). *How to win over depression.* Grand Rapids, MI: Zondervan Bible Publishers.

Lockley, J. (2002). *The practical workbook for the depressed Christian.* Bucks, England: Authentic Lifestyles.

Maxwell, J. (2000). *Failing forward: How to make the most of your mistakes.* Nashville, TN: Thomas Nelson Publishers, Inc.
McDonnell, R. (1997). *God is close to the brokenhearted: Good news for those who are depressed.* Cincinnati, OH: St. Anthony Messenger.
Minirth, F., and Meyer, P. (1994). *Happiness is a choice.* Grand Rapids, MI: Baker Books.
Truesdale, A. (2002). *When you can't pray.* Kansas City, MO: Beacon Hill Press.

Related Scriptures

> O Lord, how many are my foes! How many rise up against me! Many are saying of me, "God will not deliver him." But you are a shield around me, O Lord; you bestow glory on me and lift up my head. (Psalm 3:1-3 NIV)

> How long, O Lord? Will you forget me forever? How long will you hide your face from me? How long must I wrestle with my thoughts and every day I have sorrow in my heart? How long will my enemy triumph over me? Look on me and answer, O Lord my God. Give light to my eyes, or I will sleep in death; my enemy will say, "I have overcome him," and my foes will rejoice when I fall. But I trust in your unfailing love; my heart rejoices in your salvation. I will sing to the LORD, for He has been good to me. (Psalm 13:1-6 NIV)

> My God, my God, why have you forsaken me? Why are you so far from saving me, so far from the words of my groanings? (Psalm 22:1 NIV)

> Why are you downcast, O my soul? Why so disturbed within me? Put your hope in God, for I will yet praise him, my savior and my God. (Psalm 42:11 NIV)

> "For I know the plans I have for you," declares the LORD, "plans to prosper you and not to harm you, plans to give you hope and a future." (Jeremiah 29:11 NIV)

A D

B D

B A

B ad

What is bad about today?

What is bad about the future?

What is bad about me?

– 40 –

Peace with God

Philip J. Henry

Guiding Scripture

We have peace with God through our Lord Jesus Christ.

Romans 5:1 (NIV)

Type of Contribution: Exercise, Handout

Objective

The goal of this exercise is to lead the client into a loving relationship with God through Jesus Christ, by inviting the client to place his or her faith in Christ and receive forgiveness. This transformation is the beginning of an exciting life of faith that can change every area of the client's life.

Rationale for Use

Scripture has much to say about the changes that happen in the client's life when he or she accepts what Jesus has done for him or her, when he or she seeks forgiveness from his or her sins and surrenders his or her life to Him. Jesus used parables as a way of illustrating this new way of life. He told stories throughout the Gospels about this process: a prodigal returning home, a child being adopted, a planted seed, a found coin, a rescued sheep. All of these stories reflect a facet of the enormous change that occurs when God's grace enters the human heart. An acrostic of the word *grace* illustrates this idea:

God's

Riches

At

Christ's

Expense

The Christian Therapist's Notebook

doi:10.1300/5334_41

While many in the world go about trying to do the right things that will bring about peace or impress God, the Christian way is to recognize that this process is futile. It is not bad; it is just a dead-end street. It does not go anywhere.

Recognizing this fact and the need for change is the first step. Jesus talked of this when He said, "Blessed are those who are poor in spirit for theirs is the kingdom of God" (Matthew 5:3 KJV). The Bible compares the best a person can do to old, smelly rags—not a very pleasant picture. Rather than try to do it alone, the alternative is to realize that no one will ever measure up to God's standard. He has provided a way to find peace with Him. He has taken the initiative to move and make peace through Christ.

A person finds peace with God, then, not on the basis of anything that he or she has done, but on what Christ has accomplished on the cross. As a person accepts this, asking God to forgive him or her for not living the way that he or she ought to and surrendering his or her life to Him, this person will find peace—peace with God, peace in his or her heart and mind, and a growing sense of peace with others.

Many clients come to therapy with symptoms that connect to spiritual issues. Hosts of diagnostic categories include behaviors, feelings, and thoughts that tie directly and indirectly to greater existential questions and issues that can be answered best by understanding them in a spiritual context. Guilt and anxiety, questions of performance and value, the search for meaning and purpose—all of these questions often have spiritual roots and their solutions center on finding peace with God. Finding peace with God is wonderful.

Instructions

When introducing this exercise to a client, make sure to be equipped and prepared as a counselor. Pray to ensure peace with God, and ask God for strength and guidance. Pray for the client that God's purpose will be apparent in his or her life.

Make sure this is the proper time for this exercise. Ensure that the motivation for performing this exercise is correct and that it is in the best interest of the client. Forcing someone to move in a spiritual direction when he or she is not ready or does not wish to do so is wrong and counterproductive. A tree cannot produce fruit by force but must await its proper season; so also is there a season for individuals to consider their spiritual life and their direction. Do not pick the fruit before it is ripe.

Vignette

Sam, a forty-two-year-old accountant, began therapy once his second marriage had ended in divorce. His second wife, as had his first, received custody of the children, two daughters, ages ten and twelve. In the process of the divorce, it was revealed that Sam had been involved in multiple affairs. This was documented in gruesome detail in the court records. Sam felt a sense of surrealism as the process unfolded; it was as if he were watching someone else's life played out in front of him. His wife, his house, his children—everything he had known—was lost. Even his relationship with Rhonda, his last mistress, had taken a turn for the worse, and she had broken it off. Sam was not accustomed to this type of breakup. He had usually been in control in the relationships and was used to deciding when things began and ended.

Together, these crises motivated Sam to begin considering his choices and the way he was living his life. After several months of introspection and soul-searching, Sam began to attend a nearby Baptist church, the same denomination he had belonged to as a child. Being in church soothed him. He felt comfort from the words and messages he had heard as a child. He sought to find a compass to guide him in the storms of life and to find peace. In the bulletin, amid a myriad of announcements, Sam noticed that, as a ministry, the church offered counseling. Sam called and made an appointment the next week. He even came to the session twenty minutes early, attending the session during his lunch hour. He was eager for a different way of life.

After filling out the initial intake form and providing other related information, Sam met with Gary, a counselor at the church. At first, Sam was a little bothered by the youth of the counselor, but Gary appeared to be quite knowledgeable and professional, so Sam decided to see what he could gain from the experience.

As Gary conducted an assessment of Sam, he was struck by how many of Sam's questions were of a spiritual nature. Sam was asking serious questions; he was no dummy—he knew his life was a mess, and he was trying to find a way to make it a better life to live.

Sam kept repeating what became his mantra over several sessions: he had messed up, but he was not sure what to do. Everything he had chosen to do to fix the situation just made it worse. On top of that, his children were acting up and having trouble in school. Life seemed to be a big mess, with no help on the horizon. During this time, Sam attended church and even bought a Bible. Reading the Bible and praying soothed his mind and helped him to think clearer.

One bright, crisp October day when Sam came to therapy, Gary asked him if he felt that he was at peace with God. "I have been working on that," Sam said, "but I always come up short. I will never be as good as God wants me to be." Gary gave Sam the handout "Steps to Peace with God" and asked him to share its ideas with him. Sam agreed.

"Step 1: God loves you and wants you to experience peace and life—abundant and eternal," Gary read. Then, he had Sam read the verses that followed slowly and deliberately. After reading the verses, Gary asked, "Why don't most people have this peace and abundant life that God planned for us to have?" Sam shook his head and said, "I don't know. I guess we just lose our way." The two of them talked for a while, and Sam shared how he had held more faith when he was young, but over the years, he had drifted away.

After a few minutes, Gary continued to read: "Step 2: God created us in His own image to have an abundant life. He did not make us as robots to automatically love and obey Him. God gave us a will and a freedom of choice. We chose to disobey God and go our own willful way. We still make this choice today. This results in separation from God." Gary then read Romans 3:23 (NIV): "For all have sinned and fall short of the glory of God." Sam and Gary then talked of the choices that Sam had made. "I wish that I could start over again," quipped Sam. "I would do many things differently." They talked about this, and Gary shared that he too had done things in life that he regretted. "None of us can bridge that separation to reach God," Gary said, and then he read Proverbs 14:12 (NIV): "There is a way that seems right to a man, but in the end it leads to death." Only one bridge can reach to God.

Gary continued to read: "Step 3: Jesus Christ died on the Cross and rose from the grave. He paid the penalty for our sin and bridged the gap between God and people." Gary then read several verses, including 1 Peter 3:18 (NIV): "For Christ died for sins once for all, the righteous for the unrighteous, to bring you to God." Sam and Gary discussed this step and the verses for quite a while. Sam asserted that he did believe in God and that he was sure he was okay with the "Jesus stuff," as he put it. Sam was unable to see how any of this would make a difference. Gary explained that Jesus had made a way to reach God, but that each person had to make his or her own choice.

After a while, Gary began to read again: "Step 4: We must trust Jesus Christ as Lord and Savior and receive Him by personal invitation." He continued by reading Romans 10:9 (NIV): "That if you confess with your mouth, 'Jesus is Lord,' and believe in your heart that God raised Him from the dead, you will be saved." Gary explained that this is a choice asked Sam if he had ever done this. Sam said, "I heard about this in church, but I don't think I ever made that decision." Gary asked, "Would you like to receive Jesus Christ right now?" "What do I have to do?" asked Sam. Gary directed Sam's attention to the handout and read aloud the four steps necessary to receive Christ. After Gary had finished reading, Sam said that he would like to do this.

Gary then discussed Step 5 of the handout, which focused on prayer. He reviewed the prayer with Sam and then asked Sam to read it, as a prayer, if this expressed what he was feeling. Sam read the words of prayer aloud. As he prayed, Sam was moved emotionally, and although he was not one to cry, he sighed and breathed deeply. Following the prayer, Gary told Sam how he could grow as a Christian and invited him to attend one of the church's small groups. The session ended, and Sam left the office.

Three months later, Sam was baptized at the church he had begun to attend, and he was beginning to put some of the pieces of his life back together. There was no magic change that happened in his life, but Sam knew that his life was changing for the better and would never be the same.

Suggestions for Follow-Up

When receiving Christ, a person is born into God's family through the supernatural work of the Holy Spirit who indwells every believer. This is called regeneration, or the "new birth." This is just the beginning of a wonderful new life in Christ. To deepen this relationship, the client should be encouraged with these suggestions:

1. Read your Bible every day to know Christ better.
2. Talk to God in prayer every day.
3. Tell others about Christ.
4. Worship, be in fellowship, and serve with other Christians in a church where Christ's word is preached.
5. As Christ's representative in a needy world, demonstrate your new life by your love and concern for others.

Contraindications

Not every issue presented in counseling is a spiritual issue. Make sure not to miss anything during the intake. Consider the physical health and emotional stability of the client, whether he or she is willing and able to undertake a discussion of this magnitude. Make sure that the timing is right, that the client is ready and willing to talk about these issues, and that you proceed at a pace of the client's choosing.

Steps to Peace with God

Step 1
God's Purpose: Peace and Life

God loves you and wants you to experience peace and life—abundant and eternal.

The Bible says . . .

"We have peace with God through our Lord Jesus Christ." —Romans 5:1 (NIV)

"For God so loved the world that He gave His only begotten Son, that whoever believes in Him should not perish but have everlasting life." —John 3:16 (NIV)

"I have come that he or she may have life, and that he or she may have it more abundantly." —John 10:10 (NIV)

Why don't most people have this peace and abundant life that God planned for us to have?

Step 2
The Problem: Our Separation

God created us in His own image to have an abundant life. He did not make us as robots to automatically love and obey Him. God gave us a will and a freedom of choice.

We chose to disobey God and go our own willful way. We still make this choice today. This results in separation from God.

The Bible says . . .

"For all have sinned and fall short of the glory of God." —Romans 3:23 (NIV)

"For the wages of sin is death, but the gift of God is eternal life in Christ Jesus our Lord." —Romans 6:23 (NIV)

Our Attempts to Reach God

People have tried in many ways to bridge this gap between him or herselves and God . . .

The Bible says . . .

"There is a way that seems right to a man, but in the end it leads to death." —Proverbs 14:12 (NIV)

"But your iniquities have separated you from your God; your sins have hidden his face from you, so that he will not hear." —Isaiah 59:2 (NIV)

No bridge reaches God . . . except one.

Step 3
God's Bridge: The Cross

Jesus Christ died on the Cross and rose from the grave. He paid the penalty for our sin and bridged the gap between God and people.

The Bible says . . .

"For there is one God and one mediator between God and men, the man Jesus Christ." —1 Timothy 2:5 (NIV)

"For Christ died for sins once for all, the righteous for the unrighteous, to bring you to God." —1 Peter 3:18 (NIV)

"But God demonstrates his own love for us in this: While we were still sinners, Christ died for us." —Romans 5:8 (NIV)

God has provided the only way. Each person must make a choice.

Step 4
Our Response: Receive Christ

We must trust Jesus Christ as Lord and Savior and receive Him by personal invitation.

The Bible says . . .

"Here I am! I stand at the door and knock. If anyone hears my voice and opens the door, I will come in and eat with him, and he with me." —Revelation 3:20 (NIV)

"Yet to all who received him, to those who believed in his name, he gave the right to become children of God." —John 1:12 (NIV)

"That if you confess with your mouth, 'Jesus is Lord,' and believe in your heart that God raised Him from the dead, you will be saved." —Romans 10:9 (NIV)

Where are you?

Will you receive Jesus Christ right now?

Here is how you can receive Christ:

1. Admit your need (I am a sinner).
2. Be willing to turn from your sins (repent).
3. Believe that Jesus Christ died for you on the Cross and rose from the grave.
4. Through prayer, invite Jesus Christ to come in and control your life through the Holy Spirit. (Receive Him as Lord and Savior.)

Step 5
Prayer

How to Pray:

Dear Lord Jesus, I know that I am a sinner and need Your forgiveness. I believe that You died for my sins. I want to turn from my sins. I now invite You to come into my heart and life. I want to trust and follow You as Lord and Savior. In Jesus' name. Amen.

God's Assurance: His Word

If you prayed this prayer,

The Bible says . . .

"Everyone who calls on the name of the Lord will be saved." —Romans 10:13 (NIV)

Did you sincerely ask Jesus Christ to come into your life? Where is He right now? What has He given you?

"For it is by grace you have been saved, through faith—and this not from yourselves, it is the gift of God—not by works, so that no one can boast." —Ephesians 2:8,9 (NIV)

Receiving Christ, we are born into God's family through the supernatural work of the Holy Spirit who indwells every believer. This is called regeneration, or the "new birth."

This is just the beginning of a wonderful new life in Christ. To deepen this relationship you should:

1. Read your Bible everyday to know Christ better.
2. Talk to God in prayer every day.
3. Tell others about Christ.
4. Worship, fellowship, and serve with other Christians in a church where Christ is preached.
5. As Christ's representative in a needy world, demonstrate your new life by your love and concern for others.

Index

Page numbers followed by the letter "f" indicate figures; those followed by the letter "t" indicate tables.

doi:10.1300/5334_42

Order a copy of this book with this form or online at:
http://www.haworthpress.com/store/product.asp?sku=5334

THE CHRISTIAN THERAPIST'S NOTEBOOK
Homework, Handouts, and Activities for Use in Christian Counseling

_______in softbound at $39.95 (ISBN: 978-0-7890-2594-4)

324 pages plus index • Includes illustrations

Or order online and use special offer code HEC25 in the shopping cart.

COST OF BOOKS________

POSTAGE & HANDLING________
(US: $4.00 for first book & $1.50 for each additional book)
(Outside US: $5.00 for first book & $2.00 for each additional book)

SUBTOTAL________

IN CANADA: ADD 6% GST________

STATE TAX________
(NJ, NY, OH, MN, CA, IL, IN, PA, & SD residents, *add appropriate local sales tax)*

FINAL TOTAL________
(If paying in Canadian funds, convert using the current exchange rate, UNESCO coupons welcome)

☐ **BILL ME LATER:** (Bill-me option is good on US/Canada/Mexico orders only; not good to jobbers, wholesalers, or subscription agencies.)
☐ Check here if billing address is different from shipping address and attach purchase order and billing address information.

Signature________________________

☐ **PAYMENT ENCLOSED:** $________________

☐ **PLEASE CHARGE TO MY CREDIT CARD.**

☐ Visa ☐ MasterCard ☐ AmEx ☐ Discover
☐ Diner's Club ☐ Eurocard ☐ JCB

Account #________________________

Exp. Date________________________

Signature________________________

Prices in US dollars and subject to change without notice.

NAME________________________

INSTITUTION________________________

ADDRESS________________________

CITY________________________

STATE/ZIP________________________

COUNTRY________________ COUNTY (NY residents only)________________

TEL________________ FAX________________

E-MAIL________________________

May we use your e-mail address for confirmations and other types of information? ☐ Yes ☐ No
We appreciate receiving your e-mail address and fax number. Haworth would like to e-mail or fax special discount offers to you, as a preferred customer. **We will never share, rent, or exchange your e-mail address or fax number.** We regard such actions as an invasion of your privacy.

Order From Your Local Bookstore or Directly From

The Haworth Press, Inc.

10 Alice Street, Binghamton, New York 13904-1580 • USA
TELEPHONE: 1-800-HAWORTH (1-800-429-6784) / Outside US/Canada: (607) 722-5857
FAX: 1-800-895-0582 / Outside US/Canada: (607) 771-0012
E-mail to: orders@haworthpress.com

For orders outside US and Canada, you may wish to order through your local sales representative, distributor, or bookseller.
For information, see http://haworthpress.com/distributors

(Discounts are available for individual orders in US and Canada only, not booksellers/distributors.)

PLEASE PHOTOCOPY THIS FORM FOR YOUR PERSONAL USE.

http://www.HaworthPress.com BOF07